UNRESOLVED ISSUES AND NEW CHALLENGES TO
THE LAW OF THE SEA

Publications on Ocean Development

Volume 54

A Series of Studies on
the International, Legal, Institutional and Policy Aspects
of Ocean Development

General Editor: Vaughan Lowe
Chichele Professor of Public International Law and Fellow of All Souls College,
Oxford University

The titles published in this series are listed at the end of this volume.

Unresolved Issues and New Challenges to the Law of the Sea

Time Before and Time After

edited by

ANASTASIA STRATI
MARIA GAVOUNELI
and
NIKOLAOS SKOURTOS

MARTINUS NIJHOFF PUBLISHERS
LEIDEN / BOSTON

A C.I.P. record for this book is available from the Library of Congress.

Printed on acid-free paper.

ISBN 90 04 15191 5

© 2006 Koninklijke Brill NV, Leiden, The Netherlands
Koninklijke Brill NV incorporates the imprints Brill Academic Publishers,
Martinus Nijhoff Publishers and VSP.

<http://www.brill.nl>

Printed and bound in The Netherlands.

TABLE OF CONTENTS

ABBREVIATIONS

ADI	Annuaire de droit de la mer
AFDI	Annuaire français de droit international
AJIL	American Journal of International Law
BYBIL	British Yearbook of International Law
CAHAQ	*Ad Hoc* Committee of Experts on the Underwater Cultural Heritage
CBD	Convention on Biological Diversity
CMI	Comité maritime international
CSC	Geneva Convention on the Continental Shelf
EEnvLR	European Environmental Law Review
EEZ	Exclusive economic zone
ETS	European Treaty Series
FAO	Food and Agriculture Organisation
Georgetown IELR	Georgetown International Environmental Law Review
ICJ	International Court of Justice
ICLQ	International and Comparative Law Quarterly
ICP	United Nations Informal Consultative Process on Oceans and the Law of the Sea
ILA	International Law Association
ILM	International Legal Materials
IMO	International Maritime Organisation
ISA	International Seabed Authority
Italian YBIL	Italian Yearbook of International Law
ITLOS	International Tribunal on the Law of the Sea
IUU fishing	Illegal, unreported and unregulated fishing
LOS Convention	United Nations Convention on the Law of the Sea
MAP	Mediterranean Action Plan
MPAs	Marine Protected Areas
Netherlands YBIL	Netherlands Yearbook of International Law
NILR	Netherlands International Law Review
ODIL	Ocean Development and International Law

OJ	Official Journal of the European Community
PCIJ	Permanent Court of International Justice
PSI	Proliferation Security Initiative
PSSAs	Particularly Sensitive Sea Areas
RCADI	Recueil des cours de l'Académie de droit international
RFMOs	Regional Fisheries Management Organisations
RGDIP	Revue générale de droit international public
RHDI	Revue hellénique de droit international
San Diego LR	San Diego Law Review
SUA Convention	Convention for the Suppression of Unlawful Acts against the Safety of Maritime Navigation
TIJMCL	The International Journal of Marine and Coastal Law
TSC	Geneva Convention on the Territorial Sea and the Contiguous Zone
UKTS	United Kingdom Treaty Series
UNCED	United Nations Conference on Environment and Development
UNCHE	United Nations Conference on the Human Environment
UNCLOS III	Third United Nations Conference on the Law of the Sea
UNEP	United Nations Environment Programme
UNESCO	United Nations Educational, Scientific and Cultural Organization
UN Fish Stocks Agreement	Agreement on the Interpretation of the Provisions of the UN Convention on the Law of the Sea relating to the Conservation and Management of Straddling Stocks and Highly Migratory Fish Stocks
UNRIAA	United Nations Reports of International Arbitral Awards
UNTS	United Nations Treaty Series
Virginia JIL	Virginia Journal of International Law
WMD	Weapons of Mass Destruction
WSSD	World Summit on Sustainable Development
YBIEL	Yearbook of International Environmental Law

INTRODUCTION

The primary aim of the Conference that was organized by the Hellenic Branch of the International Law Association (ILA) and the Aegean Institute of Maritime Law and the Law of the Sea in Rhodes in 2003 under the title *"Time before and time after: Unresolved issues and new challenges to the law of the sea"* was to identify areas of the law that were not adequately addressed by the 1982 UN Convention on the Law of the Sea (hereinafter cited as "LOS Convention") or evolved after the adoption of the Convention.

The LOS Convention has been described by the President of the Third United Nations Conference on the Law of the Sea, Ambassador T.B. Koh, as a "Constitution for the Oceans", second only to the Charter of the United Nations, which would stand the test of time. Reference has been made, *inter alia,* to the promotion of the maintenance of international peace and security by replacing a plethora of conflicting claims by coastal States with universal agreed limits on the territorial sea, the contiguous zone, the exclusive economic zone and the continental shelf; the development of important new rules for the protection and preservation of the marine environment from pollution, as well as the strengthening of the world community's interest in the freedom of navigation, the peaceful settlement of disputes and the prevention of the use of force.

The LOS Convention is a comprehensive treaty that deals with practically every aspect of the uses and resources of the seas. This is illustrated in its universal language and purpose; the Preamble records the determination of the parties to settle "all issues relating to the law of the sea" on the basis that these issues are "closely interrelated and need to be considered as a whole". Nevertheless, problems – human, technical, economic and environmental – continue to arise and must be managed. The real issue is how to adjust the legal order of the oceans to changing realities, a quest that in the past has produced both great achievements and failures. It should be recalled that the

Anastasia Strati, Maria Gavouneli & Nikos Skourtos (eds.), *Unresolved Issues and New Challenges to the Law of the Sea*, Martinus Nijhoff Publishers 2006, xi-xiv.

LOS Convention has not dealt with all ocean uses successfully. Notable examples are the protection of the underwater cultural heritage, the management of transboundary fish stock, which was left for more detailed elaboration in the future, and the legal regime of internal waters that was not addressed at all following the tradition of the 1958 Geneva Conventions.

During the twenty-three years that followed the adoption of the LOS Convention there have been attempts to deal with some of these issues. Special reference should be made to the 2001 UNESCO Convention on the Protection on the Underwater Cultural Heritage, which is discussed extensively in this book and the 1995 Agreement on the Implementation of the Provisions of the UN Convention on the Law of the Sea relating to the Conservation and Management of Straddling Fish Stocks and Highly Migratory Fish Stocks. However, as pointed out by Professor Robin R. Churchill, "shared stocks" have received much less attention, their management remaining one of the greatest challenges to achieving long-term sustainable fisheries.

Most importantly, new issues arose that require the attention of the international community; preservation of marine biodiversity, bio-prospecting and access to marine genetic materials, intelligence gathering and interdiction of vessels on the high seas. The latter constitutes one of the most controversial legal issues in the post 9/11 world. Paradoxically, at present the freedom of the high seas is not challenged by its traditional opponents, the coastal States, but by the maritime powers for security reasons. Dr. Angelos Syrigos and Dr. Petros Liacouras offer two opposing views on this important and highly political subject. They both agree, however, that the "war" against terrorism should not result in any infringement of fundamental principles of international law and human rights.

Within the strict time limits of a Conference it was not possible to address comprehensively all these issues. However, the topics to which the papers are devoted reflect the diversity of contents of the present-day law of the sea. Special emphasis is paid to the protection of the marine environment, an important parameter in any attempt to regulate ocean affairs. Professor Tullio Scovazzi and Dr. Nilufer Oral discuss, from different angles, the challenging issue of the establishment of marine protected areas on the high seas as a tool for protecting vulnerable marine ecosystems, while Professor Grigoris Tsaltas underlines the importance of international and regional cooperation in this area. As pointed out, the LOS Convention promotes co-operation on a global and regional basis with the aim of achieving sustainability and a comprehensive and integrated approach to ocean management.

Last, but not least, reference is made to State practice and the related question of "uniformity" or "fragmentation" of future law of the sea. Judge Budislav Vukas discusses the establishment of exclusive economic zones in the Mediterranean. Until recently, the Mediterranean Sea was the only area where EEZs had not been established. Nevertheless, recent years have seen important developments: From the conclusion of the first delimitation agreement in Eastern Mediterranean between Cyprus and Egypt on their exclusive economic zones (2003), to the establishment of the Croatian Fisheries Protection and Ecological Zone (2003), the French *Zone de protection écologique* (2004), the Libyan Fisheries Protection Zone (2005), the Slovenian Ecological Protection Zone (2005) as well as the Syrian EEZ (2004) and the Tunisian EEZ (2005). However, this *de facto* establishment of exclusive economic zones under various other denominations has caused concern. As stated in the 2004 Report of the Secretary-General on Oceans and the Law of the Sea, "although the legal regime of these zones may as well be identical to the regime of an exclusive economic zone or not in contravention to it, the introduction of new denominations is bound to create *confusion and uncertainty*, especially as to the rights and obligations of other States. Such a potential confusion is entirely avoidable, since there are no legal impediments for any State Party that can do so in its geographical situation to proclaim an EEZ and to use the term establish in the Convention. As the entities primarily responsible for the orderly implementation of the law of the sea regime, States Parties should make sure that there is no further erosion of rights and obligations, that their actions in UNCLOS implementation are sufficiently transparent and that all their bilateral problems are dealt with on the basis of UNCLOS, through means provided by it"[1].

It is to be recalled that, as of 26 August 2005, there were 149 parties to the Convention. The future will show whether the Mediterranean States will resort to the proclamation of EEZs or continue to establish parallel regimes for fisheries and the protection of the marine environment. To a certain extent, this is an aspect of the interplay between uniformity and fragmentation, which has developed into the main issue regarding the interpretation and future adaptability of the LOS Convention.

Professor Haritini Dipla discusses the equally important role of jurisprudence in maintaining the necessary unity and coherence of the law of the sea, while the concluding essay by Professor Argyris Fatouros asserts that the LOS Convention is capable of coping with new challenges, even though it remains useful to explore its possibilities and limits.

---

[1] *Oceans and the law of the sea*, Report of the Secretary-General, A/59/62, 4 March 2004, pp. 13-14.

As far as possible the chapters reflect the law as it stood in June 2005, although some recent references have been added in the course of preparation of the book for the press.

While the authors express personal views, the editors naturally assume responsibility for errors and omissions.

Anastasia Strati
Maria Gavouneli
Nikolaos Skourtos

Part I

Unresolved Issues under
the UN Convention of the Law of the Sea

Chapter 1

THE MANAGEMENT OF SHARED FISH STOCKS:
THE NEGLECTED "OTHER" PARAGRAPH OF ARTICLE 63
OF THE UN CONVENTION ON THE LAW OF THE SEA

*Robin R. Churchill**

1. INTRODUCTION

The casual reader of the 1982 UN Convention on the Law of the Sea (hereafter cited as "LOS Convention")[1], who knew nothing about the migratory nature of fish, might be forgiven for thinking that most fish stocks were discrete stocks living either on the high seas or in the Exclusive Economic Zone (EEZ) of a single State, and that the various kinds of transboundary stocks dealt with by articles 63, 64, 66 and 67 of the Convention (namely shared, straddling, highly migratory, anadromous and catadromous stocks) were very much the exception. In fact, the position is rather the reverse. Many, possibly the majority of, fish stocks are some form of transboundary stock.

Article 63 of the LOS Convention is concerned with two types of transboundary stocks. Paragraph 1 deals with shared stocks, i.e. stocks that migrate or are distributed between the EEZs of two or more States[2], while paragraph 2 deals with straddling stocks, i.e. stocks that migrate or are distributed between one or more EEZs and the high seas. Both paragraphs of article 63 are brief and say no more essentially than that the States concerned – that

---

* Professor of International Law, University of Cardiff.

[1] 1833 UNTS 396.

[2] Unfortunately, there is no agreed terminology for this type of fish stock. The term "shared stocks" is employed in this paper on the basis that it is both widely used (especially in the legal literature) and meaningful. The term "joint stocks" has also been used, although to a lesser extent, in the literature. The FAO frequently uses the term "transboundary stocks", which seems undesirable as this term is frequently used (and will be used in this paper) to refer to all fish stocks that migrate or are distributed across man-made boundaries in the sea. For a further discussion of terminology, see A. Van Houtte, Legal Aspects in the Management of Shared Fish Stocks – A Review *in* FAO, *Papers Presented at the Norway-FAO Expert Consultation on the Management of Shared Fish Stocks, Bergen, Norway, 7-10 October 2002*, FAO Fisheries Report No. 695, Supplement, pp. 30-42, at pp. 30-31.

Anastasia Strati, Maria Gavouneli & Nikos Skourtos (eds.), *Unresolved Issues and New Challenges to the Law of the Sea*, Martinus Nijhoff 2006, pp. 3-19.

is, the States in whose EEZs the stocks are found (in the case of shared stocks) or the coastal State(s) and the States fishing on the high seas (in the case of straddling stocks) – shall seek to agree on the necessary conservation and management measures.

Since the late 1980s and early 1990s fishing on the high seas has gradually expanded, partly as a result of distant-water vessels being increasingly excluded from foreign EEZs and partly because the pressure on fish stocks in EEZs has led to a search for alternative resources in the waters beyond. This expansion of fishing effort on the high seas has led to the issue of straddling stocks and the provisions (and limitations) of article 63(2) of the LOS Convention receiving quite a lot of attention, especially in Agenda 21, adopted at the 1992 UN Conference on Environment and Development (UNCED)[3]; the 1993-1995 UN Conference on Straddling Stocks and Highly Migratory Species[4] and the resulting 1995 Agreement on the Implementation of the Provisions of the UN Convention on the Law of the Sea relating to the Conservation and Management of Straddling Fish Stocks and Highly Migratory Fish Stocks (hereinafter cited as "the UN Fish Stocks Agreement")[5]; in the practice of regional fisheries organisations[6]; and in a number of high profile disputes such as the so-called "turbot war" in 1995 between Canada and the EU in the North-West Atlantic[7]; as well as in the academic literature[8]. By contrast, shared stocks have received very much less attention. There is no specific mention of shared stocks in Agenda 21 or in the Plan of Implementation adopted at the World Summit on Sustainable Development held at Johannesburg in 2002, nor have there been any high profile political disputes over such stocks (at least with a more than local attention). There has also been

---

[3] See Chapter 17, paragraphs 17.49-17.50. Chapter 17 is reproduced in 8 *International Organisations and the Law of the Sea Documentary Yearbook* 1992, pp. 400-432.

[4] Called for by UN General Assembly Resolution 47/192 (1992), 23 *Law of the Sea Bulletin* 1992, p. 14.

[5] 34 *ILM* 1995, p. 1542.

[6] For a useful and detailed survey of such practice, see O.S. Stokke (ed.), *Governing the High Seas Fisheries* (Oxford University Press, Oxford 2001).

[7] On which see, for example, P.G.G. Davies, The EC/Canadian Fisheries Dispute in the Northwest Atlantic, 44 *ICLQ* 1995, pp. 927-939; D. Freestone, Canada and the EU Reach Agreement to Settle the *Estai* Dispute, 10 *TIJMCL* 1995, pp. 397-411; and C.C. Joyner & A. Alvarez von Gustedt, The 1995 Turbot War: Lessons for the Law of the Sea, 11 *TIJMCL* 1996, pp. 425-458.

[8] See, from an extensive literature, P.G.G. Davies and C. Redgwell, The International Legal Regulation of Straddling Fish Stocks, 67 *BYBIL* 1996, pp. 199-274; E. Melzer, Global Overview of Straddling and Highly Migratory Fish Stocks: The Non-Sustainable Nature of High Seas Fisheries, 25 *ODIL* 1994, pp. 255-344; and E.L. Miles and W.T. Burke, Pressure on the United Nations Convention on the Law of the Sea of 1982 arising from New Fisheries Conflicts: The Problem of Straddling Stocks, 20 *ODIL* 1989, pp. 343-357.

much less discussion of shared stocks than of straddling stocks in the academic literature. This lack of attention to the issue of shared stocks is regrettable. The limitations of article 63(1) of the LOS Convention are as great as those of article 63(2), and the management in practice of shared stocks, which are almost certainly more important in terms of size of catch and fishing effort than straddling stocks, has frequently been less than adequate. In the view of the FAO, the management of both straddling and shared stocks remains one of the great challenges on the way towards achieving long-term sustainable fisheries[9].

The aim of this paper is to make a small contribution to raising awareness of the shortcomings in the management of shared stocks, and to suggest some ways in which these shortcomings might be addressed. After setting out a typology of shared stocks, the paper will survey the issues involved in the management of shared stocks and the shortcomings of article 63(1). It will then go on to look at the management of shared stocks in practice, before making some suggestions as to how the shortcomings in the management of shared stocks might be addressed.

2. TYPOLOGIES OF SHARED STOCKS

In much of the literature on shared stocks the conventional paradigm of a shared stock is a stock that migrates between or that straddles the EEZs of two States. In reality the position is far more complex. Shared stocks may be divided into the following types.

(i) A stock of fish of a species that is not highly migratory (as defined in Annex I of the LOS Convention), anadromous or catadromous and that migrates between or straddles[10] the EEZs of two, but no more than two, States. Such stocks will be referred to in this paper as bilateral shared stocks. Examples of such stocks include many of the stocks of Georges Bank off the Atlantic coast of North America, which are shared between Canada and the USA, and many of the stocks of the North Sea, which are shared between the EC (which, because of its Common Fisheries Policy, may be regarded as equivalent to a single coastal State) and Norway[11].

---

[9] FAO, *Report of the Norway-FAO Expert Consultation on the Management of Shared Fish Stocks, supra* note 2, at p. iv.

[10] i.e. that occurs on both sides of a boundary at the same time in random movements or in "dynamic pool" mixing: see M. Hayashi, The Management of Transboundary Fish Stocks under the LOS Convention, 8 *TIJMCL* 1993, pp. 245-261, at p. 247.

[11] Most of the examples of shared stocks used in this paper are drawn from the North Atlantic and European waters as these are the stocks with which the writer is most familiar. Of course, many examples could be cited from other regions.

(ii) A stock of a similar kind as that in (i), except that it is found in the EEZs of three or more States. Such stocks will be referred to as multilateral shared stocks. Examples include many of the fish stocks of the Baltic and the capelin stock found in the 200-mile zones off Greenland, Iceland and Jan Mayen.

(iii) A stock of fish of a species that is not highly migratory, anadromous or catadromous and is found at various stages of its life cycle both in the EEZs of two or more States and on the high seas. Such stocks will be referred to as shared straddling stocks. Examples of such stocks include the cod and haddock stocks of the Barents Sea and many of the fish stocks found in the Mediterranean.

(iv) A stock of fish of a species that is highly migratory (as defined in Annex I of the LOS Convention) and that is found at various stages of its life cycle in the EEZs of two or more States and on the high seas. Such stocks will be referred to as highly migratory shared stocks. Examples of such stocks include most stocks of tuna.

(v) A stock of fish of a species that is anadromous and that in migrating to or from its river of origin passes through the EEZ of one or more States that is or are not the State(s) of origin. Such stocks will be referred to as anadromous shared stocks. Examples of such stocks include many of the salmon stocks of the eastern North Pacific.

(vi) A stock of fish of a species that is catadromous and that in migrating to or from the high seas passes through the EEZ of one or more States that is or are not the State(s) in whose fresh waters the stock spends the major part of its life cycle. Such stocks will be referred to as catadromous shared stocks. Examples of such stocks include some of the eel stocks of Western Europe.

Highly migratory, anadromous and catadromous (shared) stocks are regulated by articles 64, 66 and 67 of the LOS Convention[12]. These provisions may be regarded as *leges speciales*, which supplant the general provisions of article 63(1) relating to shared stocks. For this reason these kinds of stocks will not generally be considered any further in this paper, which focuses on article 63(1). On the other hand, bilateral and multilateral shared stocks are regulated exclusively by article 63(1), while shared straddling stocks would seem to be regulated both by article 63(1) and article 63(2). This paper therefore is concerned with the first three kinds of shared stocks identified above.

---

[12] And highly migratory stocks also by the UN Fish Stocks Agreement.

3. ISSUES RELATED TO THE MANAGEMENT OF SHARED STOCKS

The management of shared stocks raises a number of issues that do not arise in relation to a stock found solely in the EEZ of a single coastal State. The main such issues are as follows[13]:

(i) *Identification of shared stocks*. It is an essential pre-requisite for the effective management of a shared stock that the States concerned agree that the stock in question is indeed one that they share. This may seem not only an obvious point but one that is unlikely to cause problems in practice because it will be self-evident that a stock is shared. However, this is not always the case. For example, when in the late 1970s the EC and Norway entered into a regular system of arrangements jointly to manage the stocks that they shared, Norway argued that these stocks included the western mackerel stock; the EC, however, denied that the stock was shared and took the view that it was an exclusive EC stock[14]. It was only in the late 1980s that the EC acknowledged that the stock was indeed shared, and not until the early 1990s that both States recognised that the stock was not only shared but was also a straddling one[15]. It may also be the case that over time a stock may change its migratory pattern (for example, because of environmental factors), causing it to cease to be just a single State stock and to become a shared (strad-

---

[13] The analysis that follows is, for reasons of space, necessarily very simplified. For a comprehensive (and still the best) study of these issues, see J.A. Gulland, *Some Problems of the Management of Shared Stocks*, FAO Fisheries Technical Paper No. 206 (1980), on which this section draws heavily. Later studies, several of which also acknowledge their indebtedness to Gulland, include: J.F. Caddy, *Some Considerations relevant to the Definition of Shared Stocks and their Allocation between Adjacent Economic Zones*, FAO Fisheries Circular No. 749 (1982); *idem.*, An Objective Approach to the Negotiation of Allocations from Shared Living Resources, 20 *Marine Policy* 1996, 145-155; Hayashi, *supra* note 10, especially at pp. 247-248 and 258-260; G.R. Munro, The Management of Shared Fishery Resources under Extended Jurisdiction, *in* G. Ulfstein, P. Andersen & R. Churchill (eds.), *The Regulation of Fisheries: Legal, Economic and Social Aspects* (Council of Europe, Strasbourg 1987) pp. 27-45; G. Saetersdal, Problems of Managing and Sharing of Living Resources under the New Ocean Regime, 4 *Ocean Yearbook* 1983, pp. 45-49; and G. Munro, A. Van Houtte & R. Willman, *The Conservation and Management of Shared Fish Stocks: Legal and Economic Aspects*, FAO Fisheries Technical Paper No. 465 (2004). Unfortunately, the last of these became available to the author of this paper too late to be taken into account. However, it is said to draw "heavily" upon the Norway-FAO Expert Consultation, *supra* note 9, at p. iv, to which the author has had access.

[14] European Commission COM (82) 25.

[15] R.R. Churchill, Managing Straddling Fish Stocks in the North-East Atlantic: A Multiplicity of Instruments and Regime Linkages – but How Effective a Management?, *in* Stokke, *supra* note 6, pp. 235-272, at p. 262-263. See also D. Day, Managing Transboundary Fish Stocks: Lessons from the North Atlantic, *in* G. Blake (ed.), *Maritime Boundaries* (Routledge, London 1994) pp. 103-126, at pp. 105-106 and 114.

dling) stock: this has happened with the Norwegian spring-spawning herring in the North-East Atlantic, for example[16].

(ii) *Research.* It is, of course, axiomatic that satisfactory management of a fish stock is dependent on adequate scientific knowledge of that stock. While the States that share a stock could each manage that stock separately (although co-operative management is preferable, as will be suggested shortly), such individual management would be even less effective than it otherwise might be if the States concerned did not share their scientific knowledge of the stock. For example, if a stock spends the early part of its life cycle in the EEZ of one State but then as mature fish migrates to the EEZ of another State, the latter would be hampered in its management of the stock in its EEZ (for example, in determining a sustainable level of exploitation) if it had no knowledge of what was happening to the stock in the other State's EEZ (for example, the level of recruitment to the stock). Co-operation in scientific research of shared stocks need not necessarily be directly between the States concerned, but could take place through an international organisation concerned with fisheries research, such as the International Council for the Exploration of the Sea (ICES).

(iii) *Co-operation in management between the States concerned.* In theory each State sharing a stock with one or more other States could manage that stock separately. Such management would be likely, however, to be less than optimum, especially if the stock spent the various stages of its life cycle in the EEZs of different States or the mature fish migrated through the EEZs of several States. In the former case, if a State whose EEZ constituted the spawning and nursery ground for a particular stock took strict conservation measures, such measures would risk being undermined if the stock in whose EEZ the stock spent most of its adult life permitted too many fish to be caught. With the second type of migratory stock the States fishing for such a stock in their EEZs would have no idea of the level of catch to prescribe unless they knew what levels were being set by the other States sharing the stock. If each set a level of catch for its EEZ without reference to the other States sharing the stock, the combined levels of catch might either exceed a sustainable level for the stock as a whole (in which case there would be overfishing and the size of the stock would eventually decline), or they might be less than the level of sustainable catch (in which case there would be waste, in the sense that fish that could have been caught for human consumption without endangering the longer-term sustainability of the stock would not be caught and would die of natural causes instead). Where a stock straddles the boundary between the EEZs of two States, with little movement

---

[16] *Ibid.*, pp. 241-243.

of individuals across the boundary, there will less need for (and less benefit from) co-operative management. Overall, however, the FAO Consultation on the Management of Shared Fish Stocks, held in 2002, concluded that, with very few exceptions, non-co-operative management of shared fishery resources carried with it the threat of over-exploitation. However, while co-operative management was an essential pre-requisite for effective resource management, it did not guarantee such management[17]. The Consultation also concluded that a co-operative management arrangement would not succeed unless all the States participating in the arrangement anticipated receiving long-term benefits from it that were at least equal to the long-term benefits they would expect to receive in the absence of the arrangement[18].

If the States sharing a stock do agree to co-operate, they will need to seek agreement on management strategies (for example, whether the strategy is to be a short-term one or a long-term one, the latter being likely to involve lower catches in the short term than a short-term strategy) and on management measures (for example, technical conservation measures such as closed areas and seasons and gear regulations, and effort limitation in terms of the size of the catch, number of vessels and so on). It hardly needs to be said that reaching agreement on these issues is likely to be very difficult (and to succeed may involve the use of "side payments" such as quota trades or mutual access arrangements[19]), and will be even where more difficult where a stock is a straddling as well as a shared one.

(iv) *Allocation and Access*. Once States sharing a stock have agreed to co-operate in its management, questions of allocation of the agreed total allowable catch (TAC) or alternative forms of effort limitation (such as the number of vessels permitted to fish), and where each State may take its share of the catch or prosecute its share of the permitted effort, will arise. Such questions are particularly acute in relation to the first type of stock considered under the previous point. If the spawning and nursery grounds of a stock are located in the EEZ of one State but the fish are of mature catchable size only in the EEZ of another State, the first State would have little incentive to adopt the measures necessary to conserve the spawning and immature fish unless it was assured that its vessels would be able to take part of the mature catchable stock: This could, of course, only happen if its vessels were given access to the EEZ of the other State. Once it is acknowledged in the case of a

---

[17] *Supra* note 9. It should be noted that in this publication the FAO uses the term "shared stocks" to refer not only to shared stocks as that term is used in this paper but also to straddling stocks.

[18] *Ibid.*

[19] *Ibid.*

jointly managed shared stock (whatever the precise nature of that sharing) that both/all States that share that stock are to be permitted to harvest the stock, questions will arise as to how shares of the harvest are to be allocated (whether as a percentage of the TAC, or the number of vessels permitted to fish, or in some other way), and if allocation is in terms of a tonnage of fish to be caught, the criteria for such allocation (whether it is to reflect historic catches, zonal attachments, past contributions to conservation and enforcement, or some other basis). Where the vessels of one State are given access to the other State's (or States') EEZ, the question of what kind of conditions such access should be subject to will also arise.

(v) *Enforcement*[20]. If the States sharing a particular stock have agreed on co-operative management measures, each State needs to feel confident that its partner(s) in the co-operative arrangement is/are properly observing and enforcing the agreed measures in its/their EEZ. Such confidence may be engendered by exchanging information on enforcement, by permitting observers from other States to be placed on enforcement vessels, by joint enforcement, and so on. If the States concerned have not agreed a boundary between their overlapping EEZs, additional issues arise, notably over how enforcement is to take place in the unresolved boundary area.

(vi) *Access of third States*. If the States sharing a particular stock have agreed on co-operative management for that stock, they may also be faced with the question of whether third States should be permitted access to fish for the shared stock, and if so, under what conditions. Even if the shared stock is fully exploited by the States sharing it, one or more such States may nevertheless have an interest in permitting third States access; for example, because it desires thereby to obtain access for its vessels to the EEZ of the third State(s) concerned in order to enable its vessels to catch species not found in its own waters. This is the case with the shared stocks of the Barents Sea, where some third States are permitted to fish in the Norwegian EEZ[21].

Having examined (some of) the issues involved in the management of shared stocks, we turn now to see how these issues are addressed in the UN Convention on the Law of the Sea.

---

[20] This issue includes monitoring and surveillance as well as arrest and prosecution.

[21] R. Churchill and G. Ulfstein, *Marine Management in Disputed Areas: The Case of the Barents Sea* (Routledge, London 1992) pp. 110-111.

4. ARTICLE 63(1) OF THE UN CONVENTION ON THE LAW OF THE SEA AND ITS SHORTCOMINGS[22]

As was mentioned earlier, shared stocks are dealt with by the LOS Convention in article 63(1). This provision reads as follows:

> "Where the same stock or stocks of associated species occur within the exclusive economic zones of two or more coastal States, these States shall seek, either directly or through appropriate sub-regional or regional organizations, to agree upon the measures necessary to co-ordinate and ensure the conservation and development of such stocks without prejudice to the other provisions of this Part."

This provision requires States sharing stocks to "seek ... to agree" on measures necessary to co-ordinate and ensure the conservation and development of such stocks. These States are required, either directly or through an appropriate regional organisation, to negotiate in good faith[23] but they are not required to reach agreement on co-ordinated measures[24]. It is noteworthy that article 63(1) gives States very little guidance in conducting such negotiations. In particular, it says almost nothing about the issues just discussed in the previous section of this paper. However, it should be noted that the "without prejudice" clause at the end of article 63(1) means that the States concerned, when managing a shared stock (whether doing so co-operatively or otherwise), are still bound by their conservation duties under articles 61 and 62 of the Convention. These include promotion of the optimum utilisation of the stock, prevention of its over-exploitation, the maintenance or restoration of the population of the stock at a level that produces the maximum sustainable yield as qualified by various factors, the setting of an allowable catch, and the taking into account of the best scientific advice available. In practice, it would be difficult for a State properly to fulfil its obligations under articles 61 and 62 in respect of shared stocks without some form of col-

---

[22] For a fuller analysis of article 63(1) than that that follows, see Hayashi, *supra* note 10, especially at pp. 248-252; and International Law Association Committee on the EEZ, *Principles Applicable to Living Resources Occurring both within and without the Exclusive Economic Zone or in Zones of Overlapping Claims*, *in* International Law Association, *Report of the Sixty-Fifth Conference* (International Law Association, Cairo 1993) pp. 254 *et seq.*, at pp. 257-264.

[23] S.N. Nandan, S. Rosenne & N.R. Grandy (eds.), *United Nations Convention on the Law of the Sea 1982: A Commentary* (vol. II, Martinus Nijhoff, Dordrecht 1993) p. 646.

[24] It has been argued that co-ordinated measures amount to no more than a harmonisation of national measures relating to the shared stock in question. See ILA Report, *supra* note 22, at p. 259.

laborative arrangement with the other State(s) sharing the stock[25]. It should also be noted that in the case of shared stocks that are also straddling stocks, the principles of fisheries management set out in articles 5 and 6 of the UN Fish Stocks Agreement (including the precautionary approach) will apply to the management of such stocks in the EEZs of States that are parties to the Agreement.

It is arguable whether it is realistic to have expected the Convention to have given or have been able to give any greater guidance in the management of shared stocks than that provided in article 63(1), especially given the diverse nature of shared stocks. The Fish Stocks Agreement does provide much greater guidance for the collaborative management of straddling stocks than article 63(1) does for shared stocks, but it required the time and effort of a two-year diplomatic conference, not to mention the political pressures that prompted that conference, to achieve this. Such negotiating resources could obviously not be devoted at the Third UN Conference on the Law of the Sea ("UNCLOS III") to a single issue such as the management of shared stocks, nor did that issue have the same political profile as that of straddling stocks in the early 1990s.

The limitations and shortcomings of article 63(1) would be of little consequence if in practice all shared stocks were co-operatively managed and such management was effective. Whether this is the case is the next question we must turn to consider.

5. THE MANAGEMENT OF SHARED STOCKS IN PRACTICE

Assuming that it would be desirable for all shared stocks to be co-operatively managed, it might seem useful to begin by trying to calculate the number of shared stock co-operative arrangements that would be required. One way of doing this might be to calculate the number of potential maritime boundaries that there are and then to deduce from that the number of shared stock co-operative arrangements that might be required. One writer has indeed carried out such an exercise. Caddy suggests that there are approximately 500 potential maritime boundaries in the world, and assuming that there are at least two or three important shared stocks per boundary, arrives at a figure of some 1,000 to 1,500 actual or potential shared stocks that

---

[25] Hayashi, *supra* note 10, at p. 250. Article 56(2), which requires a coastal State to exercise its rights in its EEZ (including its right to exploit the living resources of its EEZ) with due regard to the rights of other States (including, therefore, their right to exploit the living resources of their EEZs), may also be relevant. See ILA Report, *supra* note 22, at p. 262.

would benefit from co-operative management[26]. This methodology seems flawed. First, not every maritime boundary has a shared stock or stocks. Where States are opposite one another and some distance apart, there may be no shared stocks because there is a natural boundary, such as a deep water channel, that precludes stocks crossing or straddling the boundary[27]. Secondly, a single shared stock may cross several boundaries; for example, many of the North Sea stocks cross up to a dozen boundaries. Thus, there is not necessarily any correlation between the number of boundaries and the number of shared stocks. Thirdly, if States agree on a co-operative arrangement for shared stocks, there is usually a single arrangement covering all stocks that are shared by the States concerned: this is the case for the shared stocks of the Barents and North Seas, for example. Lastly, only about half of all potential maritime boundary agreements have been agreed. Until a boundary has been definitively established, it is not always possible to be sure whether there will be any shared stocks and, if so, which States will share them. It is therefore probably impossible at the present time both to calculate how many shared stocks there are and how many of them would benefit from some form of co-operative management. It is no doubt safe to say that the number runs to at least several dozen, and probably exceeds 100, possibly by a substantial margin.

Not only is it almost impossible to calculate how many shared stocks there are, it is also very difficult to know how many shared stock co-operative management arrangements have so far actually been agreed. Owen carried out a survey of 39 arrangements in 2001. These arrangements, which are described as being selected from "a larger pool", include not only arrangements for the management of shared stocks but also arrangements that embody a management approach which is potentially applicable to shared stocks[28]. When further examined, Owen's 39 arrangements amount to 28 arrangements for the management of one or more shared stocks. The writer is aware of a further 10 arrangements, making a total of 38 in all. There are almost certainly a (possibly significant) number of further arrangements of which the writer is unaware. The main problem in trying to calculate the

---

[26] J.F. Caddy, Establishing a Consultative Mechanism or Arrangement for Managing Shared Stocks within the Jurisdiction of Contiguous States, *in* D.A. Hancock (ed.), *Joint Workshop Proceedings – Taking Stock: Defining and Managing Shared Resources*, Darwin 15-16 July 1997 (Australian Society for Fish Biology, Sydney 1998) p. 92, as quoted in D. Owen, Legal and Institutional Aspects of Management Arrangements for Shared Stocks of Marine Fish, *in* M. Fitzmaurice and M. Szuniewicz (eds.), *Exploitation of Natural Resources in the 21st Century: The Challenge of Sustainable Development* (Kluwer, The Hague 2003) pp. 271-312, at p. 272.

[27] Gulland, *supra* note 13, section 2.2.2.

[28] Owen, *supra* note 26, at pp. 273-274.

number of, not to mention study, shared stock co-operative management arrangements is that such arrangements are frequently not well publicised. Whatever the number of arrangements that actually exist may be, it is almost certainly a fairly small proportion of the total potential number of such arrangements[29]. In other words, there are a considerable number of shared stocks for which no co-operative management arrangement yet exists. These include the stocks shared between Canada and the USA in the Gulf of Maine[30] and probably numerous shared stocks in South and South-East Asia, parts of the Caribbean and the east coast of Africa.

Of the 38 or more shared stock co-operative management arrangements that actually do exist, how many have been effective in managing the stock(s) concerned? This is a very difficult question to answer. There have been a number of studies examining shared stock co-operative management arrangements, but they have tended to focus on the formal structures of such arrangements without really discussing their effectiveness[31]. There appear to be only a few studies in the academic literature that address the effectiveness of particular arrangements[32], notwithstanding the fact that Munro pointed to the need for case studies of shared stock arrangements nearly 20 years ago[33]. It may also be the case that information on the effectiveness of shared stock arrangements is available but is not well publicised or easily accessible[34]. One can only echo Munro and hope that those with an interest in international fisheries, whether they be biologists, economists, political scientists or lawyers, will produce case studies of shared stock co-operative management arrangements, evaluating their effectiveness and seeking to explain the reasons for their effectiveness or lack of it. It is therefore impossible at the pre-

---

[29] According to the FAO, "the vast majority of shared stocks are not managed jointly by neighbouring States"; see FAO, *The State of World Fisheries and Aquaculture* (1998) www.fao.org/docrep/W9900E?w9900e03.htm, Box 6.

[30] On which see Day, *supra* note 15, at pp. 106 and 111.

[31] See, for example, Hayashi, *supra* note 10, pp. 252-257; E. Hey, *The Regime for the Exploitation of Transboundary Marine Fisheries Resources* (Martinus Nijhoff, Dordrecht 1989) pp. 89-96 and Annex I; Owen, *supra* note 26; van Houtte, *supra* note 2, at pp. 4-8.

[32] For examples, see Churchill & Ulfstein, *supra* note 22, chapter 4; O.S. Stokke, The Loophole of the Barents Sea Fisheries Regime, *in* Stokke, *supra* note 6, pp. 273-301 (both on the shared stocks of the Barents Sea); Churchill, *supra* note 15 (on the shared straddling stocks of herring and mackerel in the North East-Atlantic); and some dozen case studies produced for the Norway-FAO Expert Consultation on the Management of Shared Fish Stocks, held in 2002, *supra* note 2.

[33] Munro, *supra* note 13, at p. 39.

[34] For example, the Norwegian Government publishes very detailed and informative annual reports on the shared stock co-operative management arrangements in which it participates, but these reports are only accessible to those who can read Norwegian. For recent reports, see Norwegian Parliamentary Papers, St. meld. nr. 47 (1997-98) and St. meld. nr. 50 (200-2001).

sent time to say how effective those shared stock co-operative management arrangements that do exist have been. However, given that it is well recognised that the management of stocks of fish confined to the EEZ of a single State has frequently been ineffective[35], it would be surprising if the record were any better in the case of shared stocks[36].

6. WHAT STEPS SHOULD THE INTERNATIONAL COMMUNITY TAKE TO ADDRESS SHORTCOMINGS IN THE MANAGEMENT OF SHARED STOCKS?

As suggested above, there appear to be many shared stocks for which co-operative management arrangements do not yet exist, notwithstanding the fact that such co-operative arrangements are generally desirable. Furthermore, where such arrangements do exist, they are frequently ineffective. As has also been seen, although article 63(1) of the LOS Convention requires States to enter into negotiations to seek agreement on shared stock co-operative management arrangements, it does not provide any real advice or guidance as to how such negotiations should be conducted or on the substantive content of any resulting agreement. There seems, therefore, clearly to be a need for some more helpful advice and guidance on these matters to be provided to States by the international community.

One possible way of providing such advice and guidance would be to do the same as was done with article 63(2) in the case of straddling stocks, and that is to conclude an Implementation Agreement (i.e. an agreement implementing article 63(1) of the LOS Convention). However, the Implementation Agreement for straddling stocks, the UN Fish Stocks Agreement, is probably not an appropriate model. First, that Agreement came about largely because of the political impetus generated by a number of important coastal States that felt that the fish stocks within their 200-mile zones were suffering as a result of excessive fishing for straddling stocks in the immediately adjacent high seas areas by vessels from distant-water fishing States and that this state of affairs was due to the weaknesses of article 63(2). That kind of political impetus does not currently exist in the case of shared stocks. Secondly, the UN Fish Stocks Agreement took six years to enter into force[37] and

---

[35] See Agenda 21, chapter 17, paragraph 17.72; and FAO, *infra.*

[36] According to the FAO, about 28% of all fish stocks are depleted or over-exploited: see FAO, *The State of World Fisheries and Aquaculture*, 2002, Part I (The Status of Fishery Resources), http://www.fao.org/documents/show_cdr.asp?url_file=/dorep/005/y7300e/y7300e00.htm. Statistically, the likelihood is that quite a number of these stocks are shared.

[37] It is true, however, that the Agreement had considerable influence on the practice of States and regional fisheries organisations before its entry into force: for some examples, see Stokke, *supra* note 6, *passim.*

even 10 years after its conclusion has not been widely ratified[38]. Without the same political profile as the straddling stock issue, it is likely that an Implementation Agreement on shared stocks would take longer to enter into force and might not be widely ratified. Thirdly, the kind of advice and guidance that States need in order to conclude a co-operative management arrangement for shared stocks is probably more suitably and easily expressed in a soft law or non-legal document than a hard law instrument. There is also some evidence that coastal States are resistant to hard law obligations or directions when it comes to the fisheries of their EEZs, which of course include shared stocks. This is suggested by the fact that the hard law conservation and management obligations of coastal States contained in the LOS Convention (principally in articles 61 and 62) are often not reproduced in States' domestic legislation and seem in practice to have been relatively ineffective. Furthermore, coastal States seem resistant to hard law solutions to overcome their management failures within their EEZs over the past 25 years. Thus, the Code of Conduct for Responsible Fisheries[39] and the Plans of Action adopted thereunder[40], which seek in part to improve coastal State management within the EEZ, are all soft law instruments.

In considering what would be a suitable form of soft law or non law instrument to contain the guidance to States on the management of shared stocks that is lacking in the LOS Convention it may be helpful to begin by focusing on what the principal obstacles to such management are. Such obstacles include a lack of trust between the States concerned, unresolved and/or disputed maritime boundaries, failure to agree that a particular stock is shared, the lack of funding necessary to carry out effective fisheries management, and the lack of the necessary political will to engage in co-operative management[41]. The first two obstacles do not seem amenable to easy resolution, even with the assistance of a third party. As regards the possible unwillingness of the States concerned to recognise that a particular stock is shared, the FAO could help, as could regional marine scientific organizations (such as the International Council for the Exploration of the Sea and the International Pacific Council for the Exploration of the Sea) in those

---

[38] As of 5 January 2005 the Agreement had received 52 ratifications, one third of which were from the EC and its Member States.

[39] For the text see: http://www.fao.org/documents/show_cdr.asp?url_file=/DOCREP/005/v9878e/v9878e00.htm.

[40] For the text see: http://www.fao.org/figis/servlet/static?dom=org&xml=ipoas_prog.xml &xp_lang=en. The four Plans of Action so far adopted deal with the incidental catches of seabirds in long-line fisheries; the conservation and management of sharks; the management of fishing capacity; and illegal, unreported and unregulated (IUU) fishing.

[41] Owen, *supra* note 26, p. 307.

regions where such organizations exist. As regards the lack of funding for effective co-operative fisheries management, shortage of funds is a problem that bedevils even purely national fisheries management in a number of developing, particularly African, States, and can only be addressed on a long-term basis through the much needed economic development of the States concerned for which the efforts and assistance of the international community in general are needed. The lack of the necessary political will is undoubtedly the biggest obstacle to the effective co-operative management of shared stocks[42]. To overcome this obstacle, the States concerned need to be shown that a lack of co-operative management is to their detriment and contrary to their own interests, and that it is possible to devise co-operative arrangements that will give each State greater benefits than would occur in the absence of such arrangements. The FAO does not appear to be particularly well suited to such a directly explicative role, because it is too political a body (although, of course, it is excellent at offering guidance in general terms, as will be seen below). Other States are unlikely to have sufficient interest to want to play such a role, although possibly this could be done by a regional fisheries organization or a regional marine scientific organization. It may well be that the bodies which are most suitable for playing such a role are private actors, such as environmental non-governmental organizations or possibly even fisherman's organizations.

Where there is the political will to co-operate and there are no other obstacles to co-operation, there is a range of measures and advice available to guide States both as to the substantive content of a co-operative management arrangement and as to the bargaining strategies to help achieve such an arrangement. Much such advice and guidance has been offered by the FAO. Thus, the Code of Conduct for Responsible Fisheries contains a number of provisions to guide States in the management of shared stocks. Paragraph 12.17 provides that States should develop collaborative research programmes to improve understanding of the priority, environment and status of shared stocks[43]. Paragraph 7.1.3 stipulates that States should co-operate to ensure the effective conservation and management of shared stocks, while paragraph 7.3.1 points out that for such management to be effective, it

---

[42] Interestingly, the existence of the necessary political will does not seem to be dependent on the general state of relations between the States concerned. Thus, for example, Norway and the former Soviet Union were able to co-operate quite successfully over the management of their shared stocks in the Barents Sea during more that a decade of the Cold War, whereas Canada and the USA have not engaged in co-operative management of their shared stocks in the Gulf of Maine even though their dispute over the maritime boundary was resolved by the International Court of Justice in 1984.

[43] Cf. also paragraphs 6.4 and 7.4.6.

should be concerned with the whole stock unit over its entire area of distribution. Lastly paragraph 7.3.2 states that the conservation and management measures established by the States concerned for a shared stock should be compatible[44]. Much more detailed guidance may be found in the Report of the Norway- FAO Expert Consultation on the Management of Shared Fish Stocks, held in 2002[45]. This contains a wealth of wise advice relating to the negotiation and content of arrangements for managing shared stocks, though without any intention of being prescriptive. The background papers produced for the Consultation also contain a lot of very useful information and accounts of practical experience in the management of shared stocks. Other activities of the FAO relating to the management of shared stocks include the publication of a number of very useful circulars and technical papers, such as those by Gulland, Caddy and Munro *et al.*, referred to earlier in this paper[46], and the holding of a number of workshops on the management of shared stocks, for example the workshops on shared stocks in South East Asia in 1985[47], shared fishery resources in the Lesser Antilles in 1986[48] and shared small pelagic fishery resources in North-West Africa in 2002[49]. Apart from the work of the FAO, advice and guidance on negotiating conservation and management arrangements for shared stocks may be found in various academic writings, including those cited in this paper. Finally, it should be noted that the 1978 UNEP Draft Principles of Conduct in the Field of the Environment for the Guidance of States in the Conservation and Harmonious Utilization of Natural Resources Shared by Two or More States[50] are not without relevance. Although not designed specifically with fisheries in mind or being legally binding, the Draft Principles do contain a number of provisions that are useful in the context of the management of shared fish stocks, in particular procedural principles relating to notification and consultation.

Is anything further required? One possibility might be a Plan of Action under the Code of Conduct to draw together all the existing advice and experience in the materials referred to above. Whether this would be a particularly

---

[44] This provision, like paragraph 7.11.3, applies to all kinds of transboundary stocks, and not just shared stocks.

[45] *Supra* note 9.

[46] *Supra* note 13.

[47] FAO, *Report of the FAO/SEAFDEC Workshop on Shared Stocks in Southeast Asia*, FAO Fisheries Report No. 337 (1985).

[48] FAO, *Report and Proceedings of the Expert Consultations on Shared Fishery Resources of the Lesser Antilles Region*, FAO Fisheries Report No. 383 (1986).

[49] FAO, *Report of the Workshop on the Management of Shared Small Pelagic Fishery Resources in Northwest Africa*, FAO Fisheries Report No. 675 (2002). See also the FAO Report, *supra* note 28.

[50] 17 *ILM* 1978, p. 1094.

useful exercise and add much to what already exists is perhaps debatable. Certainly there would seem to be little enthusiasm for conducting such an exercise if one is to judge from the responses to the FAO 2002 Expert Consultation on shared stocks (referred to above) that were expressed at the 25th meeting of FAO's Committee on Fisheries: these responses were generally decidedly lukewarm[51].

7. CONCLUSIONS

The title of this book is *Unresolved Issues and New Challenges to the Law of the Sea*. It is hoped that this paper has shown that the issue of the management of shared fish stocks is indeed a challenge to the Law of the Sea, although a continuing challenge rather than a new one. As was pointed out at the beginning of this paper, in the view of the FAO, the management of shared stocks remains one of the greatest challenges to achieving long-term sustainable fisheries. This paper also argues that the main provision of the LOS Convention dealing with the management of shared fish stocks, article 63(1), is inadequate and needs to be supplemented. In this sense the issue of the management of shared stocks could be said to be "unresolved". This paper suggests that the shortcomings of article 63(1) need to be resolved because, although it is generally agreed that most shared fish stocks are best managed co-operatively, few are so managed; and in the case of those that are, such management is often not effective. The weaknesses of article 63(1), it is argued, are best remedied, not through the adoption of an implementation agreement (as has been done with article 63(2) in the case of straddling fish stocks) or some other hard law solution, but rather through encouraging States that share fish stocks to follow the guidance and advice on how shared fish stocks are best managed co-operatively that are contained in various instruments and documents produced by the FAO and others, and by studying accounts of the lessons that may be learned from existing conservation and managements arrangements for shared stocks. If this is done, there are good prospects that the challenge of managing shared fish stocks can be successfully met.

---

[51] FAO, *Report of the 25th Session of the Committee on Fisheries, Rome, 24-28 February 2003*, FAO Fisheries Report No. 702, p. 6, paragraph 33.

Chapter 2

PROTECTION OF THE UNDERWATER CULTURAL HERITAGE:
FROM THE SHORTCOMINGS OF THE UN CONVENTION ON
THE LAW OF THE SEA TO THE COMPROMISES
OF THE UNESCO CONVENTION

*Anastasia Strati**

1. INTRODUCTION

On 2 November 2001, the General Conference of UNESCO adopted its fourth heritage convention, the Convention on the Protection of the Underwater Cultural Heritage[1]. The Convention was adopted by 87 affirmative votes, while four States (Norway, the Russian Federation, Turkey and Venezuela) voted against and 15 abstained from voting (Brazil, Colombia, the Czech Republic, France, Greece, Germany, Guinea-Bissau, Iceland, Israel, the Netherlands, Paraguay, Sweden, Switzerland, the United Kingdom, Uruguay). The Convention shall enter into force three months after the deposit of the twentieth instrument of ratification, acceptance, approval or accession. As yet, six States have ratified the Convention: Panama (20/05/03), Bulgaria (06/10/03), Croatia (01/12/04), Spain (06/06/05), Libyan Arab Jamahiriya (23/06/05) and Nigeria (21/10/05).

There has already been considerable delay in the adoption of legal rules to protect the underwater cultural heritage. The invention of the aqualung in 1943 made underwater sites accessible with the result that most archaeological remains in shallow water have been plundered. Modern advances in deep seabed technology and in particular the operations of salvage companies have proved to be equally detrimental to deepwater archaeological sites; unless proper precautions are taken, these too will be looted. The first legis-

---

* Law of the Sea Expert, Hellenic Ministry of Foreign Affairs. The opinions expressed in this article are strictly personal.

[1] See Annex I.

Anastasia Strati, Maria Gavouneli & Nikos Skourtos (eds.), *Unresolved Issues and New Challenges to the Law of the Sea*, Martinus Nijhoff Publishers 2006, pp. 21-62.

lative attempt to develop rules for the protection of the underwater cultural heritage was undertaken at the regional level by the Council of Europe. Regrettably, the Draft 1985 European Convention on the Protection of the Underwater Cultural Heritage (hereinafter cited as "Draft European Convention")[2] prepared by an *Ad Hoc* Committee of Experts, was not approved by the Committee of Ministers as there was no agreement on the crucial question of jurisdiction. Thus, no decision was taken to open the Convention for signature.

---

[2] Council of Europe, *Ad Hoc* Committee of Experts on the Underwater Cultural Heritage (CAHAQ), *Final Activity Report*, Doc. CAHAQ(85)5, Strasbourg, 23 April 1985 (not a public document). The Draft European Convention adopted a wide variety of measures, which encompass all aspects of the protection of underwater cultural heritage. The advocation of the fundamental principle of the *in situ* protection of underwater cultural property is accompanied by the duty of the Parties to take all appropriate measures to conserve recovered property as well as to fully record finds. Discoveries of underwater cultural property within the 'area' of a contracting State should be reported to the competent authorities, the discoverers being required to leave the property where it is situated. In addition, contracting States may require their nationals to notify the competent authorities about discoveries made in places where no State exercises control over such property. Contracting States are also required to take appropriate measures to ensure the proper documentation of recovered property, to promote public appreciation of the underwater cultural heritage and the need to protect it, and to further underwater research. The control of traffic in underwater cultural property and the restriction of its illegal circulation is another fundamental objective of the Convention. In this respect, each party shall make available evidence of any lawful export of such property and notify the other contracting states about the illegal recovery or export of such property. The proposed regime shall not interfere with property rights, the law of salvage or laws and practices with respect to cultural exchanges; nor will it prejudice any jurisdiction or rights, which contracting States may otherwise have under international law in respect of the protection of the underwater cultural heritage. The implementation of the Convention is to be kept under review by a Standing Committee.

As far as the territorial scope of application of the Draft European Convention is concerned, article 2 adopted a provision similar to article 303(2) of the 1982 United Nations Convention on the Law of the Sea (hereinafter cited as "LOS Convention"). It reads: "1. For the purposes of this Convention, the 'area' of a contracting State means its territorial sea and, in respect of a contracting State which has established it, the zone referred to in paragraph 2; 2. A contracting State which has established a contiguous zone in conformity with international law may presume that removal of underwater cultural property from the seabed in that zone without its approval would result in infringement within its territory or territorial sea of laws and regulations applied in that zone". There is, however, an important difference between the two articles. Article 2 requires the prior establishment of a general contiguous zone, while, as will be seen below, article 303(2) of the LOS Convention does not establish the declaration of the contiguous zone as a prerequisite for its application.

Finally, article 17 of the Draft European Convention enables contracting States to take all appropriate measures to protect underwater cultural property while exercising their resource-related jurisdiction on the continental shelf. Such measures should not be viewed as an expansion of coastal jurisdiction over the continental shelf, but rather as an expression of the duty to protect underwater cultural heritage.

In 1994 the International Law Association adopted the Draft Convention on the Protection of the Underwater Cultural Heritage, prepared by its Committee on Cultural Heritage (hereinafter cited as "ILA Draft")[3]. The ILA Draft Convention was subsequently submitted to UNESCO and constituted the basis of discussions that took place at UNESCO between 1996 and 2001. However, as will be seen below, the UNESCO Convention differs substantially from the ILA Draft in crucial issues, such as jurisdiction and scope of application.

2. THE PRE-EXISTING REGIME OF PROTECTION

2.1. International instruments specifically dealing with underwater cultural heritage

Recommendation 848 (1978) of the Parliamentary Assembly of the Council of Europe[4] was the first instrument to deal with the protection of underwater cultural heritage. It recognised its historical and cultural significance and suggested, *inter alia,* the drawing-up of a European Convention[5], the declaration of 200-mile national cultural protection zones and, in an Annex, the minimum legal requirements that should be incorporated into national legislation.

Twenty-two years later, Recommendation 1486 (2000) of the Parliamentary Assembly of the Council of Europe on maritime and fluvial cultural heritage[6], while noting that the Committee of Ministers failed to bring to fruition one of the main proposals of Recommendation 848 (1978), namely the elaboration of a European Convention on the protection of the underwater cultural heritage, suggested that the Council of Europe should be associated with the elaboration by UNESCO of an international convention on this subject. It also encouraged States to protect the underwater cultural heritage

---

[3] See International Committee on Cultural Heritage Law, *Report and Draft Convention on the Protection of the Underwater Cultural Heritage,* International Law Association 66th Conference, Buenos Aires, 14-20 August 1994.

[4] Council of Europe, *Texts adopted by the Assembly,* sessions 30-32 (1978-81). See also Council of Europe, *The Underwater Cultural Heritage,* Report of the Committee on Culture and Education, Doc. 4200-E, Strasbourg, 1978, pp. 1-4.

[5] The necessity of drawing up a European Convention on the protection of underwater cultural heritage was also stressed by Recommendation 883 (1984) of the Parliamentary Assembly on the United Nations Convention on the Law of the Sea and Recommendation 997 (1984) of the Parliamentary Assembly on regional planning and protection of the environment in European coastal regions.

[6] Text adopted by the Standing Committee on behalf of the Assembly on 9 November 2000. See also Report of the Committee on Culture and Education, *Maritime and fluvial cultural heritage,* Doc. 8867, 12 October 2000.

from commercial and/or unauthorized recovery operations and to promote regional co-operation by sharing information or by concluding bilateral or multilateral agreements that may be more stringent than global agreements.

In addition, a number of bilateral agreements dealt with issues relating to the protection of specific wrecks and the disposition of articles derived therefrom. One should specifically mention the Agreement between the Netherlands and Australia concerning Old Dutch Shipwrecks (1972)[7]; the Exchange of Notes between South Africa and the United Kingdom concerning the Regulation of the Terms of Settlement of the Salvaging of the Wreck of *HMS Birkenhead* (1989)[8]; the Agreement between the Government of the United States of America and the Government of the French Republic concerning the Wreck of *CSS Alabama* (1989)[9]; and more recently, the Agreement between the Government of the United States of America and the Government of the French Republic regarding the Wreck of *La Belle* (2003)[10].

2.2. *International instruments dealing with the protection of cultural heritage in general*

International and regional instruments dealing with the protection of cultural heritage in general are also relevant to the protection of the underwater

---

[7] Schedule 1 to Australian Historic Shipwrecks Act 1976 (Acts of the Parliament of the Commonwealth of Australia 1976, Australian Government Publishing Service 1978) pp. 1613-1616. This agreement, which deals with vessels that belonged to the Dutch *Vereenigde Oostindische Compagnie* (VOC) and were wrecked off the coast of Western Australia, is by far the most important bilateral agreement for the protection of underwater cultural heritage. The two parties agreed that the Netherlands should transfer to Australia all its rights, title and interest in and to wrecked vessels of the VOC lying on or off the coast of the State of Western Australia, and that Australia should accept such rights, title and interest. In addition, Australia agreed to make no claim on the Netherlands for reimbursement of any cost incurred, while it recognised the continuing interest of the latter, particularly for historical and other cultural purposes, in articles recovered from any of the vessels. To give effect to this, it was agreed to establish a Committee that would determine the disposition and subsequent ownership of the articles between the Netherlands, Australia and the State of Western Australia. Within this context, the sharing of material from an archaeological site is considered as the accommodation in several localities of a corporate entity, rather than its division into parts.

[8] UKTS 1990; South Africa Government Gazette No 12117 of 6 October 1989, Notice No 2150.

[9] *RGDIP* 1989, at p. 975.

[10] Text reprinted in R. Garabello & T. Scovazzi (eds.), *The Protection of the Underwater Cultural Heritage. Before and After the 2001 UNESCO Convention* (Martinus Nijhoff Publishers, 2003) pp. 265-266.

heritage. Some refer expressly to underwater remains[11], while others may be interpreted to include submerged sites. Nevertheless, since the vast majority of cultural conventions confine their scope of application to the national territories of contracting States, even if they were interpreted to apply to underwater cultural heritage, protection would be restricted to sites found landward of the outer limit of the territorial sea[12]. Notable exceptions are the European Convention on Offences Relating to Cultural Property (1985)[13], which permits prosecution of offences committed outside the territories of contracting States, i.e., on the high seas, and the European Convention on the Protection of the Archaeological Heritage (1992) (revised), which protects "all remains and objects and any other traces of mankind from past epochs … which are located in areas within the jurisdiction of the parties"[14].

---

[11] See, *inter alia,* the 1956 UNESCO Recommendation on International Principles Applicable to Archaeological Excavations, which extends its scope of application to the bed and subsoil of internal and territorial waters, as well as the 1978 UNESCO Recommendation for the Protection of Movable Cultural Property which encompasses "products of archaeological exploration and excavations conducted on land and underwater" within the protected property.

[12] For example, the definition of "cultural property" under the 1970 UNESCO Convention on the Means of Protecting the Illicit Import, Export and Transfer of Ownership of Cultural Property (hereinafter cited as the "1970 UNESCO Convention") is broad enough to include wrecks and other elements of underwater cultural heritage, provided that they are specifically designated as being of importance and are located landward of the outer limit of the territorial sea. Similarly, under the 1972 UNESCO Convention for the Protection of the World Cultural and Natural Heritage (hereinafter cited as the "1972 UNESCO Convention") submerged sites and monuments of outstanding universal value may be protected as part of the world cultural heritage, provided that they are of outstanding universal value and are located landward of the outer limit of the territorial sea. Mention has been made of the possible nomination of the Qait Bey/Pharos site (off the coast of Alexandria, Egypt) for the World Heritage List. However, in Prott's view, this has to be treated cautiously. The World Heritage Committee has never, so far, accepted an underwater site for inscription. This seems to be due to a variety of deterrents: the practical difficulties of delimitation; the provision of a buffer zone; monitoring; and devising an adequate management plan. None of these requirements is easy to meet, even for land sites, and is much more difficult for underwater sites. The International Council of Monuments and Sites (ICOMOS) Sub-Committee on the Underwater Cultural Heritage is in favour of their inclusion in the World Heritage List, but the World Heritage Committee will have to be convinced that it is appropriate and that proper management of such sites is possible. See further L. Prott, Legal principles for protecting the underwater cultural heritage, *Environment and development in coastal regions and in small islands* (CSI Coastal Management Sourcebooks 2); www.unesco.og/csi/pub/source/alex7.htm.

[13] ETS No. 119. The Convention has not entered into force.

[14] ETS No. 143; article 1(2). As explained in the Explanatory Report: "In itself, this is merely stating what is inherent in any international convention. Here it emphasises that the actual area of State jurisdiction depends on the individual States and in respect of this there are many possibilities. Territorially, the area can be coextensive with the territorial sea, the contiguous zone, the continental shelf, the exclusive economic zone or a cultural protection zone. Among

Overall, these instruments recognise the importance of the cultural heritage and emphasise the need to protect it by adopting the appropriate measures at national, regional and international level. The most common measures of protection are the following:

- Registration of the cultural property that constitutes the cultural heritage of contracting States;
- Creation of national inventories;
- Delimitation of archaeological sites;
- Application of scientific standards for excavations;
- Prohibition of illicit excavations;
- Prevention of illegal exportation and importation of the protected heritage;
- Duty to report the accidental recovery of cultural remains;
- Promotion of co-operation and assistance among States.

Such measures, however, are not capable of providing solutions to problems specifically related to marine archaeology, such as conflict between salvage law and heritage legislation, extent and scope of coastal jurisdiction over underwater cultural heritage, enforcement at sea of heritage legislation and, most importantly, protection of cultural heritage in international waters. Even the few instruments which encompass underwater cultural heritage within their ambit do not establish a satisfactory scheme of protection as, first, they cover only certain aspects of the archaeological issue, and, second, they deal exclusively with problems which are common to land and underwater heritage. Only international treaties specifically dealing with underwater cultural heritage can offer a more comprehensive regime of protection.

2.3. Environmental and maritime treaties

Underwater remains may also fall under the protective regimes of environmental treaties. Notable examples are the 1982 Protocol concerning Mediterranean Specially Protected Areas, which included "sites of particular importance because of their scientific, aesthetic, historical, archaeological, cultural or educational interest" among the range of protected areas[15]; the

---

the members of the Council of Europe some States restrict their jurisdiction over shipwrecks, for example to the territorial sea, while others extend it to their continental shelf. The Revised Convention recognises these differences without indicating a preference for one or another".

[15] Text reprinted in W.E. Burhenne (ed.), International *Environmental Law: Multilateral Treaties* (Berlin 1982) No. 26, pp. 11-18. The protective measures that each party is entitled to take in such areas include "the regulation of any archaeological activity and the removal of any object which may be considered as an archaeological object" and "the regulation of trade in and exportation of archaeological objects which originate in protected areas and are subject

1995 Protocol concerning Specially Protected Areas and Biological Diversity in the Mediterranean[16], which replaced the 1982 Protocol and expanded its scope of application to high seas areas, and, in the Caribbean the 1990 Protocol concerning Specially Protected Areas and Wildlife, which provides, *inter alia*, for the conservation of "areas of special archaeological value" as protected areas[17]. Similarly, of relevance to underwater cultural heritage are the IMO Guidelines for the Identification and Designation of Particularly Sensitive Sea Areas (PSSAs)[18] as well as maritime treaties dealing with private law issues, such as the International Convention on Salvage (1989)[19].

---

to measures of protection". It should be noted, however, that the territorial scope of application of the Protocol is confined to the territorial waters of the parties, with potential exclusion of internal waters extending to the watercourse up to the fresh water limit. Consequently, the Protocol is not applicable to archaeological sites found in lakes and rivers or in international waters.

[16] Reprinted in 11 *TIJMCL* 1996, pp. 101-112. The 1995 Protocol provides for the establishment of specially protected areas in order to protect, preserve and manage "areas of cultural value" in the "marine and coastal zones subject to its sovereignty or jurisdiction". Furthermore, there is provision for the drawing up of a List of Specially Protected Areas of Mediterranean Importance (SPAMI List), which may include sites which "are of special interest at the scientific, aesthetic, cultural or educational levels" even on high seas areas.

[17] Reprinted in 5 *TIJMCL* 1990, p. 369. Among the protective measures that each party is entitled to take in conformity with its national laws and regulations and international law, is "the regulation of any archaeological activity and of the removal or damage of any object which may be considered as an archaeological object".

[18] See Resolution A. 927(22) of 29 November 2001, Annex 2. The 2001 IMO Guidelines include cultural criteria for the identification of PSSAs, while the 1996 Guidelines referred to the "historical and/or archaeological significance" of the area to be identified as a PSSA. See further A. Blanco-Bazan, The IMO Guidelines on Particular Sensitive Sea Areas (PSSAs): Their possible application to the protection of underwater cultural heritage, 20 *Marine Policy* 1996, pp. 343-349. The IMO Guidelines are currently under review; however, the (draft) revised Guidelines have retained cultural criteria for the identification of a PSSA. See section 4.4.14 "cultural heritage" – "an area that is of particular importance because of the presence of significant historical and archaeological sites". MEPC 53/WP.15, 20 July 2005, Annex 1. Up till now, the existence of shipwrecks of historic importance has been taken into account in the case of the Great Barrier Reef.

[19] Reprinted in *Lloyd's Maritime & Commercial Quarterly* 1990, p. 4. According to article 30(1) of the Salvage Convention: "Any State may, at the time of signature, ratification, acceptance, approval or accession, reserve the right not to apply the provisions of this Convention: (d) when the property involved is maritime cultural property of prehistoric, archaeological or historical interest and is situated on the seabed". The inclusion of this optional clause is important, since the law of salvage provides one of the less appropriate bases for regulating underwater cultural heritage; see *infra* section 5.10. As of 31 December 2003, 18 States out of 44 States parties to the Salvage Convention had submitted such a reservation. Reference should also be made to the Draft Wreck Removal Convention, still pending at the IMO, which however contains no reference to underwater cultural heritage; IMO Doc. LEG 90/5, Annex I. Nevertheless, in August 2002 in the commentary to article 1(6) it was stated: "As regards the comment to add 'underwater cultural heritage' to the definition of 'Related interests', it is

Finally, the location of archaeological remains on and under the seabed brings them within the scope of the law of the sea. They differ, however, fundamentally – in terms of their nature and value – from natural resources, which have traditionally been its main concern. Until recently, the absence of underwater technology made the recovery of artefacts far too remote to create jurisdictional problems. As a result, the four 1958 Geneva Conventions on the Law of the Sea[20] did not include any provision on archaeological sites. It was the LOS Convention that provided for the protection of the underwater cultural heritage for the first time.

3. THE 1982 UN CONVENTION ON THE LAW OF THE SEA

The protection of the underwater cultural heritage was not one of the main issues of the negotiations at the Third United Nations Conference on the Law of the Sea (hereafter cited as "UNCLOS III"). On the contrary, in the course of negotiating the various ocean regimes, regard was paid to the accidental location of submerged archaeological objects. Initially, the discussion on this issue was limited to relics found on the seabed beyond the limits of national jurisdiction. This is not surprising since UNCLOS III had its origins in the Seabed Committee, which dealt with the deep seabed (the "Area"). The result of this was the adoption of article 149 providing for historical and archaeological objects found in the Area. In 1979 various proposals were made in the Second Committee to include provisions defining the legal status of archaeological and historical objects situated on the continental shelf and/or the exclusive economic zone (EEZ). When suggestions were made for a general duty to protect these relics wherever found, the debate was passed to the Plenary of the Conference, which adopted article 303 among the General Provisions. The regime of archaeological and historical objects found at sea was, thus, discussed by two different Committees (three, if the Plenary of the Conference is also included). The fact that three separate bodies were concerned with the same issue, even successively, had far-reaching consequences. For a considerable period of time, there was even a differentiation in the terms used employed to define the protected items. Draft article 149 referred to "objects of archaeological and historical nature",

considered that the provisions of the UNESCO Convention on the Protection of the Underwater Cultural Heritage (November 2001) provide the necessary safeguards for traces of human existence having cultural, historical or archaeological character; more in particular the articles 3, 5, 9 and 10"; IMO Doc. LEG 85/3, 17 August 2002.

[20] Convention on the Territorial Sea and the Contiguous Zone, 516 UNTS 205; Convention on the Continental Shelf, 499 UNTS 311; Convention on the High Seas, 450 UNTS 82; Convention on Fishing and Conservation of Living Resources on the High Seas, 559 UNTS 285.

while draft article 303 to "archaeological objects and objects of historical origin". It was the drafting Committee in 1982, which removed this inconsistency. Thus, articles 149 and 303 read respectively:

Article 149: *Archaeological and historical objects*
All objects of an archaeological and historical nature found in the Area shall be preserved or disposed of for the benefit of mankind as a whole, particular regard being paid to the preferential rights of the State or country of origin, or the State or country of cultural origin, or the State or country of historical and archaeological origin.

Article 303: *Archaeological and historical objects found at sea*
1. States have a duty to protect objects of an archaeological and historical nature found at sea and shall co-operate for this purpose.
2. In order to control traffic in such objects, the coastal State may, in applying article 33, presume that their removal from the sea-bed in the zone referred to in that article without its approval would result in an infringement within its territory or territorial sea of the laws and regulations referred to in that article.
3. Nothing in this article affects the rights of identifiable owners, the law of salvage or other rules of admiralty, or laws and practices with respect to cultural exchanges.
4. This article is without prejudice to other international agreements and rules of international law regarding the protection of objects of an archaeological and historical nature.

3.1. Creation of a 24-mile "archaeological" zone

The LOS regime is, no doubt, *far from satisfactory* as it limits protection to archaeological and historical objects found within 24 miles from the coast. This is the combined effect of article 303(2) and article 33 dealing with the 24-mile contiguous zone. Nevertheless, despite the limiting language of article 303(2), which confines coastal rights to the "control of traffic" in archaeological and historical objects found on the bed of the contiguous zone, in substance far more extensive rights are recognised. The combination of article 303(1) which advocates the general duty to protect archaeological objects found at sea and the legal fiction established by article 303(2) permits the extension of coastal legislation to the 24-mile zone. However, this *de facto* establishment of an archaeological zone, contiguous to the territorial sea, does not result in the transformation of the general contiguous zone into a full jurisdictional zone. The 24-mile archaeological zone has an independent character that enables its autonomous declaration[21].

---

[21] See further A. Strati, *The Protection of the Underwater Cultural Heritage: An Emerging Objective of the Contemporary Law of the Sea* (Martinus Nijhoff, 1995) at p. 167 *et seq.* In contrast J. Allain, Maritime wrecks: Where the *lex ferenda* of underwater cultural heritage

Still, the use of a *legal fiction* as a means of expanding coastal jurisdiction creates interpretation problems as to its precise scope and nature. This is also evidenced by State practice: Algeria and Cyprus claim within their contiguous zone the control necessary "to control traffic of objects of an archaeological and historical nature", while France and Tunisia apply their national heritage laws to the 24-mile contiguous zone[22]. South Africa has declared a maritime cultural zone co-extensive with the contiguous zone, over which it exercises with respect to objects of an archaeological or historical nature "the same rights and powers as it has in respect of its territorial waters"[23]. In Denmark the 24-mile limit was initially combined with the notion of the continental shelf, as the Danish legislation protected wrecks and monuments situated "on the continental shelf within 24 nautical miles" from the coast[24]. However, the present status of this 24-mile zone is unclear[25]. Finally, China exercises juris-

---

collides with the *lex lata* of the Law of the Sea Convention, 38 *Virginia JIL* 1998, pp. 747-775; B.H. Oxman, Marine archaeology and the international law of the sea, 12 *Columbia–VLA Journal of Law & the Arts* 1988, pp. 353-372; and W.G. Vitztum & S. Talmon, *Alles fließt. Kulturguterschutz und innere Gewässer im Neuen Seerecht* (Nomos Verlagsgesellschaft, 1998), who adopt a very restrictive interpretation of article 303 paragraph 2 of the LOS Convention.

[22] *Algeria:* Presidential Decree No. 04-344 of 23 Ramadan (6 November 2004) Establishing a Zone Contiguous to the Territorial Sea, Article 2; *Cyprus:* Law to provide for the Proclamation of the Contiguous Zone by the Republic of Cyprus (2 April 2004) with retroactive effect as from 21 March 2003, Article 4(c); *France:* Law No. 89-874 of 1 December 1989 on Maritime Cultural Property amending Law of 27 September 1941, Article 1; *Tunisia*: Law No 86-35 of 9 May 1988 on the Protection of Archaeological Property, Historic Monuments and Natural Urban Sites, Article 1.

[23] *South Africa:* Maritime Zones Act No. 15 of 1994, Sec. 6.

[24] *Denmark:* Conservation of Nature Act, 1978, Consolidated Act No. 435 of 1 September 1978 as amended by Act No. 530 of 10 October 1984; Section 49(1): "Ancient monuments on or in the seabed such as megaliths, graves, settlement sites, ruins, blockades, defence constructions or bridges may not be damaged or removed without the consent of the National Agency for the Protection of Nature, Monuments and Sites, if they are situated in the territorial waters or the continental shelf within 24 nautical miles from the baselines, from which the breadth of the outer territorial waters are measured". The same applies for wrecks of ships which have been wrecked for more than 100 years; sec. 49(4). Arguably, this solution was adopted in order to resolve questions of delimitation between Denmark and neighbouring countries. See further C. Lund, Beskyttelse af historicke skibsvrag og fortidmisminder pa den danske havbund in *Fortidsminder og kulturhistorie* (National Forestry and Nature Agency, Copenhagen, 1987). See further, Strati, *supra* note 21, at pp. 185-186 and 211.

[25] On the one hand, the Protection of Nature Act (No. 9 of 3 January 1992) extended Danish jurisdiction on matters of natural and cultural conservation to the 200 nm fishing zone (now EEZ), while, on the other, in the recent proclamation of a contiguous zone by Denmark it was stated that "the establishment of a contiguous zone involves no amendment to the legislation on the exclusive economic zone or the continental shelf nor the monitoring of archaeological and historical objects". Cf. Act on the Contiguous Zone, Act No. 589 of 24 June 2005; article

diction over underwater cultural relics "originating from China or from an unidentifiable country, which remain beyond China's territorial sea but within other sea areas under China's jurisdiction according to Chinese laws"[26].

3.2. Protection of the underwater cultural heritage as a freedom of the high seas

Beyond the 24-mile limit and up to the outer limit of the continental shelf there is a *lacuna*. Submerged archaeological and historical objects do not feature as natural resources of the seabed and are, therefore, not subject to the sovereign rights of the coastal State over the continental shelf and the EEZ[27]. The same applies to archaeological research, which is excluded from the scope of marine scientific research[28] and the consent regime of the coastal State (cf. article 246(2) of the LOS Convention). As a result, the protection of archaeological sites in these areas lies in principle at the discretion

---

3(2) as well as Executive Order on the Demarcation of the Danish Contiguous Zone of 29 June 2004.

[26] See Regulation on Protection and Administration of Underwater Cultural Relics, 1989, articles 2(2) and 3.

[27] Nevertheless, coastal States may take advantage of their resource-related rights over the continental shelf/EEZ and exercise control over underwater cultural heritage indirectly. The practice of some Latin-American States, which confiscate objects recovered from their continental shelf as evidence of illegitimate exercise of exploration activities in the area, is illustrative of this attitude. It has been argued that "legislators have a simple weapon to control the activities of marine archaeologists on the continental shelf, and that is to regulate the disturbance of the seabed. So, a wreck site embedded in coral could be immunized by the expedient of forbidding interference with the coral, which is a 'natural resource' of the continental shelf"; D.P. O'Connell, *The International Law of the Sea* (vol. I, Clarendon Press, 1982) at p. 918. Furthermore, there is nothing in the LOS Convention to prevent coastal States from undertaking protective measures in the exercise of their resource-related jurisdiction over the continental shelf/EEZ. The adoption of such measures should be considered as an application of the general duty to protect archaeological and historical objects under article 303(1) of the LOS Convention and not as an expansion of coastal jurisdiction in this area. It is notable that a number of States, including Norway, the Netherlands, Denmark, Israel, Libya and Thailand, oblige the licensees of oil and mineral exploration and exploitation activities to report the accidental discovery of cultural heritage on their continental shelf and to respect relevant national laws. Strati, *supra* note 21, at p. 261. Similar requirements are imposed with respect to the accidental discovery of underwater cultural heritage in the course of marine scientific research projects authorized by the coastal State, as is, for example, the case with Greece.

[28] By definition, the exploration of the seabed for the location, investigation and excavation of archaeological remains is scientific research; both the scientific knowledge acquired and the employment of scientific method contribute to this conclusion. However, within the framework of the LOS Convention, archaeological endeavour does not qualify as marine scientific research, which is confined to the natural environment and its resources. See further A.H.A. Soons, *Marine Scientific Research and the Law of the Sea* (TMC Asser Institute, Kluwer Law and Taxation Publishers, 1982) at p. 275.

of flag States[29], which even if they were willing to take the appropriate measures, lack the necessary means of enforcement. This "free-for-all" system does not acknowledge any priority to the flag State of a sunken vessel or, as the case may be, to the State of origin. Most importantly, if the flag State has not enacted specific legislation to protect underwater cultural heritage, admiralty law may govern historic wrecks and their cargoes and the finder may be considered as having a good right to such property. Admiralty courts have claimed jurisdiction over salvage operations on the high seas even in the case of derelict of foreign origin, i.e. by asserting *in rem* jurisdiction. For this reason, the reservation of the law of salvage by article 303(3) of the LOS Convention is rather unfortunate[30]. In practice, it will be the choice-of-law rules of the forum to determine which substantive law is applicable to cultural heritage found on the high seas. The applicable law could be the law of the flag of the sunken or the salving vessel, the *lex fori* or the law of the owner. However, there may be also cases where the coastal State

---

[29] A distinction, however, should be made between areas falling within and beyond the EEZ. If a coastal State has not declared an EEZ or the continental shelf extends beyond the outer limit of the EEZ, archaeological research may be exercised as a freedom of the high seas under the terms of article 87 of the LOS Convention. Nevertheless, if a coastal State has established an EEZ, the exercise of archaeological activities falls within the 'grey area' where the LOS Convention does not attribute rights and jurisdiction to either coastal or flag States. In case of doubt, the issue will be resolved on the basis of equity and in the light of all the relevant circumstances; cf. article 59 of the LOS Convention. Overall, it will be more difficult for third States to oppose the expansion of coastal jurisdiction over archaeological objects in the EEZ. In Migliorino's view, Australia's claim over historic wrecks found on the continental shelf may be regarded as compatible with article 59; L. Migliorino, *Il ricupero degli oggetti storici ed archeologici nel diritto internazionale* (Studi e documenti sul diritto internazionale del mare 15, Dott. A. Giuffre editore, Milano, 1984) at p. 182.

[30] In the writer's view, the reservation of the law of salvage under article 303(3) of the LOS Convention should be interpreted to refer to cases in which archaeological and historical objects are not involved, i.e., recent objects which do not possess historical value and which are eligible for salvage. In this respect, the use of a fixed period of 100 years underwater as a qualifying factor of protection would be a reasonable limit both for the determination of the scope of salvage law and the interpretation of "historical" and "archaeological" objects. Article 303(3) simply emphasizes the fact that the proposed scheme of protection shall not abolish the law of salvage. There is nothing in article 303 to indicate that the commercial interests of private salvage companies should be given more weight than the protection of the underwater cultural heritage. Nor does article 303(3) prevent future conventions from modifying or excluding the law of salvage; it refers specifically to the operation of this article and would appear to have been inserted as a safeguard in case of derogation. See also *The Underwater Cultural Heritage: Comparison of Relevant International Instruments and Discussions at UNESCO Expert Meeting* (CLT-96/CONF. 202/4, June 1998) at p. 4.

on whose continental shelf the wreck lies has extended its heritage legislation over this area[31].

3.3. Deep seabed cultural heritage as common heritage of mankind

Archaeological objects found in the Area are to be "preserved or disposed of" for the "benefit of mankind as a whole", while taking into consideration the preferential rights of the "State or country of origin, or the State of cultural origin or the State of archaeological and historical origin". The significance of article 149 is limited to a considerable extent by the absence of an international body to implement it. Since archaeological activities do not qualify as "activities in the Area"[32], the International Seabed Authority (hereinafter cited as "ISA"), the overall regulatory body in the Area, does not enjoy any jurisdictional powers over underwater cultural heritage. Furthermore, article 149 suffers from vagueness and ambiguity. First, it does not specify how and where deep seabed cultural heritage will be "preserved or disposed of" for the benefit of mankind as a whole, nor does it provide for the funding of such activities. Second, it fails to establish the obligation to report the accidental discovery of archaeological and historical objects and/or notify the interested parties. Third, the accommodation of the preferential rights of the States of origin is far from satisfactory, as article 149 recognises three different categories of States as claimants to these rights without defining such terms and without establishing priorities. Inevitably, conflicts will arise as to which State has priority over the items discovered. Finally, it is difficult to understand why the LOS Convention protects archaeological objects as common heritage of mankind and recognises preferential rights to their State(s) of origin, only when they are found in the Area. Is there no need for their protection and preservation for the benefit of mankind as a whole when they are found in other maritime zones? Does the international community lose its interest in the protection of cultural heritage found in

---

[31] At present only a small group of States, i.e. Australia, Morocco and Jamaica, claim jurisdiction over underwater cultural heritage on the continental shelf/EEZ. In addition, a number of States claim sovereign rights over "all resources" and/or jurisdiction over "any research" conducted in the EEZ, such as Barbados, Guyana, Mauritius, Pakistan, Seychelles, Philippines, Tanzania and Vanuatu, while Benin, Congo, Ecuador, El Salvador, Liberia, Peru and Somalia, claim 200 nm territorial seas. Strati, *supra* note 21, at pp. 270-271. Finally, Bangladesh, Cape Verde, Malaysia and Portugal have submitted declarations while ratifying the LOS Convention, whereby they require their prior notification and consent for the removal of archaeological and historical objects found within maritime areas over which they exercise sovereignty or jurisdiction.

[32] The latter are confined to mineral resource exploration and exploitation; cf. articles 1(3) and 133(b) of the LOS Convention.

areas under national jurisdiction? Apparently, the drafters of the LOS Convention did not pay the required degree of attention to the archaeological issue[33].

In concluding, the LOS Convention does not provide a comprehensive scheme of protection of underwater cultural heritage, the main deficiency being the "abandonment" of cultural heritage found beyond the 24-mile limit to flag-State jurisdiction. It should not be ignored, however, that the LOS Convention introduced new concepts, established the duty to protect the limited cultural resources of the oceans and left room for the development of more comprehensive regimes in the future.

4. NEGOTIATIONS AT UNESCO

Once it was acknowledged that the LOS Convention did not settle the underwater cultural heritage issue adequately, the question that arose was whether it would be necessary to adopt a convention on this subject. The form of instrument for protecting the underwater cultural heritage was also debated at UNESCO. The prevailing view was that a binding international instrument was essential for the protection of underwater cultural heritage, especially for the regulation of access to and the safeguarding of sites in extraterritorial waters[34]. However, the new convention should be compatible with the LOS Convention.

4.1. Compatibility of the new instrument with the LOS Convention

The issue of compatibility with the LOS Convention became the main topic of discussions both within and outside UNESCO. It is notable that the UN General Assembly Resolutions on "Oceans and the Law of the Sea" referred to this issue. According to paragraph 20 of Resolution 53/32, the General Assembly "notes with interest the ongoing work of the United Nations Educational, Scientific and Cultural Organisation towards a convention for the implementation of the provisions of the Convention, relating to the protection of the underwater cultural heritage and stresses the importance of en-

---

[33] Strati, *supra* note 21, at p. 332; *idem.*, Deep seabed cultural property and the common heritage of mankind, 40 *ICLQ* 1991, pp. 145-165.

[34] The General Conference of UNESCO adopted at its 29th session Resolution 21, which, *inter alia,* invited the Director-General to prepare a first draft of such a convention and to convene a group of governmental experts to consider this draft with a view to its submission to the General Conference at its 30th session.

suring that the new instrument to be elaborated is in full conformity with the relevant provisions of the Convention"[35].

Resolution 53/32 referred to the (then) UNESCO Draft as an instrument for implementing the relevant provisions of the LOS Convention. It should be recalled, however, that article 303(4) of the LOS Convention *permits* the elaboration of treaties on the protection of the underwater cultural heritage by recognising that its subject matter may be governed by some other existing or future international agreement. The "without prejudice" clause of article 303(4) grants priority to the other treaty which may supplement its provisions in a manner consistent with the general principles and objectives of the LOS Convention[36]. The relationship between the UNESCO Convention and the LOS Convention was finally determined by article 3, which reads: "Nothing in this Convention shall prejudice the rights, jurisdiction and duties of States under international law, including the United Nations Convention on the Law of the Sea. This Convention shall be interpreted and applied in the context of and in a manner consistent with international law, including the United Nations Convention on the Law of the Sea".

---

[35] A/RES/53/32 of 24 November 1998. See also Resolution 54/31 of 24 November 1999, par. 30; Resolution 55/7 of 30 October 2000, par. 36, as well as Resolution 56/12 of 28 November 2001, par. 43, which simply takes note of the adoption by UNESCO of the Underwater Cultural Heritage Convention.

[36] Article 303(4) should not be interpreted to refer exclusively to existing international agreements, as it primarily promotes the elaboration in the future of more comprehensive regimes of protection. It clearly covers treaties, which may be enacted in the future, as well as future rules of customary law. Furthermore, under article 311: "3. Two or more States may conclude agreements modifying or suspending the operation of provisions of this Convention, applicable solely to the relations between them, provided that such agreements do not relate to a provision derogation from which is incompatible with the effective execution of the object and purpose of this Convention, and provided further that such agreements shall not affect the application of the basic principles embodied herein, and that the provisions of such agreements do not affect the enjoyment by other States Parties of their rights or the performance of their obligations under this Convention; 5. This article does not affect international agreements expressly permitted or preserved by other articles of this Convention". As argued: "Paragraph 5 preserves the *lex specialis* of other relevant provisions of the Convention and this can be illustrated by article 237(1). Although doubts were expressed as to the necessity for this paragraph, its presence has the effect of precluding any argument of possible inconsistency between the *lex generalis* of Article 311 and the *lex specialis* of the other articles"; S. Rosenne & L.B. Sohn (eds.), *United Nations Convention on the Law of the Sea 1982 – A Commentary* (vol. V, Center for Oceans Law and Policy, University of Virginia, Martinus Nijhoff, 1989) at p. 243. Article 303(4) features among the articles, which refer specifically to the possibility that their subject matter may be governed by some other existing or future international agreement. According to Rosenne & Sohn, "[article 303(4)] which is self-explanatory is also mandated by article 311(5)", *ibid.*, at p. 161. In case of dispute over the interpretation or application of articles 303 and 311, Part XV of the LOS Convention on settlement of disputes will apply.

Article 3 does not refer to the UNESCO Convention as an implementing agreement of the LOS Convention. Nevertheless, the desire for "strict compatibility" with the LOS Convention resulted in the adoption of a legal instrument that is unnecessarily complicated and the establishment of mechanisms that it may be very difficult to be applied in practice, especially with respect to the protection of underwater cultural heritage found on the continental shelf/EEZ. Oddly enough, a number of States still consider the UNESCO Convention as an instrument non-compatible with the LOS Convention[37].

4.2. The basis of discussions: The ILA Draft

As explained, the main purpose of the ILA Draft was to provide basic protection beyond the territorial seas of coastal States for a very sensitive and precious heritage that is subject to growing threats of damage and destruction, while, at the same time, offering help to avoid and resolve jurisdictional issues involving underwater cultural heritage[38]. Accordingly, the Draft allows each State party to establish a "cultural heritage zone" coextensive with its continental shelf. Under article 1(3), "cultural heritage zone" means "an area beyond the territorial sea of the State up to the outer limit of the continental shelf as defined in accordance with relevant rules and principles of international law". A State party shall take measures to ensure that activities within its zone affecting the underwater cultural heritage comply at a minimum with the provisions of the Charter. Even though the territorial sea is excluded from the notion of the "cultural heritage zone", under article 6 State parties are encouraged to apply the provisions of the Convention and the criteria of the Charter to this are. The same applies for internal waters. In addition, article 7 prohibits the use of the territory of a State party or any other areas over which it exercises jurisdiction to be used in support of activities violating the Charter.

With respect to areas that are not subject to the jurisdiction of the parties, the Draft employs nationality as a principal jurisdictional basis to enforce its provisions. Under article 8, each State party shall prohibit its nationals and ships flying its flag from activities affecting the underwater cultural heritage in respect of any area, which is not within a cultural heritage zone or a territorial sea of another State party. There is also provision for the issuance of permits allowing entry into its territory of underwater cultural heritage exca-

---

[37] See in particular the statements made by the Netherlands, France, Norway, the Russian Federation, the United Kingdom and the United States at the 31st session of the General Conference of UNESCO.

[38] *Supra* note 3.

vated or retrieved after its entry into force so long as the State has determined that the excavation and retrieval activities have complied or will comply with the Charter (article 9); the seizure of heritage brought within its territory, directly or indirectly[39], after having been excavated in a manner not conforming with the Charter (article 10); and, finally, penal sanctions for the importation of underwater cultural heritage, which is subject to seizure (article 11). After seizure, each State party undertakes to record, protect and take all reasonable measures to conserve underwater cultural heritage, and keep it in display or otherwise ensure the fullest reasonable access to it for the benefit of the public (article 12). There is also provision for the notification of the State or States of origin, if known, of the seizure of underwater cultural heritage.

Furthermore, article 13 provides for collaboration with States, which have expressed a patrimonial interest particularly in underwater cultural heritage, in the investigation, documentation, conservation, study and cultural promotion of the heritage as well as information sharing with other States parties. An additional reference to the State of origin is to be found in the Preamble, where it is emphasized that "the underwater cultural heritage belongs to the common heritage of mankind and that responsibility for protecting it rests not only with the State or States most directly concerned with a particular activity affecting the cultural heritage or having an historical or cultural link with it, but with all States and other subjects of international law." Educating the public is advanced as a major objective of the ILA Draft[40], while disputes concerning its interpretation or application are submitted to *arbitration*, under the procedure envisaged in article 16. State parties also undertake to establish internal procedures for resolving disputes concerning the compliance of activities affecting the underwater cultural heritage with the Charter.

Most importantly, the ILA Draft excludes the law of salvage from its scope along the lines of Recommendation 848 (1978) of the Council of Europe on underwater cultural heritage. The exclusion of the law of salvage, which provides one of the most inappropriate bases for regulating access to underwater sites on the high seas, appears to be a *sine qua non* for the protection

---

[39] The "directly or indirectly" language is an attempt to expand the scope of the ILA Draft. As explained in the Commentary: "An intervening sale of excavated material can create problems. Suppose that European excavators of material excavated off the Malaysian coast proceed directly from the Far East to the Netherlands and suppose that the Netherlands is not a party to the Convention. There the excavated material is sold by auction. One of the purchasers is France and brings his ceramics home. Under the Convention, if France was a party, it could have an obligation to seize the ceramics. This obligation exists whatever the number of intervening transaction in an object".

[40] Article 14.

of underwater cultural heritage. Similarly, one of the most innovative features of the ILA Draft was the incorporation by reference of the standards
adopted by the ICOMOS Charter on the Management and Protection of the
Underwater Cultural Heritage[41].

As far as the definition of underwater cultural heritage is concerned, the
ILA Draft adopted an extensive formula, which includes all underwater
traces of human existence together with their archaeological and natural context. However, protection is limited to underwater cultural heritage which
has been lost or abandoned[42] and is submerged underwater for 100 years
with potential inclusion of more recent objects. In addition, the Draft does
not apply to warships, military remains and other vessels or aircraft owned
or operated by a State and used for government, non-commercial services.

In conclusion, the ILA Draft constitutes an ambitious attempt to deal with
the complex problems posed by the protection of underwater cultural heritage found in extra-territorial waters in a responsible and scientific manner.
Its adoption was an important development in the sphere of the law of cultural heritage and reflects heightening awareness of the need to preserve this
significant source of historical material.

5. THE 2001 UNESCO CONVENTION ON THE PROTECTION OF THE UNDERWATER CULTURAL HERITAGE

5.1. General appraisal

The UNESCO Convention, which follows in broad terms the structure of
the ILA Draft, consists of 35 articles and 36 annexed rules. The rules originate from the aforementioned 1996 ICOMOS Charter for the Protection and
Management of the Underwater Cultural Heritage, which was developed in
direct response to the need to set professional standards for the handling of

---

[41] As explained by the Chairman of the ILA Committee on Cultural Heritage Law, "the
Committee realized early in its work that States would need objective standards by which to
judge the appropriateness of actions in respect of the underwater cultural heritage. In 1991 the
newly established ICOMOS International Committee on the Underwater Cultural Heritage
was approached and asked to assist in the preparation of a set of principles which could be attached to the Draft Convention in a document called the "Charter". The relevant principles
were developed at meetings in Paris (1994) and London (1995) and forwarded to UNESCO.
The ICOMOS Committee then went further and from this set of principles developed its International Charter on the Protection and Management of Underwater Cultural Heritage ratified by the 11th ICOMOS General Assembly, Sofia, Bulgaria, in October 1996". P.J.
O'Keefe, *Shipwrecked Heritage: A Commentary on the UNESCO Convention on Underwater
Cultural Heritage* (Institute of Art and Law, 2002) at pp. 21-22.

[42] The ILA Draft employs a presumption of abandonment in article 1(2).

underwater cultural heritage. Eventually, these rules were redrafted and annexed to the Convention as "Rules concerning activities directed at the underwater cultural heritage" (hereinafter cited as "Rules"). The Rules lay down general principles of protection, such as the *in situ* preservation of underwater cultural heritage and the prohibition of its commercial exploitation, along with technical rules, such as standards for project design and scope of activity, preliminary work, funding and duration of activities, safety and environmental measures, conservation and site management, reporting and dissemination of information.

As regards the main body of the Convention, articles 2 to 6 deal with general issues, including definition of the protected cultural heritage, objectives and general principles, relationship with the LOS Convention and other bilateral, regional and multilateral agreements. Articles 7 to 12 deal with the protection of underwater cultural heritage within each jurisdictional zone, article 13 with the controversial issue of sovereign immunity of warships and public vessels, while articles 14 to 18 establish the obligation of States parties to take measures to prevent entry into their territory of underwater cultural heritage illegally exported and/or recovered; to prohibit the use of their territory, including their maritime ports, as well as artificial islands, installations and structures under their jurisdiction, in support of any activity directed at underwater cultural heritage which is not in conformity with the Convention; ensure that their nationals and vessels flying their flag are not engaged in any such activity; impose sanctions as well as provide for the seizure of underwater cultural heritage recovered not in a manner consistent with the Convention.

Articles 19-22 deal with cooperation and information sharing, public awareness regarding the value and significance of underwater cultural heritage and training. As already pointed out, these issues are equally important since the effectiveness of any scheme of protection depends to a considerable extent on the co-operation of the public particularly that of interest groups, such as underwater explorers and hobby-divers. Since legal action has its limits, educating the public may prove to be more effective than the enactment of draconian measures, which cannot be enforced. It is, therefore, important that positive action is taken not only in the legislative sphere, but also to ensure that the public is properly educated and the law is rigorously enforced. This is also acknowledged in the Preamble of the Convention, where it is stated that "cooperation among States, international organizations, scientific institutions, professional organizations, archaeologists, divers, other interested parties and the public at large is essential for the protection of underwater cultural heritage".

The remaining articles deal with institutional issues, such as meetings of States Parties and the Secretariat for the Convention, peaceful settlement of disputes, entry into force of the Convention, limitations to its geographical scope and declarations as to inland waters. More specifically, article 28 enables States to apply the Rules to "inland waters not of a maritime character", i.e. lakes and rivers, which would otherwise fall outside the scope of the Convention. The provisions on dispute settlement are particularly important, as the rather complicated system of protection of underwater cultural heritage on the continental shelf/EEZ (see *infra* section 5.3.3.) may give rise to disputes as to the applicable law. According to article 25, any dispute between two or more States parties concerning the interpretation or the application of the Convention shall be subject, as a first step, to negotiations in good faith or other peaceful means of settlement of their own choice. If negotiations are not successful within a reasonable period of time, the dispute may be submitted to UNESCO for mediation by agreement between the States Parties concerned. If, however, mediation is not undertaken or there is no settlement by mediation, the provisions on dispute settlement of the LOS Convention shall apply *mutatis mutandis*, even if the States parties concerned are not parties to the LOS Convention. In order to accommodate nonparties to the LOS Convention, article 25 allows them to elect a procedure when ratifying, accepting, approving or acceding to the Convention or at any tome thereafter, in accordance with Article 287 of the LOS Convention[43].

5.2. Definition of the "underwater cultural heritage"

According to article 1(1) a, for the purposes of the Convention, "underwater cultural heritage" means "all traces of human existence having a cultural, historical or archaeological character which have been partially or totally under water, periodically or continuously, for at least 100 years, such as (i) sites, structures, buildings, artefacts and human remains, together with their archaeological and natural context; (ii) vessels, aircraft, other vehicles or any other part thereof, their cargo or other contents, together with their archaeological and natural context; and (iii) objects of prehistoric character"[44].

---

[43] A similar procedure is envisaged by article 30 of the UN Fish Stock Agreement. It is recalled that under article 287 of the LOS Convention, States may choose one or more of four different procedures for compulsory dispute settlement: (a) the International Tribunal for the Law of the Sea, (b) the International Court of Justice, (c) arbitration, and (d) special arbitration. If no declaration is made or if the parties to a dispute have made different choices, arbitration becomes the residual procedure, unless the parties otherwise agree.

[44] There was considerable argument as to whether paleontological material should be included in the definition of underwater cultural heritage. A number of delegations suggested

The UNESCO definition includes a list of certain categories of material in addition to the general reference to "all traces of human existence", which makes it easier for administrators and courts to decide if a particular item is covered by the Convention or not. Most importantly, the context in which objects are found is itself specified as part of the underwater cultural heritage. However, the definition is qualified by the phrase "having a cultural, historical or archaeological character". The inclusion of this phrase was hotly debated and in O'Keefe's view was only admitted following what seemed to be a misreading by the Chairman of the nature of the consensus[45]. During the expert meetings in 1999 and 2000, there had been proposals by the United Kingdom and the United States to add a requirement that the underwater cultural heritage had to be "significant" before it came within the scope of the Convention. Portugal, Argentina, Greece and Colombia were strongly against any "significance criterion", as it is not clear how to determine the archaeological value of an object before its removal. One must explore first in order to assess the archaeological or historical importance of a particular site. The blanket protection of all wrecks and sites over a certain age would allow the investigation of a site to assess its importance before interference takes place. Arguably, the phrase that was eventually agreed neither adds to nor detracts from the already established scope of definition. It is meaningless[46].

Nevertheless, it may still create interpretation problems as to the precise scope of application of the Convention *ratione materiae*. It is notable that at its statement on vote the United Kingdom maintained that the reference to "character" does not limit the scope of protected areas and that the high standards of protection would apply to all underwater cultural heritage over 100 years old, this being one of the main reasons for UK's abstention, while in Greece's view it restricts unacceptably the scope of application of the

---

that the definition should not be limited to human activity, but should also include paleontological remains. The latter are protected under the terms of the 1970 UNESCO Convention and are often covered by national legislation. Others argued that much paleontological material has no relationship to humanity as such. In the end, a compromise was reached to include "objects of prehistoric character". According to O' Keefe, such objects must be related to traces of human existence and would certainly include tools, settlements and other artefacts of prehistoric humanity; O'Keefe, *supra* note 41, at p. 44.

[45] *Ibid.*, at p. 42.

[46] As pointed out by the representative of ICOMOS, something may be of archaeological interest or significance, but nothing is of an archaeological character. Whether something is "cultural" or "historical" cannot be objectively determined. There cannot be any trace of human existence, which does not have a cultural element or an historical character. Indeed, anything over 100 years of age may be said to have an "historical character" by its very nature; *ibid.*, at pp. 42-43.

Convention. A different interpretation is offered by Carduzzi[47] who argues that "as adopted, the definition rejects the proposal of some delegations to limit it through the insertion of a "significance" test. This rejection does not necessarily mean that what was occasionally stated, i.e. that the definition imposes an extreme obligation to protect any human trace with a presence in water since at least a century ago. Actually, the quality of a cultural, histori- cal or archaeological "character" does allow for some flexibility of interpre- tation which, once kept within the due limits of a *bona fide* interpretation of the Convention and the general duty to cooperate for the protection of the underwater cultural heritage should prevent such extreme readings, though the definition of underwater cultural heritage remains broad".

Time limit

The definition is further qualified by the requirement that the protected ob- jects must have been submerged for at least 100 years. The 100-year under- water rule also appears in Recommendation 848 (1978) of the Council of Europe and the ILA Draft while the Draft European Convention protected objects which are more than 100 years old. The 100-year underwater rule would appear to be more appropriate, as, first, it avoids the undesirable situa- tion in which the owner of an old vessel that has sunk cannot salvage his property, unless permission is obtained from the competent authorities; and, second, it is useful in distinguishing the scope of application of heritage leg- islation from that of salvage law. Since the protected cultural heritage is re- quired to have remained underwater for at least 100 years, it will almost cer- tainly be in equilibrium with its environment. The equilibrium is normally reached after a few decades when decomposition slows down and there is lit- tle danger of further deterioration. It is, obvious, therefore, that one of the es- sential elements of the notion of salvage, that of "marine peril" is lacking[48]. It is worth mentioning that the 100-year underwater rule was initially ac- companied by the potential discretionary inclusion of objects that had been submerged for less than 100 years. However, this reference was deleted in the final text due to objection by a number of States, in particular Japan.

---

[47] G. Carduzzi, New developments in the law of the sea: The UNESCO Convention on the Protection of the Underwater Cultural Heritage, 96 *AJIL* 2002, pp. 420-434, at pp. 422-423. Similar views are expressed by R. Garabello, The negotiating history of the Convention on the Protection of the Underwater Cultural Heritage, *in* Garabello & Scovazzi (eds.), *supra* note 10, pp. 89-192, at pp. 106-109.

[48] See further L.V. Prott & P.J. O'Keefe, *The Law and the Cultural Heritage* (vol. 1: *Discovery and Excavation*, Professional Books Ltd, 1984) at p. 178.

Abandonment

The UNESCO Convention did not retain the presumption of abandonment envisaged by the ILA Draft in an attempt to avoid the complex issues associated with ownership of underwater cultural heritage – usually wrecks[49]. Comparative legal research will show that the legal status of historic shipwrecks and their cargoes in entangled within the various wreck, salvage and heritage laws, which differ between legal systems. The absence of international principles on the question of ownership indicates the reluctance of the international community to regulate this controversial issue, which is left open to domestic legislation. The UNESCO Convention does not deal with the question of title, as it is directed at interference with cultural heritage and the quality of the work done in relation to that heritage. The inclusion of a presumption of abandonment would have affected ownership indirectly. During the meeting of governmental experts there were differences of opinion between lawyers and archaeologists over the concept of abandonment. It was argued that this concept cannot apply to underwater cultural heritage and that it does not exist in the national laws of some countries. For this reason, it should be a matter for the legislation of each State alone. As a result, the Chairman proposed to delete the term "abandoned" from the draft[50].

5.3. Jurisdictional clauses

As has already been stated, the UNESCO Convention deals with the protection of underwater cultural heritage within each jurisdictional zone separately.

5.3.1. Underwater cultural heritage in internal waters, archipelagic waters and territorial sea

According to article 7, in the exercise of their sovereignty, States parties have the exclusive right to regulate and authorize activities directed at underwater cultural heritage in their internal waters, archipelagic waters and territorial sea. In such areas and without prejudice to other international agreements

---

[49] See also Carduzzi, *supra* note 47, at p. 424, who argues that "from a technical and legal standpoint, the issue of ownership of underwater cultural heritage was too complex and time-consuming for a negotiation that was already difficult enough. Though justifiable, the exclusion of ownership is a gap in the Convention. The latter assumes ownership to be governed by the applicable (domestic) private law rules – as does the LOS Convention – and to provide title to the one who owned the underwater cultural heritage until abandonment".

[50] See further A. Strati, *Draft Convention on the Protection of the Underwater Cultural Heritage: A Commentary Prepared for UNESCO*, UNESCO Doc. CLT-99/WS/8, April 1999, at p. 18.

and rules of international law, States parties shall require that the Rules be applied to activities directed at underwater cultural heritage.

5.3.2. Underwater cultural heritage in the contiguous zone

Similarly, within the contiguous zone, States parties may regulate and authorize activities directed at underwater cultural heritage. In doing so, they shall require that the Rules be applied (article 8). However, this otherwise straightforward jurisdictional rule is qualified by the reference to articles 9 and 10. The application of the system of consultations envisaged for the continental shelf/EEZ (see *infra* section 5.3.3.) in the contiguous zone may diminish the rights that the coastal State already enjoys under article 303(2) of the LOS Convention.[51] As already stated, article 303(2) is based on a legal fiction that can be interpreted so as to recognize coastal jurisdiction over underwater cultural heritage found on the bed of the contiguous zone and establish a *de facto* 24-mile archaeological zone. The reference to articles 9 and 10 of the UNESCO Convention should, therefore, be interpreted as simply accommodating the "interests" of States parties with a cultural, historical or archaeological verifiable link to the underwater cultural heritage concerned and not affecting the otherwise applicable jurisdiction of the coastal State[52]. Such an interpretation is aligned both with the spirit and the wording of article 8:

> "Without prejudice to and *in addition to articles 9 and 10,* and in accordance with article 303, paragraph 2, of the United Nations Convention on the Law of the Sea, States Parties *may regulate and authorize ...*"

---

[51] See also the comments made by Greece at its statement on vote at the UNESCO Conference. In contrast, Carduzzi, *supra* note 47, at p. 429, claims that article 8 of the UNESCO Convention improved the protection of underwater cultural heritage afforded by article 303(2) of the LOS Convention.

[52] One reason more that this qualification was a last minute addition that was not debated at the last meeting of governmental experts in July 2001. One cannot, therefore, share the Swedish view that: "Sweden welcomes that the legal content of the rules concerning the mandate of the coastal State in its declared contiguous zone is clarified in the Convention and regards this clarification as an indication of customary law"; cf the statement made by Sweden on 29 October 2001 at the 31st session of the UNESCO General Conference. As already seen, State practice in this area is rather scarce so as to provide evidence for the existence of a customary rule both with respect to the nature of coastal rights over archaeological objects in the contiguous zone and the relationship between the general contiguous zone and the 24-mile archaeological zone.

5.3.3. Underwater cultural heritage in the exclusive economic zone and on the continental shelf

As regards the continental shelf and the EEZ, the Convention has adopted a compromise formula that combines coastal and national/flag State jurisdiction, while distinguishing between *reporting and notification* of the location of underwater cultural heritage and the actual *scheme of protection.* According to article 9, all States have a responsibility to protect underwater cultural heritage in the EEZ and the continental shelf in conformity with the Convention. A State party shall require that when its national, or a vessel flying its flag, discovers or intends to engage in activities directed at underwater cultural heritage located in its EEZ or continental shelf, the national or the master of the vessel shall report such discovery or activity to it. In the EEZ or on the continental shelf of another State party, States parties shall require the national or the master of the vessel flying their flag to report such activity or discovery to them or to that other State Party. Alternatively, a State party shall require the national or master of the vessel to report such discovery or activity to it and shall ensure the rapid and effective transmission of such reports to all other States Parties. On depositing its instrument of ratification, acceptance, approval or accession, a State party shall declare the manner in which reports will be transmitted. Furthermore, a State party shall notify the Director-General of UNESCO of discoveries or activities reported to it and the Director-General shall promptly make available to all States Parties any such information notified to him. Any State party may declare to the State party in whose EEZ or on whose continental shelf the underwater cultural heritage is located, its interest in being consulted on how to ensure the effective protection of that underwater cultural heritage. Such declaration shall be based on a verifiable link, especially a cultural, historical or archaeological link to the underwater cultural heritage concerned.

As far as protection is concerned, article 10 adopts a *system of consultations* between interested States parties. More specifically, where there is a discovery of underwater cultural heritage or it is intended that activity shall be directed at underwater cultural heritage in a State party's EEZ or on its continental shelf, that State shall consult all other States parties which have declared an interest as well as co-ordinate such consultations as the "Coordinating State", unless it expressly declares that it does not wish to do so. At the same time, however, it is provided that the Coordinating State, i.e. in principle the coastal State, may take all practicable measures and/or issue any necessary authorizations in conformity with this Convention, and if necessary prior to consultations prevent any immediate danger to the underwater cultural heritage, whether arising from human activities or any other causes, including looting. In addition, the Coordinating State shall implement the measures of protection, which have been agreed by the consulting States, unless the consulting States, which include the Coordinating State, agree that another State party shall implement those measures; issue all necessary authorizations as well as may conduct any necessary preliminary research on the underwater cultural heritage but also promptly inform the Director-General of the results. It is clarified, however, that in undertaking such activities, the Coordinating State shall act on behalf of the States parties as a whole and not on its own interest. Similarly, any such action shall not in itself constitute a basis for the assertion of any preferential or jurisdictional rights not provided for in international law, including the UN Convention on the Law of the Sea.

Undoubtedly, during the negotiations the most controversial issue was jurisdiction over underwater cultural heritage found on the continental shelf/EEZ. The majority of States were in favour of expanding coastal State jurisdiction; however, a number of States, such as the USA, the United Kingdom, Sweden, the Netherlands, France, Norway and Russia, firmly objected to any extension of coastal competence over the continental shelf. Disagreement over jurisdiction was a major drawback as most of the provisions of the Convention depended on the jurisdictional clause and inevitably could not be finalised before a decision on this fundamental issue was taken. It is notable that the compromise solution, which was finally agreed, does not even mention the term "coastal State". This was the main reason that Greece abstained from voting; namely, that the Convention leaves to the coastal State only a "co-ordinating role" on its own continental shelf. On the contrary, other States, such as Russia and Norway, voted against the Convention on the basis that it grants the coastal State excessive rights[53].

If it is considered that the extension of coastal jurisdiction over the continental shelf was also debated unsuccessfully during UNCLOS III, it is highly unlikely that a more straightforward provision could have been adopted, at least as a compromise formula acceptable to most States. Still, the adopted scheme of notification/protection is unnecessarily complicated, as it relies heavily on efficient communication between different entities; it is difficult to envisage this process as acting quickly and efficiently. There may be even cases, where the States parties to the UNESCO Convention would be notified of a discovery or an intention to engage in activities directed at underwater cultural heritage, but not the coastal State on whose continental shelf the underwater cultural heritage is found, if it is not a party to the Convention[54].

---

[53] See further Garabello, *supra* note 47, at p. 121.

[54] O'Keefe, *supra* note 41, at p. 83.

5.3.4. Underwater cultural heritage in the Area

With respect to the Area, article 11 provides that States parties have a responsibility to protect underwater cultural heritage in conformity with the Convention and article 149 of the LOS Convention. Accordingly, when a national or a vessel flying the flag of a State Party discovers or intends to engage in activities directed at underwater cultural heritage located in the Area, that State party shall require its national or the master of the vessel to report such discovery or activity to it. States parties shall notify the Director-General and the Secretary-General of the ISA of such discoveries and the Director-General shall promptly make available to all States parties. Any State party may declare to the Director-General its interest in being consulted on how to ensure the effective protection of such heritage. Such declaration shall be based on a verifiable link to the underwater cultural heritage concerned, particular regard being paid to the preferential rights of States of cultural, historical or archaeological origin.

According to article 12, the Director-General shall invite States parties, which have declared an interest to consult on how best to protect the underwater cultural heritage and to appoint a State party to co-ordinate such consultations as the "Coordinating State". The Director-General shall also invite the ISA to participate in such consultations. The Coordinating State shall implement measures of protection which have been agreed by the consulting States and issue all necessary authorizations for such agreed measures unless the consulting States agree that another State party shall implement those measures or issue the respective authorizations. The Coordinating State may also conduct any necessary preliminary research and issue all necessary authorizations therefor. However, in coordinating consultations, taking measures, conducting preliminary research and/or issuing authorizations the Coordinating State shall act for the benefit of mankind as a whole on behalf of all States Parties. In this respect, particular regard shall be paid to the preferential rights of States of cultural, historical or archaeological origin of the underwater cultural heritage concerned.

The aforementioned provisions are obviously modelled upon the scheme of protection envisaged for the continental shelf/EEZ. However, the additional reference to the "preferential rights" of the States of cultural, historical or archaeological origin complicates things further. First, there is no indication as to the nature or scope of these rights. Since States parties with a verifiable link to the underwater cultural heritage concerned already participate in the consultations for its protection, what will be the content of preferential rights? Would they be confined to the acquisition of the recovered cultural heritage? If this is the case, then the reference to "preferential rights" at the stage of declaring interest to consult on how best to protect underwater cultural heritage is meaningless. Second, article 11(4) refers to States parties with a verifiable link to the underwater cultural heritage concerned - the term "especially a cultural, historical or archaeological link" used through the Convention is omitted, arguably in order to avoid duplications. Third, from the wording of article 11(4) it appears that *all* States of cultural, historical or archaeological origin enjoy preferential rights and not only States parties to the UNESCO Convention.

As explained by Garabello, at the last Meeting of Experts the United Kingdom and Canada submitted a proposal modelled upon the scheme approved with reference to the continental shelf (notification and protection) with the Director-General of UNESCO replacing the role of the coastal State. It was this proposal, with an additional reference to preferential rights already considered by article 149 of the LOS Convention that was finally approved.[55] However, the structure of the UNESCO Convention was different from that of the LOS Convention, which recognised the interests of the States of origin only with respect to archaeological and historical objects found in the Area. The UNESCO Convention envisaged the participation of States parties with a verifiable cultural, historical or archaeological link as "consulting States" in the protection of underwater cultural heritage found in extraterritorial waters. In this context, the incorporation of the wording of article 149 of the LOS Convention in articles 11(4) and 12(6) added nothing but confusion. At least, the relationship between the different terms used by the Convention should have been clarified.

5.4. Sovereign immunity

According to article 2(8) of the UNESCO Convention, "consistent with State practice and international law, including the United Nations Convention on the Law of the Sea, nothing in this Convention shall be interpreted as modifying the rules of international law and State practice pertaining to sovereign immunities, nor any State's rights with respect to its State vessels and aircraft"[56].

---

[55] See further Garabello, *supra* note 47, at p. 153.

[56] In its statement on vote at the 31st General Conference of UNESCO, Greece criticised the reservation of both "rules of international law" and "State practice pertaining to sovereign immunities" in article 2(8). As argued: "Apart from the poor drafting of this paragraph, it is questionable whether there is consistency in State practice with respect to the legal status of sunken vessels and aircraft". Indeed, there is an absence of rules of international law, including the LOS Convention, on this issue. During UNCLOS III, a number of proposals, mainly made by eastern European countries, suggested that ships and aircraft sunk beyond the

This general principle is applied within the separate maritime zones in a manner that reflects the different compromises reached during the negotiations. Within the archipelagic waters and the territorial sea, States parties *should inform* the flag State party to the Convention and, if applicable, other States with a verifiable link, especially a cultural, historical or archaeological link, with respect to the discovery of identifiable State vessels and aircraft; article 7(3). As regards the continental shelf/EEZ, no activity directed at State vessels and aircraft shall be conducted without the *agreement* of the

---

outer limit of the territorial sea, as well as equipment and cargo on board, should be salvaged only by the flag State or within the flag State's consent. With the passage of time, the scope of these proposals was restricted to sunken warships and vessels owned or operated by a State and used only for government non-commercial purposes. However, none of these suggestions found their way into the Final Text of the Convention. It is beyond doubt that warships and State-owned or operated vessels used only on government non-commercial service, enjoy complete immunity from the jurisdiction of any State other than the flag State on the high seas; cf. articles 95 and 96 of the LOS Convention. As a corollary to the rule of immunity, they are exempted from the application of numerous international treaties, including the 1910 Brussels Convention for the Unification of Certain Rules with Respect to Assistance and Salvage at Sea, the 1989 Salvage Convention, which replaced it, and more recently the Draft Wreck Removal Convention (article 4). However, it is debatable whether *sunken* warships and public vessels still qualify as ships submitted to the exclusive jurisdiction of their flag State and enjoying immunity. Even if it is accepted that recovery operations on the high seas may be undertaken by any State, the ownership of a sunken vessel is not impaired or lost. For such a situation to occur, abandonment of the ship in question must be proven first. With respect to warships and other public vessels, abandonment is very difficult to prove, especially when national law requires the explicit renunciation of title. It has been suggested that such vessels retain their status as public property and that, therefore, "the State can prohibit any physical interference with that property even to the point of allowing its remains to lie on the bottom of the sea"; F.A. Eustis III, The *Glomar Explorer* incident: Implications for the law of salvage, 16 *Virginia JIL* 1975, pp. 117-185, at p. 186. See also L.N. Galenskaya, International co-operation in cultural affairs, *RCADI* 1986-III, pp. 265-331, at p. 302: "In particular, naval ships are the property of a State and under the rules of State succession those States have all the rights to the wrecked ships. We cannot consider them as a prize of war or a war victim because these ships were lost in battle". This conclusion is confirmed by a number of cases where coastal States had even asked the permission of the flag State to recover warships from their territorial sea. After having been denied permission, they did not recover the sunken warships. It seems, however, that in these instances in question was not the legality of the recovery operations, but the right of disposal of the wrecks concerned. In concluding, current practice suggests that public vessels used for non-commercial purposes and warships retain their status as State property so that their recovery *may* require the consent of the flag State; Strati, *supra* note 21, at pp. 220-221. Similar views are expressed by Garabello, *supra* note 47 at p. 179: "The State practice described in this section is interesting in that it shows that bilateral arrangements are the most suitable solution for settling potential disputes surrounding military wrecks, both historic and recent. They are indeed a very flexible means of solving delicate issues such as ownership, management, sharing of treasures, destiny of human bodies, etc. The lack of rules of international law (customary or conventional) concerning sunken warships – at least until the UNESCO Convention – makes the need for practical arrangements quite stringent and the bilateral solution for the right answer".

flag State and the collaboration of the Coordinating State; article 10(7). Finally, no State party shall undertake or authorize activities directed at State vessels and aircraft in the Area without the *consent* of the flag State; article 12(7). It would seem, therefore, that despite arguments to the contrary under the UNESCO Convention the legal position of the flag State is reinforced[57].

From the aforementioned provisions one should distinguish article 13 dealing with State vessels and aircraft as "finders" of underwater cultural heritage. Article 13, which came out at the very end of negotiations, *excludes* warships and other State vessels from the obligation to report discoveries of underwater cultural heritage provided that they do not operate for commercial purposes, they undertake their normal mode of operations and are not engaged in activities directed at underwater cultural heritage. Indeed, it is not unusual to conduct underwater archaeological research with State vessels, such as the nuclear submarine NR-1 – used by Robert Ballard during his research on Skerki Bank 75 miles off Sicily in 1997-1999[58]. As drafted, article 13 limits its scope of application to the "accidental" discovery of underwater cultural heritage under certain conditions[59]. Nevertheless, it still provides an important exception to the overall applicable regime.

5.5. Measures relating to nationals and vessels

Nationality is a valid basis of jurisdiction, to which States have frequently resorted to deal with situations where territorial jurisdiction is ineffective. One relevant example is the Protection of Military Remains Act 1986, under which the United Kingdom protects the site of British vessels and aircraft

---

[57] M. Aznar-Gomez, Legal status of sunken warships "revisited", 7 *Spanish Yearbook of International Law* 2001-2002. On the contrary, Garabello argues that the solution codified in the Convention leaves to the coastal State even more powers than those it actually enjoys by practice: it is not even obliged to inform the flag State that it will recover a sunken foreign military vessel in its territorial waters. *Supra* note 47 at p. 135.

[58] The "Skerki Bank Deep Sea Project" raised a lot of concern as eight ancient shipwrecks were located in deep water in the Mediterranean. No previous official information about the expedition was given to any of the Mediterranean coastal States, as Ballard justified the recovery of 150 artifacts from the wrecks as an exercise of the freedom of the high seas. See further T. Scovazzi, The application of "salvage law and other rules of admiralty" to the underwater cultural heritage: some relevant cases, *in* Garabello and Scovazzi (eds), *supra* note 10, pp. 19-80 at pp. 75-76.

[59] The original proposal, which was submitted by the United Kingdom with the support of Sweden (Non-paper 3 dated July, 3 2001) excluded all State vessels and aircraft from the general regime and – given the very broad definition of State vessels agreed upon – the risk was that an excessively high number of vessels – as finders – would be free not to apply the Convention. Garabello, *supra* note 47, at p. 156.

that sank or crashed on military service, even if the site is in international waters. It is an offence for British nationals to take any action in respect of such a site without a license[60].

The ILA Draft employed nationality as a principal jurisdictional basis to enforce its provisions in areas that were not subject to the jurisdiction of the parties, i.e. beyond the "cultural heritage zone". However, under the UNESCO Convention, which does not establish clear-cut jurisdictional rules over underwater cultural heritage on the continental shelf/EEZ, States parties have a range of obligations *vis-à-vis* their nationals and vessels flying their flag when they discover or intend to engage in activities directed at underwater cultural heritage in these areas. They may also participate in the consultations for the protection of underwater cultural heritage in such areas, provided that they have declared an interest based on a verifiable cultural, historical or archaeological link to the cultural heritage concerned. The same applies with respect to underwater cultural heritage found in the Area. On top of this, article 16 provides that States parties must take all practicable measures to ensure that their nationals and vessels flying their flag do not engage in any activity directed at underwater cultural heritage in a manner not in conformity with the Convention. Arguably, article 16 is directed at the fulfilment of a State's obligations under the provisions of the UNESCO Convention[61].

5.6. Non-use of areas under the jurisdiction of States Parties

Article 15, which originates from article 7 of the ILA Draft, prohibits the use of the territory of States parties, including their maritime ports, installations and structures under their exclusive jurisdiction or control, in support of activities directed at underwater cultural heritage which are not in conformity with the Convention.[62] Such a regulation was considered necessary, as even if all the countries in a particular region were parties to the Convention, no constraint could be imposed on activities violating its terms, but taking place in areas outside their jurisdiction. Article 15 intends to deny port-State support to such activities and supplements the mechanisms envisaged

---

[60] Protection of Military Remains Act 1986, C.35, section 3(1). In 1997, the Merchant Shipping and Maritime Security Act extended the provisions of the 1986 Act to cover non-military remains.

[61] *Supra* note 41, at p. 109.

[62] A similar regulation is to be found in article 23 of the UN Fish Stock Agreement in relation to the enforcement of conservation and management measures on the high seas.

by the UNESCO Convention for the protection of underwater cultural heritage in international waters.

As a general rule, foreign ships searching for or recovering underwater relics use local ports as operational bases. The successful completion of a research project depends, to a large extent, upon the possibility of calling at such ports. In the absence of express provisions to the contrary, there are no additional requirements for the call of archaeological vessels at foreign ports. Ports are presumed to be open unless entry is restricted or prohibited[63]. However, as the whole issue lies within the discretionary authority of the port State, the latter may make entry to its ports dependent upon compliance with conditions concerning the removal of underwater cultural heritage. Article 211(3) of the LOS Convention specifically recognizes the right of coastal States to establish particular requirements for the prevention, reduction and control of pollution of the marine environment as a condition for the entry of foreign vessels into their ports. Although its purpose is to reduce vessel-source pollution, article 211(3) is based on the assumption that the port-State has the discretionary authority to permit or deny entry of foreign vessels into its maritime ports. Under article 15 of the UNESCO Convention, the port State is not only entitled to regulate access to its ports, but must also take measures to prohibit the use of its ports and other areas under its jurisdiction for support of activities which are not in conformity with the Convention.

5.7. Control of entry into the territory, dealing and possession

Under article 14, States parties shall take measures to prevent the entry into their territory, the dealing in, or the possession of, underwater cultural heritage illicitly exported and/or recovered, where recovery was contrary to the Convention. This provision may provide an effective means of protecting underwater cultural heritage in areas beyond national jurisdiction, as the closing of the lucrative markets of some "art-importing" States may deter speculative attempts to retrieve objects from underwater sites. It is notable that in an attempt to prevent the salvaging of the wreck site of the *Titanic* by the French Institute for Maritime Research and Exploration (IFREMER), the US Congress considered a ban on the importation for commercial gain of any object from the wreck. The bill, which was never enacted, provided for termination of the embargo whenever the *Titanic* became bound by international agreement governing its exploration and salvage[64].

---

[63] See further A.V. Lowe, The right of entry into maritime ports in international law, 14 *San Diego LR* 1977, pp. 597-622.

[64] S. 1581, 100 Cong. 1st Sess., 133 Cong. Rec. SS. 1150-1151 (Aug. 3, 1987).

5.8. Seizure and disposition of underwater cultural heritage

Article 18 provides for the seizure[65] of underwater cultural heritage that has been recovered in a manner not in conformity with the Convention. This innovative provision stems from article 10 of the ILA Draft, which aimed to increase the effectiveness of the Convention by securing application of its standards to underwater cultural heritage found in international waters and brought within the territory of a State party. In case of seizure of underwater cultural heritage originating from the territorial sea or the "cultural heritage zone" of another State party, the consent of the coastal State was required. Similar clauses had appeared in earlier drafts of the UNESCO Convention with respect to underwater cultural heritage originating from the continental shelf or the EEZ of another State party. Article 18 is silent on this issue; nevertheless, it may be interpreted so as to encompass cultural heritage originating from high seas areas. As pointed out by O'Keefe, under article 18 the heritage only has to be within the State's territory; it does not matter how it got there, although the number of intervening transactions will be significant in certain respects. For example, the greater the number of such transactions, the more difficult will it be to prove that the object was recovered in a manner not in conformity with the Convention, as the evidence just will not be available. Moreover, courts may be less inclined to uphold seizure[66].

---

[65] To date, the few international instruments, which envisage seizure of cultural heritage, allow this in the general context of restitution. Thus, article 8 of the European Convention on Offences relating to Cultural Property provides for the seizure and restitution of cultural property found on the territory of the requested party subsequent to an offence relating to cultural property. Furthermore, article I(2) of the First Protocol to the 1954 Hague Convention for the Protection of Cultural Property in the Event of Armed Conflict establishes the duty of contracting States to take into their custody cultural property imported into their territory either directly or indirectly from any occupied territory, while article 7(b)(ii) of the 1970 UNESCO Convention provides that States parties undertake, at the request of the State party of origin, to take appropriate steps to recover and return any such cultural property imported after the entry into force of the Convention, provided, however, that the requesting State shall pay just compensation to an innocent purchaser or to a person who has valid title to that property. At national level, seizure of cultural heritage is designed either as a penalty or as a means of protecting cultural heritage especially in cases where it applies irrespective of ownership or punishment of the wrongdoer.

[66] *Supra* note 41, at pp. 115-116. Further problems may arise in case the identifiable owner claims the seized property or a looter exports an illegally excavated object into another State party. According to article 18, the State party must seize the underwater cultural heritage concerned and dispose of it for the public benefit. However, in such a case there may be conflict with other applicable international instruments, such as the 1970 UNESCO Convention, *supra* note 12, or the 1995 UNIDROIT Convention on Stolen and Illegally Exported Cultural Objects, 34 *ILM* 1995, p. 1322.

After seizure, each State party undertakes to record, protect and take all reasonable measures to stabilize underwater cultural heritage. The obligation to record and protect the seized material is regarded as the primary duty, but States parties are also required to take *all reasonable measures* to stabilize it. This qualification was thought to be desirable, as conservation is very expensive and could require unforeseen expenditure by a State. However, if the seized material is not rapidly and skilfully treated it may suffer irreparable damage, such as corrosion, and loss of scientific value. Relevant to this issue is also article 2(6) on the "objectives and general principles" of the UNESCO Convention, which provides that: "Recovered underwater cultural heritage shall be deposited, conserved and managed in a manner that ensures its long-term preservation".

There is also provision for the notification of the Director-General and any other State with a verifiable link, especially a cultural, historical or archaeological, to the cultural heritage concerned, of such seizure. Finally, the State party, which has seized underwater cultural heritage, shall ensure that it is disposed of for the public benefit, taking into account the need for conservation and research, the need for re-assembly of a dispersed collection, the need for public access, exhibition and education, as well as the interests of any State with a verifiable link, especially a cultural, historical or archaeological link, in respect of the underwater cultural heritage concerned.

5.9. *Cooperation and information-sharing*

Article 19 provides for the cooperation and mutual assistance of States parties in the protection and management of underwater cultural heritage, including, where practicable, collaboration in the investigation, documentation, conservation, study and presentation of the heritage[67] as well as information-sharing with other States parties concerning, *inter alia,* the discovery and location of heritage, heritage excavated or recovered contrary to the Convention or otherwise in violation of international law, pertinent scientific methodology and technology and legal developments relating to heritage. Any information shared between States parties or between UNESCO and States parties regarding the location and discovery or location of underwater cultural heritage shall, to the extent compatible with their national legisla-

---

[67] Similarly, article 4 of the Draft European Convention reads: "Where underwater cultural property is of particular interest to other contracting States, contracting States should consider providing information about the discovery of such property and collaborating in the investigation, excavation, documentation, conservation, study and cultural promotion of the property to the extent permitted by their legislation".

tion, be kept confidential and reserved to competent authorities of States parties as long as the disclosure of such information might endanger or otherwise put at risk the preservation of such underwater cultural heritage. Finally, States parties shall take all practicable measures to disseminate information about underwater cultural heritage excavated or recovered contrary to this Convention or otherwise in violation of international law.

5.10. Exclusion of the law of salvage

A highly controversial issue in the protection of underwater cultural heritage is the application of salvage law to shipwrecks of historic significance. The protection of underwater cultural heritage has never been an objective of this ancient maritime law, which evolved to provide compensation for the salvor of maritime property in distress. The salvor works for profit and this is reflected in the manner in which salvage operations are conducted. A good salvage practice might be one that destroys "piecemeal" a marine archaeological site, or neglects to record any of the finds. It is notable that in the few cases where admiralty courts required the application of archaeological principles in salvage operations, there was controversy as to whether salvors complied with it[68]. It will, no doubt, be difficult to disprove the claim of a salvor as to the nature of the work done and, in any case, this will only become an issue after the damage has been inflicted.

During the negotiations at UNESCO it was not possible to agree on an unqualified exclusion of the law of salvage as provided for by the ILA Draft. Under article 4 of the UNESCO Convention, any activity relating to underwater cultural heritage shall not be subject to the law of salvage or law of finds, unless it: a) is authorized by the competent authorities, b) is in full conformity with this Convention and c) ensures that any recovery of the underwater cultural heritage achieves its maximum protection. This qualification was considered necessary in order to bring the situation into line with that already existing in a number of national legal systems, which incorporate protective measures of the underwater cultural heritage in their admiralty laws. A permit will normally be required for any activity in relation to underwater cultural heritage. The permit will specify how the activity is to be conducted and, in many cases, what happens to the objects excavated[69]. Although article 4 is worded such that the law of salvage and the law of finds can apply in specified circumstances, if those circumstances are indeed

---

[68] To date this has not been done in circumstances involving a classic excavation. See further Strati, *supra* note 21, at p. 49.

[69] O'Keefe, *supra* note 41, at p. 63.

satisfied, there will be little left of the original concepts. In addition, article 4 should be read together with other provisions of the UNESCO Convention, such as article 2(7) prohibiting the commercial exploitation of underwater cultural heritage.

The future will show whether this compromise solution can protect cultural heritage from the devastating practices of salvage companies. As argued by Carduzzi[70], the UNESCO Convention ensures a high threshold of protection for underwater cultural heritage, *inter alia,* well beyond that afforded by the LOS Convention. The latter preserved the law of salvage and other rules of admiralty, although article 303(3) must be interpreted as not overriding the duty to protect to underwater cultural heritage and the duty to cooperate for this purpose. Furthermore, with comparison to the ILA Draft, the prohibition is not limited to the law of salvage but also to the law of finds.

5.11. Illicit traffic in underwater cultural heritage

The Convention does not deal specifically with this issue. However, as already stated, article 14 requires that States parties shall take measures to prevent the dealing in, or the possession of, underwater cultural heritage illicitly exported and/or recovered where recovery was contrary to this Convention, while article 18 provides for the seizure of underwater cultural heritage that has been recovered in a manner not in conformity with the Convention.

During the negotiations some experts suggested that the Convention should require the return of underwater cultural heritage taken from the territorial waters of a State and illegally exported when this State expressed an interest in these objects. However, according to other experts, this would occur in any event. The Convention is silent on this issue. The reason for this omission would appear to be the fact that the Convention primarily deals with cultural heritage found beyond the territorial sea. It was, therefore, thought preferable to avoid regulating this controversial issue. Inevitably, such matters will be governed by the provisions of other applicable international instruments, such as the 1970 UNESCO Convention or the 1995 UNIDROIT Convention[71].

---

[70] Carduzzi, *supra* note 47, at p. 425.

[71] See, however, Frigo, who argues that "despite the remarkable progress during the last decades in the field of legal protection of cultural property, the contemporary international practice is revealing some traces, which are very likely inspired by a relativist and alternative approach to the co-operation in our domain." In his view, the minimalist character of article 14 of the UNESCO Convention may be considered as an example of such traces and a warning sign of a trend which might emerge less elusive in the future; M. Frigo, Traces of relativism in the contemporary practice of international protection of cultural property: Reciprocal v.

5.12. Accommodation of the interests of the State(s) of origin

The accommodation of the interests of the State(s) of origin under the LOS Convention was not satisfactory so as to serve as a model for a general rule. Thus, the drafters of the UNESCO Convention attempted to deal with this issue on a different basis: First, they envisaged participation of States parties with a verifiable cultural, historical or archaeological link as "consulting States" in the protection of underwater cultural heritage in extraterritorial waters[72]. Second, within the archipelagic waters or the territorial sea of another State party such States, whether parties or non-parties to the Convention, should be informed with respect to the discovery of identifiable State vessels and aircraft. Third, there is provision for their notification in case of seizure of underwater cultural heritage. Finally, in case of disposition of the seized cultural heritage their interests should be taken into account.

The identification problem is, no doubt, acute, as in most cases the determination of the State of origin is extremely difficult. However, even if under the circumstances it is possible to identify traces of origin, the qualification of more than one States as claimants to the recovered objects may create considerable difficulties. Inevitably, conflicts will arise as to which State has priority over the discovered relics. It is recalled that article 149 of the LOS Convention refers to the "State or country of origin", "the State of cultural origin" and the "State of historical and archaeological origin" without, however, defining these terms or establishing priorities between them. The UNESCO Convention, on the other hand, uses the general term *States with a verifiable link, especially a cultural, historical or archaeological link*. This concept is not helpful either; in the writer's view, it would have been more appropriate to use the term "cultural link" alone and avoid the juxtaposition between "cultural", "archaeological" and "historical".

The situation is complicated further by the reference to the "preferential rights" of the "States of cultural, historical or archaeological origin" with respect to underwater cultural heritage found in the Area. As already stated, the incorporation of the LOS terminology in articles 11(4) and 12(6) of the UNESCO Convention added nothing but confusion. It superimposed new

---

erga omnes duties? *in* T. Scovazzi (ed.), *La protezione del patrimonio culturale sottomarino nel Mare Mediterraneo* (Giuffrè editore, Milano 2004) pp. 15-20, at p. 15.

[72] Along the same lines, a number of UN General Assembly Resolutions on the Restitution or Return of Cultural Property to the Countries of Origin invited States seeking the recovery of cultural and artistic treasures from the seabed to facilitate the participation of States having a historical and cultural link with those treasures. See, *inter alia,* Resolution 38/34 of 25 November 1973; 40/19 of 21 November 1985; 42/7 of 22 October 1987; 44/18 of 6 November 1989 and 48/15 of 2 November 1993.

concepts without clarifying their relation with equivalent terms used by the UNESCO Convention in other provisions. For example, how can one distinguish the "State of archaeological origin" from the "State with a verifiable archaeological link" or the "State of cultural origin" from the "State with an identifiable cultural link"? The only reason for the appearance of both terms in the UNESCO Convention would appear to be the desire for "compliance" with the LOS Convention, which once more did not promote the clarity of the law.

6. STATE PRACTICE IN THE AFTERMATH OF THE UNESCO CONVENTION

The UNESCO Convention is not yet in force, as only six States have so far submitted instruments of ratification. Nevertheless, the "Regulations on Prospecting and Exploration for Polymetallic Nodules in the Area"[73] require the notification of the Director-General of UNESCO of any discovery of underwater cultural heritage in the Area.

Regulation 8
A prospector shall immediately notify the Secretary-General in writing of any finding in the Area of an object of an archaeological or historical nature and its location. The Secretary-General shall transmit such information to the Director-General of the United Nations Educational, Scientific and Cultural Organization.

Regulation 34
The contractor shall immediately notify the Secretary-General in writing of any finding in the exploration area of an object of an archaeological or historical nature and its location. The Secretary-General shall transmit such information to the Director-General of the United Nations Educational, Scientific and Educational Organization. Following the finding of any such object of an archaeological or historical nature in the exploration area, the contractor shall take all reasonable measures to avoid disturbing such object[74].

Similarly, Italy incorporated the "Rules" of the UNESCO Convention in its national heritage legislation without, however, becoming a party to it. Still, the relevant Italian legislation may be interpreted as establishing a *de*

---

[73] It is notable that the so-called "Mining Code" was adopted in 2000, i.e. even before the adoption of the UNESCO Convention; ISBA/6/A18/13 July 2000.

[74] Such measures should be considered as an application of the duty to protect archaeological and historical objects found at sea under article 303(1) of the LOS Convention and not as an expansion of the competence of the ISA over archaeological remains. As already seen, the UNESCO Convention attributes a more significant role to the ISA by envisaging its participation in the consultations concerning the protection of underwater cultural heritage in the Area.

facto 24-mile archaeological zone[75]. In contrast, the States that were against the adoption of the UNESCO Convention would appear to have strengthened their opposition. It is notable that the recent UN General Assembly Resolutions on Oceans and the Law of the Sea make no reference to the UNESCO Convention. Instead, reference is made to the general duty to protect underwater cultural heritage and to co-operate therefore under article 303 of the LOS Convention[76].

7. CONCLUSIONS

The 2001 UNESCO Convention, no doubt, deals with a very complicated issue that involves a variety of interests and laws both at national and international level. The different bodies of laws involved in the protection of the underwater cultural heritage have been described as a *legal labyrinth*[77]. Regrettably, the drafters of the UNESCO Convention did not succeed in establishing an effective scheme of protection at least with respect to underwater cultural heritage found on the continental shelf/EEZ. The desire for strict compliance with the LOS Convention combined with a strict time schedule under UNESCO rules resulted in a compromise solution that is unnecessarily complicated and may involve consultations with a number of States even for the preservation of a single statue.

It is unfortunate that twenty years after the adoption of the LOS Convention it was not possible to agree on a more workable and straightforward provision on jurisdiction. Nevertheless, the UNESCO Convention should not be overlooked: it adopted legally binding measures for the protection of cultural heritage in international waters which would otherwise remain unprotected, excluded in principle the law of salvage and established scientific standards for the preservation and management of underwater cultural heritage. The future will show whether the first international agreement on the

---

[75] According to article 94 of Legislative Decree No. 41 of 22 January 2004: "Gli oggetti archeologici e storici rinvenuti nei fondali della zona di mare estesa dodici miglia marine a partire dal limite esterno del mare territoriale sono tutelati ai sensi delle "Regole relative agli interventi sul patrimonio culturale subacqueo" allegate alla Convenzione UNESCO sulla protezione del patrimonio culturale subacqueo, adottata a Parigi il 2 novembre 2001", *Gazzetta Ufficiale della Repubblica Italiana*, suppl. to No. 45 of 24 February 2004.

[76] Resolution 59/24 of 17 November 2004 "urges all States to co-operate directly or through competent international bodies to protect and preserve objects of an archaeological and historical nature from the sea in conformity with article 303 of the Convention"; paragraph 7.

[77] A. Korthals Altes, Submarine antiquities: A legal labyrinth, 4 *Syracuse Journal of International Law & Commerce* 1976, pp. 77-96.

protection of underwater cultural heritage will be applied in practice or pale into insignificance.

Pending the entry into force of the UNESCO Convention, one may consider different options for protecting the underwater cultural heritage:

- *Application of the "UNESCO Rules" in conjunction with the protective measures of the LOS Convention*

States should take advantage of the protective measures adopted by the LOS Convention in particular the duty to protect "objects of an archaeological and historical nature" found at sea which may embrace the whole spectrum of activities relating to the protection of underwater cultural heritage. In this respect, the UNESCO Rules or alternatively the ICOMOS Charter on the Management and Protection of the Underwater Cultural Heritage are of particular importance. It is notable that even States that voted against the UNESCO Convention, such as Norway, considered unilateral application of the Rules[78]. Thus, coastal States may adopt protective measures in the exercise of their resource-related jurisdiction over the continental shelf/EEZ, in addition to establishing 24-mile archaeological zones in accordance with article 303(2) of the LOS Convention. This appears to be the case with Italy, which applies the UNESCO Rules within 24-miles from its coast without being a party to the UNESCO Convention and without having declared a general contiguous zone.

However, beyond the 24-mile limit, the effectiveness of these measures would be limited, as they would be confined to specific operations and not to the actual area where operations take place. As a result, users not operating under the natural-resource jurisdiction of the coastal State will not be obliged to respect them. On the high seas, only the national/flag State could enforce such protective measures.

- *Adoption of Regional Conventions*

According to article 6(1) of the UNESCO Convention,

> "States parties are encouraged to enter into bilateral, regional or other multilateral agreements or develop existing agreements for the preservation of underwater cultural heritage. All such agreements shall be in full conformity with the provisions of this Convention and shall not dilute its universal character. States may, in such agreements, adopt rules and regulations which would en-

---

[78] Similar statements were made by Sweden at the 31st session of the UNESCO General Conference.

sure better protection of underwater cultural heritage than those adopted in this Convention".

Following the adoption of the 2001 Syracuse Declaration on the Submarine Cultural Heritage in the Mediterranean Sea[79], Italy took the initiative to propose the drafting of a regional convention for the protection of the underwater cultural heritage in the Mediterranean, pursuant to article 6 of the UNESCO Convention[80]. Despite the fact that this attempt was not successful, it provides an interesting *alternative*[81] to the UNESCO Convention. In the writer's view, such regional instruments should not necessarily be based upon the jurisdictional scheme of the UNESCO Convention; instead, they should focus on the specific needs of underwater archaeology in each particular region. It is recalled that the vast majority of Mediterranean States were in favour of extending coastal jurisdiction over the continental shelf so as to ensure an effective scheme of protection of underwater cultural heritage in this area.

Article 303(4) of the LOS Convention also acknowledges the possibility of regulating underwater cultural heritage by other international or regional instruments that would *further* and *supplement* the general principles set forth in the LOS Convention. As already stated the main reason for the failure of the UNESCO Convention to adopt a straightforward provision on jurisdiction was the desire for "strict compatibility" with the LOS Convention. It would be absurd to prevent the development of new rules by a rigid interpretation of article 6 of the UNESCO Convention calling for "full compliance" with its provisions this time.

In concluding, despite any reservations one may have with respect to the UNESCO Convention it would be in the interest of all to interpret and apply its provisions in a manner that could ensure an effective scheme of

---

[79] Adopted on 10 March 2001 during the International Conference on "Means for the Protection and Touristic Promotion of the Marine Cultural Heritage in the Mediterranean". The text is reproduced at Garabello, *supra* note 47, at pp. 274-275.

[80] See International Conference on the Cooperation in the Mediterranean Region for the Protection of Underwater Cultural Heritage, Syracuse, 3-5 April 2003. See also T. Scovazzi, Un futuro accordo sulla protezione del patrimonio culturale sottomarino del Mediterraneo, *in* Scovazzi (ed.), *supra* note 71, pp. 157-169, at pp. 164-165.

[81] It should be noted, however, that according to its drafters the draft regional convention was not meant to be an alternative to the general universal convention, but to strengthen it; see R. Garabello, Sunken warships in the Mediterranean. Reflections on some relevant examples in State practice relating to the Mediterranean Sea, *in* Scovazzi (ed.), *ibid.*, pp. 171-202, at p. 197. On the legal protection of the underwater cultural heritage in the Mediterranean see further V. Mainetti, Quelle protection pour le patrimoine culturel subaquatique en Méditerranée? En attendant l'entrée en vigueur de la Convention de l'UNESCO de 2001? *in* Scovazzi (ed.), *ibid*, at pp. 121-156.

protection. In this respect, special attention should be paid to the *acknowledgement of a full-fledged 24-mile archaeological zone* as well as the *strengthening of the role of the coastal State* in the preservation of cultural heritage found on the continental shelf/EEZ. The recognition of coastal jurisdiction in this area is by no means a *panacea* for the protection of underwater cultural heritage. However, it could provide a secure legal framework within which the UNESCO Rules will be applied[82]. The limited cultural resources of the oceans, which have been endangered recently by the development of advanced underwater technology and the devastating operations of treasure hunters/salvage companies, call for the adoption of such protective measures.

---

[82] It is recalled that a number of States, including Australia, have already expanded their jurisdiction over underwater cultural heritage on the continental shelf. For this reason Australia made a statement at the 31st session of the UNESCO General Conference that "it is understanding of Australia that in relation to Article 2 paragraph 11, the phrase "no act or activity undertaken on the basis of this Convention] shall constitute grounds for claiming, contending or disputing any claim to national sovereignty or jurisdiction" is intended only to be a reference to territorial disputes". The Chairman of the Meeting of Experts, Mr. Carsten Lund, agreed with Australia stating that article 2(11) of the UNESCO Convention should be interpreted in this limited fashion. See further Garabello, *supra* note 47 at p. 115.

Comment

THE CONTIGUOUS ZONE AS A MECHANISM FOR PROTECTING THE UNDERWATER CULTURAL HERITAGE

*Petros Sioussiouras**

1. INTRODUCTION

The contiguous zone is closely related to the territorial sea. Within the contiguous zone, the coastal State exercises jurisdiction, aiming at the protection of its territorial boundaries[1]. The contiguous zone was institutionally recognized for the first time in the 1958 Geneva Convention on the Territorial Sea and the Contiguous Zone (hereinafter cited as "TSC"). As a concept, however, the contiguous zone is rather old. It dates back to the 18th century, when a number of coastal States conceded authorities to their warships outside the boundaries of the territorial sea. Typical example of such a policy was Great Britain, which in 1718 passed a series of legal acts, the so-called "Hovering Acts", aiming at the fighting of illegal trade and the protection against customs violations. These laws remained in force for a long period of time, only to be replaced by the Customs Consolidated Act of 1876[2].

During the early 20th century, many States started to expand their jurisdiction beyond their territorial sea, which evidently did not suffice to satisfy their interests – it is worth noting that the breadth of the territorial sea, at the time, did not exceed 3 nautical miles[3]. Spain, Cuba, France and Greece were, among others, States that adopted zones of functional jurisdiction. Greece

---

* Lecturer in International Law, University of the Aegean.

[1] See R.R. Churchill & A.V. Lowe, *The Law of the Sea* (3rd ed., Manchester University Press, London 1999) at p.132.

[2] See W. Masterson, *Jurisdiction in marginal seas* (The Macmillan Company, New York 1929) at p. 7 and pp. 15-120; A.V. Lowe, The development of the concept of the contiguous zone, 52 *BYBIL* 1981, pp. 109-169; Churchill & Lowe, *ibid.*

[3] See Ch. Rozakis, *The Law of the Sea and its Formation according to the Claims of the Coastal States* (Papazisis Publications, Athens 1976) pp. 51-67 [in Greek].

Anastasia Strati, Maria Gavouneli & Nikos Skourtos (eds.), *Unresolved Issues and New Challenges to the Law of the Sea*, Martinus Nijhoff 2006, pp. 63-70.

adopted, *inter alia*, a zone of national security of 10 nautical miles[4] and a customs supervision zone of 3 kilometres[5].

Following the TSC, the 1982 UN Convention on the Law of the Sea (hereinafter cited as "LOS Convention") also recognized the concept of the contiguous zone, albeit with new improved terms and conditions[6]. The LOS Convention provided that the jurisdiction of the coastal State would also apply in the case of the protection of underwater cultural heritage.

The present paper discusses coastal State jurisdiction over underwater cultural heritage in the contiguous zone as envisaged by the LOS Convention. In addition, it examines the related issue of whether the exercise of such jurisdiction presupposes the declaration of a contiguous zone or it applies automatically.

2. COASTAL JURISDICTION WITHIN THE CONTIGUOUS ZONE

The First United Nations Conference on the Law of the Sea (UNCLOS I) concluded its proceedings in 1958 with the adoption of the four Geneva Conventions[7], which for the first time codified the law of the sea. It is worth mentioning that, up to that time, the law of the sea was primarily customary law. Furthermore, it was the first time that the contiguous zone was conventionally adopted. Until 1958, most of the coastal States were claiming contiguous zones and exercising their jurisdiction for issues relating to revenues and health interests[8].

---

[4] See Law 4141 (ΔΠΜΑ') of 26 March 1913 and a detailed analysis on the issue in M. Kladi-Efstathopoulou, *The Territorial Sea: Legal status and theories of delimitation* (Doctoral thesis, Panteion University, Athens 1992) pp. 121 and 144 [in Greek].

[5] In addition, Greece adopted a territorial sea of 10 miles for the needs of aviation; cf "Decree of 6/18 September 1931 to define the extent of the territorial waters for the purposes of aviation and the control thereof" which is still in force. It is to be recalled that the breadth of the territorial sea for general purposes remains at 6 nautical miles since 1936. See C. Economides, The contiguous zone today an tomorrow, *in* Ch. Rozakis & C. Stephanou, *The New Law of the Sea* (Elsevier Science Publishers BV, 1983) pp. 71 *et seq.*; M. Kladi-Efstathopoulou, The Contiguous Zone, *in* G. Tsaltas & M. Kladi-Efstathopoulou, *The International Status of the Seas and Oceans* (vol. I, Sideris Publications, Athens 2003) at pp. 255-256 [in Greek].

[6] Greece ratified the LOS Convention on 21 July 1995 by Law 2321/1995, Government Gazette A 130/1995.

[7] (i) Convention on the Territorial Sea and Contiguous Zone, 516 UNTS 205; (ii) Convention on the High Seas, 450 UNTS 82; (iii) Convention on Fishing and Conservation of the Living Resources of the High Seas, 559 UNTS 285; and (iv) Convention on the Continental Shelf, 499 UNTS 311.

[8] See more in Lowe, *supra* note 2, at pp. 69-109.

After the conclusion of the LOS Convention in 1982, as the outcome of the Third United Nations Conference on the Law of the Sea (UNCLOS III), the contiguous zone became of interest as a zone of national jurisdiction for reasons that do not relate only to customs, fiscal, sanitary and immigration matters. This is because the LOS Convention recognized additional jurisdictional powers to the coastal State within the contiguous zone; namely, jurisdiction for the protection of the archaeological and cultural heritage without having previously to declare a contiguous zone – a view which we support in this paper. This development is very important as, on the one hand, a number of States, such as Greece and Italy, possess considerable archaeological wealth on the sea-bed which needs protection and, on the other, the breadth of the contiguous zone was extended up to 24 nautical miles. It is evident that coastal States, such as Greece, which have maintained their territorial sea breadth to 6 nautical miles, are particularly favoured as, according to the new regime, they can extend their jurisdiction for purposes relating to the protection of the underwater cultural heritage up to 24 nautical miles.

The TSC incorporated all the relevant provisions in article 24 of Part II, according to which:

1. In a zone of the high seas contiguous to its territorial sea, the coastal State may exercise the control necessary to:
    i. prevent infringement of its customs, fiscal, immigration or sanitary regulations within its territory or territorial sea;
    ii. punish infringement of the regulations committed within its territory or territorial sea;
2. The contiguous zone may not extend beyond twelve miles from the baseline from which the breadth of the territorial sea is measured.
3. Where the coasts of two States are opposite or adjacent to each other, neither of the two States is entitled, failing agreement between them to the contrary, to extend its contiguous zone beyond the median line every point of which is equidistant from the nearest points on the baselines of which the breadth of the territorial seas of the two States is measured.

The institution of the contiguous zone was reaffirmed by article 33 of the LOS Convention, which reads:

1. In a zone contiguous to its territorial seas described as the contiguous zone, the coastal state may exercise the control necessary to:
    i. prevent infringement of its customs, fiscal, immigration or sanitary laws and regulations within its territory or territorial sea;
    ii. punish infringement of its customs, fiscal, immigration or sanitary laws and regulations within its territory or territorial sea.

2. The contiguous zone may not extend beyond 24 nautical miles from
    the baselines from which the breadth of the territorial sea is measured.

It is evident that the two definitions differ both quantitatively and qualita-
tively. Quantitatively, as under the LOS Convention the breadth of the contiguous zone is extended from 12 to 24 nautical miles. The qualitative difference emerges from the wording of article 24 of the TSC, which refers to the
contiguous zone as a "zone of the high seas contiguous to its [the coastal
State's] territorial sea". In article 33 of the LOS Convention the contiguous
zone is not referred to as a "zone of the high seas" but as a "zone contiguous
to its [the coastal State's] territorial sea". This differentiation is due to the
fact that the LOS Convention established a new jurisdictional zone, the exclusive economic zone (EEZ)[9], the boundaries of which begin immediately
after the territorial sea[10]. According to article 86 of the LOS Convention, the
high seas comprise all the parts of the sea which are not included in the EEZ,
the territorial sea or the internal waters of a State[11]. Consequently, the contiguous zone would still form part of the high seas, provided that the coastal
State concerned has not declared an EEZ. Once it adopts an EEZ, the contiguous zone would be covered by the EEZ and the coastal State shall exercise the rights recognized by international law in the contiguous zone and the
EEZ cumulatively in the overlapping part of the two zones.

Under both article 24 of the TSC and article 33 of the LOS Convention,
the jurisdiction of the coastal State within the contiguous zone has a concomitant nature[12] as far as the rights exercised by the coastal State within its
territorial sea are concerned. Thus, the main purpose of the contiguous zone
is to make the exercise of coastal jurisdiction in the territorial sea effective,
while the enumeration of the purposes for which it may be established is exhaustive[13]. A different approach must, however, be taken with respect to the

---

[9] See Part V of the LOS Convention. See also L. Alexander & R. Hodgson, The Impact of the
200-mile Economic Zone on the Law of the Sea, 12 *San Diego LR* 1975, pp. 572-577.

[10] According to article 55 "[t]he exclusive economic zone is an area beyond and adjacent to
the territorial sea…".

[11] See E.D. Brown, *The International Law of the Sea* (Vol. I, Dartmouth Publishing Company, 1994) at p. 130.

[12] See A. Papathanassiou, Adoption of archaeological zones, *in* S. Perrakis (ed.) *The Aegean Sea and the New Law of the Sea* (Ant. N. Sakkoulas Publishers, Athens-Komotini 1996)
at p. 153 [in Greek].

[13] However, according to another view, the enumeration of the purposes for which a contiguous zone may be established under article 33 is not exhaustive. In favour of this view is
the fact that many coastal States have extended their authority in the contiguous zone without
meeting any resistance by other States. It would seem, therefore, that the jurisdiction of the
coastal State within the contiguous zone is more extensive than that recognized by the LOS
Convention. See further Churchill & Lowe, *supra* note 1, at p. 117.

protection of objects of an archaeological and historical nature found on the bed of the contiguous zone. As will be discussed below, the proof of competence that article 303(2) of the LOS Convention establishes for the coastal State within its contiguous zone, leads in practice to the equalization of the status of the territorial sea and the contiguous zone as far as the "control and trade of archaeological and historical objects" are concerned[14].

3. DELIMITATION OF THE CONTIGUOUS ZONE

For its adoption, the coastal State needs to declare a contiguous zone, exactly as it has to do for the adoption of an EEZ, since the jurisdiction of the coastal State in the two zones does not apply *ipso facto* and *ab initio*[15] as is the case with the continental shelf. It is interesting to note that the LOS Convention does not refer to the delimitation of the contiguous zone in the case where "the coasts of two States are opposite or adjacent to each other", evidently due to the institution of the EEZ. On the contrary, article 24(3) of the TSC provided that in case where the coasts of two States are opposite or adjacent to each other, the delimitation shall be effected according to the rule of the "median line, every point of which is equidistant from the nearest points on the baselines of which the breadth of the territorial seas of the two States is measured". The LOS Convention too could have maintained the median line rule, in case the coastal States concerned had not adopted an EEZ and the contiguous zone would continue to constitute part of the high seas.

4. PROTECTION OF THE UNDERWATER CULTURAL HERITAGE

The interest of the LOS Convention for the protection of the underwater cultural heritage is mainly manifested in two articles.

Article 303, found in Part XVI (General Provisions) of the LOS Convention, stipulates the basic rule of protection of "archaeological and historical

---

[14] Even in the case where a violation (e.g. removal of an archaeological object) by a third State occurs within the contiguous zone of a coastal State, then the latter, in accordance with article 303(2), can exercise the right of hot pursuit, despite the fact that article 303 is not directly related to article 111 on hot pursuit, but only to article 33. The basic argument formulated is that the provision of article 111(1) on hot pursuit allows its exercise on the condition that the violation started within the contiguous zone of the State that receives the violation. The removal of archaeological objects constitutes a violation against the coastal State, according to articles 303(2) and 33 of the LOS Convention. See Brown, *supra* note 11.

[15] See the *North Sea Continental Shelf* cases, FRG v. Denmark, FRD v. The Netherlands, ICJ Reports 1969, p. 22; *Aegean Sea Continental Shelf* case, Greece v. Turkey, Provisional Measures, ICJ Reports 1976; Judgment, ICJ Reports 1978.

objects"[16] while article 149 deals with archaeological and historical objects
found in the Area[17]. However, from the wording of article 149 certain problems of interpretation may arise: First, because it does not distinguish between the "State of origin", the "State of cultural origin" or the "State of historical and archaeological origin" of the objects; and, second, because no international organization is designated to be responsible for the administration
of marine archaeological heritage (e.g. UNESCO) or for the settlement of
any disputes that might arise[18].

Article 303(2) is of interest for the purposes of the current analysis, as it
refers indirectly but clearly to the contiguous zone.

4.1. The origins of article 303 of the LOS Convention

It is worth pointing out that the adoption of article 303(2) of the LOS Convention was based on a proposal put forward by the Greek delegation in
1979[19]. This proposal was subsequently amended and jointly sponsored by
seven States: Cape Verde, Italy, Malta, Portugal, Tunisia, Yugoslavia and
Greece. It read as follows: "The coastal State exercises sovereign rights over
any object of purely archaeological and historical nature on or under its continental shelf for the purpose of research, salvaging, protection and proper
presentation. However, the State or country of origin, or the State of cultural
origin, or the State of historical and archaeological origin shall have preferential rights over such objects in case of sale or any other disposal".

The proposal was subjected to a series of amendments. The sovereign
rights of the coastal State were initially reduced to jurisdiction and subsequently to "enforcement of laws and regulations in an exclusive manner",

---

[16] It reads as follows: "1. States have the duty to protect objects of an archaeological and
historical nature found at sea and shall co-operate for this purpose. 2. In order to control traffic in such objects, the coastal State may, in applying article 33, presume that their removal
from the sea-bed in the zone referred to in the article without its approval would result in an
infringement within its territory or territorial sea of the laws and regulations referred to in that
article. 3. Nothing in this article affects the rights of identifiable owners, the law of salvage or
other rules of admiralty, or laws and practices with respect to cultural exchanges. 4. This article is without prejudice to other international agreements and rules of international law regarding the protection of objects of an archaeological and historical nature".

[17] According to article 149, "[a]ll objects of an archaeological and historical nature found
in the Area shall be preserved or disposed of for the benefit of mankind as a whole, particular
regard being paid to the preferential rights of the State or country of origin, or the State of cultural origin, or the State of historical and archaeological origin".

[18] See R.J. Dupuy & D. Vignes, *A Handbook on the New Law of the Sea* (Martinus Nijhoff
Publishers, 1991) at p. 569.

[19] See UN Doc. A/CONF.62/C.2. Informal Meeting/43 of 16 August 1979.

while there was no reference to either the continental shelf or the EEZ; coastal rights were confined to "a limit of 200 nautical miles from the baselines from which the breadth of the territorial sea is measured". Nevertheless, even this modest proposal was met with reaction by the maritime powers – mainly, the Netherlands, the United Kingdom and the USA – which argued that the rights created by the proposal in favour of the coastal State could, under no circumstances, be related to the sovereign rights of the coastal State over the continental shelf, as the latter was closely connected with the natural resources of the seabed. As a result, the compromise formula of article 303(2) was agreed.

4.2. New jurisdictional powers within the contiguous zone

From the history and the wording of article 303 it is evident that new jurisdictional powers are created in favour of the coastal State within the contiguous zone, in addition to what is envisaged by article 33. In addition, there is the general obligation "to protect objects of an archaeological and historical nature found at sea". This new jurisdiction is not incorporated in the wider framework of coastal powers under article 33, which are of concomitant nature in relation to the rights of the coastal State within its territorial sea, but rather has an autonomous character. By referring directly to the antiquities found in the contiguous zone, article 303(2) contributes substantially to the creation of a new body of law[20], according to which once objects of archaeological and historical nature are found within the contiguous zone, they will be considered, by inference, as if found in the territorial sea. As it was argued: "Under article 303(2), the removal of relics from the bed of the contiguous zone is presumed to result in the infringement of coastal customs and fiscal regulations within the territory or the territorial sea. This presumption distorts reality to such a degree that it amounts to a fiction. First, article 303(2) requires only the removal of archaeological objects from the contiguous zone; the relics concerned are, therefore, presumed to have been removed from the territory or the territorial sea of the coastal State. Second, article 303(2) assumes that removals will infringe the customs and fiscal regulations … [A]rticle 303(2) should at least be read as being based on a conclusive (absolute) presumption"[21].

---

[20] See Brown, *supra* note 11, at p. 135. Th. Halkiopoulos, *Questions juridiques de base de la Convention Européenne pour la Protection du Patrimoine Culturel Subaquatique*, Rapport préparé dans le cadre du Séminaire sur la Protection du Patrimoine Culturel Subaquatique en Méditerranée, Capri, 1 octobre 1994.

[21] See A. Strati, *The Protection of the Underwater Cultural Heritage: An Emerging Objective of the Contemporary Law of the Sea* (Martinus Nijhoff Publishers, London 1995) p. 166.

In other words, article 303 created a *de facto* maritime zone for the protection of the archaeological heritage, having as maximum breadth 24 nautical miles[22]: In the said zone the coastal State exercises new jurisdictional powers[23], additional to those envisaged in article 33 and totally independent of them.

5. CONCLUDING REMARKS

As at 26 August 2005, 74 States had adopted 24-mile contiguous zones compatible with the LOS Convention, including the USA, Canada, France, Spain, Portugal, Cyprus and more recently Denmark. In addition, one State claims a 15 nm contiguous zone; four States 18 nm contiguous zones, and one State a customs zone of 14 nm.

Very few States maintain contiguous zones established before the adoption of the LOS Convention. Saudi Arabia has adopted, since 1958, a contiguous zone of 18 nautical miles, for security, navigation, taxation and health matters, while Bangladesh has established since 1974 a contiguous zone of 18 nautical miles for security purposes. In addition, Korea has established since 1977 a security zone of 50 nautical miles[24].

As far as protection of the underwater cultural heritage is concerned, only a small group of States, including France, Tunisia, China, Cyprus and Algeria, have expanded their competence over this area (see *supra* Chapter 2).

---

[22] *Ibid.*

[23] See G. Georgakopoulou, *The Territorial Sea of Greece. Legal Status, Evolution and Prospects in the New Law of the Sea* (Approved Doctoral Thesis, University of Athens Law School, 1988) at p. 279 [in Greek].

[24] See Table of claims to maritime jurisdiction, available at www.un.org.

Part II

New Challenges to the Law of the Sea

A.

Protection and preservation of the marine environment

Chapter 3

TOWARDS A WORLD PROTECTION FRAMEWORK FOR THE
MARINE ENVIRONMENT THROUGH THE PROMOTION OF
INTERNATIONAL AND REGIONAL COOPERATION UNDER
THE UN CONVENTION ON THE LAW OF THE SEA

Grigoris Tsaltas[*]

1. INTRODUCTION

The threats that pollution poses to the marine environment are known: they
may result from human activities on land (urban waste, industrial waste,
dangerous material carried through rivers etc.) or by equivalent activities at
sea, mostly accidents and disposal of waste materials.

However, the rapid development of technology, and particularly underwater
technology, after the 1960s has contributed to the development of new forms
of marine pollution. These new forms of pollution reflect particular activities
taking place on the seabed, including the deep seabed that now constitutes a
zone of common heritage of mankind ("Area"), as a result of the unprecedented
diplomatic negotiation that took place during the Third UN Conference on
the Law of the Sea ("UNCLOS III"). Finally, there is pollution coming from
the atmosphere or through the atmosphere.

The promotion of international cooperation is the fundamental principle
and objective of the UN Charter, aiming at the peaceful resolution of all international issues, whether of economic, social, cultural or humanitarian nature[1]. More specifically, the Charter refers to international cooperation in two
chapters dealing with: a) the duties and competences of the General Assembly (Chapter IV)[2] and b) international economic and social cooperation

---

[*] Professor of International Law, Panteion University.

[1] See article 1(3) of the UN Charter.

[2] Article 13 refers more specifically: (a) to the promotion of international cooperation in
the political area aiming at encouraging the progressive development of international law as

Anastasia Strati, Maria Gavouneli & Nikos Skourtos (eds.), *Unresolved Issues and New Challenges to the
Law of the Sea*, Martinus Nijhoff 2006, pp. 73-84.

(Chapter IX)[3]. Yet in this same framework of promoting international cooperation, there is no special reference to environmental protection. This is due to the limited attention given to these issues at the time of the adoption of the Charter, at least regarding their global nature and scale. Nevertheless, environmental issues may be covered under the provisions on public health.

The rapid development of technology has brought to the fore issues that are characterised by their enormous impact on large areas, thus forcing the international community to re-examine whether compliance with the traditional international law principle of State sovereignty can address contemporary issues of such magnitude; for it is an axiom that *pollution does not recognize frontiers*.

The individual launching of activities by States or non-State actors dealing with issues of environmental degradation, wherever this is taking place, cannot provide a sufficient basis of protection. International cooperation, both at global and regional level, becomes crucial today for the promotion of a world policy in environmental protection and management.

The 1982 United Nations Convention on the Law of the Sea (hereinafter cited as "LOS Convention") promotes, in many of its provisions, international and regional cooperation in order to deal with the various and complicated issues it addresses, including lack of co-ordination between States. The protection of the marine environment from pollution constitutes but one of these issues.

2. PROMOTION OF INTERNATIONAL AND REGIONAL COOPERATION THROUGH THE LOS CONVENTION

One could assume that the method used by the States during UNCLOS III exuded the air of an international and almost general consensus[4]. This consensus is also evident in the adoption of a parallel system of international cooperation in all areas[5], whether it relates to the delimitation of zones of national jurisdiction, exploration and management of mineral resources in the

---

well as its codification; paragraph (1)a; and b) to the strengthening of international cooperation in the economic, social, cultural, educational and health fields; paragraph (1)b.

[3] 'With a view to the creation of conditions of stability and well-being' reference is made to the resolution of international economic, social, health and related problems as well as to international cultural and educational cooperation; article 55(b).

[4] The only countries that did not sign the LOS Convention were the USA, Israel, Venezuela and Turkey.

[5] For example, article 100 of the LOS Convention refers to the duty of States to cooperate in the repression of piracy on the high seas or in any other area that is not under the jurisdiction of any State.

Area[6] or, finally, protection of the marine environment. The preservation and management of natural resources, living and non-living, in conjunction with the protection of the marine environment was of special interest to the drafters of the LOS Convention, especially through the development of regional cooperation.

2.1. Regional cooperation

The meaning of 'cooperation' becomes crucial when it concerns conventional provisions on issues of regional interest[7]. Such rules apply mostly to marine areas facing serious problems because of their limited geographical and geomorphological capacity to develop a natural resistance to pollution problems. This is the case with "enclosed and semi-closed seas", i.e. a limited geographical area that is surrounded by the coastline of two or more States. The connection of these marine areas with other wider ones or with an ocean usually takes place through a narrow strip of sea[8], an element which underlines the inability of water rejuvenation of these sea areas which is enhanced by the total lack, in most cases, of sub-sea currents[9].

The LOS provisions on enclosed and semi-closed seas[10] are based upon an extended network of regional cooperation in three areas[11], namely: marine scientific research, fisheries and protection of the marine environment. The first area refers to the required coordination of all policies on marine scien-

---

[6] For example, according to the article 169 of the LOS Convention, the Secretary-General of the International Seabed Authority ("ISA") has the competence, with the approval of the Council, to conduct consultations and conclude cooperation agreements with international organisations and non-governmental organisations recognised by the UN Economic and Social Council.

[7] An important example may be found in article 129 of the LOS Convention, which encourages cooperation with the aim to construct and improve means of transport so as to facilitate land-locked States to effectively implement their freedom of transit through the transit States.

[8] Under article 122 of the LOS Convention, "'enclosed or semi-enclosed sea' means a gulf, basin or sea surrounded by two or more States and connected to another sea or the ocean by a narrow outlet or consisting entirely or primarily of the territorial seas and exclusive economic zones of two or more coastal States".

[9] See in more detail G. Tsaltas and M. Kladi-Efstathopoulou, *The International Status of Seas and Oceans* (vol. 1, I. Sideris Publications, Athens 2003) pp. 418 *et seq.* [in Greek].

[10] During UNCLOS III, there were proposals for the introduction of special rules on delimitation and the establishment of zones of national jurisdiction in such areas. However, these proposals did not make their way into the final text of the LOS Convention, which focuses only on the promotion of regional cooperation with the aim to preserve the living natural resources and protect the marine environment from pollution.

[11] See article 123 of the LOS Convention.

tific research. The second area refers to management, preservation, research and exploitation of living natural resources, while the third area concerns the implementation of rights and the fulfilment of obligations concerning the protection and preservation of the marine environment.

This system of regional cooperation among States bordering enclosed and semi-closed seas is completed with the invitation to other interested States or international organizations wishing to cooperate with the aim to implementing the appropriate provisions of the Convention[12]. Regional cooperation is further enhanced by the obligation to jointly develop and promote contingency plans for responding to pollution incidents in the marine environment[13]. Its objective is the elimination of the effects of pollution and the prevention of minimization of imminent or actual damage.

2.2. International cooperation

International cooperation in the LOS Convention is advanced primarily through policies adopted in the field of marine scientific research and the transfer of marine technology by developed to developing States. Both fields are directly and indirectly related to the development of a world strategy on environmental protection of the seas and the oceans, always based upon the consent of States.

2.2.1. Development and promotion of international cooperation in the field of marine scientific research

The vastness of the seas and the oceans could not but become the basis for developing a consolidated policy of international cooperation in the field of marine scientific research[14] through the promotion of all disciplines concerning the oceans.

Such cooperation involves all parties responsible for shaping international policy and not only its main actors, the States. Thus, international organizations, irrespective of whether they belong to the specialized system of the United Nations or constitute efforts of a regional character, are the predominant factor in developing such a policy through the provisions of the LOS Convention.

---

[12] See article 123(d) of the LOS Convention.

[13] See in particular articles 198 and 199 of the LOS Convention.

[14] For a general overview see *The Law of the Sea. Marine Scientific Research. A guide to the implementation of the relevant provisions of the United Nations Conventions on the Law of the Sea* (United Nations Office for Ocean Affairs and the Law of the Sea, New York, United Nations, 1991).

After the adoption of Agenda 21 at the 1992 Rio Summit on Environment and Development, this policy was expanded so as to include not only non-governmental organizations, but also national organizations and individuals[15].

Although the LOS Convention does not attempt to give a clear definition of marine scientific research[16], it nevertheless contains in Part XIII three articles, namely articles 242-244 dealing with international cooperation. They refer primarily to the obligation of all States and international organisations to promote international cooperation in marine scientific research for peaceful purposes on the basis of mutual benefit and in accordance with the principle of respect for sovereignty. Furthermore, States as well as international organizations are obligated to create favourable conditions for the conduct of marine scientific research through bilateral and multilateral agreements and to integrate the efforts of scientists in studying phenomena and processes occurring in the marine environment[17]. Finally, the publication and dissemination of the relevant information and knowledge by States have the primary aim to control any harmful consequences for the health and safety of persons but also to promote a general prevention scheme against the pollution of the marine environment, reflected in a continuous flow of information towards developing States so that they may gradually develop their skills and engage themselves in marine scientific research[18].

This form of international cooperation constitutes peaceful promotion of marine scientific research for the benefit of mankind, as this was reflected through the historic 1970 UN General Assembly Declaration of Principles Governing the Seabed and Ocean Floor[19].

---

[15] See in particular G. Kullenberg, Capacity-building in marine and ocean observations: a perspective on why and how, 22 *Marine Policy* 1998, pp. 185-195.

[16] Yet, one could maintain that 'marine scientific research' means any scientific activity conducted in any maritime zone by specially trained staff with scientific equipment and with the main objective to study effectively the marine environment.

[17] The study of marine phenomena would appear to include the wider scientific field of natural oceanography, chemical oceanography, marine biology as well as submarine geology. On the contrary, the study of living natural resources and marine archaeology are excluded.

[18] See G. Tsaltas, *The International Status of the Seas and Oceans* (vol. 2, I. Sideris Publications, Athens 2003) pp. 128-129 [in Greek].

[19] See General Assembly Resolution 2749 (XXV), 17 December 1970.

2.2.2. Development and transfer of marine technology and international co-operation

International cooperation is also promoted through the LOS provisions on development and transfer of marine technology[20]. In this particular case, the State prevails in the field by setting the priorities and main principles concerning the policies and the specifications that have to be met for any transfer of marine technology. This policy is promoted through bilateral or multilateral agreements or through coordinating special projects materialized through international organizations or other associations.

The developing States, which are actively involved in the exploitation of mineral resources in the Area, must also be assisted in acquiring skills and marine technology related to such activities. More specifically, under article 274 of the LOS Convention, the ISA shall ensure that: a) the selection of managerial, research and technical staff for the purposes of training also includes nationals of developing States, whether coastal, land-locked and geographically disadvantaged; b) the technical documentation on the relevant equipment, machinery, devices and processes is made available to developing States; c) developing States and their nationals will acquire the required technical assistance in the field of marine technology; d) financial assistance will be provided to developing States requesting such technical assistance. The ultimate objective of the Convention in these cases remains the promotion of specialized scientific knowledge and information to developing States, with special emphasis to the relevant needs of land-locked and geographically disadvantaged States.

3. INTERNATIONAL COOPERATION AND PROTECTION OF THE MARINE ENVIRONMENT

The pollution of the seas and oceans[21] has become the ultimate world issue in the post-war decades. Two are the main reasons: First, marine pollution has no borders, and, second, the nature of contemporary pollutants, wherever they come from, has surpassed the capabilities of any advanced technology in dealing with them directly and efficiently.

---

[20] See articles 270-274 of the LOS Convention.

[21] According to article 1(4) of the LOS Convention, 'Pollution of the marine environment" means the introduction by man, directly or indirectly, of substances or energy into the marine environment, including estuaries, which results or is likely to result in such deleterious effects as harm to living resources and marine life, hazards to human health, hindrance to marine activities, including fishing and other legitimate uses of the sea, impairment of quality for use of sea water and reduction of amenities.

Section 2 of Part XII of the LOS Convention dealing with the protection and the conservation of the marine environment refers specifically to the adoption of a policy of global and regional cooperation in addressing these kinds of issues[22].

The philosophy of the Convention in this section remains the promotion of the core principles of environmental law, with emphasis on information and prevention; thus, the provisions on the exchange of information and data acquired about pollution of the marine environment and the obligation to adopt international and national regulations for preventing marine pollution.

3.1. International cooperation in the field of information

One of the fundamental principles of environmental law is the right to information, and more specifically, to prompt notification on incidents that may cause environmental damage either originating from human intervention or from natural incidents and phenomena[23].

Article 198 of the LOS Convention reiterates the obligation of all States to show vigilance when the marine environment is in direct risk due to pollution. Accordingly, when a State becomes aware of cases in which the marine environment is in imminent danger of being damaged or has been damaged by pollution, it must inform other States, which it deems likely to be exposed to such hazards as well as the appropriate international organizations.

International cooperation in this field presupposes formulating and elaborating rules and specifications as well as recommended practices and procedures of an international character[24]. The same policy also applies in promoting the exchange of information and data concerning pollution of the marine environment[25]. The ultimate scope of this policy is the strengthening of the principles of equality and solidarity through preservation and respect of the fundamental principle of State sovereignty. However, a more realistic approach is required.

---

[22] See articles 197 to 201 of the LOS Convention.

[23] See further G. Samiotis & G. Tsaltas, *International Protection of the Environment* (Papazissis Publications, Athens 1990) 132-145 [in Greek].

[24] Article 197 of the LOS Convention.

[25] According to article 200 of the LOS Convention, this cooperation is effected through the promotion of studies, the undertaking of programmes of scientific research and the encouragement of exchange of information and data acquired about pollution of the marine environment, with the aim to "acquire knowledge for the assessment of the nature and extent of pollution, exposure to it, and its pathways, risks and remedies".

3.2. International cooperation in the field of prevention

Another fundamental principle of environmental law is the principle of prevention[26]. The notion of prevention involves two specific actions that, according to the LOS Convention, require the strengthening of international cooperation in this field.

The first action refers to the process of taking specific measures for the prevention, reduction and control of marine and ocean pollution, wherever this may originate[27]. These measures may be taken either individually or jointly, thus developing a policy for international cooperation in a field that is considered of the utmost importance. Coordination of such efforts may be achieved through the actions of the competent international organizations within the UN system, especially the IMO, or even through intergovernmental regional organizations.

The second action is related to the minimization of damages resulting from a polluting incident. In this field, international cooperation seems to be the basis for the effective treatment of any environmental injury. The cooperation established either directly or through the competent international organizations, purports to establish "appropriate scientific criteria for the formulation and elaboration of rules, standards and recommended practices and procedures"[28]. These practices are reflected in the joint development and promotion of contingency plans in order to cope with pollution incidents in the marine environment[29].

3.3. International cooperation in the adoption of rules for the prevention, reduction and control of marine pollution

The promotion of the fundamental principle of prevention is also achieved through the direct obligation[30] of States to act, individually or through the

---

[26] The principle of prevention is safeguarded in the 1972 Stockholm Declaration on the Human Environment as well as the 1972 Convention for the Protection of World Cultural and Natural Heritage, the 1975 Helsinki Final Act, the 1975 European Convention for the Preservation of Wildlife and Natural Habitats, the 1992 Rio Declaration on Environment and Development but also in the 2002 Johannesburg Declaration on Sustainable Development.

[27] According to article 194(3) of the LOS Convention, pollution may arise from (a) the release of toxic, harmful or noxious substances; (b) vessels; (c) installations and devices used in exploration or exploitation of the natural resources of the seabed and subsoil; and (d) from other installations and devices operating in the marine environment.

[28] Article 201 of the LOS Convention.

[29] See article 199 of the LOS Convention.

[30] See articles 207-212 of the LOS Convention.

competent international organisation or diplomatic Conference[31], in order to adopt rules, standards and recommended practices and procedures for the prevention, reduction and control of marine pollution[32] both at international and regional level.

The coordination of these measures presupposes a mutual recognition of the different types of marine pollution, as set out in the LOS Convention. Articles 207 to 212 analyse in detail six categories of pollution[33]. The coordinated response required led to the identification of three large systems of marine pollution, namely pollution from land-based sources, pollution from seabed activities and pollution from vessels.

The first from these systems requires coordination mostly in the field of national rules. The combating of pollution from land-based sources engages the responsibility of each and every State in an effort to reinforce and modernize the already existing domestic legislation.

In the case of pollution from seabed activities subject to national jurisdiction, the application of the relevant LOS provisions on the exclusive economic zone and the continental shelf[34] are the first substantial guarantees for conserving the marine environment and its living natural resources. The same applies for pollution from activities in the Area[35].

Pollution from vessels is quite significant because of frequent accidents usually near the coastline of coastal States. Article 211 of the LOS Convention deals with the different types of marine pollution from vessels for which States must develop appropriate institutional mechanisms and adopt regulations. Special reference is made to the necessity of adopting international rules and standards to prevent, reduce and control vessel-source pollution, mostly through the International Maritime Organization (IMO), in addition to the promotion of routeing systems on the domestic level. Such rules and standards may be re-examined from time to time as necessary.

Several conventions, agreements and protocols followed the adoption of the LOS Convention, encouraging the development of international cooperation in this field. These international agreements range from vessel-source pollution to pollution in sensitive marine areas aiming mainly at the protection of coastal zones. They include: the 1983 Cartagena Convention for the

---

[31] See in particular articles 207(4) and 211(1) of the LOS Convention.

[32] These regulations and standards are to be re-examined from time to time, if need be.

[33] They are: a) Pollution from land-based sources; b) Pollution from sea-bed activities subject to national jurisdiction; c) Pollution from activities in the Area; d) Pollution by dumping; e) Pollution from vessels; and f) Pollution from or through the atmosphere.

[34] See article 79 of the LOS Convention.

[35] See more specifically article 145 of the LOS Convention.

Protection and Development of the Marine Environment of the Wider Carib-
bean Region and the Protocol thereto Concerning Cooperation combating
Oil Spills in the Wider Caribbean Region[36]; the 1983 Quito Protocol for the
Protection of the South-East Pacific against Pollution from Land-based
Sources[37]; the 1983 Bonn Agreement for Cooperation in dealing with Pollution of the North Sea by Oil and other Harmful Substances[38]; the 1985 Nairobi Convention for the Protection, Management and Development of the
Marine and Coastal Environment of the Eastern African Region and the Protocol thereto concerning Cooperation in combating Marine Pollution in Case
of Emergency in the Eastern African Region[39]; the 1986 Noumea Convention for the Protection of the Natural Resources and Environment of the
South Pacific Region and the Protocol thereto for the Prevention of Dumping; the 1990 Lisbon Accord of Cooperation for the Protection of the Coasts
and Waters of the Northeast Atlantic against Pollution due to Hydrocarbons
or other Harmful Substances; the 1992 Agreement on the Conservation of
Small Cetaceans of the Baltic and the North Seas (ASCOBANS) and the 1996
Agreement on the Conservation of Cetaceans of the Black Sea, Mediterranean
Sea and Continuous Atlantic Areas (ACCOBAMS); the 1992 OSPAR Convention for the Protection of the Marine Environment of the North-East Atlantic. Yet, even before the adoption of the LOS Convention, 46 conventions
and protocols, with their assorted amendments and reviews, had already
been adopted regulating the protection of the marine environment and its resources.

3.4. Transfer of technology related to the protection of the marine environment to developing countries

The question of transfer of scientific and technical data on environmental
issues to developing countries was considered significant during UNCLOS
III. This was due to the importance and emergency character of the protection and preservation of the marine environment both in terms of prevention
and mitigation and in view of the inability of these States to deal with such
conditions directly and effectively.

Section 3 of Part XII ("technical assistance") of the LOS Convention promotes international cooperation with the aim to provide scientific and technical assistance to developing States by preferential treatment, so that the

---

[36] In force since 30 March 1986 and 17 January 1987, respectively.
[37] In force since 23 September 1986.
[38] In force since 1 September 1989.
[39] Both concluded on 21 June 1985.

marine environment may be protected from the risk of suffering irreparable damage or even general degradation.

Two articles are dedicated to this form of international cooperation, which must be further developed through competent international organizations; articles 202 and 203. Article 202 adopts a policy of scientific and technical assistance to developing States by: a) promoting projects of scientific, educational, technical and other assistance[40]; b) underlying the importance of the duty to provide appropriate assistance for the minimization of the effects of major incidents which may cause serious pollution to the marine environment; c) providing appropriate assistance for the preparation of environmental assessments, in particular in order to minimise pollution from land sources.

Article 203 of the LOS Convention attempts to establish preferential treatment for developing States in the field of prevention, reduction and control of pollution of the marine environment or minimization of its consequences. Such preferential treatment may be granted by the competent international organisations and refers to the allocation of appropriate funds and technical assistance, as well as to the utilisation of their specialised services.

4. CONCLUSION

Contemporary international community demands the development of co-operation in every field by all international actors and not only by States. This is due to the strong interdependence and interaction manifested in all activities taking place on our planet, which require exceptional international cooperation, especially in the field of the protection and management of the environment.

This modern form of international cooperation is reflected in the joint elaboration of specific measures for the prevention or mitigation of marine pollution, part of a general international policy for development, which should lead to the eventual convergence of all such policies in a final sustainable form.

It was the 1992 UN Conference for the Environment and Development in Rio which manifested for the first time this international cooperation through the expansion of various environmental parameters into the "development phenomenon" and in integrated terms. The preamble to the Rio Declaration

---

[40] Such assistance to developing States comprises: i) training of their scientific and technical personnel; ii) facilitating their participation in relevant international programmes; iii) supplying them with the necessary equipment and facilities; iv) enhancing their capacity to manufacture such equipment; v) advice on and developing facilities for research, monitoring, educational and other projects.

elevates such environmental concerns to the level of a development commitment both on States and individuals and civil society *per se*. Indeed, the
protection of the environment constitutes by far the area where international
cooperation by all States is required. This is especially true in the case of the
marine environment, which constitutes 72.5% of the surface of the Earth and
comprises the most sensitive habitat, indirectly affecting all other categories
of the natural environment and the global climate.

The LOS Convention constitutes a landmark in terms of international cooperation. Two particular fields became the basis for further development of
this policy. The first concerns the philosophy of the notion of "common
ownership" of seabed natural resources, manifested in the 1970 Declaration
of the Common Heritage of Mankind. The second emphasizes the necessity
for developing a similar policy for the rational management and protection
of the marine environment. Both policies reflect a new international strategy
aiming at developing and transferring marine technology as well as scientific
and technical data concerning the protection of the marine environment by
the developed to the developing States. The objective is to create strong and
solid self-sufficiency in addressing such issues in an effective manner.

In conclusion, one could maintain that both the deliberations at UNCLOS
III and the LOS Convention constitute a resounding success in establishing
international cooperation as the foundation stone for the protection of the
marine environment. It is a notion, which is also useful for enlarging the
scope of the notion of development. Moreover, it comprises the economic,
social and environmental dimension present both at the 1992 Rio Conference
and the 2004 Johannesburg World Summit on Sustainable Development.
The protection of the marine environment thus becomes a basic element of
the sustainable development process, which still necessitates the support of
all world actors.

Chapter 4

PROTECTION OF VULNERABLE MARINE ECOSYSTEMS
IN AREAS BEYOND NATIONAL JURISDICTION:
CAN INTERNATIONAL LAW MEET THE CHALLENGE?

*Nilufer Oral**

1. INTRODUCTION

There is a growing call by legal scholars, scientists and conservationists for
the greater regulation of activities threatening marine life and biodiversity in
areas beyond national jurisdiction, i.e. the high seas and deep oceans. Considering that eighty (80%) percent of the Earth's total mass is composed of
seas and oceans and some sixty (60%) percent lies beyond the national jurisdiction of States, the growing threat to future survival of the seas warrants
heightened attention. Only recently has science begun to fully appreciate the
importance of the oceans and how vulnerable the deep oceans are to human
activities such as fishing, shipping and even eco-tourism. Studies and discoveries are demonstrating the critical importance of the deep oceans for
climate regulation. Until recent scientific discoveries, the oceans were believed to be poorer in biodiversity than land. Whereas science has discovered
that, quite to the contrary, the oceans provide important biomass and greater
biodiversity than land[1]. In September 2003 the first-ever census of the
oceans was undertaken and just one month into the ten-year project 200.000
new marine life species had been discovered[2].

Yet, less than one percent of the oceans are under protection[3].

* Associate Director, Istanbul Bilgi University Marine Law & Policy Research Center.

[1] According to the 2001 GESAMP Report, during the last decade, 33 of the 34 major categories of animals (*phyla)* discovered are represented at sea whereas only 15 on land. See *infra*
note 14.

[2] The *Census of Marine Life* was established in 2003. It is a network of researchers in over
fifty countries to assess and explain distribution, biodiversity and abundance of life in the
ocean and how it will change over time. See http://www.coml.org/coml.htm>.

[3] See http://www.panda.org/about_wwf/what_we_do/marine/what_we_do/protected_areas/ in-
dex.cfm (last visited: 12 August 2004).

Anastasia Strati, Maria Gavouneli & Nikos Skourtos (eds.), *Unresolved Issues and New Challenges to the
Law of the Sea*, Martinus Nijhoff 2006, pp. 85-108.

The most dramatic impact has been witnessed in the decline, and in some cases the collapse, of fish stock as a result of the increased worldwide demand for fish and destructive fishing techniques such as driftnet fishing. Particularly popular during the 1980s, driftnet fishing allowed fishermen to sleep as nets, covering 30 miles were able to trap all living marine creatures, great and small, wanted or not[4]. In 1989 the United Nations adopted a resolution banning large-scale pelagic driftnet fishing[5]. The equally damaging method of deep-sea bottom trawling is also a commercially preferred fishing method. Once again, its indiscriminate and wasteful method has destroyed marine life, such as coral reef, that could require thousands and maybe millions of years to be restored.

The protection and conservation of marine life in the deep oceans and high seas has long been on the agenda of scientists[6]. For international law, the issue of protection of the marine environment in areas beyond national jurisdiction remains one of the greatest challenges as the high seas and deep oceans remain the last frontier of a "free zone", a *res nullius* protected by international law and relied upon by international commerce with ninety percent of international trade is transported over sea. Furthermore, technology[7], pharmacology, energy development and bioprospecting increasingly have sought the high seas and deep oceans for resources.

But can the oceans and seas survive our freedoms?

The noted marine biologist Sylvia Earle, in 1991, called for the creation of "wild ocean reserves" to protect endangered marine life[8]. Professor Michael Orbach also called for the establishment for a World Ocean Public Trust and

---

[4] L.A. Davis, North Pacific Pelagic Driftnetting: Untangling the High Seas Controversy, 64 *Southern California LR* 1991, pp. 1057 *et seq.*

[5] Large-Scale Pelagic Driftnet Fishing and its Impact on the Living Marine Resources of the World's Oceans and Seas, UN GAOR 49, UN Doc. A/Res/44/225 (1989); the United Nations General Assembly reaffirmed the ban with Resolution 46/215 the following year: UN Doc. A/Res. 46/215, paragraph 3 (1991); reaffirmed UN General Assembly A/Res/57/142 (26 February 2003).

[6] R.V. Salm, *Marine and Coastal Protected Areas: A Guide for Planners and Managers* (IUCN, Gland 1984) Chapter 7.

[7] S. Couffen-Smout & G.J. Herbert, Submarine cables: A challenge for ocean management, 24 *Marine Policy* 2000, pp. 441-448.

[8] K.M. Gjerde, High Seas Marine Protected Areas: A Participant's Report on the Expert Workshop on Managing Risks to Biodiversity and the Environment on the High Seas, Including Tools Such as Marine Protected Areas: Scientific Requirements and Legal Aspects, held in Vilm 27 February-4 March 2001, 16 *TIJMCL* 2001, pp. 515-528, at p. 515. Other scientists also called for the protection of open oceans; see C.E. Mills & J.T. Carlton, Rationale for a System of International Reserves for the Open Oceans, 12 *Conservation Biology* 1998, pp. 244-247.

the enclosure of large sections of the sea[9]. The International Union for the Conservation of Nature ("IUCN") followed with a Resolution, adopted in the year 2000, calling for international co-operation to identify areas in the high seas for collaborative conservation management[10]. The IUCN continued by instituting a plan for establishing a network of marine protected areas ("MPAs") that would include areas beyond national jurisdiction[11]. The United Nations General Assembly has called upon international law to address the growing threat to vulnerable marine areas. A new international agency is being created to co-ordinate issues related to oceans and coastal issues called the *Oceans and Coastal Areas Network* (hereinafter cited as "UN-Oceans")[12]. The challenge has been made and now international law must meet it. But can it?

The legal question to be answered by international lawyers is whether international law can protect the deep oceans and high seas, or "areas beyond national jurisdiction". Can the protection of the marine environment in the deep oceans and high seas be reconciled with the long-held freedoms of the high seas? Does the 1982 UN Convention on the Law of the Sea (hereinafter cited as "LOS Convention") provide the required legal framework? Or must amendments and new instruments be developed? Must the oceans be left to individual political will of States to ensure the sustainable use of the high seas oceans[13]?

2. VULNERABLE MARINE ECOSYSTEMS

The 2001 GESAMP Report entitled a *"A Sea of Troubles"*[14] presented an alarming assessment of the critical state of the seas and oceans including the dangers facing vulnerable marine ecosystems ("VME") such as, coral reefs, wetlands, seagrass beds, coastal lagoons, mangroves, shorelines, watersheds, estuaries, small islands, continental shelves and semi-enclosed seas. The

---

[9] M. Gorina-Ysern, World Ocean Public Trust: High Seas Fisheries After Grotius – Towards a New Oceans Ethos, 34 *Golden Gate University LR* 2004, pp. 645 *et seq.*, at p. 647.

[10] The IUCN Amman Resolution on High Seas MPAs, adopted at the Second World Conservation Congress, Amman, Jordan (2000).

[11] IUCN, *Ten-Year High Seas Marine Protected Sea Strategy: A ten-year strategy to promote the development of a global representative system of high seas marine protected areas networks*, Summary version as agreed by Marine Theme Participants at the Vth IUCN World Parks Congress, Durban, South Africa, 8-17 September 2003 (IUCN, Gland 2004).

[12] The UN Fifth Informal Consultative Process; see *infra* note 102.

[13] In her excellent and thorough treatment of the issue of high seas protection Gorina-Ysern faults governments for "a lack of will or lack of capacity" in failing to effectively govern the oceans; *supra* note 9, at p. 646.

[14] GESAMP, *Reports and Studies* No. 70 (UNEP, Nairobi 2001).

same report identified fishing, mining, and shipping activities as well as scientific exploration as the main threats to high seas VMEs. Making reference to the GESAMP Report, the Secretary-General's 2003 *Report on Oceans and the Law of the Sea* further added to this "non-exhaustive" list of vulnerable marine ecosystems, seamounts, hydrothermal vents and polar regions[15].

A general classification of VMEs can be made based on marine zones such as:

a. *Coastal VME*: Include lagoons, estuaries, mangroves, sea grass beds, warm water coral reefs and other ecosystems of close proximity to the coast.

b. *Large Marine Ecosystems*: Include semi-enclosed and enclosed seas, sea trenches, seamounts, cold water deep sea coral reefs, hydrothermal vents, sea canyons, cetaceans, seabirds, cold seeps and pockmarks, abyssal plains, continental slopes.

c. *Ecoregions*: The World Wildlife Fund established a ranking of the "most biologically outstanding terrestrial, freshwater and marine habitats", called the *Global 200*[16], which identified forty-three key ecoregional marine areas, including entire sea areas such as the Berring Sea, the Barents-Kara Sea, the Mediterranean Sea, the Yellow Sea and many more large marine areas that also encompass high seas marine zones[17].

Threats to VMEs include a number of factors, such as the location of the maritime zone and the nature of the ecosystem. The very diversity of the oceans' natural resources requires a diversified approach to devising protective measures. Land-based sources pose a greater and more immediate threat to coastal VMEs. Shipping and fishing activities, whether legal or illegal, unregulated and unreported ("IUU"), are more likely to be a threat to marine mammals and fish stock, coral reefs and sea mounts and less so to hydrothermal vents. Pollution, climate change and ozone depletion threaten VMEs in areas within and beyond national jurisdiction[18]. The reality is that science does not possess full knowledge of the deep-sea and oceans relying on limited information to assess its biodiversity. Yet, from the limited information attained, it has become abundantly clear that the oceans are brimming with marine life, natural resources both living and non-living[19].

---

[15] The Report noted that "vulnerability" was as a function of physical characteristics as well as ecological characteristics of an area; *ibid.*, paragraph 176.

[16] See http://www.panda.org/about_wwf/where_we_work/ecoregions/global200/pages/home.htm (last visited: 26 October 2003).

[17] See http://www.panda.org/about_wwf/what_we_do/marine/where_we_work/ecoregions.cfm (last visited: 26 October 2003).

[18] D.K. Anton, Law for the Sea's Biological Diversity, *Columbia Journal of Transnational Law* 1997, pp. 341 *et seq.*, at p. 350.

[19] The 10-year census of the oceans estimates discovery of over 10 million new marine species; *ibid.*

For example, seamounts were discovered just over fifty years ago, yet little is known of the estimated 30.000 that exist worldwide. Of the scientific data collected thus far, scientists have discovered that seamounts serve as a vital habitat for many species, including commercially valuable fish and other marine life such as coral reef and sponges. Seamounts have proven to be rich in biodiversity as well as in minerals and ore. Scientific data has also demonstrated that seamounts have been subject to substantial damage from human activities. A report prepared for the World Wildlife Fund by the Southampton Oceanography Institute found that protection of seamounts in the high seas was urgently needed[20].

Deep-sea coral reefs, despite their discovery over 100 years ago, have only recently become the subject matter of scientific study. Sadly, evidence has demonstrated that deep-sea trawling and deep-sea oil exploitation has also destroyed substantial portions of these fragile yet vital marine resources[21]. For example, the recently discovered deep-sea coral reef off the coast of Scotland has been seriously damaged[22]. Trawling has also been responsible for the destruction of over half of the cold water coral located in the North-East Atlantic Sea, including high sea areas[23].

Other potentially vulnerable deep-sea natural resources habitats include hydrothermal vents, deep-sea trenches, submarine canyons, gas hydrates, polymetallic nodules, cold seeps and pockmarks. However, the threats to these habitats appear to be from scientific exploitation and potential activities in bioprospecting, drilling and mining, providing a lesser degree of urgency.

3. INTERNATIONAL LEGAL FRAMEWORK FOR THE PROTECTION OF VULNERABLE MARINE ECOSYSTEMS IN AREAS BEYOND NATIONAL JURISDICTION

Freedom of the high seas without interference or proprietary claims by other States is one of the long-standing principles at the foundation of modern international law of the sea. The 1958 Geneva Convention on the High

---

[20] WWF/IUCN, *The status of natural resources on the high seas* (WWF, Gland 2001). The report provides a comprehensive overview of the various natural resources and their habitats including both actual and potential threats. The IUCN also presented a paper and report at the Fourth ICP held in New York in 2003 calling for special protection for seamounts, and that the General Assembly should assume a leadership role similar as it had assumed done for large scale pelagic driftnet fishing on the high seas.

[21] The Southampton Report also recommended urgent protection of these habitats.

[22] The *Darwin Mound* was discovered in 1998.

[23] See http://www.panda.org/about_wwf/where_we_work/europe/where/ne_atlantic/corals.cfm (last visited: 26 October 2003).

Seas (hereinafter cited as "High Seas Convention")[24] codified the customary rule of high seas freedoms in article 2, providing that the high seas were open to all nations and that no State could "validly purport to subject any part of them to its sovereignty". These freedoms included, *inter alia,* freedom of navigation, freedom of fishing, freedom to lay submarine cables and pipelines, and freedom of overflight. However, freedom of the high seas was not absolute: Immediately following the enumeration of freedoms, the last clause of article 2 included the qualifications that "these freedoms...shall be exercised by all States with reasonable regard to the interests of other States in their exercise of the freedom of the high seas". Other limitations on the 'freedom of the high seas' provided by the High Seas Convention, included the prohibition against the transport of slavery[25] and piracy[26]. These two activities were considered sufficiently odious and in violation of fundamental principles of international law (*jus cogens*) to constitute an exception to the accepted principle of freedom of the high seas. However, the High Seas Convention did no more than to codify customary international law at the time.

In addition, there was also the 1958 Geneva Convention on Fishing and Conservation of Living Resources on the High Seas[27], which imposed a duty on States to adopt and take conservation measures on the high seas. It also included provisions for an international special commission to resolve disputes arising over conservation measures in the high seas[28].

The LOS Convention marked an historical milestone in international law in many ways, one of which was the unprecedented importance it gave to the protection and preservation of the marine environment by including an entire section and detailed provisions for the protection and preservation of the marine environment. The provisions for coastal State regulation in the exclusive economic zone (EEZ) were especially 'revolutionary' allowing coastal State jurisdiction, albeit limited, in a significant territory of sea that was once classified as high seas. Declaration of an EEZ up to 200 nautical miles provided the coastal State with:

---

[24] Convention on the High Seas, 29 April 1958, 50 UNTS 82.

[25] Article 13 required all flag states to take the necessary measures to prevent slave trade on the high seas on vessels flying their flag, and article 22(b) allowed for warships to board a foreign merchant vessel suspected of transporting slaves.

[26] Article 14 requiring all States to co-operate in repressing acts of piracy on the high seas and any other place beyond their national jurisdiction. Article 22(b) allowed for a warship to board a merchant vessel suspected of engaging in piracy.

[27] Convention on Fishing and Conservation of the Living Resources of the High Seas, 29 April 1958, 559 UNTS 286.

[28] Article 9.

"sovereign rights for the purpose of exploring and exploiting, conserving and managing the natural resources, whether living or non-living, of the waters superjacent to the seabed and of the seabed and its subsoil, and with regard to other activities for the economic exploitation and exploration of the zone, such as the production of energy from the water, currents and winds"[29].

The coastal State was also provided with jurisdiction to protect and preserve the marine environment[30]. This endowed the coastal State with fairly broad regulatory authority over activities in a maritime zone that was once classified as the high seas.

Article 192 of the LOS Convention established the general duty for all States to "preserve and protect the environment". In addition, the LOS Convention recognized that certain ecosystems were more sensitive to the harmful effects of human activities than others requiring additional protective measures. Accordingly, article 194(5) specifically required that States, in taking measures to prevent, reduce and control pollution of the marine environment "shall include those [measures] necessary to protect and preserve rare or fragile ecosystems as well as the habitat of depleted, threatened or endangered species and other forms of marine life". Furthermore, the general duty to preserve and protect the environment, under article 192, was not restricted to any specific marine area but rather it extended to and encompassed marine spaces beyond the coastal State territorial sea and EEZ, including the high seas and deep oceans.

Part VII of the LOS Convention specifically addressed the high seas. Article 87 more or less reiterated article 2 of the High Seas Convention, with some additions to the non-exhaustive list of freedoms on the high seas. It also preserved the rights of third party States[31]. Article 89 emphasized the *res nullius* status of the high seas in declaring that no State could validly purport to subject any part of the high seas to its sovereignty. The LOS Convention prohibited the transport of slaves[32] and acts of piracy[33] and allowed States to interfere with the freedom of navigation rights of such vessels navigating the high seas. The above-mentioned provisions were also found in the High Seas Convention. Whereas, in addition to these, the LOS Convention also prohibited the unauthorized broadcasting from the high seas, illicit traffic in narcotic drugs or psychotropic substances and ships without nationality.

---

[29] Article 56 (1)(a).
[30] Article 56(b)(iii).
[31] Article 87(2).
[32] Articles 99 and 110(b).
[33] Articles 100, 105 and 110(a).

The LOS provisions on the high seas included a separate section on 'conservation and management of the living resources of the high seas'[34], requiring States to co-operate with each other in the conservation and management of living resources in the areas of the high seas[35]. Furthermore, article 120 extended the rights to limit, regulate or prohibit the exploitation of marine mammals more strictly than allowed under Part V of the LOS on the EEZ[36]. Consequently, article 120 provided a foundation for the high seas regulation of marine mammals based upon cooperation among States and international organizations. States bordering enclosed and semi-enclosed seas were also exhorted to co-operate and co-ordinate their activities in the sea in regard to, *inter alia*, the management, conservation, exploration and exploitation of the living resources of the sea[37].

3. REGULATION OF FISHING IN AREAS BEYOND NATIONAL JURISDICTION

The 1995 UN Fish Stocks Agreement entered into force on 11 December 2002[38] heralding what could become an important milestone in international fisheries law, particularly with regard to the high seas. Its scope of application includes areas beyond national jurisdiction[39]. The emphasis of the Agreement is on cooperation by all States[40]. Article 7(a), while recognizing the right of nationals of States to fish (straddling stock) in high seas in the adjacent high sea of a coastal State, further obligates States to co-operate to take necessary measures for the conservation of stock in adjacent high seas[41]. To ensure effective implementation of the Convention a requirement was included for the establishment of regional and sub-regional fisheries manage-

---

[34] Section 2 of Part VII on the High Seas.

[35] See articles 117 and 118.

[36] Article 65 provides that: "Nothing in this Part [Part V] restricts the right of a coastal State or the competence of an international organization, as appropriate, to prohibit, limit or regulate the exploitation of marine mammals more strictly than provided for in this Part. States shall cooperate with a view to the conservation of marine mammals and in the case of cetaceans shall in particular work through the appropriate international organizations for their conservation, management and study".

[37] Article 123.

[38] Agreement for the Implementation of the Provisions of the UN Convention on the Law of the Sea of 10 December 1982 relating to the Conservation and Management of Straddling Fish Stocks and Highly Migratory Fish Stocks, 4 August 1995, entered into force on 12 December 2002.

[39] Article 3(1).

[40] Article 7 (2).

[41] Article 7(b).

ment organizations ("RFMOs")[42]. In addition, coastal States and States fishing on the high seas, are obligated to take conservation measures using best scientific evidence[43], minimize pollution[44], protect biodiversity[45] and implement and enforce effective monitoring, control and surveillance[46].

The UN Fish Stocks Agreement not only provides for taking measures in areas "beyond" national jurisdiction for the conservation and management of highly migratory and straddling fish stocks, but also included provisions for the *enforcement* of these measures. The primary responsibility for ensuring compliance with the Convention falls upon the flag State of the fishing vessels in question[47]. However, once again the key element of the Convention is *international co-operation*, and in the case of enforcement it is directed towards assisting the enforcement actions of the flag State[48]. A significant part of the enforcement measures allowed includes the right of authorized inspectors to *board and inspect* fishing vessels in the high seas in an area that falls under the ambit of a sub-regional or regional fisheries management organization or arrangement[49]. The RFMOs provide an important mechanism for States to employ for effective regulation of high seas fisheries[50].

The 1995 FAO Code of Conduct for Responsible Fisheries[51] and the 1993 Agreement to Promote Compliance with international conservation and management measures by fishing vessels on the high seas ("Compliance Agreement") further compliment the limitations or conditions of fishing on the high seas provided under the UN Fish Stocks Agreement. Although, both instruments are soft law and do not carry the same effect and force of the UN

---

[42] Article 8.

[43] Article 5(b).

[44] Article 5(f).

[45] Article 5(g).

[46] Article 5(l).

[47] Article 19.

[48] Article 20.

[49] Article 21(1). Paragraph (2) of the same article further requires States, through subregional or regional management organizations or arrangement to establish procedures for boarding and inspection as provided by paragraph (1). See A.A. Zumwalt, Straddling Stock Spawn Fish Wars on the High Seas, 3 *University of California Davis Journal of International Law and Policy* 1997, pp. 35 *et seq.*, on Canada's use of the Convention to board and inspect foreign fishing vessels engaged in illegal fishing in the high seas adjacent to its EEZ.

[50] For a detailed discussion on the role of RFMOs and the arrangements under article 1(d) of the UN Fish Stocks Agreement for regulating high seas fishing see E.J. Molenaar, "Unregulated Deep-Sea Fisheries: A Need for Multilevel Approach" *in* K.M. Gjerde & D. Freestone (eds.) *Unfinished Business. Deep-Sea Fisheries and the Conservation of Marine Biodiversity Beyond National Jurisdiction* (Special Issue) 19 *TIJCML* 2004, pp. 223-46.

[51] FAO, *Code of Conduct for Responsible* Fisheries (Rome 1995); G. Moore, The Code of Conduct for Responsible Fisheries, *Developments in International Fisheries Law*, pp. 85-105.

Fish Stocks Agreement, they, nonetheless, represent further evidence of the
growing acceptance in the international community for limiting high seas
freedoms.

The ICJ decision in the *Case concerning Fisheries Jurisdiction* (Spain v.
Canada)[52] also deserves attention as it adopted a broad interpretation of the
meaning of "conservation and management measures" for fisheries conservation, which would include enforcement and use of force in the high seas. Although the ICJ ultimately found that it lacked jurisdiction to adjudicate the
dispute between Spain and Canada, the Court clearly condoned Canada's intervention in adjacent high seas area over Spanish- flagged fishing vessels[53].
The case arose when Canada, pursuant to an amendment to its Canadian
Coastal Fisheries Protection Act ("CFPA"), seized a Spanish-flagged fishing
boat on the high seas. Spain challenged the actions of Canada as illegal unilateral acts in an area beyond its national jurisdiction, i.e. the high seas. Canada
justified its seizure of the fishing vessel and use of force pursuant to the CFPA
as a "conservation and management measure". The Court agreed with Canada,
adopting a broad interpretation of the meaning of "measures" and also finding
enforcement measures taken in the high seas to be consistent with article
22(1)(f) of the UN Fish Stocks Agreement, even though the CFPA was not
based upon the latter[54].

3.1. Migratory Species

The earliest attempt at international regulation of high seas activities was
for whales. The International Whaling Commission ("IWC') was created in
1946 with the objective of conserving whale stocks for future generations[55].
The first high seas sanctuary was established in the Antarctic by the ICW for
regulating whaling activities. There are currently two whaling sanctuaries that
include high seas areas: the Indian Ocean sanctuary[56] and the Southern Ocean

---

[52] *Case concerning Fisheries Jurisdiction*, Spain v. Canada, Judgment, ICJ Reports 1998,
paragraphs 66, 70.

[53] Canada had argued that paragraph 2(d) of Canada's new declaration of acceptance of the
compulsory jurisdiction of the Court, deposited with the Secretary-General of the United Nations on 10 May 1994, excluded disputes arising out of or concerning conservation and management measures taken by Canada.

[54] See *supra* note 52, paragraph 84.

[55] International Convention for the Regulation of Whaling, 2 December 1946, and the Protocol thereto, 19 November 1956. The Convention was based upon the International Agreement for the Regulation of Whaling, signed in London on 8 June 1937, and the Protocols
thereto concluded on 24 June 1938 and 26 November 1945.

[56] It was established in 1979 and prohibits whaling in an area that covers the waters of the
Northern Hemisphere from the coast of Africa to 100° E, including the Red and Arabian Seas

Sanctuary[57]. In 2002 the ICW failed to establish a third sanctuary in the South Pacific[58]. Although the ICW has been shrouded in controversy and criticism, unable to effectively enforce limitations and restrictions, it, nonetheless, marks an important example of an accepted international action to limit and restrict activities in the high seas.

The Convention on the Conservation of Migratory Species of Wild Animals ("CMS Convention")[59] was adopted as a framework convention to protect migratory species. One of the first agreements adopted under the CMS Convention was the Agreement on the Conservation of Small Cetaceans of the Baltic and North Seas ("ASCOBANS")[60]. Its objective was the protection of small cetaceans on the Baltic Sea and North Sea[61]. In addition, by consensus reached during the Fourth Meeting of the Parties to ASCOBANS, the geographical scope of that Agreement was extended to include the Eastern North Atlantic[62]. Upon ratification, small cetaceans will be under the umbrella of protection of both the ACCOCAMS for the Black Sea, Baltic and the Mediterranean Seas and so that the ASCOBANS will cover five major seas. This, in turn, will afford a valuable opportunity to adopt protection and conservation measures in high seas areas as well, based upon co-operative agreements and co-ordinated actions of the Parties.

ASCOBANS was followed by the Agreement on the Conservation of Cetaceans of the Black Sea, Mediterranean Sea and Contiguous Atlantic Area

---

and the Gulf of Oman; and the waters of the Southern Hemisphere in the sector from 20° E to 130° E, with the Southern boundary set at 55° S. For details see http://www.iwcoffice.org/Schedule.htm#CAPTUREIII>.

[57] Adopted in 1994 by the 46th Annual meeting of the ICW. The sanctuary prohibits whaling in an area that covers the waters of the Southern Hemisphere southwards of the following line: starting from 40° S, 50° W; thence due east to 20° E; thence due south to 55° S; thence due east to 130° E; thence due north to 40° S; thence due east to 130° W; thence due south to 60° S; thence due east to 50° W; see http://www.iwcoffice.org/Schedule.htm#CAPTUREIII>.

[58] Proposals for sanctuaries failed to meet the required three quarters (3/4) necessary, with 24 votes for, 16 against and 5 abstentions for a sanctuary in the South Pacific and with 23 votes for, 18 against and four abstentions for a sanctuary in the South Atlantic.

[59] Adopted on 23 June 1979 in Bonn, it entered into force on 1 November 1983.

[60] Adopted in September 1991, it entered into force on 29 March 1994. ASCOBANS was established pursuant to article IV (4) of the CMS Convention.

[61] The geographic scope of the Agreement includes "the north-east by the shores of the Gulfs of Bothnia and Finland; to the south-west by latitude 48°30' N and longitude 5° W; to the north-west by longitude 5° W and a line drawn through the following points: latitude 60° N / longitude 5° W, latitude 61° N / longitude 4° W, and latitude 62° N / longitude 3° W; to the north by latitude 62° N; and including the Kattegat and the Sound and Belt passages but excluding the waters between Cape Wrath and St Anthony Head".

[62] The meeting was held in Esbjerg, Denmark, on 12-22 August, 2003. See www.ascobans.org>.

("ACCOBAMS")[63]. Given the migratory nature of cetaceans, ACCOBAMS covers a geographic area that would apply to the high seas area falling within its stated geographic scope. Article 1(a) delineated the scope of the Agreement to include all "the maritime waters of the Black Sea and the Mediterranean and their gulfs and seas, and the internal waters connected to or interconnecting these maritime waters, and of the Atlantic area contiguous to the Mediterranean Sea west of the Straits of Gibraltar". The Agreement, however, expressly preserved such rights as freedom of navigation and innocent passage[64].

Furthermore, States Parties remain under the obligation to co-ordinate measures to achieve and maintain a favourable conservation status for cetaceans including prohibiting and taking all the necessary measures to eliminate any deliberate taking of cetaceans and, to co-operate to create and maintain a network of specially protected areas to conserve cetaceans[65]. However, this obligation was restricted to areas falling within the limits of their sovereignty or jurisdiction[66]. Despite the cautious language of the Agreement, it marked an important step towards establishing co-operative agreements amongst States for the creation of protective measures in the seas, which could also include high seas areas. According to article 3 of Annex 2, Parties are under a duty to establish specially protected areas in important habitat areas for cetaceans, which necessarily would include high seas areas.

4. THE BIODIVERSITY CONVENTION AND THE JAKARTA MANDATE

The 1992 Convention on Biological Diversity ("CBD")[67] undertook a broad approach to the protection and preservation of the marine environment by providing for the conservation of the "diversity" of marine biology, including genetic resources. What is particularly noteworthy about the CBD was its equally broad jurisdictional approach to include areas beyond national jurisdiction. For example, article 4(b) extended the application of the Convention to areas beyond national jurisdiction in regard to "processes and activities", although such actions are qualified as being subject to rights of other States. Article 5 expressly obligated the Contracting Parties to co-operate

---

[63] Adopted on 24 November 1996, it entered into force on 1 June 2001. ACCOBAMS was established pursuant to Article IV (4) of the CMS Convention.

[64] Article 1(b).

[65] Article II(1).

[66] Article II (3).

[67] Adopted on 22 May 1992, it entered into force on 29 December 1993. The Cartagena Protocol on Biosafety came into force on 11 September 2004. It will regulate the transboundary movement of living modified organisms (LMOs) resulting from modern biotechnology.

in conservation and sustainable use with other Contracting Parties, as far as possible, either "directly" or through competent international organizations, for areas *beyond national jurisdiction*. Article 8(a) further required Contracting Parties to establish a "system of protected areas or areas where special measures need to be taken to conserve biological diversity". Read in conjunction with each other, articles 4, 5 and 8 not only supported the establishment of high seas MPAs but rather under certain circumstances actually required their establishment.

The Secretariat of the Convention on Biological Diversity conducted two meetings of an '*Ad Hoc* Technical Expert Group on Marine and Coastal Protected Areas' ("MCPAs"), which produced a framework for sustainable management for marine and coastal biological diversity, including a network of highly protected areas covering both areas inside and outside of national jurisdiction. The Eighth meeting of the *Ad Hoc* Technical Expert Group on Marine and Coastal Protected Areas, held in Montreal on 10-14 March 2003, stated that it was necessary to establish MCPAs in areas beyond national jurisdiction. Recognizing the extant legal hurdles under international law the Report further added that: "Consultations with relevant bodies could be initiated to identify appropriate mechanisms and responsibilities for this work, as a matter of urgency"[68]. Notwithstanding the provisions for high seas protected areas, third party rights for non-Party States remain protected, such as freedom of navigation and laying of submarine cables and pipelines. More recently, at the Seventh Session of the Conference of Parties to the CBD the Parties called on the UNGA to take action to protect the biological diversity of seamounts, cold-water corals and other VMEs.

5. International Seabed Authority

One of the major innovations of the LOS Convention was the establishment of the International Seabed Authority ("ISA"), an autonomous body whose duty is to regulate deep seabed mining activities, administer resources in the seabed area and protect the environment for what has been termed the "common heritage of mankind"[69]. The ISA provides an interesting example

---

[68] Doc. UNEP/CBD/SBSTTA/8/INF/7.

[69] The International Seabed Authority was established pursuant to the 1982 LOS Convention and the 1994 Agreement relating to the Implementation of Part XI of the United Nations Convention on the Law of the Sea.

of a quasi-regulatory authority in an area that extends beyond the national jurisdiction of any State[70].

In conformity with the authority granted, the ISA adopted on 13 June 2000 the first 'Regulations on Prospecting and Exploration of Polymetallic Nodules in the Area'[71] (hereinafter cited as "Regulations"). Part V of the Regulations addressed the protection and preservation of the marine environment. Accordingly, the Authority is to "establish and keep under periodic review environmental rules, regulations and procedures to ensure effective protection for the marine environment from harmful effects which may arise from activities in the Area". The Contractor has the responsibility to take the "necessary measures to prevent, reduce and control pollution and other hazards". The Regulations also provide other requirements and measures for the Contractor to take. In addition, the Regulations require the prospector to notify the ISA of any incidents causing "serious harm" to the marine environment[72].

Despite the appearance of an international regulatory body, close examination of the Regulations demonstrate that the foundation of the relationship between the Contractor for seabed mining and the Authority is contractual in nature. Therefore, in the case of a report of an incident causing serious harm to the marine environment, the Secretary–General, in addition to preparing a report, may also take such immediate measures as necessary to "prevent, contain and minimize serious harm to the marine environment" pending action by the Council[73]. The Council may issue emergency orders, which can include the suspension or adjustment of seabed mining operations. However, if the Contractor does not abide by these emergency orders, according to the Regulations "the Council shall take by itself or through arrangements with others on its behalf, such practical measures as are necessary to prevent, contain and minimize any such serious harm to the marine environment".

6. REGIONAL AND SUB-REGIONAL AGREEMENTS

One of the important contributions of the LOS Convention, as well as of the historic 1972 Stockholm Declaration and the 1994 Rio Declaration was

---

[70] Couffen-Smout and Herbert, *supra* note 7, at p. 444, have suggested that the UN General Assembly mandate the ISA to act as regulatory authority over the routing and management cables on the seabed in areas beyond national jurisdiction.

[71] Doc. ISBA/6/A/18.

[72] Although Regulation 31(2) adopts the "precautionary principle" in principle, the requirement of "serious harm" as the threshold would somewhat dilute the precautionary approach in actual application.

[73] Such temporary measures can only remain in effect for 90 days.

the promotion of regional co-operation as a mechanism for promoting the protection and preservation of the marine environment. Under the auspices of the United Nations Environmental Programme ("UNEP") the regional seas programmes have flourished and have proven to be effective. The first of the regional programmes was for the Mediterranean Sea, referred to collectively as the "Barcelona system"[74].

Two important developments have taken place within the Barcelona System in regard to the protection and preservation of mammals in the high seas areas of the Sea: The Protocol concerning Specially Protected Areas and Biological Diversity in the Mediterranean (hereinafter: the "SPAMI Protocol") and the 1998 Mammal Sanctuary Agreement[75]. The SPAMI Protocol provides for the establishment of "specially protected areas" to safeguard, *inter alia*, habitats which are in danger of disappearing in their natural area of distribution or which have a reduced area of distribution[76] and are critical to the survival, reproduction and recovery of endangered, threatened or endemic species of flora or fauna[77]: In short, what could also be defined as "vulnerable marine ecosystems". Of particular interest is a provision included in the SPAMI Protocol, which opened the door to establishing "specially protected areas" in the high seas.

---

[74] It comprises the 1976 Barcelona Convention on the Protection of the Mediterranean Sea Against Pollution, as amended on 10 June 1995 in Barcelona and renamed Convention for the Protection of the Marine Environment and the Coastal Region of the Mediterranean; the 1976 Barcelona Protocol for the Prevention of the Pollution of the Mediterranean Sea by Dumping from Ships and Aircraft, as amended on 10 June 1995 in Barcelona and renamed Protocol for the Prevention and Elimination of Pollution of the Mediterranean Sea by Dumping from Ships and Aircraft or Incineration at Sea; the 1976 Barcelona Protocol Concerning Cooperation in Combating Pollution of the Mediterranean Sea by Oil and Other Harmful Substances in Cases of Emergency, as amended on 25 January 2002 in Valetta, Malta and renamed Protocol Concerning Cooperation in Preventing Pollution from Ships and, in Cases of Emergency, Combating Pollution of the Mediterranean Sea; the 1980 Athens Protocol for the Protection of the Mediterranean Sea Against Pollution from Land-Based Sources, as amended on 7 March 1996 in Syracuse and renamed Protocol for the Protection of the Mediterranean Sea Against Pollution from Land-Based Sources and Activities; the 1982 Geneva Protocol Concerning Mediterranean Specially Protected Areas, as replaced on 10 June 1995 in Barcelona by the Protocol Concerning Specially Protected Areas and Biological Diversity in the Mediterranean; the 1994 Madrid Protocol Concerning Pollution Resulting from Exploration and Exploitation of the Continental Shelf, the Seabed and its Subsoil; the 1996 Izmir Protocol on the Prevention of Pollution of the Mediterranean Sea by Transboundary Movements of Hazardous Wastes and their Disposal.

[75] T. Scovazzi, Marine Protected Areas on the High Seas: Some Legal and Policy Considerations, 19 *TIJCML* 2004, pp. 1 *et seq.*

[76] Article 4(b).

[77] Article 4(c).

The 'procedures' for establishing a SPAMI includes for "two or more neighbouring Parties" to establish such an area wholly or partly on the high seas[78] or in areas where the limits of national sovereignty or jurisdiction have not yet been defined[79].

In addition to the Mediterranean Sea, other regional seas have also taken measures for the protection of vulnerable marine ecosystems that could also include areas beyond national jurisdiction such as: the Black Sea Biodiversity Protocol[80]; the Convention for the Protection and Development of the Marine Environment of the Wider Caribbean Area (hereinafter: "Cartagena Convention")[81], which includes a specific duty to take measures to protect and preserve "fragile and rare" ecosystems[82], and the Protocol Concerning Specially Protected Areas and Wildlife in the Wider Caribbean Region (SPAW)[83]; the Convention for Cooperation in the Protection and Development of the Marine and Coastal Environment of the West and Central Africa Region (hereinafter: "Abidjan Convention")[84], which requires the establishment of SPAs to protect "rare or fragile ecosystems"; the Convention for the Protection of the Natural Resources and the Environment of the South Pacific Region[85], which also includes establishment of SPAs for "rare or fragile" ecosystems; the Antarctic Convention on the Conservation of Antarctic Marine Living Resources (CCMLR)[86] which provides for MPAs; and the 1991 Antarctic Protocol for Specially Protected Areas and Managed Areas[87]; the Convention for the Protection of the Marine Environment of the North-East Atlantic (OSPAR)[88] Annex V on the Protection and Conservation of the Ecosystems and Biological Diversity of the Maritime Area; the Arrangement between the

---

[78] Article 9(2)(b).

[79] Article 9(2)(c).

[80] The Black Sea Biodiversity and Landscape Conservation Protocol to the Convention on the Protection of the Black Sea Against Pollution was signed in Sofia, Bulgaria in 2003; see http://www.blacksea-commission.org/OfficialDocuments/BLDCProtocol_main.htm

[81] Adopted on 24 March 1983, it entered into force on 11 October 1986.

[82] Article 10.

[83] Adopted on 9 June 1991, it entered into force on 18 June 2000.

[84] Adopted on 23 March 1981, it entered into force on 5 August 1984.

[85] Adopted on 24 November 1986, it entered into force on 22 August 1990.

[86] Adopted on 20 May 1980, it entered into force on 7 April 1982. See D.G.M. Miller, E.N. Sabourenkov and D.C. Ramm, Managing Marine Living Resources: The CCAMLR Approach, in Gjerde & Freestone, *supra* note 50, pp. 317- 63.

[87] The Antarctic presents a unique example of a complex set of treaties to collectively conserve and manage a large expanse of land and marine area by multiple state interests. In general see F. Francioni & T. Scovazzi (eds.), *International Law for Antarctica* (Kluwer, 1996).

[88] Adopted in September 1992; it entered into force in March 1998.

Government of Australia and the Government of New Zealand for the Conservation of Orange Roughy on the South Tasman Rise (2000)[89].

7. INTERNATIONAL SOFT LAW

The specific issue of the protection of "vulnerable", "fragile" or "rare" marine ecosystems was not included in the historic 1972 Stockholm Declaration. Not until its successor twenty years later at the 1992 Rio Earth Summit was the issue expressly addressed[90]. More specifically, Section 17.46 (f) of Chapter 17 of Agenda 21 included the objective "to preserve habitats and other ecologically sensitive areas"[91]. Furthermore, Section 17.78 exhorted States to identify marine ecosystems exhibiting high levels of biodiversity and productivity and other critical habitat areas and provide the necessary limitations on the use of these areas[92].

A decade later, the Johannesburg World Summit on Sustainable Development ("WSSD") adopted the Plan of Implementation (PoI)[93], which took a radical step by recognizing that the protection of vulnerable marine and coastal areas required the need to take action in areas *beyond* national jurisdiction[94]. Following upon Johannesburg, the UN General Assembly endorsed the Johannesburg Declaration and Plan of Implementation and followed upon this with a Resolution calling upon States "to develop national, regional and international programmes for halting the loss of marine biodiversity, in particular fragile ecosystems"[95]. The same Resolution requested the meeting of the UN Informal Consultative Process on Oceans and the Law of the Sea (hereafter cited as "ICP") to be held the following June[96] and recom-

---

[89] See E.J. Molenaar, The South Tasmanian Rise Arrangement of 2000 and other Initiatives on Management and Conservation of Orange Roughy, 16 *TIJCML* 2001, pp. 77-124.

[90] *Report of the United Nations Conference on Environment and Development*, Rio de Janeiro, 3-14 June 1992, vol. I: *Resolutions adopted by the Conference*, resolution 1, annex I; UN Publications.

[91] *Ibid.* Annex II.

[92] Section G of Chapter 17 addressing small island developing States recognized in section 17.123 that small island developing States were "ecologically fragile and vulnerable" particularly to the effects of global warming and sea-level rising.

[93] Report of the World Summit on Sustainable Development, Johannesburg, South Africa, 26 August-4 September 2002, Resolution 2, annex, A/CONF.199/20.

[94] Paragraph 31 of the PoI provided that: "[I]n accordance with chapter 17 of Agenda 21, promote the conservation and management of oceans through actions at all levels, giving due regard to the relevant international instruments to: Maintain the productivity and biodiversity of important and vulnerable marine and coastal areas, including in areas within and *beyond national jurisdiction*".

[95] GA Resolution 141, UN GAOR, 57th Session, UN Doc A/57/141 (2002).

[96] Held on 2-6 June 2003 at the United Nations in New York.

mended that the deliberations for the Report to be prepared by the Secretary General include the protection of vulnerable marine ecosystems as one of its subjects of discussion[97].

8. MARINE PROTECTED AREAS ON THE HIGH SEAS

Marine protected areas are considered by scientists to be an effective means for protecting sensitive ecosystems, if properly established and managed. However, protecting vulnerable marine areas beyond national jurisdiction raises various questions under international law. The establishment of high seas MPAs was addressed during the fourth meeting of the ICP held in New York on 9 June 2003.

During this ICP meeting there was general support for the need to protect vulnerable marine ecosystems, including those beyond national jurisdiction[98]. However, there was some difference in the approach to be taken. For example, the Netherlands supported the establishment of high seas MPAs, and recommended that "immediate action" be taken for the protection of VME beyond national jurisdiction[99]. Norway, on the other hand, asserted that high seas MPAs would be in violation of articles 89 and 137(3) of the LOS Convention[100], notwithstanding the Johannesburg Plan of Implementation[101]. Instead, Norway suggested that the long-term conservation and sustainable use of deep-sea bed "must be based on the harmonization of treaty obligations and involve all relevant international organizations and treaty bodies". Furthermore, any new regime should be based on a global agreement building upon the LOS Convention and modelled on the 1995 Fish Stocks Agreement.

The Final Report of the Fourth Meeting of the ICP noted that many delegations attending did support the use of high seas MPAs as a management tool for integrated ocean areas both within and beyond national jurisdiction but that such MPAs had to be based on the following five factors: (1) scientific evidence; (2) be enforceable; (3) be specific for each marine area and objective; (4) be consistent with the ecosystem approach; and (5) be in conformity

---

[97] GA Resolution 141, *supra* note 94, paragraph 62.

[98] *Oceans and the Law of the Sea*, Report on the work of the United Nations Open-Ended Informal Consultative Process on Oceans and the Law of the Sea, Letter from the Co-Chairpersons of the Consultative Process addressed to the President of the General Assembly, 9 June 2003; GA Resolution 95, GAOR 58th Session, UN Doc. A/58/95 (2003).

[99] UN Doc. A/AC.259/8, p. 6.

[100] The Norway position also invoked the restrictions against mining by any person or State in the Area as provided by article 137, paragraph 3 of the Convention.

[101] UN Doc. A/AC.259/10, p. 2.

with international law[102]. Delegations also supported the application of the ecosystem approach, integrated management and coastal area management as well as the application of the precautionary approach.

The Fifth ICP, which met between 7-11 June 2004 at the UN headquarters in New York, once again discussed at great length the question of the protection and conservation of the marine environment beyond national jurisdiction[103]. The use of MPAs to protect fragile ecosystems in the high seas, although not a main focus, was discussed, including the legal framework upon which it could be based. Concerns were raised, however, that high seas freedoms should be protected. Furthermore, the role of Regional Fisheries Management Organizations (RFMO) was given much importance.

The WWF and IUCN have been extremely active in promoting marine protected areas as well as exploring MPAs in areas beyond national jurisdiction. As early as 1988, the IUCN had adopted a programme to promote a global system of MPAs. In 1999 the WWF Marine Advisory Group adopted as a goal to have established effectively managed MPAs covering at least ten percent of the world's oceans by the year 2010. Both of these NGOs have held various workshops[104] and issued reports not only concerning MPAs in general but specifically addressing the issues of MPAs on the high seas. In 2000 the IUCN adopted a resolution which included high seas MPAs.

8.1. The IMO and Particularly Sensitive Sea Areas

The International Maritime Organization (IMO) is the only international governmental agency responsible for regulating shipping activities. Its scope of activities is broad and, though related to shipping, virtually limitless. The IMO has adopted numerous Conventions, Codes, Resolutions and Guidelines for the promotion of safety of navigation and the protection of the marine environment. Over nearly half a century of existence, the IMO has contributed enormously to reducing the level of maritime accidents and pollution of the seas from dangerous and hazardous cargo. However, despite these great strides, the problem of the enforcement of the standards and norms established by the international community, through the IMO, remains problematic. The weakness in the system stems from the reliance of international

---

[102] *Ibid.*

[103] UN Resolution 50, GAOR 59th Session, UN Doc. A/59/50 and Corr.1 (advance and unedited text, 2004). The Fifth UN Open-Ended Informal Consultative Process on Oceans and the Law of the Sea, pursuant to GA Resolution 58/240, addressed the issue of "New sustainable uses of the oceans, including the conservation and management of the biological diversity of the seabed in areas beyond national jurisdiction".

[104] The Cairns Workshop was held in June 2003 and the Malaga Workshop in 2004.

law on flag State enforcement and the inability to ensure a "genuine link" between the flag of the ship and its port of registry.

Nevertheless, the IMO has developed a protective mechanism for vulnerable marine areas against harmful shaping activities by the "Particularly Sensitive Sea Area" (PSSA)[105] and MARPOL 73/78 Special Areas[106]. If the IMO designates a marine area as a special area under Annexes I, II, and V of MARPOL 73/78, all ships engaged in navigation through such special area will be prohibited from engaging in discharge of oily wastes, tank washing and residue and garbage respectively. The geographical scope of a special area may include areas beyond national jurisdiction. Many vulnerable seas have been so designated, such as the Black Sea, the Baltic Sea and the Mediterranean Sea[107].

The PSSA, however, differs from the MARPOL 73/78 special area. According to the IMO a PSSA is "a comprehensive management tool at the international level that provides a mechanism for reviewing an area that is vulnerable to damage by international shipping and determines the most appropriate was to address that vulnerability"[108]. In order for a marine area to be designated as PSSA by the IMO the submitting States(s) must meet a number of criteria that include ecological, sociological, economic, vulnerability, rarity, bio-geographic importance as well as potential harm. The submitting State may then request "Associated Protected Measures" (APMs) to protect the area designated as a PSSA. According to the IMO, such measures can include ships' routing or reporting measures, discharge restrictions, operational criteria, prohibitive activities, mandatory pilotage and many more as long as they are consistent with competence of the IMO and international law, including article 211(6) of the LOS Convention.

Until recently, the PSSA was sparingly applied by States. However, there is growing recognition that the PSSA is an effective mechanism to protect vulnerable marine area from harmful shipping activities. In 2004 three new PSSAs were designated[109]: The Canary Islands, the Galapagos and the Baltic

---

[105] Guidelines for the Designation of Special Areas under MARPOL 73/78 and Guideline for the Identification and Designation of PSSAs, IMO Doc. A.927(22).

[106] International Convention for the Prevention of Pollution from Ships, 1973, as modified by the Protocol of 1978 relating thereto (MARPOL 73/78).

[107] Other seas designated as special areas include the Red Sea area, the Gulfs area, the Gulf of Aden area, the Antarctic area, the North-West European Waters and the Wider Caribbean region, including the Gulf of Mexico and the Caribbean Sea.

[108] IMO Doc. MEPC/Circ.398.

[109] The existing designated PSSAs are: the Great Barrier Reef, Australia (1990); the Sabana-Camagüey Archipelago in Cuba (1997); Malpelo Island, Colombia (2002); Around the Florida Keys, United States (2002); the Wadden Sea, among Denmark, Germany and the

Sea. However, the PSSA for the Baltic Sea, which covered the entire Baltic Sea with the exception of Russian waters, was controversial and may bring about changes to the existing IMO structure[110].

The IMO PSSA offers a very interesting model for use in seeking an effective mechanism to protect marine areas beyond national jurisdiction in activities falling outside of shipping. However, for shipping activities, the IMO PSSA mechanism exists and can be further developed, if necessary, to address the problems associated with shipping in vulnerable areas in the high seas and deep oceans. However, the IMO does not have competence over fishing activities, which is often the main threat against high seas and deep oceans vulnerable marine ecosystems.

8.2. Marine Environmental High Risk Areas

Somewhat related but different from the IMO PSSAs, are the Marine Environmental High Risk Areas (MEHRA). Following the grounding of the fully laden '*M.V. Braer*' in 1993 the United Kingdom set up the Donaldson Inquiry to study the risk of pollution from commercial shipping. The resulting report provided 100 recommendations. One of these recommendations was to establish Marine Environmental High Risk Areas. These MEHRAs would be charted on nautical maps in an advisory fashion for mariners to "voluntarily" avoid them as part of their shipping routes. The basic idea was that, if mariners were made aware of the environmental risks associated with shipping in a particular area, they would be more likely to avoid such areas[111]. This proposal highlighted the importance of both informing and including stakeholders in the debate, particularly such an important body as the international shipping industry.

9. LIMITATIONS AND REALITIES

The protection of vulnerable marine areas beyond national jurisdiction is moving beyond theory into reality. This is evident from the multiple activities taking place both at the NGO level as well as at the international governmental level. The establishment of a new interagency, the UN-Ocean, is

---

Netherlands (2002); and the Paracas National Reserve, Peru (2003). See http://www.imo.org/ index.htm>.

[110] The controversy over the designation of the Baltic Sea as a PSSA has resulted in the creation of a review procedure for Resolution A.927.

[111] L.M. Warren & M.W. Wallace, The Donaldson Inquiry and its Relevance to Particularly Sensitive Sea Areas, 9 *TIJMCL* 1998, pp. 523-534.

set to play an important role in developing the framework within which vulnerable marine ecosystems can be protected by the international community and international law. But the task is formidable as, in addition to the political foundation of regional and international co-operation, it will require an important economic component of expensive surveillance and enforcement infrastructure.

Geographically, the area of the high seas encompasses a vast area of physical space. The creation of a high seas MPA would mean the protection of a large area at a considerable distance from the shore of any one or a group of coastal States. Protection would necessarily include surveillance, most-likely satellite surveillance, of the area for possible violators, as well as needing patrol boats, helicopters etc. to pursue and capture suspected violators. Yet, even the more developed and economically developed States encounter difficulties in meeting the demands of offshore patrol and enforcement[112]. In most cases an effective system of multilateral enforcement involving multiple State co-operation would be required[113].

Furthermore, existing international instruments that do provide for some form of high seas regulation depend primarily on flag State enforcement. Establishing a new enforcement regime based upon coastal State enforcement would also require restructuring existing oceans governance under international law. The practical problem with this approach is that negotiations of agreements at the multilateral level are time-consuming, which was the case with the LOS Convention. If the state of the oceans and high seas is critical, there is then little time to be spent on costly and timely diplomatic conferences.

There is a tremendous amount of fragmentation in oceans law regarding the protection and preservation of marine life and biodiversity. Shipping, fishing, mammals, biodiversity and seabed exploration and exploitation are all subject to different legal instruments and different regulatory mechanisms. While this is by no means a criticism, the existing structure does, however, present a challenge to undertaking any unified solution – such as high seas MPAs. However, this challenge is not insurmountable but will require a great deal of political will and cooperation from the international community. For this reason, the establishment of the UN-Ocean interagency assumes great importance.

---

[112] R. Warner, Jurisdictional Issues for Navies Involved in Enforcing Multilateral Regimes Beyond National Jurisdiction, 14 *TIJCML* 1999, pp. 131 *et seq.*

[113] E.J. Molenaar, Multilateral Hot Pursuit and Illegal Fishing in the Southern Ocean: The Pursuits of the *Viarsa* 1 and the *South Tomi*, 19 *TIJCML* 2004, pp. 19-42. The author provides analyses of two separate incidents involving multilateral enforcement of illegal fishing in the EEZ of Australia.

The protection of high seas vulnerable marine ecosystems requires a clear understanding of the major threats against such ecosystems. The primary threats against the ecosystems in semi-enclosed and enclosed seas will not necessarily be the same as those against seamounts and cold water coral and the seabed. For instance, threats to the Black Sea ecosystem and biodiversity result primarily from nutrient inputs, brought by rivers, and exotic species brought by ballast water of ships whereas the major threat to seamounts and deep sea coral is deep-sea bottom trawling and IUU fishing. For this reason, the first step must be devising a clear assessment of the major threats facing identified high seas and deep oceans vulnerable ecosystems. This becomes important for assessing the impact of protective and conservation measures against high seas freedoms under international law.

10. CONCLUSION

Protection of the high seas and deep oceans presents a puzzle made up of pieces of international law, marine biology and politics. The task of the international lawyer is to assemble a complex set of legal instruments, both soft and hard, into a coherent integrated framework for the conservation and management of high seas and deep ocean vulnerable marine ecosystems. There is no reason to attempt to create a new set of rules for the high seas as the existing ones do provide the necessary foundation, albeit one that could be further refined to better meet existing needs[114]. Furthermore, the urgency of the need to protect particularly vulnerable marine life, such as deepsea fisheries would dictate against a lengthy negotiation and ratification process inevitable for any new international instrument.

In understanding the scope of the role of international law in regulating the high seas and deep oceans, it is first important to recognize that high seas freedoms and the protection of the high seas and deep oceans can be reconciled with the traditional freedoms of the high seas: International law has already recognized many limitations on high seas freedom. Furthermore, the

---

[114] There are, however, a number of international law experts who have concluded that there is an important gap in international law for regulating high seas fisheries that requires either the adoption of a new international legal instrument specifically for regulating high seas fisheries; see M. Hayashi, Global Governance of Deep-Sea Fisheries, *in* Gjerde & Freestone, *supra* note 50, pp. 289-298, or amending existing instruments such as the UN Fish Stocks Agreement to apply to *all* high seas fisheries. See L.A. Kimball, Deep-Sea Fisheries of the High Seas: The Management Impasse, *in* Gjerde & Freestone, *ibid.*, pp. 259-88; M.W. Lodge, Improving International Governance in the Deep Sea, *ibid.*, pp. 299-315. For an excellent and detailed examination of these issues by well-known international legal scholars, in general see K.M. Gjerde & D. Freestone, *ibid.*

LOS Convention provides the necessary legal infrastructure upon which to build a mechanism to protect vulnerable marine ecosystems that lie beyond national jurisdiction. The UN Fish Stock Agreement is an example of how the LOS Convention devised a method to regulate and manage straddling fish stocks on the high seas. The key lies in international and regional co-operation.

Modern international marine and environmental law requires international and regional *cooperation*. There can be no effective protection of high seas and deep oceans marine resource without a broad-based cooperation among States. Virtually every convention, agreement or resolution is structured upon "cooperation" among the participating States. Consequently, international co-operation combined with the duty to protect and preserve the marine environment leads to the legal conclusion that States must agree to limit activities in certain areas of the high seas and deep oceans designated as MPAs. International law and practice provide a number of mechanisms by which to implement regional co-operation such as RFMO, SPAMI, PSSA etc. Where the challenge lies is in provoking States to engage in these co-operative mechanism and in the implementation, surveillance and enforcement of the existing rules and regulations of international law for the protection of the marine environment beyond national jurisdictions. And herein lies the key: The political will of States to implement and enforce existing rules and regulations.

In conclusion, international law itself can meet the challenge of protecting the high seas and deep oceans but it is ultimately up to the States to act. The question of either compelling or cajoling States to act is an issue of equal importance and one that needs to be addressed from all facets including the role of law and of civil society.

Chapter 5

NEW INTERNATIONAL INSTRUMENTS FOR
MARINE PROTECTED AREAS IN THE MEDITERRANEAN SEA

*Tullio Scovazzi**

1. THE MEDITERRANEAN APPROACH TO MARINE PROTECTED AREAS

At the 2004 Fifth Meeting of the United Nations Open-Ended Informal Consultative Process on Oceans and the Law of the Sea (hereinafter cited as "ICP") the subject of "New sustainable uses of the oceans, including the conservation and management of the biological diversity of the seabed in areas beyond national jurisdiction" and its implications, such as the establishment of marine protected areas, were discussed in depth. The Final Report of the Fifth ICP meeting provides the following summary of the discussion:

"As regards the establishment of marine protected areas as a tool to protect fragile ecosystems, one delegation said that the establishment of marine protected areas on the high seas would be in keeping with the general obligation imposed by the Convention [= the United Nations Convention on the Law of the Sea] on all States to protect and preserve the marine environment (article 192), as well as the specific obligation to adopt measures necessary to protect and preserve rare or fragile ecosystems (article 194(5)). Others noted that States were obligated to cooperate under the provisions of the Convention on Biological Diversity in the conservation and sustainable use of biological diversity in areas beyond national jurisdiction (article 5). Given the existing legal framework, a number of delegations said that the international community should at this point consider specific ocean governance options. One delegation suggested the adoption of an international treaty that would provide a mechanism for the establishment and regulation on an integrated basis of marine protected areas on the high seas and the seabed beyond the limits of national jurisdiction. The treaty could be modelled on the mechanism established in the Mediterranean region under the Protocol Concerning Specially Protected Areas and Biological Diversity in the Mediterranean, which provided for the establishment of a list of specially protected areas of Mediterranean in-

---

* Professor of International Law, University of Milano-Bicocca.

Anastasia Strati, Maria Gavouneli & Nikos Skourtos (eds.), *Unresolved Issues and New Challenges to the Law of the Sea*, Martinus Nijhoff 2006, pp. 109-120.

terest, including in the high seas. Some delegations suggested that the Consultative Process should establish a working group with a mandate to begin the preparation of a legal instrument. Other delegations stressed the need to balance the protection of high seas ecosystems with freedom of navigation and other freedoms associated with the high seas. Another delegation expressed the view that marine and coastal protected areas should be considered only as one of the essential tools and approaches in the conservation and sustainable use of marine and coastal biodiversity"[1].

The fifth ICP meeting was unable to recommend to the UN General Assembly any definite action on marine protected areas beyond national jurisdiction. It merely proposed that the General Assembly welcome a decision to "explore options for cooperation" adopted by the Conference of the parties to the Convention on Biological Diversity[2]. However, the reference during the discussion to the instruments elaborated within the Mediterranean regional system, the so-called "Barcelona system", deserves further analysis. The 1995 Barcelona Protocol Concerning Specially Protected Areas and Biological Diversity in the Mediterranean is the first binding instrument in international law which explicitly envisages the creation of protected areas in the high seas.

2. THE "BARCELONA SYSTEM"

The so-called "Barcelona system" is a notable instance of fulfilment of the obligation to co-operate for the protection of the environment in a regional sea.

On 4 February 1975 a policy instrument, the Mediterranean Action Plan ("MAP"), was adopted by an intergovernmental meeting convened in Barcelona by the United Nations Environment Programme ("UNEP"). One of the main objectives of the MAP was to promote the conclusion of a framework

---

[1] Report on the Work of the United Nations Open-Ended Informal Consultative Process on Oceans and the Law of the Sea at Its Fifth Meeting, UN Doc. A/59/122, 1 July 2004, paragraphs 88-89.

[2] As a 2004 ICP agreed Recommendation stated, "it was proposed that the General Assembly: (a) Welcome decision VII/5 adopted at the seventh meeting of the Conference of the Parties to the Convention on Biological Diversity; and (b) also welcome decision VII/28 adopted at the seventh meeting of the Conference of the Parties to the Convention on Biological Diversity suggesting that the Ad Hoc Open-Ended Working Group on Protected Areas explore options for cooperation to promote the establishment of marine protected areas beyond national jurisdiction, consistent with international law, including the United Nations Convention on the Law of the Sea, and on the basis of the best available scientific information, and encourage the participation of oceans experts in the Working Group"; *ibid.*, paragraph 5.

convention and related protocols with technical annexes for the protection of the Mediterranean environment. This was done on 16 February 1976 when the Convention on the Protection of the Mediterranean Sea against Pollution and two protocols were opened to signature in Barcelona. The Convention, which entered into force on 12 February 1978, is chronologically the first of the so-called 'regional seas agreements' concluded under the auspices of UNEP. The Convention is a framework treaty, which is supplemented by implementing protocols relating to specific aspects of environmental protection.

In the last decade, the Barcelona system underwent important changes in several of its components. In 1995 the MAP was replaced by the 'Action Plan for the Protection of the Marine Environment and the Sustainable Development of the Coastal Areas of the Mediterranean (MAP Phase II)'. The Barcelona Convention and some protocols were amended. New protocols were adopted to either replace the protocols which had not been amended or cover new fields of cooperation.

The structure of the present Barcelona legal system includes the following instruments:

a) the Convention which, as amended in Barcelona on 10 June 1995, changes its name into *Convention for the Protection of the Marine Environment and the Coastal Region of the Mediterranean* (the amendments are not yet in force);

b) the Protocol for the Prevention of the Pollution of the Mediterranean Sea by Dumping from Ships and Aircraft (Barcelona, 16 February 1976; in force from 12 February 1978), which, as amended in Barcelona on 10 June 1995, changes its name into *Protocol for the Prevention and Elimination of Pollution of the Mediterranean Sea by Dumping from Ships and Aircraft or Incineration at Sea* (the amendments are not yet in force);

c) the Protocol Concerning Co-operation in Combating Pollution of the Mediterranean Sea by Oil and Other Harmful Substances in Cases of Emergency (Barcelona, 16 February 1976; in force from 12 February 1978), which is intended to be replaced by the *Protocol Concerning Cooperation in Preventing Pollution from Ships and, in Cases of Emergency, Combating Pollution of the Mediterranean Sea,* signed in Valletta on 25 January 2002 (not yet in force);

d) the Protocol for the Protection of the Mediterranean Sea against Pollution from Land-Based Sources (Athens, 17 May 1980; in force from 17 June 1983), which, as amended in Syracuse on 7 March 1996, changes its name into *Protocol for the Protection of the Mediterranean Sea against Pollution from Land-Based Sources and Activities* (the amendments are not yet in force);

e) the Protocol Concerning Mediterranean Specially Protected Areas (Geneva, 1 April 1982; in force from 23 March 1986), which has been replaced by the *Protocol Concerning Specially Protected Areas and Biological Diversity in the Mediterranean*, signed in Barcelona on 10 June 1995 (in force from 12 December 1999);

f) the *Protocol Concerning Pollution Resulting from Exploration and Exploitation of the Continental Shelf, the Seabed and its Subsoil*, signed in Madrid on 14 October 1994 (not yet in force);

g) the *Protocol on the Prevention of Pollution of the Mediterranean Sea* by Transboundary *Movements of Hazardous Wastes and their Disposal*, signed in Izmir on 1 October 1996 (not yet in force)[3].

The updating of the Barcelona system shows that the parties consider it a dynamic body capable of being subject to re-examination and improvement, if appropriate. The main objective of the updating is to adapt the Barcelona system to the evolution of international law in the field of the protection of the environment, as embodied, on the world scale, in the principles and instruments adopted at the United Nations Conference on Environment and Development (Rio de Janeiro, 1992), such as the Rio Declaration and the Action Programme 'Agenda 21'.

Besides including a number of the general principles in the Convention, the parties of the Barcelona seized the opportunity to strengthen the substantive and procedural provisions of the protocols in order to render them more effective tools. Each of the instruments of the updated Barcelona legal system contains important innovations. Some of the protocols show a certain degree of legal imagination in finding new solutions to complex problems. They could anticipate possible legal developments on the world scale and be an example of trends of cooperation in the regional seas sector.

3. THE 1995 SPECIALLY PROTECTED AREAS PROTOCOL

The 1995 Protocol Concerning Specially Protected Areas and Biological Diversity in the Mediterranean was adopted to replace the previous 1982 Geneva Protocol Concerning Mediterranean Specially Protected Areas. The 1995 Protocol is completed by three annexes, which were adopted in Monaco on 24 November 1996, namely the "Common criteria for the choice of protected marine and coastal areas that could be included in the SPAMI

---

[3] Other instruments may be elaborated in the future, for instance in the field of integrated management of the coastal zone.

List" (Annex I)[4], the "List of endangered or threatened species" (Annex II), the "List of species whose exploitation is regulated" (Annex III)[5].

The 1995 Protocol is applicable to all the marine waters of the Mediterranean, irrespective of their legal condition, as well as to the seabed, its subsoil and to the terrestrial coastal areas designated by each party, including wetlands. On the contrary, the application of the 1982 Protocol was limited to the territorial sea of the parties and did not cover the high seas. The extension of the geographical coverage of the protocol was necessary in order to protect also those highly migratory marine species (such as marine mammals) which, by definition, do not respect the artificial boundaries drawn by man on the sea.

The purpose to "go into the high seas" gave rise to some difficult legal problems which are due to the present legal condition of the Mediterranean, where most States have not yet established an exclusive economic zone and many issues of maritime boundaries are still unsettled. In order to overcome these difficulties, the 1995 Protocol includes two very elaborate disclaimer clauses, in article 2(2) and (3). The idea behind such a display of juridical devices is simple. On the one hand, the establishment of intergovernmental cooperation in the field of the marine environment should not prejudice the unsettled political and legal questions. But, on the other hand, the very existence of such questions (whose settlement is not likely to be achieved in the short term) should neither prevent nor delay the adoption of measures necessary for the preservation of the ecological balance of the Mediterranean.

The 1995 Protocol provides for the establishment of a "List of specially protected areas of Mediterranean interest" ("SPAMI List")[6]. The SPAMI List may include sites which "are of importance for conserving the components of biological diversity in the Mediterranean; contain ecosystems specific to the Mediterranean area or the habitats of endangered species; are of special interest at the scientific, aesthetic, cultural or educational levels"[7]. The procedures for the establishment and listing of SPAMIs are described in

---

[4] Under Annex I, the criteria to be used in evaluating the Mediterranean interest of an area are uniqueness, natural representativeness, diversity, naturalness and presence of habitats that are critical to endangered, threatened or endemic species, cultural representativeness (but other characteristics and factors should also be considered as favourable for the inclusion of a site in the list of SPAMI). Annex I includes also detailed provisions on the legal status of SPAMI and their protection, planning and management measures.

[5] An expert meeting convened in November 2000 in Ajaccio prepared a technical tool for the inclusion of sites in the list of SPAMIs.

[6] The existence of the SPAMI List does not exclude the right of each party to create and manage protected areas, which are not intended to be listed as SPAMIs.

[7] Article 8(2).

detail in article 9. For instance, as regards the areas located partly or wholly on the high seas, the proposal must be made "by two or more neighbouring parties concerned" and the decision to include the area in the SPAMI List is taken by consensus by the contracting parties during their periodical meetings.

Under article 9(3) "Parties making proposals for inclusion in the SPAMI List shall provide the Centre[8] with an introductory report containing information on the area's geographical location, its physical and ecological characteristics, its legal status, its management plans and the means for their implementation, as well as a statement justifying its Mediterranean importance". Annex I provides that "to be included in the SPAMI List an area will have to be endowed with a management plan. The main rules of this management plan are to be laid down as from the time of inclusion and implemented immediately. A detailed management plan must be presented within three years of the time of inclusion. Failure to respect this obligation entails the removal of the site from the List"[9].

Once the areas are included in the SPAMI List, all the parties agree "to recognize the particular importance of these areas for the Mediterranean" and – what is even more important – "to comply with the measures applicable to the SPAMIs and not to authorize nor undertake any activities that might be contrary to the objectives for which the SPAMIs were established"[10]. This gives to the SPAMIs and to the measures adopted for their protection an *erga omnes* effect, at least as far as the parties to the protocol are concerned.

As regards the relationship with third countries, the parties shall "invite States that are not Parties to the Protocol and international organizations to cooperate in the implementation" of the Protocol[11]. It is also provided that the parties "undertake to adopt appropriate measures, consistent with international law, to ensure that no one engages in any activity contrary to the principles and purposes" of the 1995 Protocol[12].

A great achievement was reached at the XIIth Meeting of the Contracting Parties (Monaco, 2001) when the first twelve SPAMIs were inscribed in the List, namely the island of Alborán, the sea bottom of the Levante de

---

[8] The Centre is the "Regional Activity Centre for Specially Protected Areas", located in Tunis, which is entrusted with a number of functions for coordinating the implementation of the 1995 Protocol; see article 25.

[9] Section D, paragraph 7.

[10] Article 8(3).

[11] Article 28(2).

[12] *Ibid.*

Almería, the Cape of Gata-Nijar, Mar Menor and the oriental coast of Murcia, the Cape of Cresus, the Medas islands, the Coulembretes islands (all proposed by Spain), Port-Cros (proposed by France), the Kneiss islands, La Galite, Zembra and Zembretta (all proposed by Tunisia), and the French-Italian-Monegasque Sanctuary (jointly proposed by the three States concerned as a result of the trilateral agreement signed in Rome in 1999 on the creation of a sanctuary for marine mammals)[13]. The last SPAMI covers also areas of high seas.

4. THE 1999 SANCTUARY AGREEMENT

On 25 November 1999 France, Italy and Monaco signed an "Agreement on the creation in the Mediterranean Sea of a sanctuary for marine mammals"[14], followed by a declaration. This is the outcome of a negotiation which made its first step with a trilateral declaration signed on 22 March 1993.

The area covered by the sanctuary, which extends over 96.000 km^2, is inhabited by the eight cetacean species regularly found in the Mediterranean, namely the fin whale *(Balaenoptera physalus)*, the sperm whale *(Physeter catodon)*, Cuvier's beaked whale (*Ziphius cavirostris*), the long-finned pilot whale (*Globicephala melas*), the striped dolphin (*Stenella coeruleoalba*), the common dolphin (*Delphinus delphis*), the bottlenose dolphin (*Tursiops truncatus*) and Risso's dolphin (*Grampus griseus*)[15]. The water currents create conditions favouring phytoplankton growth and an abundance of krill (*Meganyctiphanes norvegica*), a small pelagic shrimp that is preyed upon by pelagic vertebrates.

The Mediterranean sanctuary is a major achievement, being the first time that an international agreement has been adopted with the specific objective to establish a sanctuary for marine mammals[16].

---

[13] See *infra* paragraph 4.

[14] Hereinafter cited as the "Sanctuary Agreement". It entered into force on 21 February 2002. The parties may invite any other State or any international organisation to accede to the Agreement; article 20).

[15] Killer whale (Orcinus orca), Rough-toothed dolphin (Steno bredanensis), false killer whale (Pseudorca crassidens) and minke whale (Balaenoptera acutorostrata) can occasionally be found in the Mediterranean. Harbour porpoise (Phocoena phocoena) is found in the Black Sea.

[16] Under the 1946 International Convention for the Regulation of Whaling, the International Whaling Commission may adopt regulations with respect to the conservation and utilization of whale resources, fixing *inter alia* "open and closed waters, including the designation of sanctuary areas"; article V, para. 1c. Two vast areas were designated as sanctuaries, namely the Indian Ocean Sanctuary in 1979 and the Southern Ocean Sanctuary in 1994 (with

The main provisions of the Sanctuary Agreement, which comprises some preambular statements and 22 articles, may be summarized as follows: The parties establish a marine sanctuary in an area of the Mediterranean Sea delimited by the two lines joining Pointe Escampobariou (on the continental coast of France) to Capo Falcone (on the North-West coast of the island of Sardinia, Italy) and Capo Ferro (on the North-East coast of Sardinia) to Fosso Chiarone (on the continental coast of Italy)[17]. The area in question includes waters, which have the legal status of maritime internal waters, territorial sea, ecological zone[18] and high seas.

The parties undertake to adopt measures to ensure a favourable state of conservation for every species of marine mammals and to protect them and their habitat from negative impacts, both direct and indirect[19]. They prohibit in the sanctuary any deliberate taking[20] or disturbance of mammals. Non-lethal catches may be authorized in urgent situations or for *in situ* scientific research purposes[21].

As regards the crucial question of driftnet fishing, the parties merely undertake to comply with the relevant international and European Community regimes[22]. This seems to be an implicit reference to European Community Regulation 345/92 of 22 January 1992, laying down technical measures for the conservation of fishery resources[23], which prohibits the use of driftnets longer than 2,5 km. This also seems to be an implicit reference to the subsequent European Council Regulation 1239/98 of 8 June 1998[24], which as from 1 January 2002 prohibits the keeping on board or the use for fishing of one or more driftnets used for the catching of the species listed in an annex.

---

an objection lodged by Japan to the extent that it applies to the Antarctic minke whale stock). The measures applying to the sanctuaries are, however, limited to a prohibition of commercial whaling, whether by pelagic operations or from land stations.

[17] The coordinates of the relevant points are specified in article 3. The area has been enlarged with respect to the area envisaged by the 1993 declaration, which did not include the waters between the French island of Corsica and the Italian region of Tuscany.

[18] In 2004 an "ecological zone" was established by France along its Mediterranean shores.

[19] The level of conservation is deemed to be "favourable", if the knowledge of the populations shows that the marine mammals in the region constitute a vital element of the ecosystems to which they belong (article 1(a). The term 'habitat' means "any part of the range area of marine mammals, temporarily or permanently occupied by them, and utilised in particular for reproductive, birthing, feeding activities as well as migration route"; article 1(b).

[20] 'Taking' is defined as "hunting, catching, killing or harassing of marine mammals, as well as the attempting of such actions"; article 1(c).

[21] Article 7(a).

[22] Article 7(b).

[23] OJ L 42 of 18 February 1992.

[24] OJ L 171 of 17 June 1998.

The parties undertake to exchange their views, if appropriate, in order to promote, in the competent fora and after scientific evaluation, the adoption of regulations concerning the use of new fishing methods that could involve the incidental catch of marine mammals or endanger their food resources, taking into account the risk of loss or discard of fishing instruments at sea[25].

The parties undertake to exchange their views with the objective to regulate and, if appropriate, prohibit high-speed offshore races in the sanctuary[26]. The parties will also regulate whale-watching activities for purposes of tourism[27]. Whale-watching for commercial purposes is presently carried out in the sanctuary by a limited number of vessels. There are promising prospects for the development in the sanctuary of this kind of activities, which can be considered a benign way of exploiting marine mammals.

In the declaration annexed to the Sanctuary Agreement the parties express their desire to carry out, in conformity with the precautionary principle, studies on a certain number of issues that could improve the substance of the Sanctuary Agreement. These include considering the consequences for marine mammals of the use of seismic and acoustic means of prospecting and detection, the possible exploitation of non-living natural resources, and the noise and speed of vessels.

The parties will hold regular meetings to ensure the application of and follow up to the Sanctuary Agreement[28]. In this framework they will encourage national and international research programmes as well as public awareness campaigns directed at professional and other users of the sea and non-governmental organisations, relating *inter alia* to the prevention of collisions between vessels and marine mammals and communication to the competent authorities of the presence of dead or distressed marine mammals[29].

The Sanctuary Agreement does not establish a specific institutional framework for the management of the sanctuary. It provides that the periodical meetings of the parties are organised taking into account the already existing structures[30].

The Sanctuary Agreement includes a provision on the sovereign immunity of warships and other ships owned or operated by a State and used on government non-commercial service[31]. The parties must, however, ensure that

---

[25] Article 7(c).

[26] Article 9.

[27] Article 8.

[28] Article 2(1).

[29] Article 12(2).

[30] Article 12(1).

[31] Article 15.

vessels and aircraft, entitled to sovereign immunity under international law, act in a manner consistent with the Sanctuary Agreement.

From the legal point of view, the most critical aspect of the Sanctuary Agreement is the provision on the enforcement on the high seas of the measures agreed upon by the parties. Article 14 provides as follows:

> "1. Dans la partie du sanctuaire située dans les eaux placées sous sa souveraineté ou juridiction, chacun des États Parties au présent accord est compétent pour assurer l'application des dispositions y prévues.
> 2. Dans les autres parties du sanctuaire, chacun des États Parties est compétent pour assurer l'application des dispositions du présent accord à l'égard des navires battant son pavillon, ainsi que, dans les limites prévues par les règles de droit international, à l'égard des navires battant le pavillon d'États tiers"[32].

Most coastal States have so far been reluctant to establish exclusive economic zones (EEZ) in the Mediterranean. The absence of such zones makes the Mediterranean an old-fashioned sea, as the high seas begins just beyond the 12-mile limit of the territorial sea and is much closer to the coast than it is elsewhere. Of the three parties to the Sanctuary Agreement, Italy and Monaco have not yet claimed an EEZ, while France has established it only for its non-Mediterranean waters. Had EEZs been established, the measures provided for in the Sanctuary Agreement would fall under article 65 of the LOS Convention, which allows coastal States to prohibit, limit or regulate the exploitation of marine mammals and promotes international cooperation with a view to their conservation.

Article 14(2) gives the parties the right to enforce on the high seas the provisions of the Sanctuary Agreement with respect to ships flying the flag of third States "within the limits established by the rules of international law". This wording brings an element of ambiguity into the picture, as it can be interpreted in two different ways.

Under the first interpretation, the parties cannot enforce the provisions of the Sanctuary Agreement in respect of foreign ships, as this action would be an encroachment upon the freedom of the high seas.

The second interpretation is based on the fact that all the waters included in the sanctuary would fall within the EEZs of one or another of the three

---

[32] "1. In the part of the sanctuary located in the waters subject to its sovereignty or jurisdiction, any of the States Parties to the present agreement is entitled to ensure the enforcement of the provisions set forth by it. 2. In the other parts of the sanctuary, any of the States Parties is entitled to ensure the enforcement of the provisions of the present agreement with respect to ships flying its flag, as well as, within the limits established by the rules of international law, with respect to ships flying the flag of third States" (unofficial translation).

parties if they decided to establish such zones[33]. With the establishment of the sanctuary the parties have limited themselves to the exercise of only one of the rights which are included in the broad concept of the EEZ. However, the simple but sound argument that those who can do more can also do less *("in plus stat minus")* seems sufficient in order to conclude that the parties can enforce the rules applying in the sanctuary also in respect of foreign ships which are found within its boundaries.

If for the time being the Mediterranean is an old-fashioned sea, it is not necessarily destined to remain as such forever. If one State makes the first move towards proclaiming and effectively implementing an EEZ, several other countries are likely to follow suit. The fact that sooner or later things may change introduces an element of instability into the whole picture of the legal regime of the Mediterranean. However, the sanctuary itself does not seem to be substantially affected by a future establishment (if any) of EEZs. In this event, article 14(2) of the Sanctuary Agreement would no longer apply and the matter of enforcement could be fully covered by article 14(1).

5. CONCLUDING REMARKS

If States were to agree for the conclusion of a future Convention on high seas marine protected areas ("HSMPA") applying on a world basis, some elements for such an instrument could be drawn, *mutatis mutandis*, from the 'pioneer' 1995 Mediterranean Protocol, namely:

- the idea of a list or network of HSMPAs of world importance in the light of a number of criteria (importance for the conservation of biological diversity, ecosystems or habitats of endangered species; special interest at the scientific, aesthetic, cultural or educational level; etc.);
- a procedure for the inclusion of HSMPAs in the list or network based on a decision taken by the contracting parties, which are the trustees of the common interest for the preservation of HSMPAs;
- the adoption of a set of protection and conservation measures on a case by case basis;
- an annex where common criteria for the choice of HSMPAs are specified.

---

[33] In other words, the Mediterranean high seas (that is the waters beyond 12 nautical miles) is different from the high seas located elsewhere in the world's oceans and seas (that is the waters beyond 200 nautical miles) as it will disappear when exclusive economic zones are proclaimed.

The crucial question of free-rider States, which can undermine the effectiveness of the HSMPAs regime, should be carefully addressed. In principle, as every treaty creates rights and obligations only for its contracting parties, the protection and conservation measures agreed upon by the parties to a future HSMPA Convention could not be applicable to ships flying the flag of non-parties. However, it must be considered that every State is already under the obligations arising from customary international law and from the LOS Convention[34] to protect and preserve rare or fragile ecosystems, wherever they are located, and to cooperate for this purpose. Furthermore, special provisions on the relationship with third States, shaped on the model of the 1959 Antarctic Treaty[35] or the 1995 UN Fish Stocks Agreement[36] could be included also in the HSMPA Convention.

ADDENDUM

By Resolution 59/24 of 17 November 2004, the United Nations General Assembly decided:

> "(...) to establish an Ad Hoc Open-ended Informal Working Group to study issues relating to the conservation and sustainable use of marine biological diversity beyond areas of national jurisdiction:
> (a) To survey the past and present activities of the United Nations and other relevant international organizations with regard to the conservation and sustainable use of marine biological diversity beyond areas of national jurisdiction;
> (b) to examine the scientific, technical, economic, legal, environmental, socio-economic and other aspects of these issues;
> (c) To identify key issues and questions where more detailed background studies would facilitate consideration by States of these issues;
> (d) To indicate, where appropriate, possible options and approaches to promote international cooperation and coordination for the conservation and sustainable use of marine biological diversity beyond areas of national jurisdiction".

The Working Group will convene in 2006.

---

[34] Article 194 paragraph 5.

[35] Parties to the HSMPA Convention undertake to adopt appropriate measures, consistent with international law, to ensure that no one engages in any activity contrary to its principles and purposes; see article X of the Antarctic Treaty.

[36] Only those States which are parties to the HSMPA Convention, or which agree to apply the conservation and management measures established under such Convention, have access to activities regulated within a specific HSMPA; see article 8(4) of the Agreement on the Implementation of the Provisions of the UN Convention on the Law of the Sea relating to the Conservation and Management of Straddling Stocks and Highly Migratory Species.

Part II

New Challenges to the Law of the Sea

B.

The principle of the freedom of the high seas
in the post 9/11 world

Chapter 6

INTELLIGENCE GATHERING ON THE HIGH SEAS

*Petros Liacouras**

1. INTRODUCTION

The present paper discusses the legal issues posed by intelligence gathering activities on and underneath the surface of the high seas. Related to the operational rights acknowledged by the law of the sea, intelligence can be used, *inter alia*, as an effective tool towards eliminating surprise. In areas of inclusive jurisdiction, such as the high seas, intelligence may be collected by ships sailing the international waterways. As regards submarine surveillance, the ocean floor beyond the outer limit of the territorial sea is ideally offered for the emplacement of listening or acoustic electronic devices, the so-called "sonar or communication systems", which can observe and detect submerged transport.

User activities may be classified in two distinct categories of rights: a) operational rights and b) movement rights[1]. Under this scheme, military and other non-commercial uses, which are dealt with in this paper, fall within the notion of operational rights relating to the exploitation of the ocean space for specific functions and purposes. This category of rights includes, apart from resource-oriented activities, intelligence gathering, military exercises and manoeuvres, testing of military weapons, as well as scientific research. These specific operational rights correlate with national security activities and concerns. The other category of movement rights relates to mobility and includes navigation on the high seas outside the limit of the territorial sea, innocent passage through the territorial sea and transit passage through straits used for international navigation.

Based on the sharing of authority at sea among coastal and flag States, maritime zones may be classified in three distinct categories: a) zones of na-

---

* Lecturer in International Law, University of Piraeus.

[1] With regard to the two categories of user rights, see Ch. Pirtle, Military Uses of Ocean Space and the Law of the Sea in the Millennium, 31 *ODIL* 2000, pp. 7, 8 *et seq*.

Anastasia Strati, Maria Gavouneli & Nikos Skourtos (eds.), *Unresolved Issues and New Challenges to the Law of the Sea*, Martinus Nijhoff 2006, pp. 123-148.

tional jurisdiction, including internal waters, territorial and archipelagic waters, and to a certain extent straits used for international navigation[2]; b) zones where a coastal State exercises sovereign rights with respect to resource exploitation oriented activities, i.e. the continental shelf and the exclusive economic zone (EEZ); and, finally, c) zones of inclusive jurisdiction, i.e. high seas areas.

2. THE LEGAL REGIME OF THE HIGH SEAS

As a matter of fundamental principle, the high seas are open to use to all nations. Under article 87 of the UN Convention on the Law of the Sea (hereinafter cited as "LOS Convention"), in exercising the enumerated freedoms, i.e. freedom of navigation, overflight, scientific research, construction of artificial islands, fishing and freedom to lay submarine cables and pipelines, States must have due regard to the rights and duties of other States in their exercise of the freedom of the high seas. They must also have due regard to the rights of the coastal States with respect to their sovereign rights over the continental shelf. Most importantly, the list of high seas freedoms under article 87 of the LOS Convention is not exhaustive.

The basic concept underlining conflicting uses on the high seas is to satisfy equally, under the circumstances of each particularly case, the interests of both coastal and flag States. States may in principle satisfy their demands and be benefited without, however, undermining at the same time the public good by either diminishing or acting to the detriment of certain exclusive rights and emerging defence interests of the coastal State concerned. By the same token, self-interests and single-State benefits should be restricted if pursued in areas of common concern. Security affects mainly militarily weak coastal States, but also remain a steady concern of the international community.

2.1. Reservation of the high seas for peaceful purposes

According to article 88 of the LOS Convention, "... the high seas are reserved for peaceful purposes". This concept of peaceful purposes of the areas of inclusive jurisdiction is further elaborated in the unanimous Declaration of Principles of 1970 (GA Resolution 2749) as well as in article 301 of the LOS Convention, which equally applies to all maritime zones. The ex-

---

[2] According to Reisman, "transit passage seems more a species of innocent passage than a high seas freedom"; W.M. Reisman, The Regime of Straits and National Security: An Appraisal of International Lawmaking, 74 *AJIL* 1980, at p. 48.

pression "peaceful purposes" has undergone an evolution in meaning which, though never reaching total clarification has considerably narrowed its scope. It is a decisive factor whether the purpose of activities is or was defensive or whether such activities are consistent with the UN Charter and in particular with articles 2(4) and 51.

2.2. Self-defence and high seas

With regard to the legal treatment of the activities of our topic, the law is in general silent. We consider that both activities, intelligence gathering on the surface and on the seabed through the emplacement of acoustic devises for detection purposes of the total submarine circulation, constitute normal naval activities[3] and act for the user State's self-defence. However, the issue that arises here is whether a State is authorized to proceed to the taking of exclusive measures on high seas areas, either by blockading or by other means, thus, interfering with other' uses, by justifying it on the basis of self-defence.

The critical question is whether States in realizing their activities and strategies – objectives that definitely fall within a clear framework of lawfulness – may deviate from the general rule of either inclusive use or the commitment to have due regard to other common uses. There is a consensus on a global level in favour of undertaking every effort to prevent new wave international security threats, emerging after the end of the cold war era, and primarily terrorism. In this regard, at the domestic level, the military has been assigned the overall responsibility to operate the encountering of the terrorist threat and any other type of uncontrolled migration or any transborder organized crime[4]. As terrorism or criminal acts of the like violate *jus cogens* rules[5] counter-terrorism preventive defence measures come within the ambit of global concern matters.

Many self-defence claims include interdiction on the high seas when a vessel is suspected of carrying weapons of mass destruction or other missiles. Efforts to conclude a comprehensive legal regime have not as yet bore fruits. All the same, a concerted effort to confront suspected vessels on the high seas has been articulated by the consenting States at the 'Proliferation Secu-

---

[3] J. Astley and M. Schmit, The Law of the Sea and Naval Operations, 42 *Air Force Law Review* 1997, pp. 119, 131 and 137.

[4] P. Smith, Military Responses to the Global Migration Crisis: A Glimpse of Things to Come?, 23 *Fletcher Foreign World Affairs* 1999, pp. 77, at p. 79 *et seq.*

[5] R. Beck and A. Arend, Don't Tread on Us: International Law and Forcible State Responses to terrorism, 12 *Wisconsin International Law Journal* 1994, pp. 153, at p. 163.

rity Initiative' announced by US President G.W. Bush on 31 May 2003[6]. This initiative has been concluded only by eleven States, including the US. Support for this initiative, confronting one of the aspects of contemporary terrorism, which occurs on the high seas, has been limited to co-operation among the consenting States. Co-operation in this domain includes boarding, searching and capturing of the cargo of the vessels suspected for carrying and trafficking missiles and other weapons of mass destruction[7]. The said consenting States are under the obligation to exchange information about suspected vessels. Implemented by a series of bilateral or multilateral treaties concluded between the consenting states, the initiative is based upon the consent of the flag State to grant permission for the searching of its suspected for such illicit trafficking vessel.

Interdiction on the high seas of a suspected vessel carrying weapons to be consumed at the territory of the target State is but one aspect of self-defence claims. As regards conventional law, there has been no relevant international binding treaty yet in force suppressing high seas maritime terrorism. Only piracy is a punishable crime under the LOS Convention and the 1958 Geneva Convention on the High Seas. No convention aiming at prevention, co-operation and communication in the field of sharing information is yet in effect[8].

Reference should also be made of the so-called "ship-rider agreements", which have been concluded between the United States and Caribbean States with the aim of countering drug trafficking[9]. These agreements provide for extensive rights to boarding within other consenting States' territorial or internal waters or interdiction on the high seas of suspected vessels, in contravention to the exclusive flag State jurisdiction. These efforts lend useful ideas of how to shape a multilateral mechanism for confronting and suppressing terrorism. For the time being though, as it has been noted, there is still long way to go until these widespread conventional efforts and similar initiatives would generate any customary rule[10].

---

[6] M. Byers, Policing the High Seas: The Proliferation Security Initiative, 98 *AJIL* 2004, pp. 526, at p. 527-528.

[7] S. Murphy, 'Proliferation Security Initiative' for Searching Potential WMD Vessels, 98 *AJIL* 2004, p. 355.

[8] J. Mellor, Missing the Boat: The Legal and Practical Problems of the Prevention of Maritime Terrorism, 18 *American University International Law Review* 2002, pp. 341, at pp. 384-386.

[9] L. Davis-Mattis, International Drug Trafficking and the Law of the Sea: Outstanding Issues and Bilateral Responses with Emphasis on US-Caribbean Agreements, 15 *Ocean Yearbook* 2000, p. 280.

[10] Byers, *supra* note 6, at p. 534.

Self-defence claims are also raised with regard to acts directed against the territorial integrity and wider security interests of the assaulted State. Intelligence gathering is linked to precautionary measures taken in order to either prevent or confront sudden attacks or other international or regional friction. Information may be collected with regard to any act that either directs against a State or regards the international security and can impede the incipient development of an assault to mature.

2.2.1. Self-defence incidents

In a number of occasions, exclusive measures on the high seas have been justified on the customary rule of self-defence.

As early as 1955 Myres McDougal argued in favour of the hydrogen bomb test off shore Marshall Islands in the Pacific. The United States conducted these tests and excluded other States from using this high seas area. In fact, the United States issued the normal notice to airmen in order not to suspend or impede normal maritime traffic. Interference with navigation routes was minimal, as was interference with regard to fishing. According to McDougal, in case undue interference arises, relevant is the test of reasonableness, which underlies them all – the test that decided between fishing and navigation and all that great variety of claims, which may interfere with navigation and fishing. Paramount in the United States' considerations was the right to prepare for self-defence. That factor was deemed as the most relevant in appraising the exclusion of high seas areas and testing of weapons there. It should also be noted that it was not a claim as commonly used in cases of responding to an armed attack. As has been observed, since there was no armed attack, it was a claim to take preparatory measures under conditions comparable to those traditionally held to justify measures in self-defence. The blockade was considered a claim to take exclusive activities, including military means, arguing that, acting under conditions of necessity, it did not intend to nullify the high seas freedoms, but in fact in its exercise it caused the minimum interference with other uses. The meaning of threat, which creates the state of necessity ranges from a threat coming from a State that is viewed as an enemy – as of another camp back in the bipolar system – or by a State-sponsored terrorist group[11].

The Cuban quarantine of 1962 is the second incident in which self-defence was claimed by the United States for blockading a certain part of the high seas. The quarantine was deemed an act of a State, which was the target of

---

[11] M.S. McDougal & N. Schlei, The Hydrogen Bomb Tests in Perspective: Lawful Measures for Security, 64 *Yale Law Journal* 1955, pp. 648, at pp. 682-688.

activities by another State, and that, as was eloquently stated, such activities "imminently required reaction by unilateral action in order to protect and secure territorial integrity and human survival". Cuba's blockade was considered as an exercise of the right of self-defence on the high seas[12]. The argument in favour of self-defence was based on the rule of necessity and proportionality. In this regard, the Assistant Attorney General to the State Department had stated: "It was clearly a preventive action in self-defence and the need for it was instant, overwhelming, leaving no choice of means, and no moment for deliberation"[13]. Self-defence was claimed prior to the occurrence of an actual armed attack and in that sense the US acted in anticipation of harmful events against its vital interests.

2.2.2. The contemporary notion of self-defence

Self-defence, under article 51 of the UN Charter, is the inherent right of any State confronted with an armed attack to react. Contemporary threats or the rise of new forms of challenges for the international system, due to changes in military technology and political organization, such as "rogue States", could not have been foreseen by the drafters of the UN Charter[14]. The combined reading of articles 2 and 51 of the UN Charter cannot and shall not remain doctrinal[15]. While prohibiting use of interstate force, the drafters of the UN Charter the framer did not intend to limit the customary law of self-defence. Necessity, imminence of peril in case the attack is certain or about to occur, and proportionality of response to the armed attack should be preconditioned in order to make self-defence a legitimate means.

Anticipatory self-defence arose from the old Caroline incident[16] but has been repeatedly appraised in several other international incidents. It is a claimed right of an intended victim either to prepare for defence, when an at-

---

[12] M. S. McDougal, The Cuban Quarantine, 57 *AJIL* 1963, p. 597.

[13] N. Shlei, From the Bag: Anticipatory Self-Defense: A 1962 OLC Opinion on Lawful Alternatives for the US in the Cuban Missile Crisis, 6 *Green Bag 2d* 2003, 195.

[14] For the views of the US with regard to self-defence, see W. Nagan & C. Hammer, The New Bush National Security Doctrine and the Rule of Law, 22 *Berkeley Journal of International Law* 2004, 375.

[15] J. Yoo, Using Force, 71 *University of Chicago Law Review* 2004, p. 729, at p. 731. Yoo classifies the different views of the permission of use of force under international law. As observed, the UN drafters "designed their system to win the last war, not the next"; *ibid.*, p. 736.

[16] In the 1837 *Caroline* case, Canadian forces destroyed an American vessel, which was going to be used against Canada by Canadian insurgents and American volunteers. According to Judge Webster, the right of anticipatory self-defence arises only when there is a necessity of self-defence, instant, overwhelming, leaving no choice of means and no means and no moment of deliberation; see further Shlei, *supra*, note 13.

tack occurs, or to react in anticipation in order to avoid the attack[17]. As argued in favour of anticipatory self-defence, when the attack occurs, it could in fact deliver an unacceptable measure of damage[18]. Anticipatory self-defence may eliminate harm caused by a surprise attack, when reaction may be either meaningless or a fatally late action. It should be noted, however, that self-defence must be viewed as a constraining force in any governmental decision, as reiterated recourse to force by labelling it self-defence may leave loopholes in the system of international security. The imminence of threat or attack is the key factor for appraising the legitimacy of claims of anticipatory self-defence.

Pre-emptive self-defence is a rather novel term in the literature of international law and politics. This term is broader than the concept of anticipatory self-defence. It is a claim to use unilaterally, and without prior international authorization, such as a decision of the UN Security Council, "high levels of violence to arrest an incipient development that is not yet operational, but if permitted to mature could then be neutralized at a higher and possibly unacceptable cost"[19]. Pre-emptive action, when other means failed or have been exhausted, corresponds to a concept of flexibility to recourse to force as the certainty of a sudden attack increases, leaving to the State a margin of appreciation of the magnitude of the harm and the decision to prevent it. Pre-emptive self-defence cannot be indiscriminate. The target of the emerging doctrine remains the so-called "rogue" or "failed" States, which sponsor and nourish international terrorism as well as other similar States that possess weapons of mass destruction threatening international security[20]. Pre-emptive self-defence has been challenged by a number of academics as an arbitrary norm, which employs unauthorized force. However, it relates to the confrontation of a threat at a very early stage.

---

[17] Th. Franck, Terrorism and the Right to Self-Defence, 95 *AJIL* 2001, p. 839; *idem.*, Future Implication of the Iraq Conflict: What Happens Now? The United Nations after Iraq, 97 *AJIL* 2003, p. 607; D. Brown, Use of Force Against terrorism after September 11th: State Responsibility, Self-Defence and other responses, 11 *Cardozo Journal of International and Comparative Law* 2003, p. 1, at pp. 37-44.

[18] W.M. Reisman, Editorial comment: Assessing Claims to revise the Laws of War, 97 *AJIL* 2003, p. 82, at p. 84.

[19] *Ibid.*, p. 87. *Contra* M.E. O'Connell, Review Essay: Re-Leashing the Dogs of War: International Law and the Use of Force by Ch. Gray, Oxford University Press, New York 2000, 97 *AJIL* 2003, p. 446, at p. 452.

[20] P. Williams, Pre-emption in the 21st Century: What Are the Legal Parameters, 10 *ILSA Journal of International and Comparative Law* 2004, p. 353, at p. 354. This doctrine has served as the basis for arguing about the lawfulness of US military campaign against Iraq in March 2003. The view contained in William's note supports US positions from the point of that country's legal adviser.

Intelligence gathering is a means to assess the intentions and the capabilities of the enemy, in terms of military weapons and forces as well as other technological capabilities that may contribute to a successful enemy's sudden attack. Intelligence may trace to the enemy's harboured cell and may detect its further recruitment and its detailed overt or covert moves. Unpredictability of the moment the enemy's attack is going to occur characterizes the intended but non-warned victim's inability to react. This makes deterrence a difficult task and strengthens the necessity to take pre-emptive measures in order to avoid inflicting damage. Intelligence as a self-defence act is a means to react early to the enemy's preparations and final attack, whether certain, possible or distant, including those emanating from terrorist groups or networks, to prevent from damaging innocent civilian population and the hurting the country's integrity and stature. Further prevention may contribute to alienate and arrest an incipient development. As has been pointed out, arguing in favour of pre-emption, this doctrine includes "proactive proliferation efforts such as detection, active and passive defences, and counter-force capabilities, which are fully integrated into defence policy"[21].

2.2.3. Intelligence gathering on the high seas as self-defence in light of terrorist threats

Both intelligence gathering on the surface of the high seas and emplacement of detecting devices on the seabed constitute high seas freedoms serving the State's legitimate and vital interests in the name of self-defence[22]. Intelligence gathering should be appraised and reconsidered particularly in the light of the terrorist attacks of 11 September 2001 and in the context of substantive background to react to or prevent a future attack. Preparation based on intelligence is a relevant factor in appraising self-defence.

Terrorism has to be seen as detached from a constrained view of its punishment under conventional international law. The simultaneous September 11 attacks gave a different angle in international law[23]. It has created some confusion as to whether non-State violence deriving from terrorist activities falls within the notion of "force", which gives rise to self-defence by the

---

[21] *Ibid.*, p. 356. This is a legal view grounded at the US National Security Strategy in the frame of a reactive posture to act pre-emptively against any State that is a suspect of supporting terrorism.

[22] R. Scott, Legal Aspects of Information Warfare: Military Disruption of Telecommunications, 45 *Naval Law Review* 1998, p. 57, at p. 61. Scott deals with the issue of self-defence in organized information-gathering activities.

[23] See M. Lippman, The New Terrorism and International Law, 10 *Tulsa Journal of Comparative and International Law* 2003, p. 297, at p. 303.

State victim[24]. However, the subsequent response of the Security Council has shed ample light on this question.

2.2.4. International terrorism

In the aftermath of September 11, the Security Council unequivocally condemned terrorist attacks, with Resolution 1368 recognizing terrorism as an international crime against which any victim State maintains its inherent right to self-defence. Resolution 1368 calls upon all States to increase efforts and take all necessary measures so as to prevent as well as to suppress terrorist acts, including implementation of international antiterrorist conventions and the relevant Security Council Resolutions. In particular, the Security Council stressed the necessity to take all appropriate measures in accordance with its responsibilities under the UN Charter.

Also, subsequent UN Security Council Resolution 1373 reaffirmed the need to combat all forms of terrorism and declared it a threat to international peace and security. It also confirmed the victim's right to self-defence and all States' commitment to cooperate, through bilateral and multilateral arrangements and agreements, in order to prevent and suppress terrorist attacks. The Resolution calls upon all States to take action against perpetrators of such acts. Resolution 1373 refers to the taking of necessary measures and actions in order to prevent the further commission of terrorist attacks. Primary concern is focused on early warning and exchange of information. The UN Security Council condemns the terrorist acts against western civilization and the international community as a whole, qualifying these acts as a crime against humanity and a matter of global concern[25]. This treatment entails universal jurisdiction[26].

The aforementioned Resolutions, echoing widely shared common views, underscore the necessity of coordinating efforts and steps and taking preemptive measures in order to combat international terrorism on a global scale. This amounts to anticipatory self-defence against an elevated international crime. The victim State reserves its intrinsic right to self-defence while the implementation of UN Security Council Resolutions is considered

---

[24] K. Watkin, Controlling the Use of Force: A Role for Human Rights Norms in Contemporary Armed Conflict, 98 *AJIL* 2004, p. 1, at pp. 3-6.

[25] Lippman, *supra* note 23, pp. 358-361.

[26] M. Zaid, Universal Jurisdiction: Myths, Realities and Prospects: Will or Should the United States Ever Prosecute War Criminals?: A Need for Greater Expansion in the Areas of Both Criminal and Civil Liability, 35 *New England Law Review* 2001, p. 447.

as a measure against terrorism. In any case, preventing terrorism is less costly in terms of human lives and casualties.

Terrorists are non-State actors[27], mostly wealthy, sponsored and hosted by States, some called "rogue", "failed" or "ending", in which they operate and organize the sudden attack[28]. Their effective capacity depends chiefly on surprising a targeted, unexpectedly exposed, victim of asymmetric warfare[29], as there is no ready mechanisms to detect whether a terrorist attack is certain or about to be launched imminently and the time to respond is decreased[30]. Usually they deploy the most sophisticated weapons and high technology that command high levels of counter-terrorist responsive preparations and planning[31]; however, the September 11 terrorists employed no weapons. In addition, they mostly self-portray cosmopolitan citizens beyond any reasonable suspicion of committing an outrageous international crime. Although stressing self-perceived religious motivations and martyrdom they, at the end of the day, threaten irreparably the established international security, malevolently alienate innocent civilians' lives and mark an unprecedented global horror. Harold Koh has observed that "September 11 was an attack not just on civilians but on the very spirit of international law"[32].

Terrorism whose impact may not be easily detected is as a possible attack to occur and, thus, cannot be viewed either as occurred or imminent or *ante portas*. Terrorism is a new kind of warfare entirely unusual than any anticipated threat[33]. Pointing to the importance of immediate response and preparation based on intelligence, pre-emptive anti-terrorist self-defence of global concern[34] is mainly supported by intelligence gathering and subsequent sharing of collected information. Noteworthy that conventional law or any kind

---

[27] For a definition of the term see Watkin, *supra* note 24, pp. 6-8.

[28] W. Sharp, Sr., American Hegemony and International Law: The Use of Armed Force Against Terrorism: American Hegemony or Impotence?, 1 *Chicago Journal of International Law* 2000, p. 37, at p. 38.

[29] C. Gray, *America's Defence of the New World Order* (University Press of Kentucky, Louisville 2004) pp. 116-119.

[30] Yoo, *supra* note 15, p. 750.

[31] Watkin, *supra* note 24, pp. 8-9.

[32] H. Koh, The Spirit of the Laws, 43 *Harvard International Law Journal* 2002, p. 23, at p. 25.

[33] Gray, *supra* note 29, p. 117.

[34] M. Morris, Universal Jurisdiction: Myths and Realities and Prospects: Universal Jurisdiction in a Divided World: Conference Remarks, 35 *New England Law Review* 2001, p. 337, at p. 349; S. Sucharitkul, Jurisdiction, Terrorism and the Rule of International Law, 32 *Golden Gate University Law Review* 2002, p. 311.

of regulation cannot stop or prevent future terrorist acts and other peaceful means of reducing civilian casualties and redressing security is decreased[35].

As an example, in light of current terrorism and claims of pre-emptive self-defence as stated in its National Security Strategy, the United States has sought to extend claims of self-defence to more distant and immature challenges[36]. The necessity to react to the imminent or even distant threat of terrorism and the illicit trafficking of weapons of mass destruction may transfer implementation of self-defence at sea.

3. CHARACTERISTICS AND NATURE OF "INTELLIGENCE"

The concept of "intelligence" comprises the gathering, evaluation and dissemination of information essential to decision making. Intelligence is a critical function at all levels of better-informed decision-making[37]. Critical importance of reliable intelligence is clearly reflected in many incidents in the history of the so-called national security of the various single States[38]. In this vein, the latest terrorist attack against the twin towers and the Pentagon in the United States is of pivotal importance. To the extent that intelligence gathering can act, for any State, through knowledge in advance, as an early warning mechanism and offer any State the possibility of preventing such devastating incidents, the use of intelligence as an instrument of pre-emptive action and self-defence seems justified for the victim[39].

By 'gathering' we refer to the operations by which information can be collected and retrieved. It may be a highly sophisticated operation, such as the deduction from a number of equivocal and apparently unrelated events, of a military technological advance. Gathering may be completed either by human beings or mechanically by receptors.

---

[35] M. Halberstam, The US Right to Use Force in Response to the Attacks on the Pentagon and the World Trade Center, 11 *Cardozo Journal of International and Comparative Law* 2004, p. 851, at 861-862.

[36] M. Byers, Pre-emptive Self-Defence: Hegemony, Equality and Strategies of Legal Change, 11 *Journal of Political Philosophy* 2003, p. 171, at p. 181.

[37] G. Demarest, Espionage in International Law, 24 *Denver Journal of International Law & Policy* 1996, p. 321, at pp. 322-323.

[38] M.S. McDougal, H. Lasswell & W.M. Reisman, The Intelligence Function and World Public Order, *in* M.S. McDougal & W.M. Reisman, *International Law Essays: A Supplement to International Law in Contemporary Perspective* (The Foundation Press, New York) p. 287, at p. 298.

[39] J. Barkham, Information Warfare and International Law on the Use of Force, 34 *New York University Journal of International Law and Politics* 2001, p. 57, at p. 104.

4. INTELLIGENCE AND JURISDICTION

Each medium that is accessed through advanced technology would either be dispersed and/or be held on a sovereign territory or maritime zone of national jurisdiction (e.g. land, territorial sea and national airspace) or else be shared in common (e.g. the high seas or international airspace and outer space)[40]. As has been noted, intelligence gathering on vessels sailing in international waters is permitted in principle. It is established that apart from remote sensing, the legality of the act is predicated on the physical location and not on the activity itself[41]. Intelligence collection is essential in giving substance to the right of self-defence including all kinds of it, i.e. the anticipatory as well as pre-emptive self-defence. As has clearly been observed: "Appropriate defensive preparations cannot be made without information about physical threats"[42].

Intelligence gathering shall not be conflated with espionage. Intelligence is permitted by international law, if it is conducted in areas of common use or else of similarly inclusive jurisdiction. On the other hand, espionage refers principally to collecting critical information from a foreign territory – including zones of national jurisdiction, i.e. territorial waters, internal waters and national airspace – either in time of peace or war[43]. Espionage regularly results in violating territorial integrity and in unauthorized intervening against a State to the detriment of its integrity and of its political independence.

Collecting information in a foreign territory is considered a threat or in any event a physical invasion of that territory and in that sense it remains a breach of the territorial integrity of the intruded State. According to some academics, such an act is a clear-cut threat and invasion of that territory[44]. However, even in this case, i.e. arbitrary collection of information, claiming self-defence is a sustainable argument. Furthermore, espionage is a punishable offence only by national criminal law; international law treats it differently[45]. As has been observed, espionage is not illegal under customary in-

---

[40] S. Kanuk, Recent development: Information Warfare: New Challenges for Public International Law, 37 *Harvard International Law Journal* 1996, p. 272, at p. 286.

[41] McDougal, Lasswell & Reisman, *supra* note 38, pp. 309-310.

[42] R. Scott, Territorially Intrusive Collection and International Law, 46 *Air Force Law Review* 1999, p. 217, at p. 224.

[43] Ch. Baker, Tolerance of International Espionage: A Functional Approach, 19 *American University International Law Review* 2004, p. 1091, at p. 1094.

[44] See, *inter alia*, Scott, *supra* note 42, p. 223. It is a shared view that espionage should be conducted within normative limits.

[45] M. Robbat, Resolving the Legal Issues Concerning the Use of Information Warfare in the International Forum: The Reach of the Existing Legal Framework and the Creation of a New Paradigm, 6 *Boston University Journal of Science & Technology* 2000, p. 10.

ternational law[46]. Arguably, "espionage may be justified by corollary: in order to ensure that the right of self-defence retains substantive meaning, international law must permit States to predict armed attack. Therefore, for States to enjoy the positively-codified right to self-defence, they should retain the right to acquire in formation that would indicate whether they face imminent armed attack"[47].

Collecting information about weapons of mass destruction and about fomenting terrorist groups and networks may be considered as a lawful exercise of anticipatory or pre-emptive self-defence[48]. Observational, collection activities, even in breach of domestic regulation, can not be seen as a challenge to the non-intervention principle especially when related to self-defence in time of peace[49].

On the high seas each State is authorized to exercise its right of self-defence[50], in so far as this act creates the minimum interference to the other uses. Intelligence is principally a pre-emptive action. It includes gathering of data from any source, which is critical in preparing to the early combating as well as preventing any attack, including terrorism, prior to its damaging occurrence. In that sense it may result to a minimum scale interference of other high seas uses.

In the context of punishing international criminal acts conducted on the high seas, the law of the sea deals only with piracy, article 100 of the LOS Convention entailing universal jurisdiction by seizing the pirate vessel and by further exercising criminal jurisdiction over the persons involved, in order to punishing them[51]. Terrorism, occurring on the high seas and equally intelligence gathering or other defensive activities serving the national and international security remain not regulated matters[52].

---

[46] Kanuk, *supra* note 40, at p. 276.

[47] Baker, *supra* note 43, p. 1096.

[48] Scott, *supra* note 42, p. 225.

[49] *Ibid.*, p. 218. Further to that argument with regard to self-defence, Roger Scott stresses that espionage is not prohibited by any international conventions because all states show an interest in the activity.

[50] D. Kash, Abductions of Terrorists in International Airspace and on the High Seas, 8 *Florida Journal of International Law* 1993, p. 65, at p. 79. Douglas Kash refers to terrorist acts that occur on the high seas, which justify self-defence. Further, he refers to the three international law principles which entail jurisdiction over the terrorists, namely the protective principle, the passive personality principle and the universality principle.

[51] *Ibid.*, pp. 83-84: "Nations, victimized by terrorists, are sometimes left with no choice but to assert themselves forcefully to apprehend terrorists and bring them to the abducting State for prosecution.

[52] Pirtle, *supra* note 1, pp. 9 *et seq.*

5. INTELLIGENCE GATHERING IN AREAS OF INCLUSIVE COMPETENCE – INTERFERENCE WITH HIGH SEAS FREEDOM

It is commonly accepted that sharable resources are free to access and use by all States in order to satisfy lawful pursuits. Intelligence gathering is a lawful activity to the extent that it does not interfere with other uses or deprives other States from use. States that maintain fleets for information gathering justify their activity on the claim of self-defence. Nevertheless, intelligence, which interferes with other uses has been the target of protests by the States concerned. In such a case, intelligence gathering is deemed delictual, especially when instrumentalities cannot justify deprivations created to other users from having access to and profit from the sharable resources[53]. It would seem, however that, as argued, self-defence prevails over any disturbance or interference with other uses. But even in such a case, it is equally held that collecting should create the minimum interference.

Airspace and outer space share the same normative regime governing the high seas with regard to intelligence gathering. The stratosphere and the space beyond it, superjacent to the national air space, do not share the sovereign regime of the territory and the territorial waters[54].

On the high seas, intelligence gathering by sailing vessels is free to all States. User States are under an obligation to operate with "due regard" to other users and high seas freedoms. Intelligence gathering by ships on the high seas, with the system of remote sensing, may interfere with other uses, in particular with frequencies, which are essential for the successful function of satellites.

A further problem arises as to whether the blockade of a high seas area exclusively for intelligence gathering in defence of national interest is lawful. This brings us back to a similar legal question posed with regard to the Cuban quarantine in 1962[55]. In that particular case, the doctrine of self-defence prevailed. As maintained intensely by the United States government, States must have a proportionately greater freedom to protect their vital interests by

---

[53] McDougal, Lasswell & Reisman, *supra* note 38, p. 311. For example, the authors refer to the structuring of a tower for purposes of intelligence gathering in a customary sea-lane, which would transform a lawful act into a delictual deprivation of the others' use of the high seas.

[54] Kanuk, *supra* note 40, p. 279. In addition, the sub-stratosphere superjacent to national State territory is assimilated to its exclusive territorial jurisdiction. It is not a shared resource and it is not therefore subject to the unqualified intelligence-gathering activities of the high seas and the lower reaches of space. Insofar intelligence activities do not extend beyond passive monitoring they are assimilated to its exclusive territorial jurisdiction; see McDougal, Lasswell & Reisman, *supra* note 38, p. 311.

[55] See *supra* note 12 and accompanying text.

unilateral action of self-defence. According to the position of the United States, this is a right to protect the country itself by preventing a condition of affairs from which, if it develops, it will be too late to protect it. This underlines the acknowledged claim of anticipatory self-defence[56]. Intelligence gathering on the high seas surface can be claimed as anticipatory or preemptive self-defence. It may be maintained that States should acquire foreknowledge of the threat and its large or small, apparent or covert capabilities. It is a preparation to respond to an imminent or certain or even a possible or yet distant threat, it is a measure proportional to the goal of combating threats, which permit no choice of means and no moment for deliberation. The test of reasonableness was a prevailing concept with regard to other uses.

Sometimes intelligence vessels exclude areas of high seas. It may be recalled that quarantine or blockades in time of peace "… have been generally considered a lawful measure of self-defence to which naval powers resorted against the wrongdoer". While it is difficult to state the limits of the right of self-defence, it is clear that the immediacy of the threat and the proportionality of the response are essential to the legality of the self-defence operations, as exemplified in the Cuban and Algerian crises.

During the Cuban Missile crisis, by the presidential decision of 23 October 1962, the United States reserved the right to arrest and to inspect any vessel on the high seas that was travelling towards Cuba, in order to ascertain whether they carried missiles. For the US, this maritime quarantine was based on the Soviet Union's decision to install long-range missiles on Cuban territory[57]. The US declared that this act was a threat to its national and the western- hemisphere security. The United States wanted to stop any transfer of missiles to Cuba, and have those already installed removed[58]. However, according to the opposite view shared by Professor Quincy Wright[59], "this

---

[56] McDougal, *supra* note 12.

[57] In carrying out this order, as is noted, force shall not be used except in case of failure or refusal to comply with directions, or with regulations or directives of the Secretary of Defence issued hereunder, after reasonable efforts have been made to communicate them to the vessel or craft, or in case of self-defence. In any case, force shall be used only to the extent necessary.

[58] More specifically, any vessel or craft which may be proceeding toward Cuba may be intercepted and may be directed to identify it, to stop, to lie to, to submit to visit and search, or to proceed as directed. Any vessel or craft, which fails or refuses to respond or to comply with directions, shall be subject to being taken into custody. Any vessel or craft which is believed is en route to Cuba and may be carrying prohibited material or may itself constitute such material shall, whenever possible, be directed to proceed to another direction of its own choice All vessels or craft taken into custody shall be sent into a port of the United States for appropriate disposition.

[59] Q. Wright, The Cuban Quarantine, 57 *AJIL* 1963, p. 546.

maritime quarantine was deemed contrary to the principle of the freedom of the high seas, and even though armed force was not actually used".

France undertook a similar surveillance activity against Algeria[60]. It also intercepted and ascertained thousands of vessels suspected of trafficking illicit weapons to Algeria. Opponents argued that this act runs contrary to international law and in particular to articles 2(4) and 51 of the UN Charter in the absence of an armed attack[61].

The conclusion drawn from these international incidents is that when States are under overwhelming threat, the claim of exercising exclusive jurisdiction over foreign vessels and blocking high seas areas for exclusive use are deemed a lawful measure of self-defence. In this sense self-defence is deemed superior comparable to the obligation of due regard to the high seas common uses reserved to all States.

Particular forms of intelligence by sailing vessels, submarines or even aircraft are considered within the framework of national self-defence. The UN Charter recognizes the right to self-defence against armed aggression. The States perceive the threat of armed aggression differently and international law has not attempted to codify precisely the circumstances that justify the use of self-defence. The UN Charter cannot limit self-defence, when claimed by an imminently threatened State. As it has been maintained, the concept of threat should follow the evolution of law and correspond to the meaning given to the concept today[62]. In fact, in 1945 the drafters of the UN Charter could not have predicted that anticipatory self-defence would have been un-

---

[60] During the Algerian Revolution, French authorities arrested and submitted to inspection in the areas of high seas in the Mediterranean and elsewhere numerous foreign commercial vessels suspected of supplying arms and munitions to the Algerian rebels. This public act of the state of France was brought before the French courts by the affected shipping companies, but was "not held subject to trial, since it bore upon the international relations of the French State". In a similar case concerning a vessel flying the Italian flag, the *Duizar* case, transiting the high seas, the French Minister of Defence maintained that the boarding of the vessel was a lawful measure of self-defence, while the Paris Administrative Tribunal held that the operation of the French Navy was a "measure of police affecting the external safety of the State [which was] necessary for safety reasons, and had no vexatious character".

[61] See, *inter alia*, R.R. Churchill & V. Lowe, *The Law of the Sea* (3rd ed., Manchester University Press, Manchester 1999) pp. 65-69. The French public act of arrest and inspection of the vessel on the high seas was largely criticized first on the grounds that the area of operations was disproportionately too large and, second, the response taken in the name of self-defence was not measured to be in proportion to the perceived threat.

[62] This view has been mainly maintained by Professor W. M. Reisman, *supra* note 17. Also the ICJ in the *Aegean Sea* case stressed that "meaning ... intended to follow the evolution of the law and to correspond with the meaning attached to the expression by the law in force today"; ICJ Reports 1978, par. 77, p. 33. This Court's view was expressed with regard to the question whether the continental shelf doctrine falls within the meaning of territorial status.

avoidable. In 1945, no one could foresee the innovation and overproduction of weapons of mass destruction or even the expansion of State-supported terrorism employing such weapons. Equally, any kind of intimidation coming from asymmetric warfare could not have been thought of. Under these circumstances of military weapon development and technology innovations, it may be too late to wait for the enemy to strike the first blow. Preparation to encounter terrorism is not merely a matter of militarising the notion of national security perception. The need for intelligence to support effective exercise of the right of the anticipatory or pre-emptive self-defence is greater in today's fiction-filled, multi-polar world than it has ever been before.

As it has interestingly been noted, intelligence accomplishes the requirements in order to exercise lawful self-defence and in that sense exclusionary intelligence gathering derives from the lawfulness of self-defence[63]. Even intelligence resulting to interference with other uses is generally recognized as a freedom of the high seas, provided that the rules of reasonableness and due regard to other uses have under the circumstances been at least to a certain extent observed. This requirement is dictated by article 87 of the LOS Convention. Intelligence could be justified for self-defence purposes provided that such a right remains within the objectives of the freedom of the seas.

Exclusion for intelligence-gathering purposes of a particular area, that may interfere with other uses within the same area, may be justified on existing precedents. Self-defence was appraised as superior to any obligation of due regard to the freedoms of the high seas, even when an attack was possible or about to occur. As it has been noted, even in the case of blockade, disturbance to other high seas uses is minimal. This factor is the most relevant with respect to appraising lawfulness of certain exclusive activities on the high seas of this kind. In the 1962 Cuban quarantine incident the threat was imminent and the means necessary to confront that threat. Since intelligence gathering is necessary to eliminate international crisis and casualties and to guard against surprise, it may be considered as an act of self-defence as it detects the occurrence of the attack in anticipation.

With respect to national security concerns associated with military conflict, governments array their first class technologies; technology is a substantial indicator of current capabilities. Minimization of military involvement is an aspiring goal in order to avoid conflict and casualties. To that end, special measures to gather information from any source are considered necessary to maintain international legal order[64]. Accordingly, particular forms of

---

[63] Baker, *supra* note 43, p. 1097.

[64] J.-A. Romano, Note: Combating Terrorism and Weapons of Mass Destruction: Reviving the Doctrine of the State of Necessity, 87 *Georgetown Law Journal* 1999, p. 1023, at pp.

information gathering may give rise to a reaction in response. The right of self-defence certainly justifies the collection of intelligence. Intelligence is necessary to give substance and effect to the right of self-defence, including anticipatory or pre-emptive self-defence. Appropriate defensive preparations cannot be made without information about potential threats[65].

6. INTELLIGENCE GATHERING ON THE SEABED

Emplacement of sonar systems or other acoustic devices on the seabed is a different issue. Some of these devices are "associated with the operation of ships" and remain an essential means of collecting information essential to targeting and navigation. Sonic detection devices on the seabed help the emplacing State make more "efficient use of [its own] warships and submarines", by giving it "recourse to the best available means of locating the position and tracing the movements of" the submarines of the coastal State. As it has been noted, knowledge about the movement of submarines at the era of nuclear deterrence played an important role in preventing surprise attacks and still supports the taking of precautionary measures[66].

Communication devices emplaced on the seabed can observe and detect the route and direction of suspected submarines, especially carrying nuclear weapons, and may provide critical information about their travelling through the water column. Detecting systems may also be attached to submarines collecting information about military activities.

At first academics expressed apprehension regarding the safeguard of free access and the emplacement of detecting devises as a high seas freedom. It has thus been contended that anti-submarine warfare presumes freedom of navigation and free access to the seabed in order to emplace sophisticated listening or acoustic electronic devices. In the same vein, it has been pointed out that there is a benefit from observation and in order to contribute to the early warning about the submarines' movement, freedom of access and emplacement should be safeguarded[67]. Collection of information as a pre-emptive activity is predominant in order to avoid surprise, far prior to the

---

1039-1044. However, these measures may not be justified, if they were so intrusive or offensive as to threaten the internal order of a State in which they were employed.

[65] Scott, *supra* note 41, p. 224.

[66] T. Treves, Military Installations, Structures and Devices on the Seabed, 74 *AJIL* 1980, p. 808, at p. 810.

[67] As it is contended, these freedoms are necessary for the purpose of identifying and locating suspected submarines in order to provide the essential early warning of a possible attack as well as locating the transport of submarines. J. Wang, *Handbook on Ocean Politics and Law* (Greenwood Press, New York 1992) p. 371.

occurrence of an armed attack. As it was characteristically noted: "Anti-submarine warfare is basically a silent surveillance war game conducted below the surface of the oceans"; "surveillance of the water column should be viewed as a matter of watching the 'archer' before he fires the 'arrow'"[68].

The emplacement of detecting systems follows the distinction between the different areas of the seabed, beyond the outer limit of the bed of the territorial sea of each coastal State. On the high seas, emplacement is guaranteed free access. Several coastal States have argued that within zones of national jurisdiction emplacement could be claimed for exclusive use.

As regards the claim for exclusive use of the continental shelf for placing such devices, the law of the sea is silent. The LOS Convention does not shed light as to how this sharable use can accommodate conflicting claims and who may claim exclusive control over the detection systems emplaced on the continental shelf.

6.1. Continental shelf

In light of the doctrine of the continental shelf, emplacement of such objects on the ocean bed is perceived as a high seas freedom. The continental shelf is reserved to the coastal State for the exclusive exploitation of its natural resources. More specifically, the coastal State enjoys on its continental shelf "sovereign rights for the purpose of exploring and exploiting its natural resources". However, in exercising its sovereign rights the coastal State must have due regard to the other uses, which fall within high seas freedoms. According to article 87 of the LOS Convention, such freedoms "shall be exercised by all States with due regard to the interests of other States in the exercise of the freedom of the high seas". States wishing to emplace detection or communication devices on the continental shelf are obliged to have "due regard" to the exercise of other States' high seas freedoms. There is also an obligation for any State that acts within the framework of the high seas freedom to have due regard to the sovereign rights of the coastal State with respect to the exploration of the continental shelf and the exploitation of its natural resources. Actually, the argument in favour of coastal jurisdiction over the emplacement of detecting systems on the continental shelf focuses on the fact that placing objects would most probably interfere with the continental shelf rights of the coastal State[69].

---

[68] *Ibid.*, p. 372.
[69] Treves, *supra* note 66.

In this respect, it may be useful to refer to the *travaux préparatoires* of the First UN Conference on the Law of the Sea. An Indian proposal to reserve the right to emplacement of sonic objects and other military installations exclusively for the coastal State under the continental shelf doctrine was rejected. Thus, under the 1958 Geneva Convention on the Continental Shelf, emplacement of detecting systems is free both in terms of access and use. Nevertheless, emplacing States must have due regard to the resource exploitation activities of the coastal State. Interference is prohibited. However, as observed, it can hardly be said that all objects placed on the continental shelf may or in fact will interfere with the coastal State's sovereign rights[70].

In conclusion, under the continental shelf doctrine, emplacement of acoustic devises on the seabed is open to all States.

6.2. Exclusive economic zone

As far as the exclusive economic zone is concerned, the implication just drawn for the continental shelf, i.e. that whatever activity does not fall within the coastal State's sovereign rights (such as the emplacement of military "devices") comes under the principle of the freedom of the high seas, cannot be drawn in such an easy and unqualified way. Detecting or communicative devices are not assimilated either to the structures and installations or artificial islands provided for in article 56 of the LOS Convention – which would recognize an exclusive right of the coastal State – or to cables or pipelines or other activities related to these freedoms such as those associated with the operation of ships and the submarine cables and pipelines provided in article 58, enforcing every State's freedom. The coastal State may invoke exclusive rights stemming from the exclusive economic zone, only if it has proclaimed such a zone, regardless of being a party to the LOS Convention; this is due to the fact that the regime has reached the level of customary rule through its acceptance by a large number of States[71].

Domestic legislation of some coastal States attempts to alter their EEZ from a zone of special purposes to a zone of general purpose. In effect, these States attempt to reform this zone to an area of coastal sovereignty. It has become a common observation of the proponents of the free access, that some States use EEZ as a vehicle to assert their perceived national interests,

---

[70] R. Zedalis, Note and Comments: Military Installations, Structures and Devices on the Continental Shelf: A Response, 75 *AJIL* 1981, p. 926, at p. 930.

[71] Ch. Joyner & E. Martell, Looking Back to see Ahead: UNCLOS III and Lessons for Global Commons Law, *in* Charlotte Ku and Paul Diehl (eds.), *International Law: Classic and Contemporary Readings* (Lynne Rienner, Boulder 1998) p. 453.

whether in territorial expansion, security and self-defence, economic exploitation of the natural resources of the area and preservation of the marine environment[72]. The coastal States contest a strong national interest in order to achieve control of the EEZ for activities not falling within the ambit of articles 56 and 60 of the LOS Convention.

Flag States claiming free access invoke article 58 of the Convention, which permits them to use the EEZ for routine high seas uses, i.e. for navigation, overflight and for laying submarine cables and pipelines as well as for other uses related to these freedoms, such as those associated with the operation of the ships, aircraft and submarine cables and pipelines. These rights must be conducted with due regard to the rights and duties of the coastal State. However, naval operations in the EEZ, including the emplacement of acoustic devices on the seabed, remain a matter of an open academic debate.

The question of emplacement of acoustic devices unavoidably comes under the residuary rule of article 59 of the LOS Convention, in the context of which it should be examined. A conflict arises between on the one hand a high seas freedom and on the other hand a coastal State's claim for exclusive jurisdiction over the control of these devices. Following the residuary rule of article 59 of the LOS Convention, conflicting claims should be resolved on the basis of equity and in light of all relevant circumstance, judging the specific national interests of the coastal States and the importance of the involved interests of the international community as a whole[73]. The crucial factor at this point is taking into account the respective importance of the interests of the States, comparing them to the interests of the international community[74].

There is a strong argument in favour of the coastal State when balancing the interests of either State to a conflict, in order to gain exclusive access and exercise control over this kind of activity. Under article 59 of the LOS Convention, coastal States pursue to gain control over emplacement as their interests prevail over common interests.

Regarding emplacement of communication devices on the seabed of the EEZ, coastal States maintain that the assigned and the residual rights may be considered as belonging to the coastal States. Thus, in any kind of dispute

---

[72] G. Caldorizi & A. Kaufman, Military Activities in the Exclusive Economic Zone: Preventing Uncertainty and Defusing Conflict, 32 *California Western International Law Journal* 2002, p. 253, at pp. 278-280.

[73] S. Rosenne, *The Perplexities of Modern International Law* (Martinus Nijhoff, Leiden/Boston 2004) p. 288.

[74] Ph. Allot, Power-Sharing in the Law of the Sea, 77 *AJIL* 1983, p. 1, at pp. 15-16.

with regard to conflicting claims, the coastal State presumes jurisdiction[75]. Furthermore, the coastal States argue that military activities generate negative effects against the interests of the coastal State, which, as the argument goes, in the balance of interests prevail.

The opposite view, however, maintains that using the ocean bed for the emplacement of detection and communication devices is included within the high seas freedoms, and in particular within the freedoms recognized for all States in the EEZ[76]. In particular, as is contented in favour of the inclusive jurisdiction, all rights associated with the high seas freedoms may be perceived as pre-existing residual rights[77]. This view focuses on the permissibility of residual rights in the framework of the high seas freedoms, especially on navigational rights. Arguments for the inclusiveness of the exploitation of the seabed of the EEZ for emplacement of acoustic devises revolves around a traditional view about the postulate of the international law of the sea, according to which common interests must predominate in order to save navigation and transportation by the international waterways[78].

During the Third UN Conference on the Law of the Sea (UNCLOS III), the US, on behalf of the major maritime powers, adamantly dissented to any military activities on the EEZ, such limitations severely constraining the free access and use by flag States. It protested that if such an effort would develop, it would mean the end of any attempt to conclude the adoption of the LOS Convention[79]. In this respect, the negotiating States finally chose not to address in the LOS Convention the sensitive issues of military activities.

Some coastal States maintain that their right to control emplacement of detecting devices in the EEZ precedes or rather prevails. In fact this would lead to control EEZ for all purposes; while some other States that perceive themselves militarily weak, claim exclusive control of the EEZ for national security reasons, banning by legislation foreign States to claim inclusive use of the same area for military purposes[80].

Against this argument, the opponents rely on the meaning of "sovereign rights" of the coastal States granted by the LOS Convention: The rights are exclusive only to the extent that are related to the *stricto sensu* economic or resource oriented activities in the area. Otherwise, the coastal State's juris-

---

[75] See argument in Caldorisi & Kaufman, *supra* note 72, p. 273.

[76] Treves, supra note 66, p. 845.

[77] See Caldorisi & Kaufman, supra note 72, p. 273.

[78] Reisman, *supra* note 2, p. 49.

[79] UN Doc. A/CONF.62/SR.57-70.

[80] F. Paolillo, The Exclusive Zone in Latin American Practice and Legislation, 26 *ODIL* 1995, p. 105, at pp. 107-108.

diction is rather creeping. There is no general rule that article 59 of the LOS Convention favours the coastal State. Accordingly, it cannot be maintained that free use interests conflict with exclusive claims. Emplacement may be inhibited only in so far it interferes with the EEZ activities of the coastal State[81].

Major maritime powers at UNCLOS III objected as a matter of principle, to any kind of appropriating EEZ or continental shelf areas for the sake of safeguarding or promoting national security interests. Maritime powers have actually opposed to any expansion of exclusive jurisdiction to the zones beyond the territorial seas or the straits[82]. The US, in recognizing only those exclusive rights for national security to the limits of the territorial sea[83], protested against such an approach favouring the claims of exclusive coastal State's control over military activities, including emplacement of acoustic devises, in the EEZ[84]. Their interests remain in guaranteeing the freedom of navigation within the EEZ and other related freedoms, including surveillance of the submerged sea[85].

Under this angle, it should also be taken into account that the residuary rule of article 59 of the LOS Convention presupposes that the coastal State is a party to the LOS Convention and has proclaimed an EEZ. The residuary rule of article 59 provides the basis for arguing in favour of the coastal State's exclusive control regarding emplacement of weapons or acoustic devices. When the exclusionary claims of the coastal State to preservation of its national security conflict with the free access claimed by flag States, claiming to use this seabed for military activities on the ground of the freedom of high seas, there must be a solution based on the principle of equity. More specifically, in such a conflict there should be judged the free access provided by customary international law opposite to the contented pressing security needs of the coastal State[86]. The coastal State's claim is specific, although it gives rise to arbitrariness, while claims of inclusiveness are general. Even if we follow the rule of balancing these conflicting rights, we should not be entrapped in general interpretations. The LOS Convention points out to the solution. The claims can not be construed in the abstract.

---

[81] Zedalis, *supra* note 70, pp. 932-933.

[82] E. Miles, *Global Ocean Politics: The Decision Process at the Third United Nations Conference on the Law of the Sea* (Martinus Nijhoff, The Hague 1998) p. 89.

[83] Pirtle, *supra* note 1, p. 11.

[84] J.A. Roach & R. Smith, *Excessive Maritime Claims* (66 International Law Studies, Naval War College, Newport, Rhode Island, 1994) p. 14.

[85] E. Miles, US Security Interests in a Post-Cold War World and the Law of the Sea, 36 *Columbia Journal of Transnational Law* 1997, p. 373, at p. 381.

[86] R. Nadelson, The Exclusive Economic Zone – State Claims and the LOS Convention, 16 *Marine Policy* 1992, p. 463 at p. 483.

Each claim should be appraised under the relevant and/or specific circumstances. If the LOS Convention had attempted to satisfy the needs of the coastal State for non-resource exploitation activities, it would have disappointed the naval powers. However, such an approach would deviate from the general rule that non-resource oriented activities fall within the freedom of the seas.

The LOS Convention could not have provided for activities falling outside the frame of the economic exploitation and constrain the free deliberation of States' arrangements. It is a different question whether the LOS Convention would promote a uniform practice in the waters adjacent to a coastal State. The residuary rule conforms to the law of the sea but it equally cultivates a vacuum pointing to the rise of legal disputes and arbitrary unilateral acts instead of providing a settlement framework. The tilt in favour of either the freedom of high seas or the exclusionary control of the coastal State depends on the circumstances of each case. Accommodation of competences upon the criteria described by article 59 of the LOS Convention is obligatory towards dispute resolution outside the frame of judicial settlement, to the extent that contains issues of military nature, and it thus remains in the domain of the sole judgment of the States concerned[87].

6.3. Deep seabed

Emplacement activities normally take place on the continental shelf. In case communication devices are placed on the deep seabed, i.e. the seabed beyond the outer limit of the continental shelf ("the Area"), the question arises as to whether this activity comes under the high seas freedom or is regulated by the common heritage principle, which is overall applicable to this area.

According to article 136 of the LOS Convention, the Area is the common heritage of mankind. The Area is under the control of the International Seabed Authority (ISA) only for exploration and exploitation purposes and should be reserved for peaceful activities under articles 137 and 138 of the Los Convention.

Under the LOS Convention, the ISA exercises the overall control with regard to mining activities of the area. The new regime cannot extend its regulatory force to non-mining activities, including emplacement of communication devices. Non-mining activities remain a high seas freedom and emplacing States shall have due regard to the other uses of the same area, including

---

[87] Treves, *supra* note 66, pp. 843-844.

mining activities undertaken under the control of the ISA. This obligation originates from the high seas freedom. It is highly debatable whether a prerequisite of even optional prior permission from the ISA may be assumed. As it has been noted, it seems "reasonable the emplacing States to avoid jeopardizing the feasibility of mineral exploration and exploitation"[88]. This kind of reasonableness will not create any conflict with the Authority's organs with respect to mining activities.

7. CONCLUDING REMARKS

States have free and shared access to the high seas in order to deploy and activate intelligence gathering receptors through sailing ships. The activity is free in so far as it does not interfere with other uses in the same area or to the extent interference is minimal. Blockading of an area for exclusive use may be justified only for self-defence claims. The imminence of threat, necessity to react and proportionality of means used are the criteria for justifying such a claim. Development of terrorism differentiates the perception of threat and reaction far prior to the occurrence of an attack, in terms of prevention or exercise of self-defence than was incepted by the drafters of the UN Charter.

Intelligence gathering on the seabed beyond the outer limit of the territorial seabed is kept free for unimpeded and continuous access and use reserved though for peaceful, non-aggressive, activities. The ocean bed militarily is used mainly for emplacement of communication systems and devices. In doing so, the emplacing State must have due regard to the continental shelf or the exclusive economic zone rights of the coastal State over living and non-living resources. If the activity is conducted within 200 miles from the baselines, emplacement exclusively for the coastal State cannot be justified under the doctrine of the continental shelf. Within that limit and upon proclamation of the exclusive economic zone, coastal States would invoke the residuary rule of article 59 of the LOS Convention in order to gain exclusive control over communication systems and put aside the claim of flag States, that emplacement remains a freedom of the high seas. Article 59 of the LOS Convention deals with conflicting claims arising in the context of the EEZ with regard to non-regulated activities, such as emplacement of communication devises. It is maintained that emplacement on the bed of the EEZ is presumed for the exclusive use and control of the coastal State, as coastal defence interests on balance are more concrete and prevailing over the common interests promoted by the freedom of the high seas. On the contrary,

---

[88] *Ibid.*, p. 857.

maritime powers argue that in this area emplacing detecting devices is a freedom of high seas and in exercising this activity flag States must have due regard to the exclusive rights of the coastal States relating to the EEZ.

Finally, States emplacing detecting devices on the deep seabed must have due regard to other high seas uses and make efforts to avoid conflict with the Authority's exclusive mining activities.

Chapter 7

DEVELOPMENTS ON THE INTERDICTION OF VESSELS
ON THE HIGH SEAS

*Angelos M. Syrigos**

1. Introduction

In December 2002, two Spanish warships, acting upon information from the US intelligence[1], tried to intercept a North Korean cargo vessel, named "*So San*", in the Indian Ocean on the high seas, 600 miles east of the Horn of Africa. According to Spanish officials, no flag was flying on the vessel. The two Spanish warships were part of an eight-ship flotilla that was charged with searching for operatives of *Al-Qaeda* and terrorist contraband[2]. The Spanish warships, exercising, as they claimed, the right of *reconnaissance*, requested the captain of the vessel by radio to ascertain her type of cargo. The captain indicated that the vessel was carrying cement but resisted interception, maintained speed and did not allow anybody to board and see what the ship was indeed carrying and tried to escape. The Spanish ships fired warning shots, a Spanish helicopter intervened and a special units force landed on the deck of the vessel. The search revealed 15 Scud missiles hid-

* Lecturer in International Law, Panteion University. The author wishes to thank Judge Alexander Yankov for his comments on an earlier draft of this article; Dr. Fani Livada, Legal Advisor, and Dr. Erieta Skalieri, Rapporteur to the Legal Department of the Hellenic Ministry of Foreign Affairs, for their valuable information on recent developments concerning co-operation between States against terrorism; and Dr. Anastasia Strati for her comments, assistance and patience. All opinions expressed in this paper are strictly the author's personal views.

[1] According to the Spanish Defence Minister, Frederico Trillo, "*the intelligence services of the US obtained information on the fact that that there was a suspicious vessel, which they thought was illegally trading arms...*", Spanish Authorities hold news conference on Scud missile interception, CNN, Transcript 121101CN.V54, 11 December 2002.
[2] M.R. Gordon, German and Spanish Navies take on major role near Horn of Africa, *The New York Times*, 15 December 2002.

Anastasia Strati, Maria Gavouneli & Nikos Skourtos (eds.), *Unresolved Issues and New Challenges to the Law of the Sea*, Martinus Nijhoff Publishers 2006, pp. 149-201.

den beneath sacks of cement. The vessel was turned over to the US Navy and American explosive experts secured the missiles.

Although there was some criticism concerning the fact that the seizing of a non-national vessel on the high seas that has not committed any offence could be considered an act of piracy[3], at first sight the discovery of the hidden cargo appeared to justify the interception. There was clear evidence that North Korea was involved in illegal proliferation of weapons of mass destruction, which were probably connected either with Al-Qaeda, Iraq or a private buyer like a militant group[4]. The worse came when Yemen's government declared that it had bought the missiles and wanted them to be delivered as originally planned. Furthermore, Yemen had notified the US in advance of the shipment. White House spokesman, Ari Fleischer, accepted that "there was no provision under international law prohibiting Yemen from accepting delivery of missiles from North Korea"[5]. Under these circumstances President Bush ordered the US Navy to release the North Korean ship.

The whole incident raised a number of political and legal questions. Was it an isolated and unfortunate event? Was it deliberately staged to show to potential buyers of North Korean missiles that US intelligence follows closely every contact with Pyongyang? Did the US wanted to dramatize the whole incident in order to show that there is an imperative need to intercept suspicious ships on the high seas? Or did the US want to make a point for a new right of pre-emptive action against terrorism on the high seas[6]? Whatever the real aim was, one thing is certain.

The incident touched upon the issues of the freedom of the high seas, maintenance of order on the high seas and prevention of maritime terrorism. Despite the fact that all these issues are addressed by the 1982 Law of the Sea Convention (hereinafter cited as "LOS Convention"), it is obvious that there are attempts to change the system of maintenance of order in areas beyond national sovereignty. These attempts are directly related with the 11 September 2001, terrorist attacks in the US. Many fear that the shipping industry and seaports may be the next terrorist target or that terrorist groups

---

[3] Nevertheless, it has been suggested that the "cargo and vessel could be subject to forfeiture under the doctrine of piracy and prize" since "it is not considered polite, in international shipping circles, to sail on the high seas in ghost vessels, without a flag, flaunting a false cargo manifest"; R. Wedgwood, A pirate is a pirate, *Wall Street Journal*, 16 December 2002.

[4] For the initial reactions of American intelligence officials see T. Shanker, Scud missiles found on ship of North Korea, *The New York Times*, 11 December 2002.

[5] D.E. Sanger & T. Shanker, Reluctant US Gives Assent for Missiles to Go to Yemen, *The New York Times*, 12 December 2002.

[6] See the relevant leading article "High seizures: Silly stunts are not a serious policy", *The Guardian*, 12 December 2002.

may be using traditional seaways to transfer illicit arms. In either case maritime security is considered to be at risk as a potential target of international terrorism.

2. THE RULE OF FLAG STATE JURISDICTION AND ITS EXCEPTIONS

2.1. Freedom of navigation

Freedom of the high seas is a general and long established principle of international law[7]. It applies both in time of peace and during armed conflicts[8]. One of the freedom of the high seas is freedom of navigation[9]. Freedom of navigation and equality of States lead to the exclusivity of the flag State jurisdiction. Consequently, ships on the high seas are only subject to the exclusive jurisdiction and authority of the State under whose maritime flag they are sailing. Only the flag State has the power to exercise control over these ships on the high seas and apply its national laws. The Permanent Court of International Justice affirmed the exclusivity of the flag State jurisdiction in the *Lotus* case: "Vessels on the high seas are subject to no authority except that of the State whose flag they fly. In virtue of the principle of the freedom of the seas, that is to say, the absence of any territorial sovereignty upon the high seas, no state may exercise any kind of jurisdiction over foreign vessel upon them"[10].

The exclusivity of flag State jurisdiction has been codified in the 1958 Geneva Convention on the High Seas (hereafter cited as "High Seas Convention") and repeated in the LOS Convention: "Ships shall sail under the flag of one State only and, save in exceptional cases expressly provided for in interna-

---

[7] See D.P. O'Connell, *The International Law of the Sea* (Vol. II, Shearer (ed.), Clarendon Press, Oxford 1984) pp. 792-801; I. Brownlie, *Principles of Public International Law* (6th edition, Oxford University Press, Oxford 2003) pp. 223-227; R. Jennings & Sir Arthur Watts (eds.), *Oppenheim's International Law* (9th ed., Vol. I: *Peace*, Parts 1-4, Longman Group, Avon 1992) pp. 731-735.

[8] The present article does not examine interdiction of vessels and intelligence activities on the high seas during armed conflicts at sea. On this issue see *San Remo Manual on International Law applicable to armed conflicts at sea* (International Institute of Humanitarian Law, Grotius Publications, Cambridge University Press, Cambridge 1995) pp. 187-223.

[9] According to article 87 of the Law of the Sea Convention, freedom of the high seas comprises *inter alia* (i) freedom of fishing, (ii) freedom to lay submarine cables and pipelines, (iii) freedom to fly over the high seas, (iv) freedom to construct artificial islands and other installations and (v) freedom of scientific research. The last two freedoms were not included in article 2 of the 1958 Geneva Convention on the High Seas.

[10] *The S.S. Lotus* case, France v. Turkey, PCIJ Series A, No. 9, 1927, p. 25.

tional treaties or in these articles, shall be subject to its exclusive jurisdiction on the high seas"[11]. Thus there can be no interference with freedom of navigation on the high seas. Consequently, the maintenance of order on the high seas under the law of the sea is minimal and limited to ensuring that all vessels are flying the maritime flag of the State under which they are registered.

2.2. Flags of convenience

Relevant to this issue is also the problem with flags of convenience. Article 91 of the LOS Convention provides: "1. Every State shall fix the conditions for the grant of its nationality to ships, for the registration of ships in its territory, and for the right to fly its flag. Ships have the nationality of the State whose flag they are entitled to fly. There must exist a genuine link between the State and the ship"[12].

Nevertheless, in many cases the genuine link between the State and the ship is absent. This problem has arisen in two cases before the International Tribunal on the Law of the Sea in Hamburg (hereafter cited as "ITLOS")[13]. In practice many States have developed open registers which enable vessels to claim nationality of the State with which the vessel has few or no connections. Thus, open registries or registries of flags of convenience are States that allow "the registration of foreign-owned and foreign controlled vessels under conditions which, for whatever reasons, are convenient and opportune for the persons who are registering the vessels"[14]. Several factors led the ship-owners to register their ships under flags of convenience. Lower taxes,

---

[11] Article 92 of the LOS Convention; article 6 of the 1958 Geneva Convention on the High Seas.

[12] See also United Nations Convention on Conditions for Registration of Ships, Geneva, 7 February 1986, *ILM* 1987, p. 1229.

[13] *The M/V "SAIGA"* case, Saint Vincent and the Grenadines v. Guinea, Case No. 1, Judgment of 4 December 1997; *The "Grand Prince"* case, Belize v. France, Case No. 8, Judgment of 20 April 2001. For more see T. Treves, Flags of convenience before the Law of the Sea Tribunal, 6 *San Diego International Law Journal* 2004, p. 179.

[14] B.A. Boczek, *Flags of convenience: An international legal study* (Harvard University Press, Cambridge MA, 1962) p. 2. The following 32 countries are considered as 'flags of convenience' by the International Transport Workers' Federation Fair Practices Committee: Antigua and Barbuda, Bahamas, Barbados, Belize, Bermuda (UK), Bolivia, Burma, Cambodia, Canary Islands (Spain), Cayman Islands (UK), Comoros, Cook Islands (New Zealand), Cyprus, Equatorial Guinea, French International Ship Register (FIS), Georgia, German International Ship Register (GIS), Gibraltar (UK), Honduras, Jamaica, Lebanon, Liberia, Malta, Marshall Islands (USA), Mauritius, Mongolia, Netherlands Antilles, Panama, St. Vincent, Sri Lanka, Tuvalu, Vanuatu, in http://www.itfglobal.org/flags-convenience/flags-convenien-183.cfm, last visited on 31 August 2005.

crewing standards and salaries, less stringent shipping regulations, volume discounts and relief of manning requirements are the most important among them[15].

Since flags of convenience offer relatively easy registration, it is obvious that they attract all kinds of maritime fraud and they are often connected with maritime violence on the high seas. More specifically, a vessel sailing on the high seas is under the exclusive jurisdiction of the flag State. Therefore, maritime violence and terrorism related to this specific vessel, fall exclusively under the jurisdiction of the flag State. If the flag State is not a signatory to a convention against maritime violence and terrorism, little can be done to combat these crimes[16].

Moreover, it is easy for a ship to change registry. For example, the US and its allies consider that vessels flying the North Korean flag are potential target for illicit cargos, like drugs, missiles or nuclear weapon fuel. At present, western intelligence monitors North Korea flag vessels around the world. Nevertheless, the owners of suspicious vessels may seek, with relative easiness, other more convenient registries. These States register everything that floats and can pay the fee. The recent example of the world's largest landlocked country, Mongolia, which introduced in 2003 an open registry, is illuminating. More than 250 ships were flying Mongolia's colours, a year after the introduction of the registry[17]. The reason of the increase was probably the fact that Japan, a traditional trading partner of North Korea, introduced stringent checks on ships flying the North Korean flag. Port calls of North Korean vessels dropped whereas those of Mongolian ships increased[18].

2.3. The exceptions to the rule

International law accepts that under certain circumstances the rule of the exclusivity of the flag State jurisdiction may bend. Since the 19th century it was admitted that: "The right of a vessel of one State to visit and search a vessel of another State on the high seas, in any case, is therefore an exception to the general rights of property, jurisdiction, equality and independence of sovereign States, and to justify such an act it must be shown that the par-

---

[15] J.A. Perkins, Ship registers: An international update, 22 *Tulane Maritime Law Journal* 1997, p. 197.

[16] T. Garmon, International Law of the Sea: Reconciling the law of piracy and terrorism in the wake of September 11th, 27 *Tulane Maritime Law Journal* 2002, pp. 268-269.

[17] J. Brooke, Landlocked Mongolia's seafaring tradition, *The New York Times*, 2 July 2004.

[18] *Ibid.*

ticular case comes clearly within the exceptions to this rule which have been established by the positive law of nations, or by treaty stipulations between the parties"[19].

Thus, under very specific and exceptional circumstances, which will be examined later, a State may interfere with the ship of another State on the high seas. This interference may take several forms and can be classified under two general categories, the first being the right of approach and the second being the right of search and visit.

The right of approach is a customary rule of international law. According to this right, any warship of every State may approach a ship on the high seas in order to verify her identity and nationality. This is a very simple action and the least obstructive to the voyage of a ship. Nowadays, warships normally request the identification of commercial ships by radio. The right of approach is a standard right and forms an everyday practice on the high seas.

In contrast, the right of visit and search is rather controversial. . Gidel wrote in 1932 that "le droit de 'visite' en temps de paix n'existe pas, sauf exceptions strictement limitées et résultant d'accords conventionnels"[20]. Both the High Seas Convention and the LOS Convention depict the limited circumstances in which action can be taken against non-national ships on the high seas. Both conventions also describe to a certain extent the exercise of this right. Nevertheless, it has to be pointed out that many scholars often confuse the actions taken under this right and the right of approach[21]. The

---

[19] H.W. Halleck, *International Law; or Rules regulating the intercourse of States in peace and war* (H.H. Bancroft & Company, San Francisco, 1861, in reproduction of the original edition, Rodopi, Amsterdam, 1970) p. 593.

[20] G. Gidel, *Le Droit International Public de la Mer: Le Temps de Paix* (Établissements Mellottee Chateauroux, Paris 1932) p. 292.

[21] Oppenheim includes in the notion of the verification of flag the actual boarding upon the ship in certain cases "since a suspicious vessel may still be a pirate although it shows a flag, it may further be stopped and visited for the purpose of inspecting its papers and thereby verifying its flag"; Oppenheim, *supra* note 7, pp.736-737. Colombos takes a similar view; C.J. Colombos, The *International Law of the Sea* (6th edition, Longmans, London 1967) p. 311. The same view is shared by A. van Zwanenberg, Interference with ships on the High Seas, 10 *ICLQ* 1961, pp. 791-792. Evans does nor refer to the right of approach but only to the right of visit; M. Evans, *International Law* (Oxford University Press, 2003) pp. 638-641; an approach which is followed by R.R. Churchill & A.V. Lowe, *The Law of the Sea* (3rd edition, Manchester University Press, 1999) pp. 210-213. *Contra* Brownlie considers that "the right of approach exists in all circumstances but does not involve the actual examination of papers or seizure of the vessel"; Brownlie, *supra* note 7, p. 232 & fn. 56; R. Reuland, Interference with non-national ships on the High Seas: Peacetime exceptions to the exclusivity rule of flag jurisdiction, 22 *Vanderbilt Journal of Transnational Law* 1989, pp. 1169-1171. Daillier & Pellet make a very short but very precise description of the actions undertaken during the intervention of a ship on the high seas; P. Daillier & A. Pellet, *Droit International Public* (7e edition,

right of visit and search can be distinguished from the right of approach in the following phases:

i. *Right of investigation of flag / droit d'enquête ou vérification du pavillon*: During this stage, the warship sends a boat under the command of an officer to check the documents of the suspected ship. Instead, the master of the ship may be ordered to bring his papers for inspection to the warship[22].

ii. *Right of search / droit de visite et inspection*: If after the documents have been checked suspicion remains, the warship may proceed to a further examination on board of the ship. If the master of the ship refuses to stop for search, two blank canon shots may be fired and if the ship continues to refuse search the warship can fire across suspect ship's bow[23]. It is obvious that the right of search disturbs the life of the ship and therefore the examination has to be carried out with all possible consideration and no damage must be done to the cargo.

iii. *Right of seizure / droit de saisir et immobilisation*: In case there is evidence that the ship is engaged in one of the activities that are punishable on the high seas, the warship has the right to arrest the ship and confiscate her goods. Nevertheless, if after the search suspicions prove to be unfounded the ship shall be compensated for any loss or damage. In order to avoid the unnecessary exercise of the visit and search of foreign ships on the high seas, the International Law Commission in its comment on the relevant article of the High Seas Convention stated that the severe penalty of the State to which the warship belongs "seems justified in order to prevent the right of visit being abused"[24].

The right of visit and search can be exercised only under very specific and limited circumstances. According to both the 1958 Geneva Convention and the LOS Convention, specific mutual jurisdictional rights of visit and search are given by the flag State to another State by virtue of a treaty. Moreover, the principle of universal jurisdiction provides the prosecuting State with jurisdiction to try a case in its own courts without regard to territorial or any other links (e.g. where the actions in question took place or which is the nationality of any of the people involved)[25].

LGDJ, Paris 2002) p. 1201. Both the 1958 Geneva Convention on the High Seas and the LOS Convention use the expression "boarding/arraisonnement".

[22] Oppenheim, *supra* note 7, pp.738.

[23] *Ibid.*; Reuland, *supra* note 21, pp. 1173-1175.

[24] *ILC Yearbook* 1956-II, p. 284.

[25] M. Morris, Universal jurisdiction in a divided world: Conference remarks, 35 *New England LR* 2001, p. 35.

This principle applies in cases where there is a universal agreement that a specific act is so repugnant to the humankind that all States have an interest and consequently the authority to arrest and prosecute the perpetrators of that act. These perpetrators are regarded as *hostis humanii generis*, enemies of all mankind. Up to the early 20th century this term was exclusively connected with two crimes that take place on the seas, namely piracy – "because the international community regarded piracy as damaging the interests of all"[26] – and slavery[27]. Nevertheless, as will be shown later, universal jurisdiction was recognized only for the case of piracy.

2.4. List of activities exempted from exclusive flag State jurisdiction

Article 110 of the LOS Convention provides a list of specific activities whose exercise gives to a warship[28] the ground to implement the rights of search and visit. Therefore, a warship is not justified in boarding a foreign ship unless "there is reasonable ground" for suspecting that the ship (a) is engaged in piracy; (b) is engaged in the slave trade; (c) is engaged in unauthorized broadcasting and the flag State of the warship has jurisdiction under article 109; (d) is without nationality; or (e) though flying a foreign flag or refusing to show its flag, the ship is, in reality, of the same nationality as the warship. With the exception of cases (c) and (d), the other provisions were contained in article 22 of the High Seas Convention. In addition to these activities, article 108 of the LOS Convention refers to the suppression of drugs trafficking by vessels on the high seas. Nevertheless, this is an anaemic provision since the suppression is limited to co-operation between the flag State and other States in cases where there are reasonable grounds to believe that a specific ship is engaged in illicit drug trafficking[29].

Although the circumstances under which a warship may interfere with non-national ships on the high seas are specifically addressed in the LOS

---

[26] *Arrest Warrant of 11 April 2000* case, Democratic Republic of Congo v. Belgium, Preliminary objections and merits, Judgment, ICJ Reports 2002, Separate Opinion of Judges Higgins, Kooijmans and Buergenthal, paragraph 61.

[27] C. Bassiouni, Universal jurisdiction for international crimes: Historical perspectives and contemporary practice, 42 *Vancouver Journal of International Law* 2001, pp. 108-115.

[28] The term "warship" is used for reasons of convenience and because it is common practice to use mainly warships for interception, search and visit of a ship on the high seas. Nevertheless, not only warships but also "military aircraft, or other ships or aircraft clearly marked and identifiable as being on government service" can be used for the exercise of the right of visit and search; articles 107 and 110(5) of the LOS Convention.

[29] See relevant comment by Evans who describes article 108 as "an anodyne provision"; Evans, *supra* note 21, p. 641.

Convention, the limits of the actions taken are not uniform: "Classic international law is highly restrictive, for it recognizes universal jurisdiction only in cases of piracy and not of other comparable crimes which might also be committed outside the jurisdiction of coastal States, such as trafficking in slaves or in narcotic drugs or psychotropic substances"[30].

Since piracy is considered as the most serious of all crimes on the high seas, all States may take action against such acts. On the contrary, this is not the case with slavery. Although slave-trading is one of the most appalling crimes against individuals[31], it falls short of giving jurisdiction to any State to repress the offenders on the high seas, regardless of the flag shown on the ship. The LOS Convention merely provides that every State shall take "effective measures to prevent and punish the transport of slaves in ships authorized to fly its flag and to prevent the unlawful use of its flag for that purpose"[32]. As it has been correctly pointed out, "it remains difficult to see why those involved in the trade, and the vessel itself, should not be capable of arrest under such circumstances without the express authorization of the flag State"[33].

In the case of unauthorized broadcasting from a ship or installation on the high seas not all States have jurisdiction to intervene. The States that have jurisdiction to intervene are exclusively (a) the flag State of the ship, (b) the State of registry of the installation, (c) the State of which the person is a national d) any State where the transmissions can be received; or (e) any State where authorized radio communication is suffering interference[34].

As it concerns stateless ships, jurisdiction derives from the simple fact that the international regime of the high seas is based upon the nationality of ships. The flag State has exclusive jurisdiction over ships flying its flag. Therefore, ships without a flag fall outside the scope of protection of commercial ships on the high seas[35]. Illustrative of this principle is the decision about the stateless vessel "Asya". *Asya* was engaged in illegal transportation

---

[30] *Arrest Warrant of 11 April 2000* case, Democratic Republic of Congo v. Belgium, Preliminary objections and merits, Judgment, ICJ Reports 2002, Separate Opinion of President Guillaume, par. 5.

[31] Slavery Convention, Geneva, 25 September 1926 & Protocol, New York, 7 December 1953. The amended Convention entered into force on 7 July 1955.

[32] Article 99 of the LOS Convention.

[33] Evans, *supra* note 21, p. 641.

[34] Article 109 of the LOSC.

[35] For more see A.W. Anderson, Jurisdiction over Stateless Vessels on the High Seas: An Appraisal under Domestic and International Law, 13 *Journal of Maritime Law and Commerce* 1981-82, pp. 323-343.

of Jews to Palestine. In 1949 a British warship stopped her. During the exercise of the rights of approach and visit *Asya* hoisted the Zionist flag (that later became the flag of Israel but at the time was not the flag of any State) whereas no documents were found to link her with any State. The court observed that: "Having no usual ship's papers which would serve to identify her ... hoisting a flag which was not the flag of any State in being, the *Asya* could not claim the protection of any State nor could any State claim that any principle of international law was broken by her seizure"[36].

Last but not least is the case of a ship which, though flying a foreign flag or refusing to show its flag, is in reality of the same nationality as the warship. This exception derives from the very principle of flag State jurisdiction. From the moment that a ship is registered with a State, this State has exclusive jurisdiction over it. Thus, the warship has the right to confirm that the ship is registered under its flag.

2.5. "...except where acts of interference derive from powers conferred by treaty"

Both articles 22 of the High Seas Convention and 110 of the LOS Convention provide that interference on the high seas may derive from powers conferred by treaty. Therefore, greater powers of extraterritorial jurisdiction may be acquired by treaty and the right of search and visit may be allowed under the terms of a specific treaty between two States. It is understandable that the contracting States cannot confer more powers than they actually possess under international law. Thus, in the case of vessels on the high seas they can confer the powers they possess as flag States.

In the past such treaties were used to prevent the importation of arms[37] or drug trafficking[38]. As it will be seen, nowadays this provision tends to be the rule for interference on the high seas even in cases of alleged terrorism. The United States have entered in several agreements with States to intercept ships registered under a foreign flag. Whereas in the past the emphasis was placed on bilateral agreements enabling the US Coast Guard to intercept

---

[36] *Molgan v. Attorney General for Palestine*, Appeal Cases, 1948 (England), p. 370.

[37] e.g. the two Conventions on Arms Traffic between Great Britain and France in 1919 and 1925, as referred in van Zwanenberg, 1961, *supra* note 21, p. 793, fn. 35.

[38] See the 1982 exchange of notes between Britain and the USA permitting the US authorities to board private British vessels on the High Seas in the Gulf of Mexico and the Caribbean Sea; J. Siddle, Anglo-American co-operation in the suppression of drug smuggling, 31 *ICLQ* 1982, pp. 726-747.

ships heading towards the American north subcontinent, recent agreements have a universal application.

Moreover, in a number of cases the right to interfere was not conferred upon by a treaty. The US claimed the existence of "special arrangements" or "informal agreements" which allow boarding of a foreign vessel, if consent of the flag State was obtained even informally[39]. In some cases consent was obtained by telephone after the actual boarding of the vessel[40] or until two days after the initial boarding[41]. In 1986 the US Congress introduced into an act these informal communications: "Consent or waiver of objection by a foreign nation to the enforcement of United States law by the United States ... may be obtained by radio, telephone, or similar oral and electronic means, and may be proved by certification of the Secretary of State or the Secretary's designee"[42].

Clearly these cases do not fall within the proviso of the High Seas Convention and the LOS Convention, which refer to "acts of interference deriv[ing] from powers conferred by treaty". Neither radio, nor telephone, nor any other oral and electronic means can replace a treaty. The use of these "special arrangements", endemic between the United States and Central and Southern American States, is rather motivated by the political relationship between these countries. Thus, they have very little, if any value as a precedent on interdiction on the high seas.

3. SELF-DEFENCE ON THE HIGH SEAS

3.1. Disagreement on the scope of self-defence

Having considered the exceptions to the freedom of navigation provided in the LOS Convention[43], it is important to note that customary international

---

[39] C. Sorensen, Drug trafficking on the High Seas: A move towards universal jurisdiction under international law, 4 *Emory International Law Review* 1990, pp. 220-225.

[40] See *United States v. Gonzalez*, US Federal Court, 629 F.2d 1081, 1083 (5th Cir. 1980).

[41] See *United States v. Barrio Hernandez*, as referred in Sorensen, *supra* note 38, p. 224, at footnote 86.

[42] Section 1903(c)(1) of the 1986 Act as it is referred in J.D. Stieb, Survey of United States Jurisdiction over High Seas Narcotics Trafficking, 19 *Georgia Journal of International and Comparative Law Quarterly* 1989, p. 141.

[43] In addition to these exceptions, another exception with regard to fisheries is contained in the Implementation Agreement on Straddling Fish Stocks and Highly Migratory Fish Stocks. Article 21 provides that one party is allowed to board fishing vessels of another party and to carry out inspection in areas of high seas covered by regional fisheries management organizations or schemes for improving enforcement of agreed conservation and management meas-

law accepts as a general proposition that a warship may proceed in visit and search of foreign ships on the high seas on the ground of national self-defence. Under the traditional view as emerged in the *Caroline* incident[44], a State is permitted to take measures of self-defence when there exists "a necessity of self-defence, instant, overwhelming, leaving no choice of means and no moment for deliberation". Moreover, the action taken in pursuance of self-defence must not be unreasonable or excessive "since the act, justified by the necessity of self-defence must be limited by that necessity and kept clearly within it"[45].

Nevertheless, there exists a long controversy over the precise scope of the right of self-defence[46]. As O'Connell observed, "if that were so it would be difficult to justify a regime of visit and search unconnected with immediate threats and which is really intended to create a *cordon sanitaire*"[47]. The controversy does not involve an actual armed attack against any ship on the high seas which touches upon the core of the existence of the State and offers it the ground to exercise the right of self-defence and to resort to force in order to repel the attack. The exercise of the right of self-defence under these specific circumstances includes, *inter alia*, search and visit on the high seas.

On the contrary, the situation is not so clear-cut in the case where the exercise of force takes place solely in the interest of national self-defence, under circumstances that do not amount to an actual armed attack. Is there any right of "anticipatory" or "pre-emptive" or "preventive"[48] self-defence?

The fundamental provision of the UN Charter is article 51:

---

ures. Moreover, the LOS Convention acknowledges another indirect exception to the rule of freedom of navigation on the high seas. Articles 216 and 220 of the LOS Convention provide, *inter alia*, that the coastal State is entitled to take measures against vessels substantially polluting the marine environment within its exclusive economic zone (EEZ). The LOS Convention follows the relevant provision of the 1969 Convention on Intervention on the High Seas in Cases of Oil Pollution Casualties. The Convention was the result of the *Torrey Canyon* incident.

[44] In the *Caroline* incident, the British seized and burned the American vessel *Caroline* in 1837 when she was on the US shore of the Niagara River. The ship was supplying Canadian revolutionaries. In the correspondence that followed the incident, the American Secretary of State laid down the requirements for self-defence.

[45] Letter from Mr. Daniel Webster to Lord Ashburton, 17 July 1842, reprinted in R. Jennings, The *Caroline* and *McLeod* cases, 32 *AJIL* 1938, p. 89.

[46] It has been argued that the standard of necessity set in the *Caroline* case exaggerates necessity in a time when war was a permissible option for States that had actually been attacked; A.R. Coll, The legal and moral adequacy of military responses to terrorism, 81 *ASIL Proceedings* 1987, pp. 297-298.

[47] O'Connell, *supra* note 7, p. 804.

[48] A term used by M. Sapiro, Iraq: The shifting sands of pre-emptive self-defence, *AJIL* 2003, p. 599.

"Nothing in the present Charter shall impair the inherent right of individual or collective self-defence, if an armed attack occurs against a Member of the United Nations, until the Security Council has taken measures necessary to maintain international peace and security. Measures taken by Members in the exercise of this right of self-defence shall be immediately reported to the Security Council and shall not in any way affect the authority and responsibility of the Security Council under the present Charter to take at any time such action as it deems necessary in order to maintain or restore international peace and security".

One school of thought maintains the view that article 51 simply states that nothing contained in the UN Charter restricts the inherent and customary right of a State to use force in self-defence. The only restrictions are related "to the procedures for settlement available to the parties to a dispute and the powers of settlement granted to the Security Council under Chapters VI and VII of the Charter and to the General Assembly under Chapter IV. But it is clear that if these procedures do not prove adequate, a residual power to act in self-defence must remain even when no actual armed attack has taken place"[49]. Thus, customary self-defence goes beyond the right to respond to an armed attack. In such a case a state is allowed to take anticipatory measures for its own defence. One of these measures is interference with freedom of navigation on the high seas[50].

According to another school of thought, article 51 imposes certain restrictions on the right of self-defence in cases of an armed attack. It is odd to impose restrictions in the case of an actual armed attack and from the other side to give an unlimited right of self-defence in all other circumstances. The advocates of the unrestricted exercise of the right of self-defence invoke its

---

[49] D. Greig, *International Law* (Butterworth, London 1976) p. 336-337. See also D. Bowett, *Self-defence in International Law* (Manchester University Press, Manchester 1958) pp. 185-186; J.L. Brierly, *The Law of Nations. An introduction to the international law of peace* (Oxford University Press, Oxford 1963) pp. 416-421; D.W. Greig, Self-defence and the Security Council: What does Article 51 require, 40 *ICLQ* 1991, pp. 366 *et seq.*; R. Higgins, *Problems and process. International law and how we use it* (Clarendon Press, Oxford 1996) pp. 242-243; D.P. O'Connell, *International Law* (Stevens & Sons, London 1970) pp. 315-320; M. Shaw, *International Law* (5th edition, Cambridge University Press, Cambridge 2003) pp. 1024-1031; J. Stone, *Aggression and World Order: A critique of United Nations theories of aggression* (Stevens & Sons, London 1958) pp. 95-96; C.H.M. Waldock, The regulation of the use of force by individual States in international law, 81 *RCADI* 1952-II, pp. 496-498.

[50] "The right of self-defence ... will confer on a State, in a case where its safety is threatened, a self-protective jurisdiction which will entitle it to visit and arrest a vessel on the high seas..."; Colombos, *supra* note 21, p. 315. "Once the proposition is accepted that self-defence is available as a basis for action in the absence of an actual armed attack, it is clear that some form of interference with the freedom of passage of foreign vessels on the high seas may be justifiable"; Greig, *International Law*, *supra*, p. 341.

customary character simply because article 51 imposes restrictions. Therefore, under article 51 of the UN Charter, in conjunction with Article 2(4),
self-defence can only be resorted to "if an armed attack occurs" and in no
other circumstances[51].

The International Court of Justice examined article 51 and it seems that it
has left the issue open: "... the United Nations Charter ... by no means covers the whole area of the regulation of the use of force in international relations. ... the Court therefore finds that article 51 of the Charter is only meaningful on the basis that there is a "natural" or "inherent" right of self-defence
and it is hard to see how this can be other than of a customary nature...
Moreover, the Charter ... does not go on to regulate directly all aspects of its
content. For example, it does not contain any specific rules whereby self-
defence would warrant only measures which are proportional to the armed
attack and necessary to respond to it, a rule well established in customary international law"[52]. "[T]here is a specific rule whereby self-defence would
warrant only measures which are proportional to the armed attack and necessary to respond to it, a rule well established in customary international law...
This dual condition applies equally to article 51 of the Charter, whatever the
means of force employed"[53].

The divided views on whether self-defence can be employed against an
armed attack that has not yet occurred but seems to be imminent are also reflected in the International Law Commission's remarks on the High Seas
Convention: "The question arose whether the right to board a vessel should
be recognized also in the event of a ship being suspected of committing acts
hostile to the State to which the warship belongs, at a time of imminent danger to the security of that State. The Commission did not deem it advisable
to include such a provision, mainly because of the vagueness of terms like
'imminent danger' and 'hostile acts', which leaves them open to abuse"[54].

---

[51] J. de Arechaga, International law in the past third of a century, 159 *RCADI* 1978-I, pp.
87-98; Brownlie, *supra* note 7, pp. 699-702; Ian Brownlie, *International Law and the use of
force by States* (Clarendon Press, Oxford 1963) pp. 264-280; L. Henkin, *How nations behave:
Law and foreign policy* (Council on Foreign Relations, Columbia University Press, New York
1979) pp. 141-144; Oppenheim, *International Law. Disputes, War and Neutrality* (Volume II,
7th edition, Longmans, London-New York 1955) pp. 154-157.

[52] *Military and Paramilitary Activities in and against Nicaragua*, Nicaragua v. United
States of America, Merits, ICJ Reports 1986, par. 176.

[53] Advisory opinion on the *Legality of the Threat of Use of Nuclear Weapons*, ICJ Reports
1996, par. 41.

[54] Article 46, comment 4, Report of the International Law Commission to the General Assembly, 11 UN GAOR Supp. (No. 9), UN Doc. A/3159 (1956), as reprinted in *ILC Yearbook*
1956-II, p. 284.

Thus, the International Law Commission recognized that there might be other circumstances which could legalize deviation from the freedom of navigation. Nevertheless, the vagueness and uncertainty of these circumstances led the International Law Commission to follow a cautious approach to the issue.

3.2. State practice and incidents on the high seas prior to 11 September 2001

a. The Algerian emergency

During the Algerian Emergency between 1956 and 1962 the French Navy conducted operations, which included visit and search of non national vessels on the high seas. The aim was to stop the infiltration of weapons to the Algerian insurgents. Initially, the operations took place within a zone of twenty to fifty kilometres from the coastline[55]. Later on they were extended over wide areas of the high seas not only in the Mediterranean Sea[56] but also in the English Channel[57]. The French government argued that the operations constituted a police measure affecting the external safety of the State. They were necessary for safety reasons and had no vexatious character[58]. The French activities were met with vigorous protests by many of the flag states of the affected vessels[59].

b. The Cuban Quarantine

On 22 October 1962, US President J.F. Kennedy announced "a strict Quarantine of all offensive military equipment under shipment to Cuba". The interdicted shipping was to be identified, searched and visited and, if found to carry prohibited material to Cuba, to be "turned back". This was a

---

[55] See e.g. the incidents with the Italian vessel *Duizar* in D.P. O'Connell, International Law and contemporary naval operations, 40 *BYBIL* 1970, p. 37 *et seq.*; or the *West Breeze* on 23 February 1961 while she was off 32 miles from the coast of Algeria, referred in van Zwanenberg, *supra* note 21, p. 791.

[56] E.g. the Polish ship *Wisla* was intercepted on 3 February 1958 while being between Gibraltar and Casablanca; O'Connell, *supra* note 49, p. 36.

[57] The German ship *Bilbao* while sailing in the English Channel was intercepted by the French navy and conducted to the French port of Cherbourg.

[58] As it is referred in O'Connell, *supra* note 7, p. 805.

[59] *Ibid.*

response towards the supply of missiles to Cuba by Soviet Union[60]. The quarantine was to "be extended, if needed, to other types of cargo and carriers"[61]. The announcement of the President was followed the next day by a resolution of the Organization of American States. The US Navy was ordered to intercept any vessel heading towards Cuba, while warships from Argentina, the Dominican Republic and Venezuela joined the operation. The Soviet Union described the maritime quarantine as "piracy"[62]. During the quarantine, a number of third State vessels, under Soviet charter, were inspected and boarded while other vessels simply altered course to avoid inspection[63].

The United States employed various arguments in order to justify the legality of their action[64]. The most relevant arguments to the present study were: (a) the exercise of their right of self-defence in provocative circumstances[65] and (b) the sanctions by a regional organization, such as the Organization of American States. In this context, it was argued that the US action fell within the meaning of "regional arrangements" of article 52 of the UN Charter[66], which it clearly did not. In any case as it has been observed: "Whatever be the plausibility of these justifications the Cuban Quarantine was a highly exceptional matter with little value as a precedent in situations of self-defence which fall short of global deterrence".

c. Interdiction of illegal aliens on the high seas

On 29 September 1981, US President Ronald Reagan issued a proclamation declaring that "the entry of undocumented aliens from the high seas is hereby suspended and shall be prevented by the interdiction of certain vessels carrying such aliens"[67]. The interdiction programme was based on the

---

[60] For a chronological list of the events see Mallison, Limited naval blockade or quarantine interdiction: National and collective self-defence claims valid under international law, 31 *George Washington University Law Review* 1962, pp. 339-343.

[61] Interdiction of the Delivery of Offensive Weapons to Cuba, President John F. Kennedy's speech announcing the quarantine against Cuba, 22 October 1962, 47 *Department of State Bulletin* 1962, p. 717.

[62] C.Q. Christol & C.R. Davis, Maritime Quarantine: The naval interdiction of offensive weapons and associated materiel to Cuba, 1962, 57 *AJIL* 1963, p. 528.

[63] *Ibid.*, p. 530.

[64] For a summary of these points see O'Connell, *supra* note 7, at p. 808.

[65] Christol & Davis, *supra* note 62, p. 533-536.

[66] A. Chayes, Law and the Quarantine of Cuba, 41 *Foreign Affairs*, p. 550.

[67] United States Proclamation 4865 on High Seas interdiction of illegal aliens, 29 September 1981, 20 *ILM* 1981, p. 1263.

finding that the illegal migration "was a serious problem detrimental to the interests of the United States". The real reason to interdict vessels on the high seas was the fact that the asylum provision of the US Refugee Act of 1980 applied exclusively to aliens "physically present in the United States or at land border or port of entry". Thus, aliens on the high seas and not "physically present or at land border or port of entry" did not have any rights under the US Refugee Act of 1980[68].

The executive order of the Proclamation authorized the US Coast Guard to interdict ships "outside the territorial waters of the United States", "to stop and board" suspect vessels, to make inquiries of those on board and to return the vessel and its passengers to the country from which it came[69]. The proclamation intended to stop the illegal transport of persons from Haiti to the USA[70], although in subsequent years the same law was used for immigrants from Cuba[71]. Initially, there was a screening process for those of the immigrants eligible to apply for political refugee status. On 24 May 1992, US President George Bush allowed the Coast Guard to interdict Haitians and immediately return them to Haiti[72].

Most importantly, interdiction and boarding could take place only on the following vessels:

a. vessels under the US flag;
a. vessels owned "in whole or in part by the United States, a citizen of the United States or a corporation incorporated under the laws of the United States". Vessels, that have been granted nationality by a foreign nation in accordance with article 5 of the High Seas Convention, were expressly exempted;

---

[68] See *Haitian Refugee Centre, Inc. v. Gracey*, US District Court, DDC, 10 January 1985, 79 *AJIL* 1985, pp. 744-746.

[69] United States Executive Order 12324 on interdiction of illegal aliens, 29 September 1981, *ibid*. In November 1991 the USA opened the base at Guantanamo Bay in Cuba for the purpose of interviewing interdictees.

[70] The issue of the Haitian refugees has been raised several times in the US courts. See M. Leigh, *Haitian Refugee Center, Inc. v. Gracey*, 600 F.Supp. 1396, 79 *AJIL* 1985, pp. 744-746; Jonathan Harris, *Haitian Centers Council, Inc. v. McNary*, 87 *AJIL* 1993, pp. 112-117; T.D. Jones, *Sale v. Haitian Centers Council, Inc.*, 88 *AJIL* 1994, pp. 114-126; see also For Haitians, justice denied, *The New York Times*, 30 August 1992 (editorial).

[71] See T.D. Jones & J.H. Bello, *Cuban-American Bar Association, Inc. v. Christopher*, 43 F.3d 1412; *Haitian Refugee Center, Inc. v. Christopher*, 43 F.3d 1431, 90 *AJIL* 1996, pp. 477-483; see also Sean Murphy, Ability of detainees in Cuba to obtain federal Habeas Corpus review, 96 *AJIL* 2002, pp. 481-482.

[72] Executive Order 12807, 24 May 1992 (Kennebunkport Order), 57 *Federal Registry* 1992, p. 133.

c. vessels without nationality;

d. vessels assimilated to vessels without nationality because of an attempt to fly more than one flag;

e. vessels flying the flag of a State with which the US had an arrangement authorizing such action.

The same day of the Proclamation it became known that, following an exchange of notes, the United States agreed with Haiti on the establishment of a programme of interdiction of Haitian vessels on the high seas[73]. A representative of the Haitian Navy was to be aboard the US warship engaged in the implementation of the programme.

Serious issues as to the validity of these actions were raised under international law. The most relevant to the present study[74] were the following: (a) the case of a vessel owned in part or in whole by a US national but being under the flag of another State. In such a case it is uncertain whether the United States could claim lack of a genuine link between the flag State and the owner of the ship[75]; (b) the question whether States may enter into agreements that restrict the movement of persons (even when these persons are refugees) on the high seas[76]. The flag State cannot confer by treaty to another State more rights that it possesses over its citizens on the basis of the principle of nationality, while they are on the high seas.

d. Drug trafficking on the high seas

In 1980 the United States modified their existing legislation governing seizures of drug smuggling foreign vessels on the high seas[77]. In 1986 the Maritime Drug Law Enforcement Act passed by the US Congress. Under the new legislation US warships could visit, search and seize foreign vessels while being outside the territorial sea but within the so-called "customs waters".

---

[73] For a basic points of the exchange of notes see M.N. Leigh, Contemporary practice of the United States relating to international law, 76 *AJIL* 1982, pp. 374-376.

[74] Some other points were related to the definition of a refugee under international law and the obligatory return of the refugees which conflicts with the principle of *non-refoulement*; for more see C. Gutekunst, Interdiction of Haitian migrants on the high seas: A legal and policy analysis, 10 *Yale Journal of International Law* 1984, pp. 151-184.

[75] L. Sohn, Interdiction of vessels on the high seas, 18 *International Lawyer* 1984, pp. 418-419.

[76] Jones, *supra* note 71, pp. 122-123. Nevertheless, article 110 of the LOS Convention provides an exception when "acts of interference derive from powers conferred by treaty".

[77] See the 1970 Comprehensive Drug abuse Prevention and Control Act, passage 21 USC section 955a, as it is referred in Sorensen, *supra* note 39, p. 211, fn. 19; see also C. Connoly, 'Smoke on the water': Coast Guard authority to seize foreign vessels beyond the Contiguous Zone, 13 *International Law and Policy* 1981, pp. 249-332.

"Customs waters" have been established in the 1920s during the period of the prohibition of alcohol; they extended between three to twelve miles from the coast[78] thus corresponding to the 12-mile contiguous zone established after World War II. Nevertheless, "customs waters" are not limited in this area. As specifically provided for: "The term "customs waters" means, in the case of a foreign vessel subject to a treaty or other arrangement between a foreign government and the United States enabling or permitting the authorities of the United States to board, examine, search, seize, or otherwise to enforce upon such vessel upon the high seas the laws of the United States, the waters within such distance of the coast of the United States as the said authorities are or may be so enabled or permitted by such treaty or arrangement and, in the case of every other vessel, the waters within four leagues of the coast of the United States"[79].

Thus, "customs waters" could extend far beyond the outer limit of the contiguous zone, which today extends to 24 nautical miles[80], subject to an arrangement with the flag State. For that purpose, the relevant provision "except where acts of interference derive from powers conferred by a treaty" of both article 22 of the High Seas Convention and article 110 of the LOS Convention has been employed. However, as it has already been mentioned, this condition has not always been followed. The US authorities simply require informal expression of the consent by the flag State which could be a telephone call or a radio message[81]. In some cases even the consent requirement has been ignored on the grounds that US jurisdiction was derived from the objective territorial principle, since drug smuggling intended to affect US citizens[82]. More recently, US Courts used the "protective principle" in order to justify extraterritorial jurisdiction: "...under the "protective principle" of international law, a nation is permitted 'to assert jurisdiction over a person whose conduct outside the nation's territory threatens the nation's security' ... Consistent with this principle, Congress specifically found in the Maritime Drug Law Enforcement Act that 'trafficking in controlled substances aboard vessels is a serious international problem and is universally condemned[, and] ... presents a specific threat to the security ... of the United

---

[78] *Ibid.* See also Stieb, *supra* note 42, p. 140.

[79] US Code, Title 19 (Customs Duties), Chapter 4, Subtitle III, Part I, subpart a, par. 1401.

[80] See Proclamation by the President of the United States of America, http://www.un.org/Depts/los/LEGISLATIONANDTREATIES/STATEFILES/USA.htm.

[81] See further Sorensen, *supra* note 39.

[82] See the Case of *United States v. Postal*, where the US courts acted in derogation of the High Seas Convention, in S.P. Bodner, *United States v. Postal*, 6 *Brooklyn Journal of International Law* 1980, pp. 134-158.

States.' …Therefore, application of the Maritime Drug Law Enforcement Act to the defendants is consistent with the protective principle of international law because Congress has determined that all drug trafficking aboard vessels threatens our nation's security"[83]. Or, as the US court held in a previous case: "Inasmuch as trafficking of narcotics is condemned universally by law-abiding nations, we see no reason to conclude that it is 'fundamentally unfair' for Congress to provide for the punishment of persons apprehended with narcotics on the high seas"[84]. Thus "even absent a treaty or arrangement, the United States could under the 'protective principle' … prosecute foreign nationals on foreign vessels on the high seas for possession of narcotics"[85].

References such as "a serious international problem" or "trafficking of narcotics is condemned universally", made by the US courts, are used to provide the basis for the universality principle. The aim is to consider drug trafficking as a crime universally condemned and thus assimilated with piracy. The application of the universality principle to drug smuggling will allow a State to claim extraterritorial jurisdiction on the high seas, irrespective of the nationality of the vessel. Nevertheless, such claims "are being received by other States with apparent equanimity"[86]. Repression of drug smuggling continues to be dependent on international co-operation[87].

4. SELF-DEFENCE AND TERRORISM

4.1. State practice prior to 2000

Under which circumstances can a State lawfully respond to terrorism[88] with armed force? Since the '80s this is one of the fundamental questions in international law of armed conflict. This question is related with the present

---

[83] *United States v. Julio-Cardales*, United States First Circuit, Court of Appeals, No 97-2383, 26 February 1999.

[84] *United States v. Martínez- Hidalgo* , 993 F.2d 1052 (3d Cir. 1993).

[85] *United States v. Romero-Galue*, 757 F. 2d 1147 (11th Cir. 1985).

[86] Churchill & Lowe, *supra* note 21, p. 218.

[87] e.g. the seizure of the *Privilege* carrying 5 tones of cocaine. *Privilege* was stopped and boarded 200 nautical miles southwest of the Canary Islands, in the Atlantic Ocean, on 1 September 2000. The raid was part of *Operation Orinoco*, which involved police forces from Venezuela, Colombia, the United States, Italy, Panama, France, Greece and Spain.

[88] It is out of the scope of the present article to examine problems related with the legal definition of terrorism. Quite often "freedom fighters" are considered as "terrorists" and *vice versa*; for more see A.C. Arend & R.J. Beck, 'Don't read on us': International law and forcible state responses to terrorism, 12 *Wisconsin International Law Journal* 1994, p. 172.

practice of interference of ships on the high seas. It was raised several times in the last two decades of the 20th century in relation to state practice of both Israel and the USA[89]. These were the only states in the world that have used force in response to terrorist acts. Their practice was followed by international criticism, although this criticism was frequently inconsistent and was reflecting ideological considerations analogous to the mood prevailing during the Cold War era[90].

From the rather scare practice, the interception of two civilian aircrafts in 1973 and 1986 by Israeli fighter jets represent the most relevant examples to the present problem posed by the interception, visit and search of ships on the high seas without the permission of the flag State on the grounds of suspected terrorism. In both cases Israeli fighter jets intercepted two civilian flights and forced them to land in territory under Israeli control. In 1973 the incident involved an aircraft flying from Beirut to Baghdad. In the second case, in 1986, it was a Libyan civilian airplane flying from Tripoli to Damascus. It has been intercepted while being on international airspace, over the high seas[91]. In both cases the Israelis thought that there were "terrorists" aboard. All passengers and crew were forced to disembark and were interrogated for several hours. When it has been proved that the interception of the planes was based on false information, the civilian aircrafts were allowed to depart[92].

---

[89] In the past both the US and Israel have claimed self-defence for use of force in response to 'terrorist' attacks. Israel attacked PLO headquarters in Tunis in 1985 as a response to an attack against an Israeli agent in Cyprus. The action was condemned by the Security Council and regarded as a violation of the UN Charter; see Security Council Resolution 573 (1985). On the contrary, the reactions were not the same when the US attacked on Tripoli in 1986 in response to the bombing of the death of American citizens in Berlin, the so-called *Operation El Dorado Canyon*. The US argument to the UN Security Council was that the action was self-defence under article 51 of the UN Charter, as it was intended to protect nationals abroad and to deter future terrorist attacks. A similar reasoning was used in 1998 when the US claimed to have acted in self-defence in response to embassy bombings in Kenya and Tanzania by striking at targets in Sudan and Afghanistan.

[90] See e.g. the relevant discussion during the 1987 annual meeting of the American Society of International Law: Views by F. Boyle, Military Responses to Terrorism: Remarks, 81 *ASIL Proceedings* 1987, pp. 288-297; also C. Gray, The use of force and the international legal order, in M. Evans (ed.), *International Law* (Oxford University Press, Oxford 2003) p. 603.

[91] H. Kamm, Rabin defends air interception: Vows more 'unconventional'' acts, *The New York Times*, 6 February 1986.

[92] For more see A. Cassese, The international community's 'legal' response to terrorism, 38 *ICLQ* 1989, pp. 601, 603-604; D. Kash, Abductions of terrorists in international airspace and on the high seas, 8 *Florida JIL*, pp. 90-93; also A.C. Arend & R.J. Beck, *International Law and the Use of Force. Beyond the UN paradigm* (Routledge, New York 1993) pp.148-149.

Both cases were discussed in the UN Security Council. Israel claimed that it was acting in self-defence and exercising its inherent right to use force to protect its nationals from terrorist attacks: "[A] nation attacked by terrorists is permitted to use force to prevent to pre-empt future attacks … it is simply not serious to argue that international law prohibits us capturing terrorists in international waters or international airspace"[93]. While the US criticized the Israeli action in 1973[94], it held a different view in 1986 agreeing with Israel's interpretation of the law: "…there may arise exceptional circumstances in which an interception may be justified… A State whose territory or citizens are subjected to continuing terrorist attacks may respond with appropriate use of force to defend itself against further attacks… We believe that the ability to take such action in carefully defined and limited circumstances is an aspect of the inherent right of self-defence recognized in the United Nations Charter"[95]. For these reasons the draft Security Council Resolution condemning Israel's action was vetoed by the US. Nevertheless, this interpretation of law was not supported by any other Security Council member[96].

During all this period the international law community was divided over the question of the victim State's right to defend itself in case of a terrorist act. There were disagreements as to what constituted a "timely response" to a terrorist act; how proportionate the response should be; which were the proper targets for response; and how focused the action of the victim State could be upon the actual attackers or upon a State possibly sponsoring terrorism[97].

4.2. "A revolutionary challenge to the doctrine of self-defence"[98]

Following the 11 September 2001 terrorist attacks, the doctrine of preemptive self-defence was seen from a totally different angle. The reassessment of the law in this area was pursued by the US administration. A day after the tragedy the Security Council adopted Resolution 1368. The Resolution reaffirmed in its preamble "the inherent right of individual and collective self-

---

[93] UN Doc S/PV.2651, 4 February 1986, pp. 19-20.

[94] See statement by the US delegate according to which "Actions such as Israel's diversion of civil airliner on 10 August 1973 are unjustified and likely to bring about counter-action on an increasing scale…", UN Doc S/PV.1738, 14 August 1973, p. 30.

[95] Relevant UN Doc S/PV.2655/Corr.1, 18 February 1986, pp. 112-113.

[96] Arend & Beck, *supra* note 92, p.149; Cassese, *ibid.*, pp. 604-606; G.M. Borkowski, Recent developments. Use of force: Interception of Aircraft, 27 *Harvard International Law Journal* 1986, pp. 765-766.

[97] Arend & Beck, *ibid.*, pp. 147-173.

[98] Gray, *supra* note 90, p. 603.

defence in accordance with the Charter". It also urged the world community to suppress terrorism and hold accountable all who aid, support or harbour the perpetrators, organizers and sponsors of terrorist acts, and stated that the UN was prepared to combat all forms of terrorism. On 28 September 2001 the Security Council issued Resolution 1373, which set out the methods whereby member States were to root out terrorists and terrorist organizations and deprive terrorists of the funds and materials necessary to conduct their operations. In its preamble it also included express reference to the "inherent right of individual or collective self-defence". The Security Council has never before recognized the right to use force in self-defence against terrorism.

The US invoked article 51 of the UN Charter as well as Security Council Resolutions 1368 and 1373 and the relevant anti-terrorist treaties in order to find support for the "war on terror": "In addition to US pressure to end State sponsorship, we will strongly support new, strict standards for all States to meet in the global war against terrorism. States that have sovereign rights also have sovereign responsibilities. Security Council Resolution 1373 clearly established States' obligations for combating terrorism... Together, Resolution 1373, the international counter-terrorism conventions and protocols and the inherent right under international law of individual and collective self-defence confirm the legitimacy of the international community's campaign to combat terrorism"[99].

The greater emphasis, nevertheless, was placed on the inherent right of individual and collective self-defence. This was the official reasoning used to justify the attack on Afghanistan[100]. The reasoning of the actions against Afghanistan were the attacks of the 9/11: In "response to these attacks and in accordance with the inherent right of individual and collective self-defence, United States armed forces have initiated actions designed to prevent and deter further attacks on the United States". At this point it has to be pointed out that although there may be doubts as to the accuracy of the information provided by the unilateral fact-finding mission of the US intelligence, it is beyond doubt that the 9/11 incidents were clearly falling under the category of "large scale, continuing attacks" which could be considered as justifying the use of force[101].

---

[99] *National Strategy for combating terrorism*, February 2003, http://www.white house.gov/news/releases/2003/02/counter_terrorism/counter_terrorism_strategy.pdf, p. 19.

[100] Letter dated 7 October 2001 from the Permanent Representative of the United States of America to the United Nations addressed to the President of the Security Council, UN Security Council Document S/2001/946, 7 October 2001.

[101] J.P. Rowles, Military Responses to Terrorism: Substantive and Procedural Constraints in International Law. Military Responses to Terrorism, 81 *ASIL Proceedings* 1987, p. 314.

Following the overthrowing of the *de facto* Taliban regime, the US administration declared the "second stage" of the war on terror. This second stage had two goals: impede *Al-Qaeda* to regroup outside Afghanistan and prevent 'rogue States'[102] and terrorist groups from developing weapons of mass destruction ("WMD") or gaining access to them[103]. The emphasis on terrorist groups which develop WMD was supporting so broad a conception of self-defence that it was giving a *carte blanche* to the US armed forces to include pre-emptive strikes against terrorist networks and States with WMD, irrespective of whether they were connected with the attacks of 9/11. In 2002 and 2003 two official papers presenting the US national strategy were published. According to these papers, the basic elements of the new US strategy were the following:

- The terrorist attacks of 9/11 were "acts of war" against the United States of America and its allies.

- There exists an inherent right under international law of individual and collective self-defence.

- This right was allowing the US and its allies to act pre-emptively even to "emerging threats before they are fully formed"[104] rather than waiting to respond to an actual or imminent armed attack.

The critical point in the new *National Strategy* was the right to pre-emptive self-defence. This right was expressed in various forms: "The United States has long maintained the option of pre-emptive actions to counter a sufficient threat to our national security. The greater the threat, the greater is the risk of inaction-and the more compelling the case for taking anticipatory action to defend ourselves..."[105]. "The United States will constantly strive to enlist the support of the international community in this fight against a common foe. If necessary, however, we will not hesitate to act alone, to exercise our right to self-defence, including acting pre-emptively against terrorists to prevent them from doing harm to our people and our country..."[106]. "We cannot wait for terrorists to attack and then respond. The

---

[102] According to the US National Strategy "The United States currently lists seven state sponsors of terrorism: Iran, Iraq, Syria, Libya, Cuba, North Korea and Sudan", *National Strategy for combating terrorism*, February 2003, http://www.whitehouse.gov/news/releases/2003/02/counter_terrorism/counter_terrorism_strategy.pdf, p. 18.

[103] Remarks on the Six-Month Anniversary of the September 11th Attacks, 38 *Weekly Comp. Pres. Doc.*, 11 March 2002, p. 391.

[104] *National Security Strategy of the United States of America*, September 2002, http://www.whitehouse.gov/nsc/nss.pdf>, Introduction.

[105] *Ibid.*, p. 15.

[106] *National Strategy for combating terrorism*, February 2003, http://www.whitehouse.gov/news/releases/2003/02/counter_terrorism/counter_terrorism_strategy.pdf, p. 18.

United States and its partners will disrupt and degrade the ability of terrorists to act… Once we have identified and located the terrorists, the United States and its friends and allies will use every tool available to disrupt, dismantle, and destroy their capacity to conduct acts of terrors…"[107].

The view that the US had to act pre-emptively divided contemporary legal scholarship[108]. Nevertheless, the US are using this argument to justify their global activities against terrorism, including interdiction of ships on the high seas. It has also to be noted that, days before the 9/11 attacks, the UN Secretary General's Report on the implementation of the UN Millennium Declaration referred to measures that have to be taken in order to promote human security, especially in situations where the rule of law fails. One of the challenges was to "replace the culture of reaction by one of prevention"[109]. The question at issue is the extent of that prevention.

4.3. NATO and the "war on terror"

In addition to the US reaction, NATO is also active on the "war against terror". A day after the terrorist attacks, NATO invoked article 5 of the North Atlantic Treaty for the first time in its history. Article 5 provides that: "The Parties agree that an armed attack against one or more of them in Europe or North America shall be considered an attack against them all and consequently they agree that, if such an armed attack occurs, each of them, in exercise of the right of individual or collective self-defence recognised by Article 51 of the Charter of the United Nations, will assist the Party or Parties so attacked by taking forthwith, individually and in concert with the other Parties, such action as it deems necessary, including the use of armed force, to restore and maintain the security of the North Atlantic area".

The attack against the USA was considered as an attack against all the then 19 member States of NATO. Since then, all NATO decisions to combat ter-

---

[107] *Ibid.*, pp. 15, 18.

[108] See Gray, *supra* note 90, p. 603-604; Brownlie, 2003, *supra* note 7, pp. 701-702, 713-714; Sapiro, *supra* note 48, pp. 599-607; L. Feinstein, A duty to prevent, 98 *ASIL Proceedings* 2004, pp. 89-94; L. Feinstein & A.-M. Slaughter, A duty to prevent, 83 *Foreign Affairs* 2004, pp. 136-150; C.M. Bassiouni, Legal control of international terrorism: A policy-oriented assessment, 43 *Harvard International Law Journal* 2002, pp. 97-103; R. Turner, State responsibility and the war on terror: The legacy of Thomas Jefferson and the Barbary pirates, 4 *Chicago Journal of International Law* 2003, pp. 121-140.

[109] *Roadmap towards the implementation of the United Nations Millennium Declaration*, Report of the Secretary General, UN Doc A/56/326, 6 September 2001. See also Shaw, *supra* note 49, p. 1101.

rorism were based on the collective defence provision. In this framework, the NATO member States agreed, *inter alia*, to provide (a) individually or collectively assistance to Allies and other States which are or may be subject to increased terrorist threats; (b) blanket overflight clearances for the US and other Allies' aircraft for military flights related to operations against terrorism; and (c) access for the US and other Allies to ports and airfields on the territory of NATO States for operations against terrorism, including the deployment of part of NATO's Naval Forces to the Eastern Mediterranean[110].

5. TERRORISM AND PIRACY

5.1. Piracy: Change of pattern

The International Maritime Bureau's Piracy Reporting Centre states that the pattern of pirate attacks has changed. Whereas in the past pirates tended to board ships to steal money or valuable items of cargo, today they try to hijack entire vessels or cargoes. According to the Piracy Reporting Centre at the dawn of the 21st century there are three types of piracy: (a) persons boarding ships in port or at anchor who are stealing anything handy; (b) organized, well armed and determined gangs boarding ships alongside, at anchor or underway in order to steal money from the crew or valuable items of cargo or ship's equipment; and (c) hijackers of ships and cargoes[111].

Hijacking of ships and cargoes is on the increase[112]. This type of attack is also the most serious and life threatening to the crews.

---

[110] They also agreed to enhance intelligence sharing and co-operation, relating to the threats posed by terrorism; take necessary measures to provide increased security for facilities of the United States and other Allies on their territory; backfill Allied assets in NATO's area of responsibility that are required to directly support operations against terrorism; for more see *Statement to the Press by NATO Secretary General, Lord Robertson, on the North Atlantic Council Decision on Implementation of Article 5 of the Washington Treaty following the 11 September Attacks against the United States.*

[111] See International Maritime Bureau's Piracy Reporting Centre, *Attacks on Ships. Background Information*, http://www.marisec.org/piracy/background.htm#IMO (last visited: 27 April 2005). See also M.W. Brauchli, High Seas scourge: Pirates return in Asia armed with AK 47s instead of bolo knives, *Wall Street Journal*, 2 June 1993.

[112] See e.g. the case of the Malaysian tanker *Petchem*, carrying a mixed cargo of light fuel oil and aviation spirit. On 25 September 2000 a gang of armed pirates took control of the ship off East Malaysia. The pirates painted a false name on the ship's stern, changed the colour of its funnel, and then navigated near Johore, where they pumped the light fuel oil onto a second vessel; Piracy in southeast Asia getting out of control, *Jane's Terrorism & Security Monitor*, 1 November 2000. See also C. Glass, Terror on the High Seas? Piracy is up, increasing fears of terror attacks at sea, *ABC News*, 10 September 2003.

Hijacking of ships and cargoes is most prevalent in the South China Sea area and off Somalia. Since, the LOS Convention describes as piracy an act that takes place on the high seas or outside the jurisdiction of any State[113], attacks within the territorial sea of a State cannot be described as "piracy" according to the LOS Convention. Attacks taking place in the territorial sea fall within the jurisdiction of the littoral State and they are that State's responsibility to address. From the three types of "piracy", hijacking of ships and cargoes is the type that more often takes place on the high seas. Thus, the naval forces that control the area have jurisdiction to deal with these incidents.

Hijacking of ships and cargoes can link pirates with terrorists. The existence of pirates stealing entire ships reveals a collaboration between criminal gangs and unknown patrons, who may well be international terrorists[114]. The fear is that ships carrying fuel or chemical cargoes could be hijacked and used in indiscriminate terrorist attacks. This is one of the aspects of the relationship between piracy and terrorism. The other is the attempt to equate terrorists with pirates.

5.2. "Terrorists today, like pirates of old"[115]

The first attempt to address the issue of maritime terrorism in a convention was made after the *Achille Lauro* incident in 1985. In this incident, a group of Palestinians from the Popular Liberation Front seized an Italian registered cruise ship in Egyptian territorial waters, kept five hundred passengers and crew as hostages for two days and demanded the release of some Palestinian prisoners from Israel. During the seizure of the ship a wheel-chair-bound American-Jew was murdered[116]. One of the legal questions raised in relation to the *Achille Lauro* was whether the seizure of the ship constituted piracy.

---

[113] According to article 101 of the LOS Convention: "Piracy consists of any of the following acts: (a) any illegal acts of violence or detention, or any act of depredation, committed for private ends by the crew or the passengers of a private ship or a private aircraft, and directed (i) on the high seas, against another ship or aircraft, or against persons or property on board such ship or aircraft, (ii) against a ship, aircraft, persons or property in a place outside the jurisdiction of any State; (b) any act of voluntary participation in the operation of a ship or of an aircraft with knowledge of facts making it a pirate ship or aircraft; (c) any act inciting or of intentionally facilitating an act described in sub-paragraph (a) or (b)".

[114] T. Ország-Land, Fighting terrorism at sea, *Jane's Terrorism & Security Monitor*, 1 July 2003.

[115] M. Halberstam, Terrorism on the High Seas: The *Achille Lauro*, Piracy and the IMO Convention on Maritime Safety, 82 *AJIL* 1988, p. 289.

[116] See A. Cassese, *Terrorism, politics and the law: The* Achille Lauro *Affair* (Princeton University Press, Princeton 1989).

The exclusion of political objectives from the definition of piracy in the LOS Convention and its restriction on private acts led to the exemption of a terrorist act, such as the *Achille Lauro* incident, as an act of piracy.

Since then there is a trend towards equating terrorism (or at least certain forms of terrorism[117]) with piracy[118]. This trend became more obvious following the 9/11 attacks. It is based on the argument that the definition of piracy in both the 1958 and 1982 Conventions is not exhaustive. As O'Connell noted: "Because of its elliptical nature, article 15 is one of the least successful essays in codification of the law of the sea, and the question is open whether it is comprehensive so as to preclude reliance upon customary law, where this may differ, or has superseded customary law. If … article 15 [of the 1958 Convention] is not exclusive of other definitions of piracy, then a number of questions are opened up".

In any case, the aim is to reconsider piracy and terrorism and extend universal jurisdiction recognized under international law for piracy to also cover terrorism. The principle of universality provides a prosecuting State with jurisdiction, irrespective of where the acts take place or the nationality of any people involved[119]. Thus, if terrorists are held to be guilty of piracy, any State could validly seize their vessel on the high seas. For that purpose, it has even been suggested to consider terrorism as a crime against humanity or even as genocide[120].

In reality and with the exception of piracy, genocide, crimes against humanity and the crime of aggression[121], State practice is very reluctant to recognize the existence of universal jurisdiction. It is interesting to note that, as already mentioned, the crime of slavery is not considered as a crime against humanity in the LOS Convention. Even the ICJ in the *Congo v. Belgium* case

---

[117] e.g. to include single ship seizures; G.R. Constantinople, Towards a New Definition of Piracy: The *Achille Lauro* Incident, 6 *Vancouver JIL* 1985, pp.748-749.

[118] In addition to the above mentioned passage by Halberstam, see also F.W. Paasche, who also considers that "acts of terrorism, like acts of piracy, should be declared crimes against humanity'"; The use of force in combating terrorism, 25 *Columbia Journal of Transnational Law* 1987, p. 380; also S.P. Menefee, Piracy, terrorism and the insurgent passenger: A historical and legal perspective, *in* N. Ronzitti (ed.), *Maritime terrorism and International Law* (Martinus Nijhoff, Dodrecht 1990) pp. 43-68.

[119] See M.H. Morris, Universal jurisdiction in a divided world: Conference remarks, 35 *New England Law Review* 2001, p. 2001; also M.P. Scharf, Application of treaty-based universal jurisdiction to nationals of non-party States, *ibid.*, p. 361.

[120] See e.g. J.D. Fry, Terrorism as a crime against humanity and genocide: The backdoor to universal jurisdiction, 7 *UCLA Journal of International Law & Foreign Affairs* 2002, pp. 190-197.

[121] In 1946 the UN General Assembly codified the universality principle as applied in the Nuremberg tribunal to war crimes, crimes against humanity and the crime of aggression, General Assembly Resolution 95, UN Doc. A/64/Add.1 (1946).

avoided to rule on the question of a State's exercise of universal jurisdiction[122]. With the exception of some European States that have adopted legislation that provides their courts with varying degrees of universal jurisdiction[123], the US is generally sceptical to the general principle of universality[124].

A further problem is that, with the exception of certain types of terrorism such as hijacking[125] and crimes against diplomats[126], international law does not provide a universal definition of terrorism. Different States have different perspectives on what constitutes terrorist acts, which is often depended on political orientation. Although it can be said that the term 'terrorism' refers to violence with a political motive and that the international community clearly condemns terrorism in general, international law prohibits only specific terrorist acts occurring at a particular time. Thus, it is very difficult to assert universal jurisdiction over terrorism on the high seas, since it is unclear who is a terrorist and what constitutes a terrorist act especially under circumstances where there is absence of proof of an attack and "uncertainty

---

[122] M.A. Summers, The International Court of Justice's decision in *Congo v. Belgium*: How has it affected the development of a principle of universal jurisdiction that would obligate all states to prosecute war criminals?, 21 *Boston University International Law Journal* 2003, pp. 65, 67-68.

[123] Belgium, Austria and Denmark have adopted legislation which provides their courts with varying degrees of jurisdiction based on universality; see e.g. M. Holdgaard Bukh, Prosecution before Danish Courts of foreigners suspected of serious violations of human rights or humanitarian law, 6 *Revue Européenne de Droit Public* 1994, pp. 339-352. Spain requested the extradition of Chilean General Augusto Pinochet from Britain on the basis of universal jurisdiction; W.J. Aceves, Liberalism and international legal scholarship: The *Pinochet* case and the move towards a universal system of transnational law litigation, 41 *Harvard International Law Journal*, pp.162-164.

[124] Brownlie, *supra* note 7, p. 303. Another remark in relation to the reluctance of the USA to accept universal jurisdiction is that prosecution of suspected terrorists in other States might be considered as inadequate due to the fact that convicted terrorists may not receive the death penalty, which has been abolished in all the European Union countries; Fry, *supra* note 120, p. 198.

[125] Convention on Offences and Certain Other Acts Committed on Board Aircraft, Tokyo, 1963, *ILM* 1963, pp. 1042-1046; Convention for the Suppression of Unlawful Seizure of Aircraft, Hague, 16 December 1970, *ILM* 1971, pp. 133-136; Convention for the Suppression of Unlawful Acts Against the Safety of Civil Aviation, Montreal, 23 September 1971, 10 *ILM* 1971, pp. 1151-1156.

[126] See Convention on the Prevention and Punishment of Crimes against Internationally Protected Persons, including Diplomatic Agents, General Assembly of the United Nations, 14 December 1973, 13 *ILM*, p. 41; International Convention against the Taking of Hostages, General Assembly of the United Nations, 4 December 1979, 18 *ILM*, pp. 1456-1462.

remains as to the time and place of the enemy's attack", as it was stated in the US National Security Strategy in 2002[127].

6. RECENT STATE PRACTICE ON INTERDICTION OF VESSELS ON THE HIGH SEAS

6.1. Abuse of the UN trade embargo against Iraq

The legality of maritime interceptions in cases where warships acted under the terms of resolutions adopted by the UN Security Council is not contested. Thus cases like the blockade in Rhodesia based on Security Council Resolutions 221 and 232 in 1966[128] or Iraq, Haiti[129] and Serbia[130] in the 1990s were perfectly legal. Nevertheless, attempts were made to use the UN embargo in order to acquire a broader jurisdiction to visit and search vessels under foreign flags. More specifically, in 1990 the UN imposed sanctions on Iraq, after the invasion of Kuwait. Various States contributed forces to enforce the trade embargo imposed on Iraq by UN Security Council Resolutions 661 (1990) and 687 (1991)[131]. Naval and air units were sent by 18 countries[132]. The Fifth Fleet of the US Navy assumed leadership of the international naval force. Naval units were deployed in the Straits of Hormuz and the Horn of Africa. All the ships leaving or heading for Iraqi ports were li-

---

[127] *National Security Strategy of the United States of America*, September 2002, http://www.whitehouse.gov/nsc/nss.pdf, p. 15.

[128] See J.E.S. Fawcett, Security Council Resolution on Rhodesia, 41 *BYBIL* 1965-66, pp. 118 *et seq.*; for the case of the two Greek ships attempting to run the blockade see H.L. Cryer, Legal aspects of the *Joanna V* and *Manuela* Incidents, *Australian Yearbook of International Law* 1966, pp. 85-98.

[129] UN Security Council, acting under Chapter VII of the Charter, adopted Resolution 841/1993 which imposed an arms and oil embargo on Haiti. The Security Council decided to reimpose sanctions with Resolution 873/1993. Resolution 917/1994 tightened sanctions with a general trade embargo.

[130] UN Security Council, acting under Chapter VII of the Charter, adopted Resolution 757/1992 in relation to the events in the former Socialist Federal Republic of Yugoslavia and imposed a trade embargo. Resolutions 713/1991 and 727/1991 have imposed an arms embargo.

[131] Security Council Resolution 661 (1990) imposed economic sanctions on Iraq, including a "full trade embargo barring all imports from and exports to Iraq, excepting only medical supplies, foodstuffs, and other items of humanitarian need". Security Council Resolution 687 (1991) declared that "the full trade embargo against Iraq would remain in place", pending periodic reviews every 60 days (par. 21) and every 120 days (par. 28) of Iraqi compliance with the obligations imposed under it. Security Council Security Council Resolutions 1134 & 1137 (1997) "imposed travel restrictions" on all Iraqi officials.

[132] British, Canadian, Dutch, German, Greek, French, Italian, Japanese, Polish, Spanish, and US naval assets were regularly assigned to operate in the area.

able to be searched. Only cargo falling within "oil for food" program could leave for Iraq[133]. Imports had to be approved by the UN Sanctions Committee.

The bulk of the work of the naval forces was the monitoring of commercial traffic and boarding of suspicious vessels. Various tactics have been employed. Maritime patrol aircraft conducted surveillance on the seas next to Iraq. Suspicious ships were queried on the high seas and if suspicions remained, boarding was taking place. Since illicit cargo was often hidden in concealed oil tanks that could not be easily found by onboard teams, the vessels could be diverted to a holding area for detailed survey. If there was hidden cargo, the vessel was seized[134].

During the enforcement of the UN trade embargo against Iraq, the US were tempted to use the embargo regime in order to search ships headed for other countries not subject to embargo. On 21 February 1992 it became known that US intelligence agencies tracked a North-Korean government-owned ship, the "*Dae Hung Ho*", with a shipment of advanced missiles and missile-manufacturing equipment. The ship was heading for Syria[135]. The shipment was prohibited under the Missile Technology Control Regime[136]. Nevertheless, North Korea has never signed to this regime and thus the

---

[133] Security Council Resolution 712 (1991) allowed a partial lifting of the embargo, which would have enabled Iraq to sell some oil to use the proceeds for humanitarian purposes. Resolution 986 (1995) enabled Iraq to sell up to $1 billion of oil every 90 days. On 20 May 1996 the UN and the Government of Iraq concluded the Memorandum of Understanding that codified the practical arrangements for the implementation of the oil-for-food agreement. Resolutions 1241 & 1281 (1999) extended the oil-for-food programme. Resolution 1284 (1999) removed the ceiling on Iraqi oil exports and provided for additional specific arrangements for facilitating humanitarian supplies to Iraq. Following Resolution 1302 (2000), the Security Council repeatedly extended the "oil for food" programme for 180-day periods over the following years.

[134] According to Captain Mark Buzby, commander of US Destroyer Squadron Thirty One, who led the maritime interdiction operations in the northern and southern Gulf during the latter half of 2002: "In a typical week we do 500 queries of ships and make 150-200 boardings. At the top of the Gulf we make seizures every night… Every week 10-30 dhows and five or six large ships are boarded and diverted to a holding area for detailed survey so [that] we can investigate them"; T. Ripley, Middle East maritime embargo patrols maintain pressure, *Jane's Navy International*, 1 January 2003.

[135] E. Sciolino, US tracks a Korean Ship taking missile to Syria, *The New York Times*, 21 February 1992.

[136] The Missile Technology Control Regime is an informal and voluntary association of thirty four countries (as of April 2005) which seek to coordinate national export licensing efforts aimed at preventing the proliferation of unmanned delivery systems capable of delivering weapons of mass destruction. It was originally established in 1987 by Canada, France, Germany, Italy, Japan, the United Kingdom and the United States.

shipment did not violate any of (the limited, in any case) North Korea's international pledges. The US were prepared to intercept the ship on the high seas of the Persian Gulf and board her. This was going to be a symbolic gesture, hoping to create diplomatic and public pressure that might deter North Korea delivering the shipment. The American Navy could query the ship only if it was entering the Persian Gulf. If it was confirmed that the shipment was not bound for Iraq, the US Navy did not have UN authority to seize either the ship or its cargo[137]. Nevertheless, there was severe criticism to any action against the North Korean vessel on the high seas: "It would make a mockery of international law to use American warships that are helping enforce a trade embargo against Iraq, sanctioned by the UN, to search ships headed for other countries not subject to embargo"[138]. Finally, the decision to search the ship was considered as wholly unjustified and was never initiated.

6.2. Operation "Enduring Freedom"

Immediately after the 11 September 2001 terrorist attacks and responding to the Taliban's refusal to surrender *Al-Qaeda* leaders, including bin Laden[139], the USA began a military operation against Afghanistan. The operation was part of the war against terrorism and its name was Operation "Enduring Freedom"[140]. The short-term goals of the Operation included the destruction of terrorist training camps and infrastructure within Afghanistan, the capture of *al Qaeda* leaders, the cessation of terrorist activities in Afghanistan and the prevention of the use of Afghanistan as a safe haven for terrorists[141]. Long-term goals included the end of terrorism and the deterrence of State sponsorship of terrorism[142].

---

[137] A. Rosenthal, No orders to stop arms ship, *The New York Times*, 9 March 1992.

[138] Misguided machismo on the High Seas, leading article in *The New York Times*, 7 March 1992.

[139] See also the relevant UN Security Council Resolutions 1267/1999 & 1333/2001.

[140] The initial name was "Operation Infinite Justice". It became "Operation Enduring Freedom" when Islamic scholars complained that only God was capable of dispensing infinite justice and the US administration worried that people in the Middle East would take offence by the use of this name. For more see E. Becker, Renaming an Operation to Fit the Mood, *The New York Times*, 26 September 2001. It was supported by the Canadian Operation "Apollo".

[141] See President George W. Bush Address to a Joint Session of Congress and the American People, 20th September 2001, http://www.whitehouse.gov/news/releases/2001/09/2001 0920-8.html; also President George W. Bush Speaks to America After the Strikes Begin, Address made from the Treaty Room in the White House, 7 October 2001.

[142] As expressed by the British Prime Minister, Tony Blair, in Her Majesty's Government Campaign Objectives, 16 October 2001, http://www.globalsecurity.org/military/library/news/ 2001/10/uk-011016-terror-objectives.htm.

Planning involved not only destruction of the *Al-Qaeda* network inside Afghanistan but also maritime interdiction operations in support of "Operation Enduring Freedom". For that purpose naval forces were deployed to the Gulf or Arabian Sea. At this point it has to be noted that the mandates for the enforcement of the Iraqi embargo and of the Operation "Enduring Freedom" were distinct and separate. Nevertheless, forces of the countries participating in both operations were routinely rotated between the two. France and Japan deployed naval forces in the Indian Ocean and NATO naval forces supported the operation in the Eastern Mediterranean[143]. The aim of the naval forces was: a) to search for Taliban and *Al-Qaeda* leaders fleeing from Afghanistan and Pakistan especially in the Straits of Hormuz[144]; b) to protect international waterways and navigation channels[145]; c) to watch for about twenty merchant ships known to have ties with *Al-Qaeda*[146]; and d) to eliminate the threat of attacks on shipping by small craft operated by terrorists.

During these operations the allied forces in the northern Arabian Sea and the Gulf of Oman were tracking all passing merchant vessels. They questioned the captains of every merchant vessel by radio. The answers were transmitted to a command centre where they were checked against a database. If there was a refusal of answer or suspicions due to incomplete answers, a search could take place. It seems that allied forces were more aggressive towards local tiny fishing boats (known as 'dhowls'). Teams of sailors boarded them and searched the cargo and the passengers. On the contrary, the allied forces were much more cautious with international shipping. There was seldom any boarding on these ships and cooperation by the captain was always needed[147].

Following the defeat of the Taliban regime in Afghanistan and the formation of a provisional government on 23 December 2001, naval forces remained *in situ* protecting international waterways. The attack against a French oil super-tanker, the *"Limburg"*, in October 2002, confirmed terrorist

---

[143] As provided by the International Institute of Strategic Studies, *Naval Forces in the Gulf/Arabian Sea and in Support of Operation Enduring Freedom*, 6 May 2003, http://www.iiss.org/iraqCrisis-more.php?itemID=137.

[144] See D.S. Cloud, US Navy, allies patrol sea off Somalia, in search of fleeing *Al Qaeda* fighters, *The New York Times*, 4 January 2002.

[145] One of the threats to the sea lanes were sea mines. In October 2002 Britain dispatched a Mine Countermeasures Group; Ripley, *supra* note 134.

[146] See W.K. Rashbaum & B. Weiser, *Al Qaeda*'s fleet, *The New York Times*, 27 December 2001. According to other information by 2003 23 merchant vessels were linked to Osama bin Laden. All of them were registered in Arab countries and with flags of convenience, see Ország-Land, *supra* note 114.

[147] J. Dao, Coalition widens its ocean manhunt, *The New York Times*, 17 March 2002.

interest in maritime targets[148]. It seems that Osama bin Laden took responsibility for this attack. In addition to this, other *Al Qaeda* leaders declared that they wanted to cut the economic lifelines of the world's industrialized societies[149]. One year earlier, on 30 October 2001, the Liberation Tigers of Tamil Eelam claimed responsibility for suicide bombers destroying the oil tanker "Silk Pride" 12 nautical miles north of Point Pedro off Sri Lanka[150]. These incidents and threats further disturbed the world's seagoing States, especially in relation to the vulnerability of oil tankers.

The growing tension between the USA, Britain and their allies with Iraq reinforced the requirement for a strong international maritime presence in the region. During the war in Iraq, the naval forces participating in Operation "Enduring Freedom" continued tracking merchant vessels and conducting maritime interdiction operations. These operations continued even after the formal ending of the UN embargo on Iraq[151]. The Red Sea is considered a prime area for *Al-Qaeda* ship-borne terrorist activity. Maritime interdiction operations continue to be at the centre of international naval operations in the Middle East. Although few details of the exact behaviour of the naval forces have entered the public domain, it seems that they have respected freedom of navigation on the high seas. This is even proved by the outcome of the North Korean cargo vessel, "*So San*", which has finally been released.

6.3. NATO's Active Endeavour

A day before the beginning of Operation "Enduring Freedom", on 6 October 2001, NATO deployed its Standing Naval Forces to the Eastern Mediterranean. This was one of the early measures agreed upon by the Allies after 9/11. Some 20 days later, the operation was named "Active Endeavour". The initial goal of the Operation was to survey the trade routes of the Eastern Mediterranean and keep them open and safe. For that purpose NATO's naval forces were carrying out route surveys in important waterways. The aim of

---

[148] A French oil tanker, the *Limburg*, was attacked by a small boat on 6 October 2002 while docking to take on crude oil in Mina al-Dabah port in Yemen. The Aden Abyan Islamic Army (AAIA) claimed the attack. For more see E. Sciolino, Preliminary investigation indicates oil tanker was attacked, *The New York Times*, 11 October 2002. The attack against *Limburg* followed a previous attack in October 2000 against "*USS Cole*" in Yemen.

[149] K. Bradsher, Warnings from *Al Qaeda* stir fear that terrorist may attack oil tankers, *The New York Times*, 12 December 2002.

[150] Sri Lankan suicide attack at sea, 30 October 2001, CNN News, http://edition.cnn.com/ 2001/WORLD/asiapcf/south/10/30/slanka.tiger.attack.

[151] All sanctions, "except those related to the sale or supply to Iraq of arms and related material", were formally ended by the Security Council Resolution 2483 (2003).

the operation was to detect ships transporting WMD or terrorists. In case they discover ships carrying illegal immigrant or refugees, they do not intervene but pass the information to the nearby coastal NATO States[152]. Operation "Active Endeavour" was the first time that NATO forces have been deployed in order to implement article 5 of the North Atlantic Treaty.

In March 2003 the Operation was extended to cover the western area of the Mediterranean Sea. Naval forces, provided upon request, escort through the straits of Gibraltar commercial ships flying the flag of NATO's member States. The aim was to prevent terrorist attacks similar to the one against the French oil tanker, the "*Limburg*", in October 2002. A month later NATO expanded the mandate of the naval operation from surveillance to include boarding and searching of vessels[153]. A week after the terror attacks in Spain, in March 2004, NATO ordered the extension of anti-terrorist surveillance patrols to the whole of the Mediterranean[154]. For the coordination of operations under "Active Endeavour", an Operations Training Centre has been established in Souda, Crete in Greece.

According to a US official[155], merchant ships passing through the eastern Mediterranean are queried by the patrolling NATO warships to identify themselves. The information is reported to Allied centres in Italy and Britain. In case there is something suspicious, the Allied forces are asking permission to board the ship in order to inspect documentation and cargo. The most suspicious ships are general cargo vessels between 2,000-4,500 tones, over 20-25 years old, that have been sold several times and have switched to flags, which do not respect the requirement for the existence of a genuine link between the State and the ship (not necessarily flags of convenience).

The boarding of ships on the high seas is taking place with the consent of the ship's master[156]. In practice, teams between 15-20 soldiers are boarding the vessel. It seems that 7,9% of ships are unwilling to grant permission for the boarding. In such a case the vessel enters on a kind of a black list and she

---

[152] NATO sources speaking on condition of anonymity.

[153] All the information concerning Operation "Active Endeavour" was provided by NATO briefing, *Active Endeavour. NATO naval operations. Proliferation Security Initiative*, NATO Public Diplomacy Division, Brussels, December 2003.

[154] A NATO spokesman said that the decision to extend the Operation "was not directly a response to last week's terror attacks in Madrid", *Agence France Presse*, 16 March 2004.

[155] Information provided by Thad Moyseowicz, Captain of the US Navy during interview held on 25 May 2004.

[156] It seems that US, German and French warships consider that they are allowed to board as long as they get the captain's consent. British and Greek warships need also to know the flag State's position about the boarding.

is followed by NATO warships while an official authorization by the flag State to board is requested. Between April 2003[157] and January 2005 the NATO naval forces hailed almost 59,000 vessels and conducted 80 compliant boardings[158].

During the NATO summit in Istanbul in June 2004, heads of State and government of the NATO member States responded positively to proposals for participation of Russia and Ukraine in the Operation "Active Endeavour". Although there initially some problems due to the fact that article 5 of the North Atlantic Treaty did not envisage participation of States other than NATO, the whole issue was settled and Russian warships practiced joint manoeuvres with NATO as part of anti-terrorist operations[159]. In January 2005 Russia decided to participate in the Operation, though not on a permanent basis. The aim was to conduct anti-terrorist operations in the Black Sea[160]. By March 2005 the process of participation was likely to be completed by the end of 2005, in order for the Black Sea fleet warships to join the operation in the Mediterranean in 2006[161].

6.4. Minor incidents and developments as part of the "War on Terrorism"

The North Korean "*So San*" interdiction was just one of the incidents that took place on the seas following the 9/11 terrorist attacks and the initiation of the "war on terrorism". Nevertheless, it is interesting to note that although US intelligence knew of the cargo at least four weeks before its interception by the Spanish Navy, they were searching for a justification to board the ship which would be valid under international law. In late November they considered that they found this justification. Although the hull of the ship read "*So San*" in letters freshly painted, no ship under this name was registered. Thus US officials considered that it was a ship without nationality. More-

---

[157] The first boarding took place on 29 April 2003. Merchant vessels "*Nino Star*" and "*Dimo*" both flagged by Comoros were boarded in international waters near Cyprus,; NATO ships start boarding operations in Mediterranean, *M2 Presswire*, 1 May 2003.

[158] NATO briefing, *Response to terrorism. Active Operating against terrorism. Strengthening cooperation and capabilities*, NATO Public Diplomacy Division, Brussels, March 2005, p. 5.

[159] Russian warships head for Mediterranean to join NATO drills, *BBC Monitoring International Reports*, 26 November 2004.

[160] Russian warships to take part in NATO's Active Endeavour operation, *BBC Monitoring International Reports*, 12 January 2005.

[161] Black Sea fleet may join NATO Active Endeavour operation in 2006, ITAR-TASS News Agency, 15 March 2005.

over, while on the high seas, no flag was flying over the vessel. On these grounds they decided that they could proceed with the boarding[162].

The "*So San*" incident was not the only one. A few weeks after the 9/11 attacks the Italian authorities found a container which was fitted with a bed, toilet, laptop computer and mobile and satellite phones[163]. Following this incident, the US designed the Container Security Initiative (CSI). Under the CSI, the US authorities have entered into bilateral agreements with other States[164] with the aim to identify high-risk cargo containers at the port of departure instead of at the port of arrival[165].

On 23 June 2003 the Greek Coast Guard interdicted and boarded a vessel named "*Baltic Sky*", registered in the Comoros and owned by a company in the Marshall islands, while it was in Greek territorial waters. The vessel was packed with explosives, since about 680 tonnes of explosives and 8,000 detonators were discovered on board. The vessel was destined for a company in Sudan that was later discovered to be a simple box office address. The vessel itself was acting suspiciously since it appears that she had re-entered Greek territorial waters some days before the interdiction. With the exception of the Sudanese government that complained about the incident claiming, *inter alia*, that the explosives were to be used for road constructions, no other company raised concerns about the interdiction of the vessel[166]. In this case, the Greek authorities acted in conformity with the applicable rules of international law relating to innocent passage.

In early October 2003 a German ship, the "*BBC China*", while on the high seas en route to Libya, was diverted to an Italian port so that US investigators could search and seize the cargo, which included a thousand components used to enrich uranium. The German company, *BBC Chartering and Logistic*, which owned the ship co-operated with the German authorities that received information by US and British intelligence agents. The captain of "*BBC China*" was ordered by its company to divert the vessel which was es-

---

[162] Information provided by A. Robbins, The UN searching for relevance; operation bypass: why US gave UN no role in plan to halt ships, *Wall Street Journal*, 21 October 2003.

[163] The container was found on 18 October 2001 in the Italian port of Gioia Tauro; Is terrorism heading for the high seas?, *Financial Times*, 7 October 2003.

[164] Other countries participating in CSI are Belgium, China (& Hong Kong), France, Germany, Italy, Japan, Singapore and the UK.

[165] For more see J. Romero, Prevention of maritime terrorism: The Container Security Initiative, 4 *Chicago Journal of International Law* 2003, pp. 597-605; also F. Booth & L. Altenbrun, Maritime and port security, piracy and stowaways: Renewed concerns over old problems, 15 *USF Maritime Law Journal*, pp. 2-47; T. Schoenbaum & J.C. Langston, An all hands evolution: Port security in the wake of September 11, 77 *Tulane Law Review*, pp. 1333-1370.

[166] Greece traces route of seized ship, *CNN*, 24 June 2003.

corted by a US warship to an Italian port. US officials have refused to state who sold the centrifuges or where they originated from. The operation took place in the framework of the PSI. On 19 December 2003 Libya agreed to destroy all of its chemical, nuclear and biological weapons. US officials expressed the view that the discovery of the cargo might have helped Libya towards agreeing to stop its weapons programme[167].

Amongst the most important incidents and developments referred to in this section is the imposition of a 1000-mile "terror exclusion zone" by Australia. On 15 December 2004 Australian Prime Minister, John Howard, announced the creation of a 1000-mile security ring around the coastline of his country. All vessels entering this zone en route to Australia would be requested to give details of the "ship identity, crew, cargo, location, course, speed and intended port of arrival". In case the ships are considered suspicious, Australian authorities will intercept and board them and inspect their cargo and crew[168]. Given the fact that Australia was supportive of the view that pre-emptive self defence is a legitimate response to terrorist threats, the announcement of the new security zone was met with criticism and anger by its neighbours. Indonesia has emphatically rejected Australia's plan as breaching Indonesian maritime jurisdiction and international law[169]. The zone, a clear contravention of international law, has not been enforced during the first months of 2005.

7. PROLIFERATION SECURITY INITIATIVE

The frustrating experience with the North Korean vessel in November 2002, led US President George W. Bush to announce on 31 May 2003 in Krakow, Poland, a new initiative against shipments of WMD and missile-related equipment in transit via air[170], land and sea: "When weapons of mass destruction or their components are in transit, we must have the means and authority to seize them"[171]. This initiative was in harmony with the US "Na-

---

[167] German Ship Seized with Uranium-Making Parts for Libya, *Deutche Welle*, 1 December 2004, http://www.dw-world.de/dw/article/0,1075724,00.html.

[168] K. Marks, Australia to impose 1000-mile terror exclusion zone, *The Independent*, 16 December 2004.

[169] M. Moore, Indonesia rejects plan for security zone as breach of maritime boundaries, *The Sydney Morning Herald*, 18 December 2004.

[170] The PSI refers also to interdiction of planes. The questions related with these interdictions are not discussed.

[171] Remarks by President George W. Bush to the People of Poland, 31 May 2003, http://www.usinfo.pl/bushvisit2003/wawel.htm

tional Strategy to combat Weapons of Mass Destruction"[172], which aimed at stopping WMD to get into the hands of terrorists as well as into States that support terrorism or "have demonstrated records of supporting international instability and tension"[173]. The initiative was named 'Proliferation Security Initiative' ("PSI"). Although it did not explicitly refer to any State, it was obviously directed against North Korea[174] but also against Iraq, Iran as well as Libya, Syria, Sudan and Cuba[175].

Besides the USA, the PSI was initially launched by 10 more States, namely Australia, France, Germany, Italy, Japan, the Netherlands, Poland, Portugal, Spain and the United Kingdom. These States were "*chosen*" with three different criteria: a) they have shown a strong support for non-proliferation; b) they have been involved in active efforts to prevent proliferation, e.g. Spain and Germany in the incident with the motor vessel "*So San*"; and c) they are located in geographically important locations in relation to proliferation pathways, e.g. Japan and Australia[176]. Nevertheless, the PSI was not only limited to the founding States. Cooperation "from any state whose vessels, flags, ports, territorial waters, airspace, or land" might be used both by States and non-State actors for proliferation purposes[177]. From this perspective the PSI cannot be considered as an organization with members. It is open to all States of the world that adopt the very principles of the PSI.

---

[172] *National Strategy to Combat Weapons of Mass Destruction*, NSPD-17 / HSPD 4 [unclassified version], December 2002, http://www.fas.org/irp/offdocs/nspd/nspd-17.html.

[173] B. Coceano, *The Proliferation Security Initiative: Challenges and Perceptions*, The Atlantic Council of the United States, Occasional Paper, Washington, DC, May 2004, p. 3.

[174] See the press release issued by Alexander Downer, Australia's Foreign Affairs Minister, who stated that "the initiative is global in nature and while it is not directed at any one country, it is relevant to the government's concerns about North Korea, including its declared nuclear weapons programme"; Australia to host forum on mass destruction weapons 9-10 July, *BBC Monitoring International Reports*, 26 June 2003.

[175] Testimony of John R. Bolton, Under Secretary for Arms Control and International Security, U.S. Department of State, Committee on International Relations, United States House of Representatives, 4 June 2003, http://wwwa.house.gov/international_relations/108/bolt0604.htm.

[176] See Question: How were the founding PSI countries *chosen*" [emphasis added], *Proliferation Security Initiative Frequently Asked Questions*, Fact Sheet, Bureau of Non-Proliferation, Washington, DC, 11 January 2005. Nevertheless, South Korea has not joined the PSI "due to the peculiar and political and security situation of the Korean peninsula"; Interview with Song Young Wan, South Korea's Deputy Director General for Disarmament, *Asian Export Control Observer*, Center for Non-Proliferation Studies, Monterey Institute of International Studies, Issue 3, August/September 2004, p. 21.

[177] *Proliferation Security Initiative: Statement of Interdiction Principles*, 4 September 2003, Office of the Press Secretary, The White House, Washington, DC., reprinted in Annex II(a).

The initial aim of the PSI seems to be the taking of action against suspicious vessels on the high seas. US Under-Secretary of State for Arms Control, John Bolton, declared that the States participating to the PSI "had the authority to intercept any suspect ships and aircraft in international waters and airspace"[178]. However, it was obvious that this was not consistent with international law[179]. The founders of the PSI claimed that their initiative was based on the Statement made by the President of the Security Council on 31 January 1992, at the conclusion of the 3046th meeting of the Security Council, in connection with the item entitled: "The responsibility of the Security Council in the maintenance of international peace and security"[180]. According to this statement: "The proliferation of all weapons of mass destruction constitutes a threat to international peace and security. The members of the Council commit themselves to working to prevent the spread of technology related to the research for or production of such weapons and to take appropriate action to that end".[181]

Nevertheless this statement was quite vague as to the exact actions that could be undertaken for its implementation. Furthermore, Presidential Statements do not enjoy the same status as Security Council Resolutions. Thus, the statement could not legitimise actions of pre-emptive interdiction of vessels on the high seas on the ground of shipment of WMD.

The problem with the legal issues involved was shown during the first meeting of the PSI founding members in June 2003, where there was an initial disagreement between the US and the other participating States. US Under Secretary of State, John Bolton, stated that there existed authorization to interdict on the high seas in three cases, namely a) when ships do not display a State flag, they effectively become pirate ships that can be seized; b) when ships use a "flag of convenience" and the State chosen gives the United States or its allies permission, the ships can be stopped and searched and; c) when there is a serious belief that the vessels carry WMD material. In the last case the authority for interdiction was based on a "general right of self-defence"[182]. On the contrary, the majority of the participating States were of

---

[178] Michael Evans, US plans to seize suspects at will, *The Times*, 11 July 2003.

[179] See the reaction of British diplomats on the US statement concerning authorisation to take action on the high seas and in international airspace: "All 11 participants agreed that any action that might be taken would have to be consistent with international law"; Evans, *ibid.*

[180] The USA stated that: "The PSI is consistent with and a step in the implementation of the UN Security Council Presidential Statement of January 1992"; US Department Fact Sheet, 4 September 2003, Proliferation Security Initiative Meeting, Paris, 3-4 September 2003.

[181] UN Security Council Statement, Project on Chemical and Biological Warfare, S/23500, 31 January 1992

[182] G. Sheridan, US 'free' to tackle N. Korea, *The Australian*, 9 July 2003.

a different opinion. Finally a consensus was reached[183] on the search of ship-ment as soon as suspicious vessels and aircraft enter territory, territorial wa-ters or airspace of the participating States. Thus, and provided that the right of innocent passage was respected, within the territorial waters, only national laws would be enforced.

On 4 September 2003 the eleven States finally agreed on a general state-ment of interdiction principles. Apart from the exchange of information, PSI participants were committed to take actions in support of interdiction efforts regarding cargoes of WMD and more specifically:

(i) to prohibit transport or assistance to transport of cargoes of WMD by them or by persons under their jurisdiction;

(ii) to interdict, board and search any suspicious vessel flying their flag in their internal waters or territorial seas, or areas beyond the territo-rial seas of any other State;

(iii) to "seriously consider providing consent" to the boarding and searching by other States, of its own flag vessels that are suspicious;

(iv) to stop and search "in their internal waters, territorial seas, or con-tiguous zones" suspicious vessels carrying WMD cargoes to or from States or non-State actors of proliferation concern and to seize such cargoes; and

(v) to enforce conditions on suspicious vessels entering or leaving their ports, internal waters or territorial seas such as requiring that such vessels be subject to boarding, search, and seizure of such cargoes prior to entry.

These actions could be undertaken provided that they were consistent with the obligations of participating States under international law.

The statement showed that all States participating in the PSI accepted that no interdiction or seizure of ship could take place on the high seas. Even the US changed their policy and wanted to "base…efforts on the inventive use of national laws"[184]. As American officials accepted, cargoes with WMD "could not be seized in international waters. But if they entered the waters of a coalition member, they could be grabbed under a variety of national laws"[185]. Nevertheless, interdiction, search andseizure of a ship within the territorial waters is not something that it is left entirely at the discretion of

---

[183] See R. Weiner, Proliferation Security Initiative to Stem Flow of WMD Matériel, 16 July 2003, http://cns.miis.edu/pubs/week/030716.htm.

[184] D.E. Sanger, When laws don't apply: Cracking down on the terror-arms trade, *The New York Times*, 15 June 2003

[185] *Idem.*

the coastal State. Under both customary and conventional law, when a ship exercises the right of innocent passage through the territorial sea, the coastal State cannot hamper this passage. Only when the passage is non-innocent, i.e. "prejudicial to the peace, public order or security of the coastal State", the coastal State may take the necessary steps to prevent it[186]. In addition, the LOS Convention enumerates in article 19 specific activities, which automatically render passage as non-innocent.

After the announcement of the general statement of interdiction principles, the States parties to the PSI started conducting exercises on the seas in order to work out gathering of intelligence information, procedures and techniques for interdicting WMD cargoes. In spite of the fact that it was accepted that all participating States to the PSI have agreed that there exist strict limitations to interdict a ship on the high seas, it is interesting to note that, during the PSI exercise "Sea Saber" which was held in the Arabian Sea in January 2004, the Spanish Navy forcibly boarded a target ship on the high seas. According to the exercise scenario, the master of the vessel refused to give permission which was finally granted by the State whose flag the vessel was flying[187].

The limitations to interdict ships on the high seas led the States parties to the PSI to rely on bilateral agreements with flag States. The idea was to stop and search ships (identified as being involved in WMD trading) on the high seas after getting permission from the country that issued the ship's flag and not from the master of the ship. It was within this scope that the US signed a series of agreements with Liberia[188], Panama[189], the Marshall Islands[190], Croa-

---

[186] See articles 17-26 of the LOS Convention. Article 23 of the LOS Convention even allows the right of innocent passage through territorial seas to "ships carrying nuclear or other inherently dangerous or noxious substances" as long as they "carry documents and observe special precautionary measures established for such ships by international agreements". The aim of the present paper is not to examine interdiction of ships in the territorial waters.

[187] At least three interdictions in international anti-WMD effort, *Agence France Presse*, 15 January 2004.

[188] Agreement between the Government of the United States of America and the Government of the Republic of Liberia concerning cooperation to suppress the proliferation of weapons of Mass Destruction, their deliver systems and related material by sea, Washington, 11 February 2004, http://www.state.gov/t/np/trty/32403.htm; reprinted in Annex II(b). The Liberian agreement was regarded by US officials as a model for similar agreements; see: High time to stop terrorists on the high seas, *Financial Times*, 27 February 2004.

[189] Amendment to the Supplementary Arrangement between the Government of the United States of America and the Government of the Republic of Panama to Arrangement between the Government of the United States of America and the Government of the Republic of Panama for support and assistance from the United States Coast Guard for the National Maritime Service of the Ministry of Government and Justice, 12 May 2004, http://www.state.gov/

tia[191], Cyprus[192] and Belize[193]. With the exception of Croatia, all the other States have registers that are listed as flags of convenience by the International Transport Workers' Federation. More specifically, Panama has more ships flying its flag than any other country in the world. Liberia is second in this list, Cyprus[194] and the Marshall Islands registries are ranked among top 10 merchant fleet of the World, when measured in gross tonnage.

All agreements referred to in their preambles to customary international law of the sea as well as to the provisions of the LOS Convention. Nevertheless, they fall into two different categories as far as boarding and inspection arrangements are concerned: On the one hand, there are the agreements with Croatia and Cyprus. These two agreements establish a system of consultation between the contracting Parties concerning transportation by sea of items of proliferation concern. If a suspect vessel claiming nationality of one of the contracting Parties is on the high seas, the other Party may request authorization to board and search the vessel. The other Party, after examining the information forming the basis for the suspicion, may authorize or deny permission to board and search. There is no implied authorization to board and search in case the State of the suspect vessel does not reply to the request.

On the other hand, there are the agreements with Liberia, the Marshall Islands, Belize and Panama. The agreements between the US and the first three countries have identical structure and, with few minor exceptions, fol-

---

t/np/trty/32858.htm. See also: Panama joins Accord to stem ships' transport of illicit arms, *The New York Times*, 11 May 2004.

[190] Agreement between the Government of the United States of America and the Government of the Republic of the Marshall Islands concerning cooperation to suppress the proliferation of weapons of Mass Destruction, their deliver systems and related material by sea, Washington, 13 August 2004, http://www.state.gov/t/np/trty/35237.htm; reprinted in Annex II(c).

[191] Agreement between the Government of the United States of America and the Government of the Republic of Croatia concerning cooperation to suppress the proliferation of weapons of mass destruction, their delivery systems, and related materials, 1 June 2005, http://www.state.gov/t/np/trty/47086.htm.

[192] Agreement Between the Government of the United States of America and the Government of the Republic of Cyprus Concerning Cooperation to Suppress the Proliferation of Weapons of Mass Destruction, Their Delivery Systems, and Related Materials By Sea, Washington, 25 July 2005, http://www.state.gov/t/np/trty/50274.htm; reprinted in Annex II(d).

[193] Agreement Between the Government of the United States of America and the Government of Belize Concerning Cooperation to Suppress the Proliferation of Weapons of Mass Destruction, Their Delivery Systems, and Related Materials By Sea, Washington, 4 August 2005, http://www.state.gov/t/np/trty/50809.htm.

[194] Although registered as a flag of convenience, Cyprus is adopting various measures to improve its record, including the imposition of additional conditions for registration of vessels over 15 years of age.

low the same boarding and inspection arrangements[195]. The Agreement with Panama was an amendment to an existing maritime cooperation agreement aiming at drug interdiction. Under this second category of agreements, the US should contact the registers of Liberia, the Marshall Islands, Belize and Panama and request the right to board on suspect ships flying the flags of these States anywhere on the high seas. If there is no response within a limited period of time, 2 to 4 hours, the interdiction could proceed. The same rights enjoyed by the US and the four contracting States could be extended to all participating States to the PSI. With the four ship-boarding agreements with Liberia, Panama, the Marshall Islands and Belize plus the agreements from the PSI participating States, more than 50 percent of international commercial shipping fleet was in 2005 subject to boarding and search procedures by the US.

Thus, interdiction could take place on the high seas according to national authorization by the flag State, as it is prescribed in the agreements[196]. The basis of interdiction was the jurisdiction enjoyed by each State over ships flying its own national flag and not any vague notion of self-defence as part of the war against terrorism that was giving the right to intercept foreign ships on the high seas.

The PSI gained some momentum a few months after its launching when Canada, Denmark, Greece, Norway, Singapore and Turkey joined the loose affiliation of countries. It is interesting to note that, with the exception of the USA and Turkey, which has neither signed nor ratified the LOS Convention all other States parties to the PSI are members to the LOS Convention.

In June 2004 the G-8 adopted the "Action Plan for Non-Proliferation". This plan singled out eight major areas that required special attention, one of them being the PSI[197]. On the first anniversary of the PSI, some 80 States gathered in Poland. During this anniversary, Russia, the only G-8 member

---

[195] e.g. Liberia and Belize are under the obligation to reply within two hours whereas the Marshall Islands can reply within four hours on the nationality of the suspected ship. If there is no answer within this time limit, the requesting party will be deemed to have been authorized to board the suspect vessel; article 4.3.c. d. & e. The safeguards are slightly different between the agreements; article 8. In the Liberian agreement the use of force refers also to the case that the suspect vessel does not stop; article 9.5.

[196] "This would make the PSI appear multilateral, when it, in essence, is unilateral"; A. Persbo, *The Proliferation Security Initiative: Dead in the water or steaming ahead?* Prospects for the 16-17 December 2003 PSI meeting in Washington, 12 December 2003, http://www.basicint.org/pubs/Notes/BN031212.htm.

[197] G-8 Action Plan for non-proliferation, White House, Office of Press Secretary, 9 June 2004, http://www.whitehouse.gov/news/releases/2004/06/20040609-28; http://www.fmprc.gov.cn/eng/xwfw/2510/2511/t25626.htm.

still outside the initiative, also joined it[198]. Although the Russian decision was followed by a statement that the PSI was regarded as "a supplement rather than a replacement to the existing non-proliferation mechanisms"[199] and that the PSI "should not and will not create any obstacles to the lawful economic, scientific and technological co-operation of States"[200], it was an important development since Russia was one of the countries that were critical to the Initiative. In February 2005 US President Bush said that sixty governments around the world cooperate in the PSI to detect and stop the transit of dangerous materials[201].

Nevertheless, other States were very sceptical towards the initiative. China was the most prominent State that was uneasy towards PSI. In spite of the fact that China was kept informed of the PSI[202], it voiced concern over the legality of the Initiative. The spokesman of the Chinese Ministry of Foreign Affairs stated that China "can understand the worries by some countries over the proliferation of weapons of mass destruction... Some countries of the world have doubts over the legality and effectiveness of the measure"[203]. The Chinese concerns were shown during winter 2003 when the US introduced Security Council Resolution 1540. The US draft resolution aimed at finding support for the PSI from the UN or, according to one commentator, "the original intent of Washington [was] to use the UN to change international law and criminalize behaviour involving WMD proliferation"[204]. During the negotiations prior to the adoption of the Security Council Resolution 1540/2004 on the non-proliferation of WMD, a provision authorizing countries to intercept suspected foreign ships on the high seas was dropped in order to secure China's position in favour of the Resolution[205].

---

[198] *On Russia's participation in Proliferation Security Initiative*, Ministry of Foreign Affairs of the Russian Federation, Press Department, Press Release no 1224, 31 May 2004; see also: Russia joins Proliferation Security Initiative, *Asia Export Control Observer*, Issue 3, August/September 2004, http://cns.miis.edu/pubs/observer/asian.

[199] *Ibid.*

[200] Russia joins Proliferation Security Initiative, *Arms Control Today*, July/August 2004.

[201] We must pass reforms that solve the financial problems of social security, *The New York Times*, 3 February 2005.

[202] Australia hosts talks on US plan to halt North Korean arms trade, *Agence France Presse*, 9 July 2003.

[203] Foreign Ministry Spokesperson's Press Conference, 4 September 2003.

[204] W. Hawkins, Chinese Realpolitik and the Proliferation Security Initiative, 5 *China Brief – A Journal of Analysis and Information*, Jamestown Foundation, 1 February 2005.

[205] Security Council adopts WMD Resolution, *Facts on File World News Digest*, Section Pg. 322D2, 6 May 2004;

North Korea also complained about the PSI. The Initiative was described as "brigandish naval blockade [akin to] terrorism in the sea and a gross violation of international law"[206]. During the PSI international naval interdiction drill, "Team Samurai 2004", in the Pacific south of Tokyo Bay, which was clearly aiming to send a signal to North Korea, the government of Pyong Yang considered that this was "a serious infringement upon the sovereignty of Democratic People's Republic of Korea and an intolerable military provocation to it"[207].

8. THE SUA CONVENTION

8.1. The 1988 Convention

Following the *Achille Lauro* incident, the UN General Assembly adopted in 1985 Resolution 40/61. This Resolution requested, *inter alia*, the International Maritime Organization "to study the problem of terrorism aboard or against ships with a view to making recommendations on appropriate measures"[208]. Subsequently to this request the International Maritime Organization adopted in 1988 the Convention for the Suppression of Unlawful Acts against the Safety of Maritime Navigation[209]. The SUA Convention applies to ships navigating or scheduled to navigate into, "through or from waters beyond the outer limit of the territorial sea of a single State, or the lateral limits of its territorial sea with adjacent States".

Article 6 provides that States shall take measures to establish jurisdiction over the offence described in the convention when the offence is committed:

(a) against or on board of a ship flying the flag of the State at the time the offence is committed;

(b) in the territory of that State, including its territorial sea;

(c) by a national of that State;

(d) by a stateless person whose habitual residence is in that State; or

(e) when, during the commission of the offence a national of that State is seized, threatened, injured or killed (passive personality principle[210]); or

---

[206] S. Maiden, *The Advertiser*, 14 July 2003.

[207] US-led naval exercise sends clear message to North Korea, *The New York Times*, 27 October 2004.

[208] Article 13, General Assembly, A/RES/40/61, 9 December 1985.

[209] The Convention for the Suppression of Unlawful Acts against the Safety of Maritime Navigation is reprinted in 27 *ILM* 1988, pp. 672 (hereinafter cited as the SUA Convention). See also Halberstam, *supra* note 115, pp. 269-310.

[210] e.g. jurisdiction is based on the nationality of the victim.

(f) when the offence is committed in an attempt to compel that State to do or abstain from doing any act (protective principle[211]).

Thus, it is obvious that the SUA Convention has the competitive advantage of being fairly broad as it concerns jurisdiction[212]. This permits effective legal action to be undertaken against those who are engaged in offences related with maritime terrorism.

Nevertheless the offences in the 1988 text were limited to activities that were directed against the ship *per se* (including its cargo), the safe navigation of that ship, persons on board and maritime navigational facilities[213]. However, these acts were more related to the traditional notion of piracy and were setting the framework to punish the offenders irrespective of the political or terrorist purpose they might have. They did not include activities on the high seas, which are simply supportive of terrorist acts and which would be lawful if committed by other individuals. Moreover, they did not include terrorist activities which are not sufficiently precise to be considered as piracy and of course, they did not include transfer of WMD.

---

[211] The rationale of the protective principle applies to acts committed in an attempt to coerce the will of a State or in cases where the nationals are attacked simply due to their nationalities.

[212] See also UN General Assembly resolution 55/7, urging States to become party to the 1988 Convention for the Suppression of Unlawful Acts against the Safety of Maritime Navigation and its Protocol and to ensure their effective implementation.

[213] According to article 3 of the SUA Convention: "1. Any person commits an offence if that person unlawfully and intentionally: (a) seizes or exercises control over a ship by force or threat thereof or any other form of intimidation; or (b) performs an act of violence against a person on board a ship if that act is likely to endanger the safe navigation of that ship; or (c) destroys a ship or causes damage to a ship or to its cargo which is likely to endanger the safe navigation of that ship; or (d) places or causes to be placed on a ship, by any means whatsoever, a device or substance which is likely to destroy that ship, or cause damage to that ship or its cargo which endangers or is likely to endanger the safe navigation of that ship; or (e) destroys or seriously damages maritime navigational facilities or seriously interferes with their operation, if any such act is likely to endanger the safe navigation of a ship; or (f) communicates information which he knows to be false, thereby endangering the safe navigation of a ship; or (g) injures or kills any person, in connection with the commission or the attempted commission of any of the offences set forth in subparagraphs (a) to (f). 2. Any person also commits an offence if that person: (a) attempts to commit any of the offences set forth in paragraph 1; or (b) abets the commission of any of the offences set forth in paragraph 1 perpetrated by any person or is otherwise an accomplice of a person who commits such an offence; or (c) threatens, with or without a condition, as is provided for under national law, aimed at compelling a physical or juridical person to do or refrain from doing any act, to commit any of the offences set forth in paragraph 1, subparagraphs (b), (c) and (e), if that threat is likely to endanger the safe navigation of the ship in question".

8.2. The Draft Protocol

Following the terrorist attacks on the United States of America on 11 September 2001 and resolutions 1368 of the Security Council and 56/1 of the UN General Assembly, the IMO decided in November 2001 to update the SUA Convention[214]. The aim was to broaden the range of offences included in article 3. The IMO Legal Committee was charged with the revision of the Convention. The Legal Committee held several sessions between 2002 and 2005. Two new protocols were drafted to be adopted by a diplomatic conference to be held in autumn 2005. The first of the two Protocols concerns provisions specifically addressed to suppress additional terrorist acts against the safety and security of maritime navigation. The other Protocol concerns terrorist acts on platforms attached to the seabed.

The legal framework of the Protocol is set by the relevant international legal instruments against terrorism as well as the LOS Convention and the "customary international law of the sea". The reference to customary law could be explained by the fact that some States have not yet ratified the LOS Convention[215] whereas the USA and Israel, the two most proponent States of the fight against terrorism, have not even signed it. Nevertheless, in the light of the debate about article 51 of the UN Charter and whether it reserves or not a right of self-defence allegedly existing in customary international law and therefore legitimising anticipatory self defence, the reference to the "customary international law of the sea" becomes more significant.

During the works of the Committee, the USA and other western countries tried to widen up the scope of the SUA Convention. For that purpose they introduced new provisions for boarding vessels suspected of being involved in terrorist activities. Concerns have been expressed by other States, like China, India, Pakistan, Japan and Brazil, that the new provisions should not jeopardise the principle of freedom of navigation and the right of innocent passage. Since the present discussion is based on draft versions of Protocol prepared by the Legal Committee until April 2005, the impression seems to be that some exaggerated proposals concerning interception of ships on the high seas will be omitted from the final text.

---

[214] Review of measures and procedures to prevent acts of terrorism which threaten the security of passengers and crews and the safety of ships, IMO\Assembly\ 22\RES\924.DOC, adopted on 20 November 2001.

[215] Estonia was the 149th State that ratified on 26 August 2005 the LOS Convention; see *Chronological list of ratification of, accession and succession to the Convention*, Division for Ocean Affairs and the Law of the Sea, Oceans and Law of the Sea, http://www.un.org/Depts/los/reference_files/chronological_lists_of_ratifications.htm#The%20United%20Nations%20Convention%20on%20the%20Law%20of%20the%20Sea.

The "Draft Protocol to the Convention for the Suppression of Unlawful Acts against the Safety of Maritime Navigation" is not limited to activities directed against the ship, its navigation or against maritime navigational facilities. It enlists activities which derive from a ship and destruct a place of public use, a State facility, a public transportation system[216], resulting in major economic loss. It is obvious that these potential targets may be on land and are not necessarily connected with ports or maritime navigational facilities. Moreover, the draft Protocol applies in cases of substantial damage to the environment. Last but not least, under the draft Protocol the transportation of biological, chemical and nuclear weapons or their equipment is prohibited, with the exception of activities undertaken by States that are parties to the relevant treaties concerning these weapons[217].

The draft Protocol attempts to indirectly define some aspects of international terrorism. Thus a person is committing an offence when he uses a ship (or transport aboard a ship explosives or other prohibited material) with the purpose "to intimidate a population or to compel a government or an international organization to do or to abstain from doing any act". This is a wording that was first used in the Convention for the Suppression of the Financing of Terrorism[218]. This wording differentiates both the Financing of Terrorism Convention and the draft Protocol from previous treaties and protocols on terrorism. In such legal instruments, we had a list of specific activities, which are described as 'terrorist activities' irrespective of the motive. The first serious attempt to change this was made during the negotiations for the

---

[216] The meaning of these terms is given in article 1 of the International Convention for the Suppression of Terrorist Bombings, New York, 15 December 1997, 37 *ILM* 1998, pp. 249-252.

[217] Treaty on the Non-Proliferation of Nuclear Weapons, London-Moscow-Washington, 1 July 1969, 7 *ILM* 1968, p. 809; Convention on the Prohibition of the Development, Production and Stockpiling of Bacteriological and Toxin Weapons and on their Destruction, London-Moscow-Washington, 10 April 1972, 1015 UNTS, p. 163; Convention on the Prohibition of the Development, Production, Stockpiling and Use of Chemical Weapons and on their Destruction, Paris, 13 January 1993, 32 *ILM* 1993, p. 800.

[218] See similar wording in International Convention for the Suppression of the Financing of Terrorism, 10 January 2000, Article 2: "Any person commits an offence within the meaning of this Convention if that person by any means, directly or indirectly, unlawfully and wilfully, provides or collects funds with the intention that they should be used or in the knowledge that they are to be used, in full or in part, in order to carry out: (a) An act which constitutes an offence within the scope of and as defined in one of the treaties listed in the annex; or (b) *Any other act intended to cause death or serious bodily injury to a civilian, or to any other person not taking an active part in the hostilities in a situation of armed conflict, when the purpose of such act, by its nature or context, is to intimidate a population, or to compel a government or an international organization to do or to abstain from doing any act*", UN General Assembly Resolution 109, 54th Sess., 76th plen. mtg., UN Doc. A/RES/54/109, 39 *ILM* 2000, p. 270 (emphasis added).

Rome Statute to International Criminal Court but it was unsuccessful[219]. Since December 1999, when the Convention for the Suppression of the Financing of Terrorism was adopted[220], the objective is to take into consideration the real aim, the motive, of the perpetrator, since a terrorist act is simply the means to achieve it.

Moreover, according to the draft Protocol, it is an offence to intentionally transport persons who have committed acts, which are considered as offences under the other international legal instruments against terrorism. These include all the treaties and protocols that have been developed since 1970 under the auspices of the United Nations and its specialized agencies[221]. The same approach was followed by the Convention for the Suppression of the Financing of Terrorism. It is clear that the draft Protocol on Maritime Navigation comes as a supplement not only to the SUA Convention but also to all the other anti-terrorism conventions and protocols.

The draft Protocol applies not only within the territorial sea but most importantly "seaward of any State's territorial sea" and involves a ship flying the flag of a State party to the draft Protocol. In case that another State party to the draft Protocol "has reasonable grounds" to suspect this ship as committing one of the offences referred to in the draft Protocol, it may request permission to board. The flag State may either authorize the requesting party to board or conduct the boarding with its own officials or decline any such

---

[219] In the initial draft Statute "crimes of terrorism" meant "understanding, organising, sponsoring, ordering, facilitating, financing, encouraging or tolerating acts of violence against another State directed at persons or property and of such a nature as to create terror, fear or insecurity in the minds of public figures, groups of persons, the general public or populations, for whatever considerations and purposes of a political, philosophical, ideological, racial, ethnic, religious or such other nature that may be invoked to justify them"; see Draft of the Rome Statute to International Criminal Court, http://www.un.org/ law/icc/n9810105.pdf.

[220] It entered into force 23 May 2001.

[221] i. Convention for the Suppression of Unlawful Seizure of Aircraft, The Hague, 16 December 1970; ii. Convention for the Suppression of Unlawful Acts against the Safety of Civil Aviation, Montreal, 23 September 1971; iii. Convention on the Prevention and Punishment of Crimes against Internationally Protected Persons, including Diplomatic Agents, UN General Assembly, 14 December 1973; iv. International Convention against the Taking of Hostages, UN General Assembly, 17 December 1979; v. Convention on the Physical Protection of Nuclear Material, Vienna, 3 March 1980; vi. Protocol for the Suppression of Unlawful Acts of Violence at Airports Serving International Civil Aviation, supplementary to the Convention for the Suppression of Unlawful Acts against the Safety of Civil Aviation, Montreal, 24 February 1988; vii. Protocol for the Suppression of Unlawful Acts against the Safety of Fixed Platforms located on the Continental Shelf, Rome, 10 March 1988; viii. International Convention for the Suppression of Terrorist Bombings, UN General Assembly, 15 December 1997; ix. International Convention for the Suppression of the Financing of Terrorism, UN General Assembly, 9 December 1999.

request. It is expressly provided that the requesting party shall not board the ship without the express authorization of the flag State.

Nevertheless, a State Party to the Protocol may notify to the Secretary General that with respect to ships flying its flag, authorization is granted to any requesting State to board and search the ship, its cargo and persons on board subject to no negative response from the ship's flag State within a specific period of time. Moreover, a State may authorize in advance all requesting parties to board and search any ship flying its flag. There is no reference that this authorization in advance is given on condition of reciprocity. Thus, on this specific point, the draft Protocol uses the same pattern adopted in the agreements between the US and Liberia, Belize, the Marshall Islands and Panama, under the PSI.

It is unclear the level of evidence needed either to prove an ongoing violation of the draft Protocol or to be presented prior of taking action. The expression "reasonable grounds" is quite vague. Since most of the evidence will come from intelligence activities as part of the "war" against terrorism, a lot of emphasis will be given to secrecy. It is beyond doubt that there are sensitive areas of intelligence that have to remain classified or secret. Thus, it is very difficult for the flag States to be able to value, if there are sufficient indications for the request to visit and search a ship.

In any case, the draft Protocol provides for certain safeguards like treatment of all the persons on board in a manner preserving their basic human dignity; taking due account of the safety and security of the ship and its cargo; assurance that the master of the ship is advised of the intention to board; taking reasonable efforts to avoid unduly detainment or delay of the ship. Moreover, the draft Protocol refers to "effective recourse" that a State party is obliged to provide in respect of damage attributable to the boarding and search of that ship if the grounds for such measures proved to be unfounded. Nevertheless, the draft Protocol does not clarify the exact form of this effective recourse; it leaves it upon the discretion of States parties.

In summarizing, the draft Protocol, follows in general terms the pattern of the Convention for the Suppression of the Financing of Terrorism. It is obvious that, if adopted, it will form part of the international legal instruments related to States' responsibilities for combating terrorism. On the specific aspect of fighting terrorism on the high seas, the draft Protocol follows to a certain extent the pattern of the agreements signed under the PSI between the US and Liberia, Belize, the Marshall Islands and Panama. After its adoption, boarding and search of ships on the high seas may not be subject exclusively to the authority of the State whose flag they fly. The ships may also be boarded and searched by States parties to the draft Protocol. This depends on the acceptance of this procedure, the circumstances and the readiness of the flag State to respond within a specific but limited period of time to such a request by another State party to the draft Protocol.

9. CONCLUSION

When the LOS Convention was drafted more than two decades ago, the most important criminal activities at sea included piracy, armed robbery against ships, narcotic drugs and illegal dumping and discharge of pollutants. Since 1982, and especially after the 9/11 attacks, the importance of other crimes at sea, like terrorism or transportation of WMD, rose dramatically. The need to take drastic measures in order to prevent and suppress these activities is imperative and as a result naval operations are endemic in many areas of the world. Nevertheless, State practice proves that the ancient principle of freedom of navigation on the high seas as well as the rule of the exclusivity of flag State jurisdiction managed to survive. The release of the North Korean vessel "*So San*" was a clear indication that the USA, the main power behind the "war on terrorism", remains sensitive to the importance of freedom of navigation[222].

The attention is now focused on the first part of article 110 of the LOS Convention, which bends the rule of exclusive flag State jurisdiction in cases of "acts of interference deriv[ing] from powers conferred by treaty". It would seem that the principle of freedom of navigation is still acceptable to the USA, because the general rule of non interdiction of vessels on the high seas may be modified by treaty. The first application of this exception took place in the 80s in the Caribbean Sea, when the US government signed bilateral agreements with the aim to curb trade of illegal narcotic substances. The same model was used in the PSI. The States parties to the PSI are seeking the permission, given (as in the cases of Croatia and Cyprus) or implied (as in the cases of Liberia, Belize, the Marshall Islands and Panama), of the government of the flag State. Again the USA has signed agreements with six countries five of are considered as flags-of-convenience. The draft Protocol amending the SUA Convention (to be adopted probably in autumn 2005) shows that this is the pattern preferred by the USA.

The new trend towards modification by treaties of the exclusive jurisdiction of the flag State over its vessels on the high seas is a clear indication of

---

[222] J.E. Noyes, American Hegemony, US political leaders and general international law, 19 *Connecticut Journal of International Law* 2003, p. 301.

what has been termed as "hegemonic international law"[223]. As it has been observed, hegemonic international law "jettisons or severely undervalues the
formal and de facto equality of States, replacing pacts between equals
grounded in reciprocity, with patron-client relationships"[224]. Bilateral agreements under the PSI are reciprocal to the extent that it is theoretically possible for Liberian or Panamanian warships to stop, visit and search US commercial vessels in the Mediterranean, the Indian Ocean or the Arabian Sea[225].
The same applies more or less for the draft SUA Protocol, at its current
form; however, as work is still in progress, the final outcome is unknown.

The reason that the draft Protocol preceded the PSI, although they both
employ the same means, is explained by John Bolton, Under Secretary of
State for Arms Control: "The idea we could have ... a nice international
treaty is fine if you have unlimited time. We don't, not with the threats out
there...We didn't want to engage in an endless legal seminar"[226]. PSI followed the pattern of bilateral agreements as long as the draft Protocol of the
SUA Convention was under formation and negotiation. From the moment
that the draft Protocol would be adopted, the pressure upon States would be
to ratify or accede to it and even to accept the proviso granting in advance
authorization to board and search suspicious ships.

Thus, vessel interdictions on the high seas would be legal, following either
the conclusion of a bilateral agreement providing for the right to board and
inspect foreign flag vessels or the ratification of or accession to the Protocol
of the SUA Convention, should it enter into force. The role of the USA in
signing bilateral agreements or in drafting the new rules of the SUA Protocol
is evident. As argued, the US foreign policy increasingly presents States with
strong incentives to surrender parts of their sovereignty through bilateral
agreements or multilateral treaties[227]. Under these circumstances, the most
promising element is that despite the attacks, the freedom of navigation continues to exist as the common minimum legal denominator.

---

[223] D.F. Vagts, Hegemonic international law, 95 *AJIL* 2001, pp. 843-848.

[224] J.E. Alvarez, Hegemonic international law revisited, 97 *AJIL* 2003, p. 873.

[225] Nevertheless, as explained above, the terms of the agreements with Croatia and Cyprus
are significantly different from the other four agreements under the PSI.

[226] Robbins, *supra* note 162.

[227] See relevant comment in J.E. Kramke, Bilateral maritime counter-drug and immigrant
interdiction agreements: Is this the world of the future?, 31 *University of Miami Inter-
American Law Review* 2000, p. 146.

Part III

The Future of the Law of the Sea:
Uniformity or Fragmentation?

Chapter 8

FROM UNIFORMITY TO FRAGMENTATION?
THE ABILITY OF THE UN CONVENTION ON THE LAW OF THE
SEA TO ACCOMMODATE NEW USES AND CHALLENGES

*Maria Gavouneli**

The Law of the Sea Convention (hereinafter cited as the "LOS Convention") has been called "a Constitution for the Oceans"[1]. In truth, it is more than a constitution[2]: It provides a comprehensive regulatory regime for all matters maritime, without being the typical framework convention so frequently encountered in other branches of international law; it prevails in practice over other incompatible rules and regulations, without enjoying any priority as of its nature; it is generally construed by its own judicial forum, without this being necessarily the only means of judicial adjudication possible. Adhered to by 149 States[3], created by consensus after a protracted and strenuous negotiation[4], it remains the one example of a successful integral document[5], which has come to prevail over any other expression of State power by the sheer force of its existence.

Comprehensive as it might be, the LOS Convention is still growing old. In the 20 years of its presence in the legal world, a number of things have changed. And although it is certainly tempting to suggest that the rules con-

---

* Lecturer in International Law, University of Athens Law School.

[1] See the statement of Tommy T.B. Koh, President of the Third UN Conference on the Law of the Sea, see www.un.org/Depts/los/convention_agreements/texts/koh_english.pdf.

[2] For an excellent description of the evolutionary character of the LOS Convention see Alan Boyle, Further development of the Law of the Sea Convention: Mechanisms for change, 54 *ICLQ* 2005, pp. 563-584, at pp. 563-567.

[3] As of 16 September 2005; see www.un.org/Depts/los/reference_files/status2005.pdf.

[4] See, among others, B. Buzan, Negotiating by consensus: Developments in technique at the UN Conference on the Law of the Sea, 75 *AJIL* 1981, pp. 324-348; P.J. Allott, Power-sharing in the Law of the Sea, 77 *AJIL* 1983, pp. 1-30.

[5] It is to be reminded that article 309 of the LOS Convention allows for no reservations; as to the complementarity clause of article 311, see more *infra*.

Anastasia Strati, Maria Gavouneli & Nikos Skourtos (eds.), *Unresolved Issues and New Challenges to the Law of the Sea*, Martinus Nijhoff Publishers 2006, pp. 205-233.

tained therein have been general enough – and wise enough – to cater for any eventuality, it would still be interesting to examine whether the Convention can stand up to the new challenges arising in the world today or can even cover new uses of the seas developing over time.

At first glance the system created by the LOS Convention is quite simple. On a horizontal level, there is a balance between the customary freedom of the seas on the one hand and the pronounced State tendency to expand towards the high seas. On a vertical level, the LOS Convention, being an (admittedly non-typical) umbrella convention[6], allows for an infinite number of implementing agreements, complementary provisions and regional rules, which may modify or suspend the operation of its provisions "provided that such agreements do not relate to a provision, derogation from which is incompatible with the effective execution of the object and purpose of this Convention, and provided further that such agreements shall not affect the application of the basic principles embodied herein, and that the provisions of such agreements do not affect the enjoyment by other States Parties of their rights or the performance of their obligations under this Convention"[7]. It will be through this crossroads that I will attempt to discern instances of development through uniformity or strains to the inherent flexibility of the system leading to fragmentation. The uniformity of unilateral action will be examined first (under I), before turning to the substantial issues of complementarity and innovation through new agreements and the authoritative means of interpretation provided by the LOS Convention itself (under II).

1. UNIFORMITY UNDER THE FLAG: THE LIMITS OF UNILATERAL ACTION

The horizontal structure of the LOS Convention is evident in the interplay between the flag State and the coastal State jurisdiction over the ship. Navigation gave rise to the first truly international rules and regulations in the Law of the Sea, establishing a quest for uniformity while preserving the sovereign powers of the State, already present in the customary formulation of the freedoms of the high seas.

1.1. *Nationality of ships and the requirement of 'genuine link'*

One of the more solid customary rules, incorporated into the LOS Convention, relates to the primacy of flag State jurisdiction over vessels. The provi-

---

[6] But see also Boyle, *supra* note 2, at p. 564.
[7] Article 311(3) of the LOS Convention.

sion seems unconditional, in spite of this strange clause in article 91 paragraph 1 of the LOS Convention, where it is stated that "[t]here must be a genuine link between the State and the ship". It is generally admitted that each State retains exclusive jurisdiction over the granting of its nationality to ships[8], especially since such registration seeks to establish a permanent legal relationship between the ship and the State, on the basis of which the State undertakes specific duties and obligations, summarily set out in article 94 of the LOS Convention. They include the obligation to *effectively* exercise its jurisdiction and control in matters administrative, technical and social, ranging from the construction, equipment and seaworthiness of ships to the manning, labour conditions and the training of crews on board. It becomes clear, therefore, that the failure of a flag State to carry out its obligations of implementation and enforcement may dramatically affect compliance with the rule of law on the seas. Indeed, defective implementation of national and international rules or even the complete lack of any attempt at supervision lies at the heart of the flags of convenience issue[9] and the substandard shipping[10] problems usually encountered under such registries. The LOS Convention has no solution to offer: It demurely states that "a State which has clear grounds to believe that proper jurisdiction and control with respect to a ship has not been exercised may report the facts to the flag State"[11]. Somehow, I do not believe that such an announcement would be exactly news to the State concerned…

One way to redress the lack of effective exercise of jurisdiction would have been to adopt specific terms and conditions for the granting of nationality to ships, although the International Tribunal on the Law of the Sea has expressly reiterated that "[d]etermination of the criteria and establishment of the procedures for granting and withdrawing nationality to ships are matters

---

[8] See PCA, *Boutres de Mascate*, France v. UK, award of 8 August 1905, XI *UNRAA* 92 *et seq.*; *Lauritzen v. Larsen*, 345 US 571, 73 SCt 921 (1953).

[9] For a brief overview see, among many others, Emmanuel Roucounas, Facteurs privés et droit international public, 299 *RCADI* 2002, pp. 9-19, at pp. 205-207; G. Athanassiou, *Aspects juridiques de la concurrence maritime* (Paris 1996); Moritaka Hayashi, Toward the elimination of substandard shipping: The Report of the International Committee of Shipping, *TIJMCL* 2001, pp. 501 *et seq.*

[10] Defined by the OECD Maritime Transport Committee as: "A vessel that, through its physical condition, its operation or activities of its crew, fails to meet basic standards of seaworthiness and thereby poses a threat to life and/or the environment. This would be evidenced by the failure of the vessel to meet regulations contained in international maritime conventions to the extent that it would be considered unfit to sail by a reasonable flag State or port State inspection"; OECD Maritime Transport Committee, *Policy Statement on Substandard Shipping*, 2002, at www.pecd.org/dataoecd/18/37/2080990.pdf.

[11] Article 94(6) of the LOS Convention.

within the exclusive jurisdiction of the flag State"[12]. However, an attempt to organise international rules on the subject was unsuccessful. The 1986 UN Convention on Conditions for Registration of Ships[13] remains an exercise in ineffectiveness as it never entered into force. It is a rather vague text, which seeks to strengthen the genuine link between the flag State and the ship by means of nationality requirements as to the level of participation in owner-ship[14] or the manning of the ship[15].

On the other hand, it seems unclear whether the mere act of registration suffices to establish a 'genuine link' with the flag State[16]. Although the IT-LOS has not as yet directly addressed the question, it has considered the af-firmation of nationality as a prerequisite for jurisdiction, to be examined *propio motu*[17]. In the *M/V Saiga* no. 2 case, the Tribunal held that "the pur-pose of the provisions of the Convention on the need for a genuine link be-tween a ship and its flag State is to secure more effective implementation of the duties of the flag State and not to establish criteria by reference to which the validity of the registration of ships in a flag State may be challenged by other States"[18]. However, Judge Anderson in his Separate Opinion seems to construe an element of good faith in this dictum[19] and thus slightly amends the unequivocal disassociation of the genuine link from registration. A ten-dency to distance themselves from a mechanical application of registration as the sole evidence of genuine link is also evident in the Declaration by

---

[12] ITLOS, The *M/V Saiga* (no. 2) case, Saint Vincent and the Grenadines v. Guinea, 1999, paragraph 65, available at www.itlos.org.

[13] 28 *ILM* 1987, pp. 1229 *et seq.* For a general overview see G. Kasoulides, The 1986 UN Convention on the Conditions for the Registration of Vessels and the question of open regis-try, 20 *ODIL* 1989, pp. 543-576; M.L. McConnell, 'Business as usual': An evaluation of the 1986 UN Convention on Conditions for Registration of Ships, 18 *Journal of Maritime Law & Commerce* 1987, pp. 435 *et seq.*; H. Wefers Bettink, Open registry, the genuine link and the 1986 Convention on Registration Condition for Ship, 18 *Netherlands YBIL* 1987, pp. 68-119.

[14] Article 8 of the 1986 UN Registration Convention.

[15] Article 9 of the 1986 UN Registration Convention.

[16] For a general overview of the effectiveness of the genuine link requirement see, among others, Robin Churchill (with Christopher Hedley), *The meaning of the 'genuine link' re-quirement in relation to the nationality of ships*, A study prepared for the International Trans-port Workers' Federation, October 2000; Alex Oude Elferink, The genuine link concept: Time for a *post mortem*?, in I.F. Dekker & H.H.G. Post (eds.), *On the foundations and sources of International Law* (T.M.C. Asser Press, The Hague 2003) pp. 41-63; Maurice Kamto, La nationalité des navires en droit international, *La mer et son droit. Mélanges offer-tes à Laurent Lucchini et Jean-Pierre Quéneudec* (Paris 2003) pp. 343-373.

[17] ITLOS, *The Grand Prince*, Belize v. France, 2001, paragraph 77, available at www.itlos.org.

[18] See *supra* note 12, paragraph 83.

[19] *Ibid.*

Judge Wolfrum[20] and the Separate Opinion by Judge Treves[21] attached to the judgment in the *Grand Prince* case. Nevertheless, the Tribunal seems to generally accept formal registration as sufficient in order to establish a genuine link between the ship and the State. The international rule remains uniform, in recognising the exclusive jurisdiction of the flag State to decide the extent of its jurisdiction as it sees fit. Resigned almost to the inevitable, the UN General Assembly keeps a record of the situation[22] and, in its annual omnibus resolution on the law of the sea, "once again urges flag States without an effective maritime administration and appropriate legal frameworks to establish or enhance the necessary infrastructure, legislative and enforcement capabilities to ensure effective compliance with, and implementation and enforcement of, their responsibilities under international law and, until such action is undertaken, to consider declining the granting of the right to fly their flag to new vessels, suspending their registry or not opening a registry"[23].

1.2. *Labour standards and the manning of ships*

If international standards remain illusive in the definition of a genuine link between the State and the ship, it is also true that, as free as vessels are to roam the seas, they still need to be subject to the same rules and regulations, share the same rights and duties. A hint to that effect is acknowledged by the LOS Convention in article 94 paragraph 3(b), where the injunction to the flag State to effectively exercise its jurisdiction and control over the manning of ships, labour conditions and the training of crews according to its national laws is tempered by the additional obligation to also take into account any applicable international instruments. Indeed, although the protection of seafarers and the setting of labour standards fall essentially within the ambit of the flag State[24] and all attempts by the port State to assert a similar jurisdiction have been summarily rebuffed[25], the relevant international rules and

---

[20] See paragraph 3: "… the registration cannot be reduced to a mere fiction … - an empty shell"; *supra* note 15.

[21] See paragraph 2: "It was an artificial creation, a fiction …"; *ibid.*

[22] See the report of the Consultative Group on Flag State Implementation, UN Doc. A/59/63 (2004).

[23] General Assembly Resolution A/Res/59/24, *Oceans and the law of the sea*, 4 February 2005, paragraph 38.

[24] For an overview of the international and domestic rules safeguarding seafarers' rights in selected jurisdictions see Deirdre Fitzpatrick & Michael Anderson (eds.), *Seafarers' Rights* (Oxford 2005).

[25] The application of the Jones Act, the US maritime labour legislation, was found not to apply to foreign vessels, even those beneficially owned by US interests; *Lauritzen v. Larsen*, 345 US 571 (1953). A proposal along those lines brought before the US Congress in 1994

regulations remain both the more ancient and the more recent rules in the field.

The International Labour Organisation (ILO) has set standards in the maritime sector and adopted conditions of employment of seafarers since the 1920s in a series of special maritime sessions[26], long before the International Maritime Organisation (IMO) entered the field in the 1970s, essentially with the 1978 International Convention on Standards of Training, Certification and Watch-keeping for Seafarers (STCW)[27]. Both organisations work currently together with a view to elaborate a Consolidated Maritime Labour Convention[28], encompassing the *acquis* in terms of maritime labour standards and identifying the fundamental principles at work. At the same time, the IMO has promoted the Voluntary Audit Scheme[29] as a tool in order to assess how effectively States member to the Organisation implement and enforce conventional standards on the basis of a draft Code for the implementation of such mandatory IMO instruments[30]. Being developed by an IMO Subcommittee on Flag State Implementation and although it contains only a passing reference to the LOS Convention, there is no doubt that the draft Code finds its legal basis in the obligations of the flag State to effectively exercise its jurisdiction and control over ships flying its flag[31].

1.3. *Design and construction standards*

Much stricter in their uniform unilateralism remain the regulations relating to the design, construction and seaworthiness of ships. There is no reference to international rules in article 94 paragraph 3(a) of the LOS Convention,

---

gave rise to a diplomatic protest by the European Community, which in turn withdrew a draft directive on manning conditions proposed in 1998; see Alan Boyle, EU unilateralism and the Law of the Sea, 20 *TIJMCL* 2005, pp. 1-17, at pp. 6 and 9.

[26] See Nicolas Valticos, La protection internationale des travailleurs de la mer, *La Mer et son droit*, *supra* note 16, pp. 611-617.

[27] Available at www.imo.org/Conventions.

[28] Cleopatra Doumbia-Henry, The Consolidated Maritime Labour Convention: A marriage of the traditional and the new, *Les normes internationales du travail: Un patrimoine pour l'avenir*, *Mélanges en l'honneur de Nicolas Valticos* (BIT, Genève 2004) pp. 319-334. See also the Report by the Secretary-General to the General Assembly on the implementation of the LOS Convention, Addendum, *Oceans and the law of the sea*, UN Doc. A/60/63/Add.2, 15 August 2005, pp. 10-11.

[29] Approved by the IMO Assembly in Resolution A.946 (23) on 27 November 2003.

[30] Report by the Secretary-General, *Oceans and the law of the sea*, *supra* note 28, at p. 12. See also www.imo.org.

[31] For more see www.imo.org; Veronica Frank, Consequences of the *Prestige* sinking for European and International Law, 20 *TIJMCL* 2005, pp. 1-64, at pp. 50-51.

which establishes the fundamental obligation of the flag State to take all measures necessary to ensure safety at sea for ships flying its flag. Indeed, there is an express prohibition to the coastal State to assume any such jurisdiction over ships in innocent passage through territorial waters "unless [...] giving effect to generally accepted international rules and standards"[32]. Such international construction, design, equipment and manning (CDEMs) standards are indeed adopted by the IMO, the competent international organisation, in order to prevent, reduce and control pollution of the marine environment from vessels[33]; they are to be found mostly in the 1973 International Convention for the Prevention of Pollution from Ships as amended in 1978 (MARPOL 73/78)[34] and the 1974 International Convention for the Safety of Life at Sea (SOLAS 74)[35]. In contrast, the coastal States remain free to adopt national *pollution control* measures applicable on ships flying their flag[36] or in their territorial waters stricter than the relevant international regulations but the application of such measures "cannot hamper innocent passage of foreign ships"[37]. In the Exclusive Economic Zone (EEZ), their corresponding power is significantly reduced to rules and regulations "conforming to and giving effect to generally accepted international rules and standards established through the competent international organisation"[38].

Nevertheless, the port State retains fully its sovereign right to set conditions for[39] or even deny access to their ports[40]. Thus affirmed the ICJ in the *Nicaragua* case[41], confirming in essence what the domestic courts had already considered a rule of customary law[42]. The discretionary power of the port State is also presumed in articles 25, 211 paragraph 3 and 255 of the LOS Convention. The exercise of this right is subject to the general restric-

---

[32] Article 21(2) of the LOS Convention.

[33] Article 211 of the LOS Convention.

[34] For the text of the Convention and the 1997 Protocol thereto, see www.imo.org.

[35] For the text of the Convention and the protocols thereto, see www.imo.org.

[36] Article 211(2) of the LOS Convention.

[37] Article 211(4) of the LOS Convention.

[38] Article 211(5) of the LOS Convention.

[39] Including the obligation to prevent from sailing a vessel which does not conform to the international standards of seaworthiness; article 219 of the LOS Convention.

[40] For a thorough discussion of this issue see A.V. Lowe, The right of entry into maritime ports in international law, *San Diego LR* 1977, pp. 597-622; Louise de la Fayette, Access to ports in International Law, 11 *TIJMCL* 1996, pp. 1-22.

[41] ICJ, *Case concerning military and paramilitary activities in and against Nicaragua*, Nicaragua v. US, Merits, ICJ Reports 1986, paragraphs 212-213.

[42] *Patterson v. Bark Eudora*, 190 US 169 (1903); *Lauritzen v. Larsen*, 345 US 571 (1953); *McCulloch v. Sociedad Nacional de Marineros de Honduras*, 372 US 10 (1963); *Incres Steamship Co. Ltd. v. International Maritime Workers' Union*, 372 US 24 (1963).

tions of proportionality, non-discrimination and abuse of right. Indeed, the latter, along with the requirement of good faith, is clearly incorporated into the system of the LOS Convention[43] and as such it was invoked both before the ITLOS by the European Community in the *Swordfish* case[44] and by Australia and New Zealand in the *Southern Bluefin Tuna* case[45] as well as by Ireland in the *MOX Plant* arbitration[46]. It is regrettable that both judicial instances refrained from elaborating on the exact content and extent of the rule.

It is on the combined authority of the exclusive jurisdiction to regulate entry to port and protect one's waters from pollution that individual States have acted unilaterally to matters pertaining to the design and structure of vessels. Under the Oil Pollution Act 1990, the United States banned from its ports single-hull vessels from 2005 onwards on the basis of age limits set for new and existing oil tankers, which would lead to a total phasing-out of all such vessels by 2010 and 2015 respectively. Alarmed by both this precedent in unilateralism and the resulting exposure of European waters to the risk of pollution caused by the old single-hull tankers excluded from American waters, the European Community[47] kept sustained pressure to the IMO to synchronise the regional and the international regimes by threatening to undertake in its turn unilateral action. As a result, the MARPOL Convention was amended in 2001, introducing a new global timetable accelerating the phasing-out of single hull oil tankers. Community legislation followed[48], primar-

---

[43] Article 300 of the LOS Convention.

[44] ITLOS, *Case concerning the Conservation and Sustainable Exploitation of Swordfish Stocks in the South-Eastern Pacific Ocean*, Chile v. European Community, 2000, available at www.itlos.org.

[45] ITLOS, *Southern Bluefin Tuna* cases, New Zealand v. Japan, Australia v. Japan, Provisional measures, 1999, available at www.itlos.org; see also ICSID, *Bluefin Tuna cases*, available at www.worldbank.org/icsid/bluefintune/award080400.pdf.

[46] ITLOS, The *MOX Plant* case, Ireland v. UK, Provisional measures, 2001, available at www.itlos.org; see also PCA, Arbitral Tribunal constituted pursuant to article 287 and article 1 of Annex VII of the UN Convention on the Law of the Sea for the dispute concerning the MOX Plant, international movements of radioactive materials and the protection of the marine environment of the Irish Sea, *The MOX Plant* case, Ireland v. UK, 2003, available at www.pca-cpa.org. For an overview see R.R. Churchill & J. Scott, The MOX Plant litigation – The first half-life, 53 *ICLQ* 2004, pp. 643-676.

[47] The member States of the European Community have delegated their jurisdiction in matters pertaining to transport and environment, including maritime transport, to the organisation, thus authorising the European Commission to act on their behalf.

[48] Yves van der Meensbrugghe, Sécurité maritime et protection de l'environnement marin en l'an 2000 : Des réactions de la Communauté européenne à l'affaire de l'*Erika* et *de quibusdam aliis...*, 5 *ADM* 2000, pp. 177-201; *idem.*, De l'*Erika* au *Prestige* : La réaction de la Communauté européenne en matière de sécurité maritime et de protection de l'environnement marin en 2002, *ADM* 2003, pp. 333-345; Catherine Roche, Prévention et la lutte contre la pol-

ily in the form of Regulation 417/2002 on the accelerated phasing-in of dou-
ble hull or equivalent design for single-hull oil targets[49]. Thus, on a protracted *valse hésitation*, the world community paid lip service to the need for
international coordination while affirming the ultimate authority of each
State to act unilaterally[50].

1.4. *Access to port reversed: Places of refuge*

A further exception lies in the equally well-established customary right of
entry to ports for ships in distress, defined strictly as danger to human life[51].
Whether such a right exists for reasons of environment distress, where there
is imminent danger of grave damage to the marine environment, is a novel
proposition, clearly not covered in the LOS Convention. Indeed, the opposite
argument could even be true; namely, that a State has a right to self-defence
when its territory, including maritime zones under its jurisdiction, is threatened by pollution[52]. On the other hand, article 192 of the LOS Convention
reaffirms a customary duty of States to protect and preserve the marine environment; article 194 paragraph 2 instructs States to ensure that pollution created by incidents under their jurisdiction and control does not spread beyond
areas under such jurisdiction and control; article 195 prohibits any transfer,
direct of indirect, of damage, hazards or pollution from one area to another;
and article 225 insists that, in exercising their powers of enforcement against
foreign vessels, States shall not expose the marine environment to an unreasonable risk. A legal basis for international action may thus exist, founded
on the fundamental principles of environmental protection enshrined in the
LOS Convention[53].

---

lution des mers par les hydrocarbures : Les derniers développements communautaires, *Revue
du Marché commun et de l'Union européenne* 2003, pp. 598-609; Wang Hui, The EU marine oil
pollution prevention regime – Recent developments, *EEnvLR* 2004, pp. 292-303, at 300-301.

[49] OJ L 64/1, 7 March 2002.

[50] Boyle, *supra* note 25, at 6; Françoise Odier, Le droit de la mer doit-il être remis en question par les accidents des navires?, *ADM* 2003, 303-312, at 307-308.

[51] See R.R. Churchill & A.V. Lowe, *The Law of the Sea* (3rd ed., Manchester 1999) at 63.

[52] See article 221 of the LOS Convention; article V of the 1969 Intervention Convention;
and also *ACT Shipping (OTE) Ltd. v. Minister for the Marine, Ireland and the Attorney-
General (The MV Toledo)*, [1995] 2 *ILRM* 30.

[53] See, for instance, Simon Marr, *The precautionary principle in the Law of the Sea* (Martinus Nijhoff 2003) especially at pp. 41-45.

The question of balancing conflicting interests in not new in either the law of the sea or environmental law[54]. A precedent, taking also into consideration the significant financial interests involved, could be found in article 11 of the 1989 Salvage Convention. With this in mind, the *Comité maritime international* undertook in 2001 an investigation among its members in order to ascertain State practice, particularly in regard to the liabilities attached to such action[55]. It is clear that both the coastal States and the industry were unwilling to undertake obligations with significant financial cost, without sufficiently objective criteria. Thus when on 5 December 2003 the IMO Assembly adopted 'Guidelines on places of refuge for ships in need of assistance'[56], the coastal States were simply "recommended … [to] endeavour to establish procedures…by which to receive and act on requests for assistance with a view to authorizing, where appropriate, the use of a suitable place of refuge"[57] although even "[w]hen permission to access a place of refuge is requested, there is no obligation for the coastal State to grant it, but the coastal State should weigh all the factors and risks in a balanced manner and give shelter whenever reasonably possible"[58]. This is clearly not the most resolute of languages, even for a non-binding instrument.

There is no question that the traditional rule of coastal State jurisdiction over access to port remains unchallenged in the LOS Convention. Yet, a new reading, allowing for an environmental distress exception, is possible on the letter of the relevant provisions but also fully compatible with the spirit and the purpose of the treaty. Indeed, there are already conventional rules along the same lines, admittedly not drafted in very strong language. Article 16 of the 2002 Valetta Protocol to the Barcelona Convention on cooperation in preventing pollution from ships and, in cases of emergency, combating pol-

---

[54] Henrik Ringbom (ed.), *Competing norms in the law of marine environmental protection* (Kluwer Law International 1997); Maria Gavouneli, Obbligazioni alternative e contrastanti nel diritto internazionale dell'ambiente, *Rivista giuridica dell'ambiente* 2001, pp. 527-551.

[55] The International Sub-committee on places of refuge identified the following main issues to be addressed by the IMO: rights and obligations of States; impartiality and objectivity of decision-makers; civil and criminal liability in conjunction with immunity; compulsory insurance, financial compensation and security for the States granting refuge; predestination and publicity of identified places of refuge and availability of funds to meet the gaps of existing liability regimes; *CMI Yearbook* 2002, pp. 117-146. See also G.J. Timagenis, Places of refuge as a legislative problem, available at www.comitemaritime.org/future/futuridx.html; E. Van Hooydonk, The obligation to offer a place of refuge to a ship in distress, *CMI Yearbook* 2003, pp. 379-445; A. Chircop, Ships in distress, environmental threats to coastal States, a place of refuge: New directions for an *ancien régime?*, 33 *ODIL* 2002, pp. 207-226.

[56] IMO Resolution A.949(23).

[57] Paragraph 3.4 of the Guidelines; *ibid.*

[58] Paragraph 3.12 of the Guidelines; *ibid.*

lution of the Mediterranean Sea requires States parties "to define national, subregional or regional strategies concerning reception in places of refuge, including ports, of ships in distress presenting a threat to the marine environment"[59]. Similar is the obligation under Regulation 12 of Annex IV to the 1992 Helsinki Convention on the protection of the Baltic Sea[60]. European Community regulations seem to go one step further: Under article 20 of Directive 2002/59/EC of 27 June 2002 on a Community Vessel Traffic Monitoring and Information System[61], the member States shall draw plans to accommodate ships in distress, taking into account the relevant guidelines of IMO. Such arrangements, "taking into account operational and environmental constraints", are "to ensure that ships in distress may immediately go to a place of refuge" but always "subject to authorisation by the competent authority", including – one presumes – the possibility of outright refusal. The Commission is contemplating infringement proceedings against those who did not communicate the relevant list on time, i.e. almost all the member States with the exception of Denmark, Germany and Spain. This reluctance to commit oneself makes even more precarious the encouragement offered by the UN General Assembly to States to draw up their national plans and establish procedures for the implementation of the IMO Guidelines[62]. Even the Parliamentary Assembly of the Council of Europe, not the most obvious source of such regulations, invited member States to adopt the necessary measures to receive ships in distress in their territorial waters, provide places of refuge and draw up appropriate action plans[63].

Could we detect an erosion of the traditional jurisdiction of the coastal State, affirmed and safeguarded by the LOS Convention? Perhaps – but it would still be an erosion already built into the system, with a legal basis solidly found in the balance of interests inherent in the Convention and subject

---

[59] For the text see www.unepmap.gr; Maria Gavouneli, New forms of cooperation in the Mediterranean system of environmental protection *in* Myron H. Nordquist, John Norton Moore & Said Mahmoudi (eds.), *The Stockholm Declaration and the Law of the Marine Environment* (Martinus Nijhoff Publishers, The Hague/London/New York 2003) pp. 223-235.

[60] Regulation 12 reads: "Places of refuge. The Contracting Parties: a) shall, following-up the work of EC and IMO, draw up plans to accommodate, in the waters under their jurisdiction, ships in distress in order to ensure that ships in distress may immediately go to a place of refuge subject to authorisation by the competent authority; and b) shall exchange details on plans for accommodating ships in distress"; available at www.helcom.fi/Convention/en_GB/annexes/#annex4.

[61] Of the European Parliament and of the Council of 27 June 2002 repealing Council Directive 93/75/EEC, OJ L. 208/10, 5 August 2002.

[62] GA Resolution 59/24, *supra* note 23, paragraph 35.

[63] PACE, Resolution 1439 (2005) of 29 April 2005, available at www.coe.int.

to judicial review under article 297 of the LOS Convention. "Evolution, not revolution"[64] would indeed be the order of the day.

2. INNOVATION THROUGH FRAGMENTATION

The idea of contractual schemes containing their own in-built systems of evolution is certainly not new. The concept of an umbrella convention setting out the bare minimum of communal life with specific provisions to be concluded at a later stage and/or date through protocols and (more or less simplified) amendments has become the stereotypical format in the environmental field, although it remains by no means restricted to it. The Law of the Sea Convention is clearly not such an open-ended agreement: the compelling "desire to settle, in a spirit of mutual understanding and cooperation, all issues relating to the law of the sea"[65] could hardly have been accommodated with the flexibility of a system in perennial flux. And yet ...

2.1. *A system of institutional complimentarity*

At first sight, the LOS Convention remains a fairly strictly defined text. Article 309 solemnly states that "No reservations or exceptions may be made to this Convention unless expressed permitted by other articles of this Convention". No reservation is permitted under any other article of the Convention and the possibility of an exception is only entertained in article 298, where States are given the option not to submit certain categories of disputes to compulsory procedures entailing binding decisions. One could be justified to believe that the integrity of the text, an integrity which the package deal to be agreed upon by consensus employed for its adoption sought to maintain[66], would be fully secured.

Yet, on the very next line it is further noted that

> "Article 309 does not preclude a State, when signing, ratifying or acceding to this Convention, from making declarations or statements, however phrased or named, ..., provided that such declarations or statements do not purport to exclude or to modify the legal effect of the provisions of this Convention in their application to that State"[67].

---

[64] Boyle, *supra* note 2, at p. 584.

[65] As clearly stated in the first preambular paragraph of the LOS Convention.

[66] In the words of Sir Robert Jennings: "A package deal subject to reservations in no longer a package or a deal"; R.Y. Jennings, Law-making and the package deal, *Mélanges offertes à Paul Reuter* (Paris, Pedone, 1981) pp. 347-355, at p. 352.

[67] Article 310 of the LOS Convention.

A large number of States have taken advantage of this facility to produce an impressive number of declarations and statements, ranging from simple interpretative declarations to conditional interpretative declarations to objections and even 'disguised reservations'[68]. This long list of pronouncements, from the innocuous to the illicit, depict in the clearest possible way the almost atavistic will of the States to break the confines of their conventional existence and interpret the common obligations enshrined in the Convention in the way they see fit.

Such attempts at unilateralism constitute the last bastion of defence, as the LOS Convention remains typically cumbersome in its amendment procedures. It could not have been otherwise: the balance of interests achieved at the end of a long negotiated process cannot be easily disturbed by anything less than an equally fully negotiated amendment[69]. Still, article 313 allows for a limited possibility of amending the Convention without convening a diplomatic conference[70]; the consent of the States, however, remains sacrosanct and one objection is sufficient to derail the system.

Nevertheless, practice has repeatedly shown that the exigencies of real life may create new routes where none existed before: se hace camino al andar. To a certain extent, the 1994 Agreement relating to the Implementation of Part XI of the LOS Convention[71] is nothing more than an amendment explicitly agreed upon by the States parties to it and acquiesced to by States non parties[72]. In contrast, neither the 1995 Agreement for the Implementation of the provisions of the UN Convention on the Law of the Sea Relating to the Conservation and Management of Straddling Fish Stocks and Highly Migratory Fish Stocks[73] nor the 1993 FAO Agreement to Promote Compliance with international Conservation and Management Measures by Fishing Vessels on the High Seas[74] constitute such amendments although they were

---

[68] For a thorough discussion of the matter, see L.D.M. Nelson, Declarations, statements and 'disguised reservations' with respect to the Convention on the Law of the Sea, 50 *ICLQ* 2001, pp. 767-786.

[69] Article 321 of the LOS Convention.

[70] See also a similar amendment procedure for provisions relating exclusively to activities in the Area in article 314 of the LOS Convention.

[71] UN General Assembly Resolution A/RES/48/263 (1994), 33 *ILM* 1994, p. 1309.

[72] Boyle, *supra* note 2, at p. 565; Churchill & Lowe, *supra* note 51, at p. 20.

[73] 34 *ILM* 1995, at p. 1542. See, in general, Peter G.G. Davies & Catherine Redgwell, The international legal regulation of straddling fish stocks, *BYBIL* 1996, pp. 199-274; Djamchid Momtaz, L'Accord relatif à la conservation et la gestion des stocks des poissons chevauchants et grands migrateurs, 41 *AFDI* 1995, p. 676.

[74] 33 *ILM* 1994, p. 968. On this unique combination of a binding text implemented by a non-binding Code of Conduct see Gavouneli, *supra* note 54, at pp. 543-544; Gerald Moore, Enforcement without force: New techniques in compliance control for foreign fishing opera-

clearly conceived and promoted as such. Indeed, the Straddling Stocks Agreement remains a fairly typical convention, applicable as between the parties to it, without creating rights or extending obligations to third parties[75]; such obligations could only be created as a result of a potential customary rule with the same content. This is already acknowledged in the text, which obligates the States parties to "take measures consistent with [the] Agreement and international law to deter the activities of vessels flying the flag of non parties, which undermine the effective implementation of this Agreement"[76].

However, these more or less formal means are not the only methods whereby the conventional rules may be amended or simply extended. The LOS Convention contains numerous references to regional cooperation in furtherance of various tasks, including the treatment of enclosed seas[77], fisheries management[78] and – most prominently – environmental protection[79]. The notion of regional seas, an issue of the 1972 Stockholm Declaration, predated the Convention and, to a certain extent, served as a blueprint for novel ideas and practical solutions[80]. Regional systems of environmental protection were already in place when the LOS Convention emerged from the long negotiation process and it made sense to integrate their policies, activities and mechanisms of implementation into the new world order just developing[81]. This was in essence what article 237 of the LOS Convention accom-

---

tions based on regional cooperation, 24 *ODIL* 1993, pp. 197-204; Francisco Orrego Vicuña, *The Changing International Law of High Seas Fisheries* (Cambridge 1999) at pp. 227-233.

[75] See, instead of many others, Erik Franckx, *Pacta Tertiis* and the Agreement for the Implementation of the Straddling and Highly Migratory Fish Stocks Provisions of the UN Convention on the Law of the Sea, 8 *Tulane Journal Of International & Comparative Law* 2000, pp. 49-81, at p. 73; Moritaka Hayashi, The 1995 Agreement on the Conservation and Management of Straddling and Highly Migratory Fish Stocks: Significance for the Law of the Sea Convention, 29 *Ocean and Coastal Management* 1995, pp. 51-69.

[76] Article 33 paragraph 2 of the Straddling Stocks Agreement. See also Laurent Lucchini & Michel Voelckel, *Droit de la mer* (Pedone, Paris 1996) p. 642; Moritaka Hayashi, Enforcement by non-flag States on the high seas under the 1995 Agreement on Straddling and Highly Migratory Fish Stocks, 9 *Georgetown IELR* 1996, pp. 1-36.

[77] Articles 122-123 of the LOS Convention.

[78] Articles 118-119 of the LOS Convention; article 21 of the Straddling Stock Convention. See also, among many others, Serge Pannatier, Problèmes actuels de la pêche en haute mer, 101 *RGDIP* 1997, pp. 421-446; Franckx, *supra* note 75, at p. 56.

[79] Especially in Part XII of the LOS Convention.

[80] There are currently 14 regional seas action plans: for the Red Sea and the Gulf of Aden; the West and Central Africa; the Caribbean; the East Asian States; the South-East Pacific; the South Pacific; Eastern Africa; the Black Sea; the North-West Pacific; the South Asian Seas; the North-East Pacific; and the Upper South-West Atlantic; see http://www.unep.ch/seas.

[81] Erik Franckx, Regional marine environment protection regimes in the context of UNCLOS, 13 *TIJMCL* 1998, pp. 307 *et seq.*; Günther Handl, Regional arrangements and third

plishes: States remain free to conclude "in furtherance of the general princi-ples set forth in [the] Convention" special conventions and agreements relat-ing to the preservation and protection of the marine environment, provided that such agreements as well as any similar obligations already assumed will "be carried out in a manner consistent with the general principles and objec-tives of the Convention". It follows that agreements or obligations "incom-patible with the effective execution of the object and purpose of the Conven-tion" or affecting "the application of the basic principles embodied therein" or even affecting "the enjoyment by other States Parties of the their rights or the performance of their obligations under the Convention" would fall within the ambit of article 311 paragraph 3 of the LOS Convention.

There has been as yet no adjudicated case on the compatibility of a re-gional agreement with the LOS Convention. The possible incompatibility of the 2000 Galapagos Framework Agreement for the Conservation of the Fishery Resources of the Southeast Pacific High Seas, concluded among Chile, Peru and Ecuador, was brought before a Special Chamber of the In-ternational Tribunal on the Law of the Sea, in a dispute between Chile and the European Community on measures to ensure conservation of swordfish in the high seas adjacent to Chile's EEZ[82]. The case remains currently sus-pended, along with the entry into force of the Galapagos Agreement, while the parties negotiate a compromise agreement[83]. The question was also touched upon in the *Southern Bluefin Tuna* case, where again the arbitral tri-bunal decided that it lacked jurisdiction to decide the merits of the case[84]. Consequently, the question whether an incompatible agreement remains valid as between the parties to it, while they are liable for breach of their ob-ligations under the LOS Convention; or whether such an agreement *subse-quent* to the LOS Convention is invalid *ab initio* will have to be authorita-tively decided on another occasion[85].

2.2. *Shades of an umbrella convention in the deep seabed?*

The legal regime applicable in the deep seabed, an area which constitutes the 'common heritage of mankind'[86], was the one issue that almost sent the Law

---

state vessels: Is the *pacta tertiis* principle being modified?, *in* Ringbom (ed.), *supra* note 54, at pp. 217 *et seq.*

[82] See *supra* note 44, Order 2000/3 of 20 December 2000.

[83] *Ibid.*, Order 2001/1 of 15 March 2001.

[84] See *supra* note 45.

[85] For a general discussion on the matter see Boyle, *supra* note 25, at pp. 15-17.

[86] Article 136 of the LOS Convention. For an overview of the context and the content of this notion see, instead of many others, Arvid Pardo, *The Common Heritage – Selected papers*

of the Sea Convention overboard. The detailed financial and organisational provisions of Part XI and the controversy they created somehow managed to obscure the fact that large gaps remained both in our knowledge of the deep seas and consequently in the regulation of activities undertaken in the Area. As a result the International Seabed Authority (hereinafter cited as "ISA"), an international organisation in its own right created by the LOS Convention[87], is entrusted with the delicate task to delineate existing information, define emerging needs and produce new rules and regulations on the subject on the basis of what amounts to a general authorisation granted by the Convention itself[88].

The first regulations were developed in rather predictable areas. In 2000 the Assembly approved the Regulations on Prospecting and Exploration for Polymetallic Nodules in the Area[89], the Mining Code. Once the regulatory framework was in place, the ISA was able to sign contracts for exploration with the first seven pioneer investors[90]; one cannot but note with some asperity that, in spite of all the big words and grand gestures of the 1980s, commercial deep seabed mining is still a long way into the future[91]! Similar regulations[92] are currently being drafted for hydrothermal polymetallic sul-

---

on oceans and world order (Valetta 1975); Charles-Alexandre Kiss, La notion du patrimoine commun de l'humanité, 243 RCADI 1982-II.

[87] Established by article 156 of the LOS Convention. For an overview of its functions see Satya Nandan, David Lodge & Shabtai Rosenne, The development of the regime for deep seabed mining (ISBA, Kingston 2002); Levy, Le destin de l'Autorité International des Fonds Marins (Pedone, Paris 2002).

[88] Article 160 of the LOS Convention.

[89] Doc. ISBA/6/A/18, available at www.isa.org.jm. Polymetallic nodules are defined as "one of the resources of the Area consisting of a deposit or accretion of nodules, on or just below the surface of the deep seabed, which contain manganese, nickel, cobalt and copper"; Regulation 1 paragraph 1(d). For an overview see M.W. Lodge, International Seabed Authority Regulations on Prospecting and Exploration for Polymetallic Nodules in the Area, 20 Journal of Energy & Natural Resources 2002.

[90] These were consortia sponsored by China (COMRA), France (Ifremer-Afernod), the Government of India, Japan (DORD), the Government of the Republic of Korea, the Russian Federation (Yuzhmorgeologiya) and Poland in cooperation with Bulgaria, Cuba, the Czech Republic, the Russian Federation and Slovakia (ICM). A new contract was granted in August 2005 to the Federal Republic of Germany in the Clipperton-Clarion zone in the North-East Pacific Ocean; Decision of the Council relating to a request for approval of a plan of work for exploration by the Federal Republic of Germany represented by the German Federal Institute for Geosciences and Natural Resources, Doc. ISBA/11/C/10 of 23 August 2005, available at www.isa.org.jm.

[91] See, instead of many others, Lyle Glowka, The deepest of ironies: Genetic resources, marine scientific research and the Area, 12 Ocean Yearbook 1996, pp. 154-178.

[92] For the latest version see Draft Regulations on prospecting and exploration for polymetallic sulphides and cobalt-rich ferromanganese crusts in the Area, Doc. ISBA/10/C/WP.1/Rev.1 of 6 September 2005, available at www.isa.org.jm.

phides[93] and cobalt-rich ferromanganese crusts[94] while methane hydrates are set to follow. The Mining Code is further complemented by Recommendations for the Guidance of Contactors for the Assessment of Possible Environmental Impacts Arising from Exploration for Polymetallic Nodules in the Area[95].

More than the Mining Code (in its various manifestations), these Recommendations denote the extent of the competences enjoyed by the ISA and its crucial regulatory role. States already have the obligation to "adopt laws and regulations to prevent, reduce and control pollution of the marine environment from activities in the Area undertaken by vessels, installations, structures and other devices flying their flag or of their registry or operating under their authority, as the case may be"[96]; but these rules must be no less effective than international rules, regulations and procedures established in accordance with Part XI of the LOS Convention. It is clear that the intention of both the framers of the Convention and of the 1994 Implementation Agreement was to grant to the ISA a preferential role of administrator in the Area[97], an administrator further endowed with all "incidental powers, consistent with [the] Convention that are implicit in and necessary for the exercise of its powers and functions with respect to activities in the Area"[98]. In essence, the Regulations build upon the environmental standards set out in Part XII of the LOS Convention, as further developed over time, most notably in view of the precautionary principle and the Agenda 21 in the 1992 Rio Declaration on Environment and Development[99].

Perhaps the best illustration of both the prospects and the limitations of the ISA may be found in the treatment of the genetic resources of the deep seabed. It appears that organisms found around hydrothermal vents have developed the capacity to survive extreme temperatures and other manifestations

---

[93] Defined as "hydrothermally formed deposits of sulphide minerals which conain concentrations of metals including, inter alia, copper, lead, zinc, gold and silver"; draft Regulation 1 paragraph 3(f).

[94] Defined as "hydroxide/oxide deposits of cobalt-rich iron/manganese (ferromanganese) crust formed from direct precipitation of minerals from seawater onto hard substrates containing minor but significant concentrations of cobalt, titanium, nickel platinum, molybdenum, tellurium, cerium, other metallic and rare earth elements"; draft Regulation 1, paragraph 3(b).

[95] Approved on 4 July 2001 by the Legal and Technical Commission; Doc. ISBA/7/LTC/1/Rev.1 of 10 July 2001, available at www.isa.org.jm.

[96] Article 209(2) of the LOS Convention.

[97] See article 157(1) of the LOS Convention.

[98] Article 157(2) of the LOS Convention.

[99] For a comprehensive overview see Tullio Scovazzi, Mining, protection of the environment, scientific research and bioprospecting: Some considerations on the role of the International Sea-bed Authority, 19 *TIJMCL* 2004, pp. 383-409, at pp. 392-394.

of extreme maltreatment; genetic material from these thermophiles, hyper-
thermofiles and assorted extremophiles is increasingly in use in a number of
industrial processes, including drug delivery, molecular biology and waste
treatment. Bioprospecting becomes, therefore, a major lucrative resource of
the deep seabed and, moreover, one that is immediately exploitable. Yet, the
term does not even appear in the Law of the Sea Convention. Defined as "the
exploration of biodiversity for commercially valuable genetic and biochemi-
cal resources" or "the process of gathering information from the biosphere
on the molecular composition of genetic resources for the development of
new commercial products"[100], bioprospecting does not fit easily into the categories of activities already recognised by the LOS Convention. It is, nevertheless, clear that, whatever the nature of the beast, it is an activity carried
out in the Area, where the ISA holds sway. As such it would have been un-
thinkable, to my mind, to consider exploiting this resource without involving
in some manner the Authority.

It is true that the ISA administers the common heritage of mankind in the
Area, which consists of "all activities of exploration of and exploitation of
the resources of the Area"[101], the latter being defined as "all solid, liquid or
gaseous minerals resources *in situ* in the Area or beneath the sea-bed, including polymetallic nodules"[102]. It is also true that the hydrothermal vents species are living resources and as such do not fall within the ambit of article
133 of the LOS Convention. Nevertheless, the critical element here does not
involve the harvesting of a readily exploitable species, in a manner reminis-
cent of fishing[103]. It pertains rather to the use of such genetic material for scientific research[104], which may eventually produce financial advantages as
well – which is indeed possible for all kinds of research, if not the purpose of
the whole exercise[105]. Indeed, the link between scientific research on the one

---

[100] As defined by the Subsidiary Body on Scientific, Technical and Technological Advice
(SBSTTA) in a report prepared in 2003 in response to Decision II/10 (1995) of the Conference of the Parties to the Convention on Biological Diversity; doc. UNEP/CBD/SBSTTA/
8/INF/3/Rev.1 of 22 February 2003, paragraph 49.

[101] Article 1(1)(3) of the LOS Convention.

[102] Article 133 of the LOS Convention.

[103] Armas Pfirter, *Legal implications related to te management of seabed living resources
in the Area under the LOS Convention*, paper submitted to the ISA Legal and Technical Commission in 2004, as quoted by Scovazzi, *supra* note 99, at pp. 400-401.

[104] As such bioprospecting falls also within the ambit of the Convention on Biological Diversity, which considers the conservation of biological diversity a common concern of humankind; see Tullio Scovazzi, The evolution of the International Law of the Sea: New issues,
new challenges, 286 *RCADI* 2000, pp. 39-244, at pp. 213-220; Michael W. Lodge, Improving
international governance in the deep sea, 19 *TIJMCL* 2004, pp. 299-316, at pp. 308-313.

[105] See also Scovazzi, *supra* note 99, at p. 402.

hand and commercial exploitation on the other becomes evident in the regulation of marine scientific research on the continental shelf/EEZ, where the coastal State may withhold its consent, if a project proposed by another State or international organisation "is of direct significance for the exploration and exploitation of natural resources, whether living or non-living"[106] but is not to unreasonably refuse such consent, if the project is to be carried out "exclusively for peaceful purposes and in order to increase scientific knowledge of the marine environment for the benefit of all mankind"[107]. The same rules apply on marine scientific research conducted in the Area[108]; the central role of the Authority in coordinating such research is again reiterated and States parties are empowered not only to carry out research but also to promote international cooperation by "effectively disseminating the results of research and analysis when available, through the Authority or other international channels when appropriate"[109].

There is no reason to believe that bioprospecting, being a specific form of marine research, would fall under the same regulatory regime and would have to be carried out under the same conditions, to be guaranteed by the Authority[110]. In doing so, the Authority would need to elaborate and adopt specific rules and regulations in implementation of the general principles of the LOS Convention but essentially developing a new branch of the law of the sea. These rules would effectively go beyond the original framework of the Law of the Sea Convention, encompassing intervening developments in the protection of the marine environment and biodiversity. It would be most interesting to see a new generation of law-making in this area and monitor differences and similarities with the well-documented practice of almost 20 years ago.

2.3. Evolution through authentic interpretation

---

[106] Article 246(5)(a) of the LOS Convention.

[107] Article 246(3) of the LOS Convention.

[108] In a very interesting interplay article 256 of the LOS Convention stipulates that marine scientific research shall be carried out in the Area "in conformity with the provisions of Part XI" whereas article 143 explicitly states that such research shall be carried out in the Area "in accordance with Part XIII".

[109] Article 143(3) of the LOS Convention.

[110] Thus also Scovazzi, *supra* note 99, at p. 402; C.H. Allen, Protecting the Oceanic Gardens of Eden: International Law Issues in Deep-Sea Vent Resource Conservation and Management, 13 *Georgetown IELR* 2003, pp. 565-660. For the historical thinking see Jon Van Dyke & Christopher Yuen, 'Common heritage' v. 'Freedom of the high seas': Which governs the seabed?, 19 *San Diego LR* 1982, pp. 493 *et seq.*

In creating a compulsory system of judicial resolution of disputes, the Law of the Sea Convention joined a select club of two instruments of constitutive character, founded on a delicate equilibrium of rights, duties and legitimate interests in a comprehensive, integral regulatory framework with a view to stabilize and maintain the compromises made. Conscious of the exceptional character of such compulsory third party dispute resolution mechanisms[111], the framers of the LOS Convention provided a veritable cornucopia of venues, including two permanent international courts and two arbitral formations. Nevertheless, the perception remained that the bulk of the disputes involving the Law of the Sea Convention could be addressed by the International Tribunal on the Law of the Sea, which could evolve into a veritable maritime chamber of international adjudication.

Almost 12 years and 13 cases later, the ITLOS has not made as yet the major contribution to the development of the law of the sea that would justify the expense necessary for its existence. Only one case was decided on the merits by the Tribunal: the *M/V Saiga* (no. 2) case[112]. A further case, the *Swordfish* case between Chile and the European Community[113], has been suspended, pending negotiations between the parties. The *MOX Plant* case was referred to an Annex VII Tribunal, which promptly suspended the proceedings before it, albeit allowing the provisional measures granted by ITLOS to continue[114]. An Annex VII Tribunal was also constituted for the *Land Reclamation* case[115], before which the case is currently pending. Another Annex VII Tribunal found in the *Southern Bluefin* case[116] that it lacked jurisdiction to hear the case. What remains are four cases where provisional measures were requested, under article 290 paragraph 1 of the LOS Convention – and seven cases of a request for the prompt release of vessels and crews. On the basis of this meagre harvest, little could be detected as to the contribution of ITLOS to the authentic interpretation of the Convention, let alone its substantive development. One would need perhaps to wait as ITLOS becomes

---

[111] See, among many others, A.E. Boyle, Dispute settlement and the Law of the Sea Convention: Problems of Fragmentation and Jurisdiction, 46 *ICLQ* 1997, pp. 37-54; G. Guillaume, Dispute settlement prospects in the Law of the Sea, 44 *ICLQ* 1995, pp. 848 *et seq.*; J. Charney, The implications of the International Dispute Settlement System of the 1982 Convention on the Law of the Sea on International Law, 90 *AJIL* 1996, pp. 69-75.

[112] See *supra* note 12.

[113] See *supra* note 44.

[114] See *supra* note 46.

[115] ITLOS, *Case concerning Land Reclamation by Singapore in and around the Straits of Johor*, Malaysia v. Singapore, Provisional measures, 2003, available at www.itlos.org

[116] See *supra* note 45.

increasingly the judicial formation of choice[117]: other instruments relevant to law of the sea issues designate it as the appropriate forum for the settlement of disputes arising under these conventions. Among them, the 1993 Agreement to promote Compliance with International Conservation an Management Measures by Fishing Vessels on the High Seas[118] under article IX; the 1995 Straddling Fish Stocks Agreement[119] under article 30; the 1996 Protocol to the Convention on the Prevention of Marine Pollution by Dumping of Wastes and Other Matter[120] under article 16; the 2000 Convention on the Conservation and Management of Highly Migratory Fish Stocks in the Western and Central Pacific Ocean[121] under article 31; the 2001 Convention on the Conservation and Management of Fishery Resources in the South-East Atlantic Ocean[122] under article 24; and the 2001 UNESCO Convention on the Protection of the Underwater Cultural Heritage[123] under article 25.

Nevertheless, even in these few cases of provisional measures that the Tribunal has actually produced for the time being, it was still able to give an indication of the manner in which it – and its members – would see the Convention developing. The starting point was already significantly improved as compared with the standard required by other judicial formations: Under article 290 paragraph 1 of the LOS Convention, "the court or tribunal may prescribe any provisional measures [...] it considers appropriate under the circumstances", first: in order "to preserve the respective rights of he parties to the dispute"; and second, "to prevent serious harm to the marine environment". The preservation of the *status quo* constitutes an inherent part of the rationale for granting provisional measures and it is frequently combined with the requirement of urgency in order to justify the freezing of a particular situation in a specific moment in time. Urgency, conceived evidently as a time parameter, is mentioned in the ITLOS context only in relation to provisional measures prescribed in anticipation of the constitution of an arbitral tribunal, which will adjudicate on the main argument[124]; one could be justi-

---

[117] For more see Robin Churchill, The International Tribunal for the Law of the Sea: Survey for 2003, 19 *TIJMCL* 2004, pp. 369-382, at pp. 380-382; Shabtai Rosenne, *Provisional measures in International Law* (Oxford 2005) pp. 58-61.

[118] See *supra* note 74.

[119] See *supra* note 73.

[120] 36 *ILM* 1997, p. 1.

[121] For the text see 16 *TIJMCL* 2001, pp. 402 *et seq.*

[122] For the text see 17 *TIJMCL* 2002, pp. 50 *et seq.*

[123] See Annex I. For a general overview see Guido Camarda & Tullio Scovazzi (eds.), *The protection of the underwater cultural heritage. Legal aspects* (Giuffrè Editore 2002); Roberta Garabello & Tullio Scovazzi (eds.), *The protection of the underwater cultural heritage. Before and after the 2001 UNESCO Convention* (Martinus Nijhoff 2003); see also *infra* Chapter 2.

[124] Article 290(5) of the LOS Convention.

fied to consider it an element of comity from one institution to another. Nevertheless, it has to be read into the phrase "under the circumstances" in paragraph 1 as the element of urgency is implicit in the need take immediate action to protect the rights being claimed until such time as a final decision is made[125].

The second element constitutes a novelty introduced by the Law of the Sea Convention. Being the first comprehensive global environmental treaty that it is, it was appropriate for it to recognise the intrinsic value of the environment and thus allow for the possibility of prescribing provisional measures in cases where serious harm to the marine environment may be at stake. The elaboration of a standard of risk, a threshold of what constitutes 'serious harm' would have been a very significant contribution to both the substantive rights of environmental protection as well as to the on-going work in the International Law Commission on principles of prevention of transboundary damage from hazardous activities.

It remains unclear in the cases heard by the Tribunal to which of the two parameters it relied in granting (or refusing to grant) provisional measures. In the *Southern Bluefin Tuna* case[126], the Tribunal accepted the Australian and New Zealand contention that Japan's experimental fishing programme was in beach of the total allowable catch agreed under the 1993 Convention for the Conservation of Southern Bluefin Tuna and imposed *de facto* provisional measures by submitting the effective continuation of the programme to the consent of the applicants. In doing so, the Tribunal noted that the parties should act "with prudence and caution to ensure that effective conservation measures are taken to prevent serious harm to the stock of southern bluefin tuna"[127]. Was this a reference to the procedural prerequisite of article 290 paragraph 1 of the LOS Convention or rather a substantive issue, a *prima facie* confirmation that the precautionary principle was at play[128] in the application of the Law of the Sea Convention as authoritatively construed by the Tribunal? Judge Warioba noted that the parties have not even argued

---

[125] Rosenne, *supra* note 117, at p. 135. On the possible different standard generated by the different formulation of the two paragraphs see Natalie Klein, *Dispute settlement in the UN Convention on the Law of the Sea* (Cambridge 2005) pp. 69-85.

[126] See *supra* note 45.

[127] *Ibid.*, Order of 27 August 1999, paragraph 77; available at www.itlos.org.

[128] Thus, for instance, David Freestone, Caution or precaution: A rose by any other name, 10 *YBIEL* 1999, pp. 25 *et seq.*; Moritaka Hayashi, The Southern Bluefin Tuna cases: Prescription of provisional measures, 13 *Tulane Environmental Law Journal* 2000, pp. 361 *et seq.*; Adriana Fabra, The Law of the Sea Convention and the implementation of the precautionary principle, 10 *YBIEL* 1999, pp. 15-24.

along those lines[129]. Judge Laing is unease about the possible use of this un-
tried formulation and insists that "reliance on the preservation of rights formula of article 290 paragraph 1 must continue to be the main engine of this
aspect of the provisional measures"[130]. Judge Treves finds that the two parts
must be addressed together "whenever the measures, although requested for
the preservation of the rights of a party, concern rights whose preservation is
necessary to prevent serious damage to the environment"[131].

The situation did not become any clearer in the next case brought before
the Tribunal. In the *MOX Plant* case[132], Ireland argued for the application of
the precautionary principle as a means for the Tribunal to assess the urgent
need to grant provisional measures[133], although without any direct reference
to the environmental risk requirement of article 290 paragraph 1 of the LOS
Convention. The Tribunal disagreed[134]; Judge Treves in his Separate Opinion[135] as well as Judges Caminos, Yamamoto, Park, Akl, Marsit, Eiriksson
and Jesus in a joint declaration[136] put the emphasis on the shortness of the
time period required before the constitution of an Annex VII Tribunal rather
than on any possible risk to the marine environment in application (or not) of
the precautionary principle proper. Only Judge Wolfrum in his Separate
Opinion distinguished clearly between the substantive and the procedural issue, cautioning that a broad application of the precautionary principle would
render the affirmation of the article 290 paragraph 1 requirements auto-
matic[137]. Although this approach might err on the side of prudence rather
than caution[138], it is nevertheless important to maintain the purity of the procedural argument, keeping in mind at all times that the level of certainty required for granting provisional measures remains lower than the judicial
conviction necessary for the adjudication on the merits.

It is interesting to note, however, that the Tribunal seems to have developed a further reading of article 290 of the LOS Convention, involving the

---

[129] *Ibid.*, Separate Opinion of Judge Warioba, final paragraph.

[130] *Ibid.*, Separate Opinion of Judge Laing, paragraph 18.

[131] *Ibid.*, Separate Opinion of Judge Treves, paragraph 6.

[132] See *supra* note 46.

[133] *Ibid.*, Order of 3 December 2001, paragraph 71.

[134] *Ibid.*, paragraph 81.

[135] *Ibid.*, Separate Opinion of Judge Treves, paragraph 8.

[136] *Ibid.*, Joint Declaration, paragraph 2.

[137] *Ibid.*, Separate Opinion, paragraph 13.

[138] Thus Gwenaele Rashbrooke, The International Tribunal for the Law of the Sea: A forum for the development of principles of International Environmental Law?, 19 *TIJMCL*
2004, pp. 515-535, at pp. 528-529; Chester Brown, Provisional measures before the ITLOS:
The MOX Plant case, 17 *TIJMCL* 2002, pp. 267 *et seq.*

duty to cooperate, affirmed as "a fundamental principle in the prevention of pollution of the marine environment under Part XII of the Convention and general international law"[139]. The Tribunal considers the rights arising from the application of the principle as appropriate to be preserved under article 290 of the LOS Convention and has set "prudence and caution" as the applicable standard of implementation[140]. The same formulation was again used in the *Land Proclamation* case[141], without any further reference to environmental risk although Malaysia argued on that point. Indeed, both President Nelson[142] and Judge Chandrasekhara Rao[143] in their respective Separate Opinions seemed to integrate the environmental risk requirement with the obligation to cooperate in matters environmental.

As far as progressive development of the law goes, this is certainly not on the grand scale. Nevertheless, it is increasingly becoming clear that although the Tribunal is not exactly inundated with cases, it has developed into a default instance of first call for issues relevant to the law of the sea[144]. Its procedures are user-friendly, its time-limits are short, provisional measures granted under its jurisdiction are binding[145], all the elements are present to attract the kind of clientele, which would prefer an expeditious first act in dispute settlement while at the same time freezing, at the very least, the respective rights and conditions of the situation. The jurisprudence of the Tribunal, even in this fast and hard manner of delivering justice, could be indicative of new trends in the Law of the Sea, as it is singularly placed to ascertain and address the vagaries and eventually the shortfalls of the system. ITLOS has been very cautious so far in building slowly its expertise and also its reputa-

---

[139] *The MOX Plant* case, *supra* note 46, Order of 3 December 2001, paragraph 82.

[140] *Ibid.*, paragraph 84.

[141] See *supra* note 114, Order of 8 October 2003, paragraph 92.

[142] *Ibid.*, Separate Opinion of President Nelson, paragraph 7: "[t]he Tribunal has once again stressed the fundamental role and central importance of cooperation in he protection of the preservation of the marine environment".

[143] *Ibid.*, Separate Opinion of Judge Chandrasekhara Rao, paragraph 13: "[i]t is to be specially remembered that the Malaysian concerns primarily relate to allegations of environmental damage and that the duty to cooperate is a fundamental principle in the prevention of pollution of the marine environment under Part XII of the Convention and general international law".

[144] On the shortcomings of the provisional measures approach see Malcolm D. Evans, The Southern Bluefin Tuna Dispute: Provisional thinking on provisional measures?, 10 *YBIEL* 1999, pp. 7 *et seq.*

[145] See article 290(6) of the LOS Convention. For an overview see Rosenne, *supra* note 119, pp. 44-61, at p. 49; Antonios Tzanakopoulos, Provisional measures issued by international courts: Emergence of a general principle of international law, 57 *RHDI* 2004, pp. 53-84.

tion; and at this stage it seems that caution remains the best part of valour. The future, however, could be exciting.

2.4. *New procedural tools of enforcement*

The procedures so far examined are not unique to the Law of the Sea Convention and its judicial organ and, to that extent, present problems and perspectives not uncommon to those encountered in other conventional contexts. Yet, the Law of the Sea Convention has established a unique system of recourse before the Tribunal in providing in article 292 of a mechanism of the prompt release of vessels and crews. Conceived as yet another balancing act between the respective interests of the flag State and the coastal State, this State-to-State recourse finds its most frequent application in fisheries cases[146] and eventually protects the primary users of the sea, the seafarers. As such, it constitutes the only person-oriented mechanism available in the field; in fact, a human rights clause in the law of the sea.

The prompt release procedure is founded on an original, non incidental[147] jurisdiction, compulsory for the States parties to the Convention, irrespective of whether they have accepted the jurisdiction of ITLOS under article 287 of the LOS Convention[148]. The case brought before the Tribunal pertains only to the very specific matter of "release from detention", when a State Party, having detained a vessel flying the flag of another State party, "has not complied with the provisions of [the] Convention for the prompt release of the vessel or its crew upon the posting of a reasonable bond"[149]. It does not constitute an appeal procedure against a domestic court decision[150]. Indeed, it does not impact at all upon the merits of the case before the competent domestic fo-

---

[146] For an overview see D.R. Rothwell & T. Stephens, Illegal Southern Ocean fishing and prompt release: Balancing coastal and flag state rights and interests, 53 *ICLQ* 2004, pp. 171-187.

[147] ITLOS, The *M/V Saiga* (no.1) case, Saint Vincent and the Grenadines v. Guinea, 1997, paragraph 50; G. Eiriksson, The International Tribunal for the Law of the Sea (Martinus Nijhoff 2000) at p. 205.

[148] Yoshifumi Tanaka, Prompt release in the UN Convention on the Law of the Sea: Some reflections on the ITLOS jurisprudence, 31 *NILR* 2004, pp. 237-271, at p. 240.

[149] Article 292(1) of the LOS Convention.

[150] Thus affirmed the Tribunal in the *Camouco* case, Panama v. France, 2000, paragraph 58; The *Monte Confurco* case, Seychelles v. France, 2000, paragraph 72; both available at www.itlos.org..

rum[151]; and although the Tribunal has been consistent in respecting the restraints of each particular case[152], a number of commentators recognise in this function a general review of legality[153], "la fonction générale de gardien de la légalité maritime"[154].

Yet, even in keeping within the strict confines of the law, the Tribunal does have a general understanding of the merits of the case when deciding on the 'reasonableness' of the bond requested by the detaining State. In successive cases, ITLOS has developed a series of criteria of what constitutes a "reasonable" bond[155], creating an autonomous notion of its own[156]. Starting from a simple statement in the *M/V Saiga* (no.1) case that the "overall balance" of "the amount, the nature and the form of the bond or financial security" must be reasonable[157], it proceeded in the *Camouco* case to enumerate a series of criteria: "[T]he gravity of the alleged offences, the penalties imposed or imposable under the laws of the detaining State, the value of the detained vessel and of the cargo seized, the amount of the bond imposed by the detaining State and its form"[158]. In reiterating the "overall balance" formula in appreciating this non-exhaustive list, the Tribunal seems to have introduced in the *Monte Confurco* case an element of proportionality into the system[159].

Would these elements suffice to bring into the purview of the Tribunal the wider issues involved in each case, so that the decision finally reached may reflect their gravity? On the face of it they seem to be capable to do so. Indeed, in the *Volga* case, it got out of its way to note the importance of measures undertaken by coastal States in the wider area covered by the Convention on the Conservation of Antarctic Marine Living Resources (CCAMLR)[160],

---

[151] Article 292(3) of the LOS Convention.

[152] See *supra* note 149, paragraph 74.

[153] ITLOS, The *Volga* case, Russian Federation v. Australia, 2002, Separate Opinion of Judge Cot, paragraph 24, available at www.itlos.org. See also Shigeru Oda, Dispute settlement prospects in the Law of the Sea, 44 *ICLQ* 1995, at p. 866.

[154] Jean-Pierre Queneudec, À propos de la procédure de prompte mainlevée devant le Tribunal international du Droit de la mer, *ADM* 2003, pp. 79-92, at pp. 87-92.

[155] For an overview see Erik Franckx, "Reasonable bond" in the practice of the International Tribunal for the Law of the Sea, 32 *California Western ILJ* 2002, pp. 303-342.

[156] Queneudec, *supra* note 154, p. 89. For a general discussion of reasonableness see Olivier Corten, *L'utilisation du 'raisonnable' par le juge international. Discours juridique, raison et contradictions* (Bruylant, Bruxelles 1997).

[157] See *supra* note 147, paragraph 82.

[158] See *supra* note 150, paragraph 67.

[159] See *supra* note 150, paragraph 66.

[160] For an overview of the system see Rosemary Rayfuse, Enforcement of High Seas Fisheries Agreements: Observation and Inspection under the Convention on the Conservation of Antarctic Marine Living resources, 13 *TIJMCL* 1998, pp. 579-605.

presumably including the detention of vessels engaged in illegal fishing[161]. Judge *ad hoc* Shearer took the case one point further: "A new 'balance' has to be struck between vessel owners, operators and fishing companies on the one hand and coastal States on the other"[162]. It would be interesting to see whether the Tribunal would follow this admonition in the years to come, especially since new challenges would arrive before its portals.

This is not the only direction in which ITLOS may choose to extent its writ. Article 292 paragraph 1 of the LOS Convention stipulates that the prompt release procedure applies only where "it is alleged that the detaining State has no complied *with the provisions of this Convention* for the prompt release of the vessel or its crew"[163]. Which are these provisions is not immediately clear. The Tribunal itself identified them in the *M/V Saiga* (no.1) case as article 73 paragraph 2 on the enforcement of the laws and regulations of the coastal State with respect to living resources; article 220 on the enforcement by the coastal State of laws and regulations or the applicable international rules and standards for the prevention, reduction and control of pollution from vessels; and article 226 paragraph 1(c) on the detention of unseaworthy vessels presenting "an unreasonable threat of damage to the marine environment"[164].

All seven prompt release cases brought before ITLOS allege a violation of article 73 paragraph 2 of the LOS Convention, which makes the prompt release procedure the necessary corollary to the enforcement of fishing rules and regulations. The environmental protection provisions have never been invoked before the Tribunal so far, although article 226 paragraph 1(c) of the LOS Convention, in essence the legal basis of memoranda of understanding for port State control, was mentioned in the *Volga* case as one of the possible instances where the prompt release procedure would apply[165]. They are, however, liable to encompass a wide range of enforcement procedures, both national as well as international: Article 220 paragraph 6 of the LOS Convention provides for the detention of the vessel as a possible means of enforcement "where there is clear objective evidence that a vessel navigating in the exclusive economic zone or the territorial sea of a State has, in the exclusive

---

[161] See *supra* note 153, paragraph 68.

[162] *Ibid.*, Dissenting Opinion of Judge *ad hoc* Shearer, paragraph 19.

[163] Emphasis added.

[164] See *supra* note 147, paragraph 52.

[165] See *supra* note 153, paragraph 77; Anne-Katrin Escher, release of vessels and crews before the International Tribunal for the Law of the Sea, 3 *The Law and Practice of International Courts and Tribunals* 2004, pp. 205-374, at pp. 271-274. See in general Christoph Schwarte, Environmental concerns in the adjudication of the International Tribunal for the Law of the Sea, 16 *Georgetown IELR* 2004, pp. 421-439.

economic zone, committed a violation [...] resulting in a discharge causing major damage or threat of major damage to the coastline or related interests of the coastal State or to any resources of its territorial sea or exclusive economic zone..."; whereas paragraph 7 stipulates the release of the vessel "whenever appropriate procedures have been established, either through the competent international organisation or as otherwise agreed". In such a way any breach of the international conventions on civil liability for marine pollution or indeed any other environmental protection convention, which provides for detention, may be submitted to the jurisdiction of he Tribunal under the prompt release procedure. Under such circumstances, the human rights parameter of the procedure will become evident as seafarers, often trapped for long periods of time in interminable proceedings in countries far way from home, will, through the flag State or agents acting on its behalf[166], be able to have access to the short delays of the Tribunal.

Whether this enumeration is restrictive or the prompt release mechanism would be open to any case where a vessel is detained for breach of the Convention is a subject of intense debate[167]. Judges Park, Nelson, Chandrasekhara Rao, Vukas and Ndiaye noted in their Dissenting Opinion in the M/V Saiga (no.1) case opted for a restricted approach[168], relying also on the legislative history of the provision[169]. Vice President Wolfrum and Judge Yamamoto concurred in their own Dissenting Opinion: article 292 was a unique

---

[166] Indeed, the practice of the Tribunal has shown that it is usually the company managing the ship rather than the flag State that takes the initiative to bring a case to court; misgivings were expressed by Judge *ad hoc* Cot in his Declaration in the Grand Prince case, *supra* note 17, paragraph 14. See generally Tanaka, *supra* note 148, p. 251 at footnote 50; Queneudec, *supra* note 154, p. 91; J.-P. Cot, Appearing "for" or "on behalf of" a State: The role of private counsel before international tribunals, *Liber amicorum Judge Shigeru Oda* (Kluwer Law International 2002) pp. 835-847, at p. 842.

[167] Tanaka, *supra* note 148, pp. 241-248; Tullio Treves, The proceedings concerning prompt release of vessels and crews before the International Tribunal for the Law of the Sea, 11 *TIJMCL* 1996, pp. 179-200; Rainer Lagoni, The prompt release of vessels and crews before the International Tribunal for the Law of the Sea: A preparatory report, 11 *TIJMCL* 1996, pp. 147-164; J. Akl, La procédure de prompte mainlevée du navire ou prompte libération de son équipage devant le tribunal international du droit de la mer, 6 *ADM* 2001, pp. 219-246; Klein, *supra* note 125, pp. 103-108.

[168] See *supra* note 147, Dissenting Opinion of Judges Park, Nelson, Chandrasekhara Rao, Vukas and Ndiaye, paragraphs 21-25. See also V. Lowe, The *M/V Saiga*: The first case in the International Tribunal for the Law of the Sea, 48 *ICLQ* 1999, pp. 187-199, at p. 195.

[169] See M.H. Nordquist *et al.* (eds.), *United Nations Convention on the Law of the Sea 1982: A Commentary* (vol. 5, Martinus Nijhoff 1989) pp. 68-69.

and self-contained procedure with specific rules and very precise limits[170]. The subject was never again brought before the Tribunal.

Equally interesting might be the expansion of article 292 procedures to disputes under the 1995 Straddling Stock Agreement. Under article 30 paragraph 1 of the Agreement "The provisions relating to the settlement of disputes set out in Part XV of the Convention apply *mutatis mutandis* to any dispute between States Parties to this Agreement concerning the interpretation or application of this Agreement, whether or not they are also parties to the Convention". The Agreement provides expressly in article 21 paragraph 12 for the possible detention of inspected vessels at the request of the flag State. It is not inconceivable that the release of the crew may become an issue and there is, in my mind, no reason to exclude *a priori* the availability of the prompt release mechanism from the Straddling Stock Agreement[171].

3. CONCLUDING REMARKS

What could be the outcome of this overview? Perhaps what was evident from the starting point. The product of a compromise, the LOS Convention contains provisions expressing the most traditional ideas of allocation of powers along the lines of State sovereignty and even flag State sovereignty. On the other hand, in the 20 years of its existence things *have* changed in the world. The mechanisms established by the Convention, both as decision-making processes, especially in the deep seabed, and as enforcement procedures, including the prompt release of vessels and crews, could indeed adjust to the new realities and allow for significant evolution in these fields.

To a certain extent, the development of the Convention towards one direction or another would depend on several criteria, which would differ over time. The first would certainly be the evolving needs of the world community, which would create priorities and allocate resources for future expansion. Another one would be the prospective with which we view the Convention and the system it created. If one is to consider the compromises achieved several years ago as cast in stone, without any further possibility of revision, then, sooner or later, the Law of the Sea Convention would ground to a standstill. Restrictive approaches will suffocate possible new aspects of implementation and eventually marginalise the existing procedures. If, how-

---

[170] See *supra* note 147, Dissenting Opinion of Vice-President Wolfrum and Judge Yamamoto, paragraphs 14-18.

[171] Thus also Treves, *supra* note 167, pp. 186-187. *Contra* E.D. Brown, The *M/V Saiga* case on prompt release of detained vessels: The first judgment of the International tribunal for the Law of the Sea, 22 *Marine Policy* 1998, pp. 307-327, at p. 312.

ever, we move on with a flexible interpretation of the rules and regulations we have, in full respect of both the letter and the spirit of the Convention, we will be able to make this elaborate creation breathe and live along with the times; it will then become a most effective tool for the comprehensive management of maritime spaces, of marine resources and the wealth of the oceans. As it seems that our future lies in the water, this evolution might be not only recommended but indeed the only possible.

Chapter 9

THE ROLE OF THE INTERNATIONAL COURT OF JUSTICE AND THE INTERNATIONAL TRIBUNAL FOR THE LAW OF THE SEA IN THE PROGRESSIVE DEVELOPMENT OF THE LAW OF THE SEA

*Haritini Dipla**

1. INTRODUCTION

The principal role of courts and tribunals is to resolve the disputes submitted to them by applying the existing rule of law[1]. However, in every legal system, and most prominently in the international legal order, their contribution to the law-making process, be it customary or conventional, is fundamental. The term "progressive development", borrowed from the United Nations Charter, is closely related to the codification of international law, it being one of the missions of the General Assembly through the creation of the International Law Commission and the organization of international conferences. Within the United Nations *fora*, States have indeed the last word. But if one looks at the results of such a process, one is impressed by the impact on codification, usually in the form of international conventions, of the decisions of international courts and tribunals.

Major issues of the law of the sea have been put both before the Permanent Court of International Justice (PCIJ) and the International Court of Justice (ICJ), each of them having been for a long time the only international judicial forum with broad jurisdiction. In the *S.S. Wimbledon* case (1923), the Permanent Court has had the opportunity to declare that an artificial channel used for international navigation between two parts of the high seas should be assimilated to an international strait, where freedom of navigation exists

---

* Professor of International Law, University of Athens.

[1] Statement of M. Bedjaoui, (former) President of the International Court of Justice to the General Assembly, 15 October 1996, p. 3, www.icj-cij.org/ Statements of the President; Statement of D. Nelson, President of the International Tribunal of the Law of the Sea to the General Assembly, 9 December 2002, paragraph 19, www.itlos.org/ Statements of the President.

Anastasia Strati, Maria Gavouneli & Nikos Skourtos (eds.), *Unresolved Issues and New Challenges to the Law of the Sea*, Martinus Nijhoff Publishers 2006, pp. 235-250.

even for warships of belligerent States[2]. In the *Lotus* case (1927), the PCIJ discussed the exercise of criminal jurisdiction of States vis-à-vis foreign nationals in the case of collision in the high seas. The Court held that jurisdiction of the national State of the responsible person (France) runs concurrent to the jurisdiction of the State of the victims (Turkey)[3]. It should be noted, though, that the decision of the Court was eventually reversed by international practice and later codification, which reserves the exercise of criminal jurisdiction only to the flag State and the national State of the person responsible for the collision (article 11 of the 1958 Geneva Convention on the High Seas and article 97 of the 1982 United Nations Convention on the Law of the Sea, hereinafter cited as "LOS Convention")[4].

2. THE CONTRIBUTION OF THE INTERNATIONAL COURT OF JUSTICE TO THE CODIFICATION OF THE LAW OF THE SEA

In its early days already, the International Court of Justice was seized with cases concerning the law of the sea. In the *Corfu Channel Case* (1949) the parties, United Kingdom and Albania, had discussed the elements necessary for a natural strait to qualify as a strait in the legal sense. The Court admitted that both criteria, "the geographical situation as connecting two parts of the high seas and the fact of its being used for international navigation", were important and declared that innocent passage could not be suspended therein[5]. The Court's *dicta* were subsequently included in article 16 paragraph 4 of the 1958 Geneva Convention on the Territorial Sea and the Contiguous Zone (hereinafter cited as "TSC") and later incorporated in the relevant articles of Part III of the LOS Convention on straits used for international navigation, *inter alia* articles 37 and 45.

In the *Anglo-Norwegian Fisheries* Case (1951), the Court innovated by admitting the validity in international law (and its opposability to the United Kingdom) of the outer limit of the territorial sea of Norway, drawn by reference to the new, at the time of the judgment of the Court, straight baselines system. Against strong reaction by three dissenting judges[6], the Court's deci-

---

[2] PCIJ, Series A, 1923, No 1, p. 28 .

[3] PCIJ, Series A, 1927, No 10, p. 30.

[4] R.R. Churchill and A.V. Lowe, *The Law of the Sea* (3nd ed., Manchester University Press, 1999) p. 208; T. Treves, La navigation, *in* R.-J. Dupuy and D. Vignes (éds.), *Traité du nouveau droit de la Mer* (Economica, Paris 1985) p. 732.

[5] Judgment of 9 April 1949, Merits, ICJ Reports 1949, p. 28.

[6] Judges Hsu Mo, Sir Arnold MacNair and Read, ICJ Reports 1951, pp. 154, 185 and 186 respectively.

sion contributed in introducing the straight baselines system in article 4 of the TSC and eventually in article 7 of the LOS Convention.

The Court's case law contributed further to the definition of the continental shelf, this being made in the context of its delimitation between States. After the 1958 Geneva Convention on the Continental Shelf (hereinafter cited as "CSC") has been adopted and entered into force, in the *North Sea Continental Shelf* cases (1969) the Court defined the continental shelf as being "the natural prolongation of the land territory under the sea"[7]. Even though the law on the delimitation of the continental shelf has been through a dramatic evolution since the 1960s, one can still trace these terms in article 76 of the LOS Convention[8].

Other cases were related, *inter alia*, to the liberty of navigation on the high seas[9] as well as the extension of the jurisdiction of the coastal State's fishing zone[10].

In the continuous interaction between the Court's decisions and international law-making, the case law on the maritime zones delimitation between States constitutes the richest and most interesting contribution of the Court to the law of the sea. Its impact consists, among other, on the one hand, in the *clarification* of the principles and rules of delimitation through the reconciliation between customary and conventional law and, on the other hand, in the *unification* of the rules concerning the delimitation of all the maritime zones.

i. As far as *clarification* of the law is concerned, the Court's work has been the result of a long and difficult course, which began with the *North Sea Continental Shelf* cases (1969)[11]. In that case, the first to be submitted to it in this area, the Court pronounced in favour of the discrepancy between customary and conventional law and introduced in the legal scene of general international law the equitable principles as being something different from the rule expressed in the conventional law of 1958, that mentioned the line of equidistance/special circumstances[12].

---

[7] ICJ Reports 1969, p. 6.

[8] The text reads as follows: "1. The continental shelf of a coastal State comprises the seabed and subsoil of the submarine areas that extend beyond its territorial sea throughout the natural prolongation of its land territory to the outer edge of the continental margin…".

[9] *Military and Paramilitary Activities in Nicaragua*, Jurisdiction and Admissibility, Judgment of 26 November 1984, ICJ Reports 1984, paragraph 73; and Judgment of 27 June 1986, Merits, ICJ Reports 1986, paragraph 174.

[10] *Fisheries Jurisdiction* cases, Germany/UK v. Iceland, ICJ Reports 1974, pp. 3 and 175.

[11] *Supra* note 7.

[12] Article 6 of the CSC.

Coupled with the definition given by the Court of the continental shelf, as being the natural prolongation of the coastal State's territory under the sea, this discrepancy inevitably led to a theoretical and practical controversy between those States that adhered to the median line/special circumstances rule and those that preferred the equitable principles rule. It also led to legal uncertainty, since the casuistic application by the judge of the equitable principles has proven to be highly approximate and unpredictable. Last but not least, in the next cases, for example *Tunisia/Libya* (1982), in which the parties pleaded the geological characteristics of the seabed in order to defend their case, those criteria proved difficult if not impossible to verify and apply[13].

The awkwardness of the situation was acknowledged by the President of the Court Judge Guillaume, who declared at his speech before the Sixth Committee of the United Nations General Assembly on 31 October 2001:

> "At this stage, case law and treaty law had become so unpredictable that there was extensive debate within doctrine on whether there still existed a law of delimitation or whether, in the name of equity, we were not ending up with arbitrary solutions. Sensitive to these criticisms, in subsequent years, the Court proceeded to develop its case law in the direction of greater certainty"[14].

By then, the Third UN Conference for the Law of the Sea ("UNCLOS III") had reached consensus on the introduction in the law of the sea of the Exclusive Economic Zone (EEZ), the definition of which was not based on physical characteristics but mainly on the distance, 200 nautical miles from the baselines used for the measurement of the territorial sea. In view of the fact that the legal regime of the continental shelf is intimately related to that of the EEZ[15], the Court abandoned the bed of the sea in favour of its surface and from the geological factors turned to geography. The judgment in the *Libya/Malta* case (1985) was a turning point[16], the one in the *Maritime Delimitation in the Area Between Greenland and Jan Mayen* case (1993) proved to be a break with the past[17]. In this last case, the Court found that the rules on the delimitation of the continental shelf and the EEZ in the LOS Convention[18] and the 'line of equidistance /special circumstances' rule in article 6 of the CSC have the same finality, to obtain an equitable delimitation. The special circumstances of conventional law and the relevant circum-

---

[13] ICJ Reports 1982, p. 7.

[14] For the text, see www.icj-cij.org/Statements of the President of the Court.

[15] This has been expressly admitted through the drafting of article 56 paragraph 3 of the LOS Convention, according to which "the rights set out in this article with respect to the seabed and subsoil shall be exercised in accordance with Part VI [on the continental shelf]".

[16] ICJ Reports 1985, p. 4.

[17] ICJ Reports 1993, p. 4.

[18] Articles 74 and 83 of the LOS Convention with identical texts.

stances of customary law, that have to be taken into account in order to achieve an equitable result (an expression inherited from the ICJ case law and codified in the relevant articles of the LOS Convention), have the same meaning and are mostly of geographical nature. The median line in both must be the point of departure, in cases where continental shelf and/or EEZ delimitation takes place within a area where the distance is shorter than 400 miles between opposite coasts.

From this point on, in the subsequent cases, the Court applied almost automatically the median line at the first stage of the delimitation process, then corrected it in order to serve equity. In the *Qatar/Bahrain* case (2001)[19] the Court applied also this solution in a situation where the coasts of the two States are adjacent.

In the case concerning the *Land and Maritime Boundary Between Cameroon and Nigeria* (2002), where applicable law were for the first time the LOS Convention rules on delimitation, the Court proceeded also by drawing a line of equidistance between the (adjacent) coasts of the two States. In this application of the equidistance line, it went even further by refusing to correct it, having denied to retain criteria that it had admitted as relevant in its previous case law, such as the concavity of the coasts, oil practice, even the existence of an important island, Bioko Island, belonging to a third State, namely Equatorial Guinea.

ii. In its recent case law, the Court also seized the opportunity to make a step further towards the *unification* of the rules of delimitation by declaring that the above method is to be followed, not only for continental shelf and exclusive economic zone delimitation purposes but also for the delimitation of the territorial sea.

Thus, in the *Qatar/Bahrain* case (2001) delimitation issues involved all three maritime zones: The territorial sea in the South, the continental shelf and the EEZ in the North, where the coasts of the parties begin by being opposite and then become adjacent. In this case, the Court declared that the essence of the rules contained in articles 74 and 83 has transcended also the one inserted in article 15 of the LOS Convention. All three provisions aim at an equitable delimitation and lead to a unity of law, providing that in the three cases a median/equidistant line is to be drawn first, then corrected, if needed, in order to achieve an equitable result. Thus, the Court in this case used the median line as a point of departure and corrected it in order to take into consideration certain insular features and other geographical irregularities in the delimitation area. Before that, a similar approach had been followed by the Arbitral Tribunal on the *Maritime Delimitation between Eri-*

---

[19] ICJ Reports 2001, p. 6.

trea and Yemen (1999), which had decided for a "single-all-purpose boundary", thus being the first to contribute to the unification of the rules on maritime delimitation contained in articles 15, 74 and 83 of the LOS Convention[20].

To sum up, one might observe that the interrelation between the Court's judicial activity and the law-making process passed through different stages. Having started from a more or less precise conventional framework, that of article 6 of the CSC, the Court introduced in customary law the equitable principles that resulted in legal uncertainty. The latter is being reflected in the text of both articles 74 and 83 of the LOS Convention, which were "consciously designated to decide as little as possible"[21]. To redress this situation, the ICJ interpreted the provisions of these articles, to which it added, as stated above, article 15 on the delimitation of the territorial sea, by reintroducing in the legal landscape the principle of the median line.

For a long time the ICJ was the only international judicial body with broad jurisdiction and the choice of States was necessarily focused between the Court and international arbitral tribunals. Their contribution to the law of the sea is also of importance. Let us simply recall the Arbitral Tribunal between France and the UK on the *Delimitation of the Continental Shelf in the English Channel and North Western Approaches* (1977), which was the first international tribunal that tried to reconcile the conventional rule of article 6 of the CSC and customary law[22].

3. THE CONTRIBUTION OF THE INTERNATIONAL TRIBUNAL
FOR THE LAW OF THE SEA

The proliferation of norms, through codification and regionalization, in many fields of international law gave birth to a multiplication of judicial organs[23]. The law of the sea is an interesting example. Since 1996 the contribu-

---

[20] Award of 17 December 1999, paragraph 132; for the text, see www.pca-cpa.org. The Award has been commented by S.M. Reisman, Case Report on the Eritrea-Yemen Arbitration (Phase II), 94 *AJIL* 2000, pp. 721-736; Ph. Weckel, CPA, Sentence du 17 septembre 1999, *RGDIP* 2000, pp. 189-192; M.D. Evans, The Maritime Delimitation Between Eritrea and Yemen, 14 *Leiden Journal of International Law* 2001, pp. 141-170; and B. Kwiatkowska, The Eritrea-Yemen Arbitration, 32 *ODIL* 2001, pp. 1-25.

[21] According to the Arbitral Tribunal on Eritrea/Yemen Maritime Delimitation case, *ibid.*, paragraph 116.

[22] Award of 1977, *La Documentation française* (1977) p. 80.

[23] For a multidisciplinary approach of this issue, see the Acts of a Meeting on 'The Proliferation of International Tribunals', 1-2 October 1998, 31 *New York University Journal of International Law and Politics* 1999. Also M. Couston, La multiplication des juridictions internationales. Sens et dynamique, *Journal du droit international* 2002, pp. 5-53; and S. Karagiannis, La multiplication des juridictions internationales: Un système anarchique?, *La*

tion of the ICJ to the law of the sea is being enriched and completed by the case law of the International Tribunal for the Law of the Sea (ITLOS)[24]. It is expected that arbitral tribunals, to be constituted under the dispute settlement system of the 1982 LOS Convention, will also play an important role in this regard[25].

3.1. Prompt Release of Vessels and their Crews

The International Tribunal for the Law of the Sea had up to this date the opportunity to clarify, through the cases adjudicated[26], the rules on the prompt release of vessels arrested for (alleged) violations of the legislation adopted by coastal States in exercising their rights to explore, exploit, conserve and manage the living resources in the EEZ. Under article 73 paragraph 1 of the LOS Convention, enforcement measures in accordance with such legislation may consist in boarding, inspection, arrest and judicial proceedings. But arrested vessels and their crews must be promptly released "upon the posting of reasonable bond or other security" (paragraph 2) and the penalties for fisheries laws and regulations may not include imprisonment or other corporal punishment (paragraph 3). Under article 292 of the LOS Convention, the disputes related to the duty to release and the assessment of the reasonableness of the bond fall, as a last resort, within the compulsory jurisdiction of the ITLOS[27].

---

juridictionnalisation du droit international (Société française pour le droit international, Colloquium of Lille, Pedone, Paris 2003) pp. 559-562.

[24] For the Tribunal see, among others, Th. Mensah, The International Tribunal for the Law of the Sea: Its Role for the Settlement of Law of the Sea Disputes, *African Yearbook of International Law* 1998, pp. 227-242; Sh. Rosenne, Establishing the International Tribunal for the Law of the Sea, 89 *AJIL* 1995, pp. 806-814; *idem.*, The International Tribunal for the Law of the Sea, 13 *IJMCL* 1998, pp. 487-514; M. Marsit, *Le Tribunal du droit de la mer* (Pedone, Paris 1999); T. Treves, Le règlement du Tribunal international du droit de la mer entre tradition et innovation, 43 *AFDI* 1997, pp. 342-367.

[25] For the settlement of disputes in the framework of the LOS Convention see E.D. Brown, Dispute Settlement and the Law of the Sea: The UN Convention Regime, 21 *Marine Policy* 1997, pp. 17-43; J. Charney, The Implications of Expanding International Dispute Settlement Systems: The 1982 Convention on the Law of the Sea, 90 *AJIL* 1996, pp. 69-75.

[26] Judgments in the following cases on prompt release: The *Saiga* I, St. Vincent and the Grenadines v. Guinea, 4 December 1997; the *Camouco*, Panama v. France, 7 February 2000; the *Monte Confurco*, Seychelles v. France, 18 December 2000; the *Grand Prince*, Belize v. France, 20 April 2001; the *Volga*, Russia v. Australia, 23 December 2002; and the *Juno Trader*, Saint-Vincent and the Grenadines v. Guinea-Bissau, 18 December 2004; see www.itlos.org/cases.

[27] This is an independent, not an incidental procedure, since the Tribunal's jurisdiction is limited to the question of release of the ship upon the posting of a reasonable bond.

Using a teleological interpretation, the ITLOS declared that the object of both articles 73 and 292 of the LOS Convention is to reconcile the interests of the coastal State in enforcing its laws and regulations with those of the flag State to see its vessel and crew promptly released. The bond serves the interest of the detaining State to secure appearance in its courts and the payment of penalties and for its assessment this compromise must be born in mind[28].

The Tribunal further clarified the factors that have to be taken into account in order to assess the reasonableness of the bond for the release of a vessel under article 292 of the LOS Convention: The gravity of the alleged offences; the penalties imposed or imposable under the laws of the detaining State; the value of the detained vessel and the cargo seized; the amount of the bond imposed by the detaining State and its form[29]; this list being not exhaustive[30] but excluding the right for the detaining State to impose non-financial conditions as components of a bond or other financial security, e.g. the obligation for the vessel to carry a Vessel Monitoring System (VMS)[31]. The form of the bond will be a bank guarantee from a bank operating in the detaining State or a bank having corresponding arrangements with it[32].

In the last case on prompt release, the *Juno Trader*, the ITLOS ruled on the nature of the obligation of the prompt release of vessels and crews in relation to the amount of the bond. It declared that this obligation "includes elementary considerations of humanity and due process of law" and the requirement of the reasonableness of the bond is dictated by a concern for fairness[33]. This statement seems extremely important at a time when one witnesses extremely severe inhuman penalties, including imprisonment, imposed to the crew members of vessels, who happen to be the least responsible for violations of conservation and management measures, including those on the preservation of the marine environment, in the EEZ.

3.2. Nationality of Ships and Claims

According to article 292 paragraph 2 of the 1982 LOS Convention, an application for release may only be made by or on behalf of the flag State of

---

[28] Judgment in the case of the *Monte Confurco*, paragraphs 70-73.

[29] Judgment in the case of the *Camouco*, 7 February 2000, paragraph 67.

[30] See for example the judgments in the cases of the *Monte Confurco*, paragraph 76; and of the *Juno Trader*, paragraph 83.

[31] Judgment in the case of the *Volga*, paragraph 77.

[32] *Ibid.*, paragraph 93; and Judgment in the case of the *Juno Trader*, paragraph 101.

[33] Judgment in the case of the *Juno Trader*, paragraph 77.

the vessel. In its case law, the Tribunal seized the opportunity to examine the issue of the nationality of the vessel and to weigh the relevant evidence put before it[34]. Due to the importance of the issue, in the *Grand Prince* case, brought before the ITLOS by Belize against France, the Tribunal examined *proprio motu* the nationality of the detained vessel, taking as a point of departure article 91 of the LOS Convention, which, according to the Tribunal, "codifies a well established rule of general international law" and leaves to each State the exclusive jurisdiction to fix the conditions for the grant of its nationality to ships[35]. It looked at the conditions under which the flag State attributes its nationality – in the case of Belize, upon registration. It noted that when it had been arrested, on 26 December 2000, the *Grand Prince* was under a provisional patent of navigation issued by the competent authority of Belize and expiring on 29 December 2000 and that at the date of the filing of the application for prompt release, on 21 March 2001, the vessel was under de-registration[36]. The Tribunal thus decided, albeit at a weak majority, that the documentary evidence submitted by the applicant did not permit to establish that Belize was the flag State at this date and consequently that it had no jurisdiction to hear the application[37].

Thus, the Tribunal, in interpreting article 292 paragraph 2 of the LOS Convention, applied in the specific context of the prompt release procedure the rule of general international law on diplomatic protection, according to which the person in favour of whom the protection is exercised must possess the nationality of the applicant State both at the date of the violation of his/her rights and at the date of the filing of the application[38]. Transposed to the procedure before the ITLOS, this means that the applicant State must be the flag State, not only at the time of the arrest of the vessel but also at the date of the filing of the application.

Another issue that the ITLOS was faced with in the case of *Saiga* 2 (Merits) concerned the genuine link between the arrested vessel and the applicant State. The Tribunal refused to admit that the (alleged) absence of a genuine link between the flag State and the ship allows third States to refuse to rec-

---

[34] Judgment in the case of the *Saiga* 2, Merits, paragraph 66; Judgment in the case of the *Grand Prince*, paragraph 81.

[35] Judgment in the case of the *Saiga* 2, Merits, paragraph 63.

[36] This was asserted in a Note Verbale of the Ministry of Foreign Affairs of Belize addressed to France on 4 January 2001. De-registration was imposed as a punitive measure with effect from the date of the Note Verbale for violations of fisheries regulations committed by the vessel.

[37] Judgment in the case of the *Grand Prince,* paragraph 93; but see also the dissenting opinion of nine judges on this point.

[38] N. Ros, La France, le TIDM et les légines. A propos de l'Arrêt rendu le 20 avril 2001 dans l'affaire du *Grand Prince*, 5 *Annuaire du droit de la mer* 2000, p. 277.

ognize the nationality of the ship. It inferred, from the provisions of the LOS and other international conventions, that the need for a genuine link is not a condition for the grant and validity of the nationality of a ship vis-à-vis other States but it rather aims at ensuring more effective implementation of the duties of the flag State[39].

Finally, in the same case, the ITLOS pronounced also on the issue of the nationality of claims. It considered that the applicant State, namely St. Vincent and the Grenadines, had the right to protect not only the vessel flying its flag but also the crew serving on board, irrespective of their nationality. The Tribunal explained that in modern shipping ships have crews of a multinational composition and, if each person having suffered damage were obliged to seek protection from his or her national State, "undue hardship would ensue"[40]. Here too, the ITLOS emphasized the attention that should be given to the crew of arrested vessels and their protection under the law of the sea rules.

3.3. Means of Enforcement of Laws and Regulations of the Coastal State

In the *Saiga* 2 (Merits) case, where the issue put before the Tribunal was the lawfulness of the arrest and detention of the vessel *Saiga*, the ITLOS had the opportunity to pronounce on the conditions of the exercise of the right of hot pursuit and the use of force as means of arresting a vessel. The Tribunal found that the conditions contained in article 111 of the LOS Convention are cumulative: The vessel has to be warned that it will be pursued, the pursuit has to be uninterrupted and force has to be resorted to only as the last resort and after warning[41].

The use of force is not mentioned among the means of enforcing protection measures by the coastal State within the EEZ provided for in article 73 of the LOS Convention. Let us be reminded that the ICJ, in the *Fisheries Jurisdiction case* (1998), had simply declared that recourse to use of force, if authorized by the coastal State's legislation, "falls within the ambit of what is commonly understood as enforcement of conservation and management measures"[42].

The ITLOS proceeded a step further and pronounced that international law prescribes that use of force should be avoided, as far as possible, that it "must not go beyond what is reasonable and necessary in the circumstances

---

[39] Judgment in the Case of the *Saiga* 2, Merits, paragraph 83.

[40] *Ibid.*, paragraph 107.

[41] *Ibid.*, paragraph 146.

[42] *Fisheries Jurisdiction* case, Spain v. Canada, Jurisdiction, Judgment of 4 December 1998, paragraph 84.

and also that considerations of humanity must apply in the law of the sea, as they do in other areas of international law"[43]. This declaration, together with those mentioned above on the considerations of humanity that underline the obligation of the prompt release and the extent of the protection of the flag State to the members of the crew, irrespective of their nationality, undoubtedly shows the sensitivity and the will of the judges of the ITLOS to play an active role in the development of the law of the sea through the incorporation into it of principles safeguarding the protection of seamen and their rights.

3.4. Preservation and Protection of the Marine Environment

In the case law of the International Court of Justice, environmental concerns have been treated with restraint, the Court having confined itself to limited declarations on the existence of very general obligations concerning the protection and the preservation of the environment. It is true that in its early jurisprudence it had acknowledged the existence of the principle according to which "a State must not allow its territory to be used for acts contrary to the acts of other States"[44], and more recently that "the existence of a general obligation of States to ensure that activities within their jurisdiction and control respect the environment of other States or of areas beyond national jurisdiction as being part of the *corpus* of international law relating to the environment"[45]. It admitted also that vigilance and prevention are required in order to avoid damage that might be irreversible[46]. But it simply conceded to the idea of sustainable development a conceptual character rather than a genuine legal identity, by acknowledging that this idea underlines the need to reconcile economic development with the protection of the environment[47]. Finally, although it recognized that new environmental standards, including that of assessment of the risks, have been developed over the last years, the Court adopted a rather "minimalist approach"[48] by failing to admit the existence in positive customary international law of the precau-

---

[43] Judgment in the case of the *Saiga* 2, Merits, paragraph 155.

[44] *Corfu Channel* case, UK v. Albania, Merits, Judgment of 9 April 1949, ICJ Reports 1949, p. 22.

[45] Advisory Opinion on the *Legality of Threat or Use of Nuclear Weapons*, ICJ Reports 1996, paragraph 29.

[46] *Gabčikovo-Nagymaros* case, Hungary v. Slovakia, Judgment of 25 September 1997, ICJ Reports 1997, paragraph 140, 3.

[47] *Ibid.*, paragraph 140.

[48] P.-M. Dupuy, The Danger of Fragmentation or Unification of the International Legal System and the International Court of Justice, 31 *New York University Journal of International Law and Politics* 1999, p. 804.

tionary principle, pleaded by New Zealand in the *Nuclear Tests* II case (1995) and by Hungary in the *Gabcikovo-Nagymaros* case (1997)[49].

Several cases submitted to the ITLOS and the arbitral tribunals under the LOS Convention system have a central or side environmental aspect. Among those, two were genuine fisheries disputes, namely the *Southern Bluefin Tuna* cases and the *Swordfish Stocks in the South Eastern Pacific* case. Also in many prompt release cases the detained vessel had been arrested following alleged violations of fisheries laws in the EEZ or fisheries zone.

The contribution of the ITLOS to the development of the law of the sea concerning the marine environment is to be found in the Orders on provisional measures the Tribunal may prescribe under article 290 of the LOS Convention. Paragraph 1 of this article gives the Tribunal, or indeed another *prima facie* competent court or tribunal, the power to prescribe provisional measures to preserve the rights of the parties or to prevent serious harm to the marine environment, pending its final decision. Paragraph 5 gives the ITLOS, or any other court or tribunal agreed upon by the parties, the power to prescribe provisional measures, pending the constitution of an arbitral tribunal to which the dispute is submitted, if it considers that the tribunal under constitution has *prima facie* jurisdiction and that the urgency of the situation so requires. In this case, the ITLOS may prescribe provisional measures, assuming that another international tribunal has jurisdiction[50].

From the examination of its case law, it appears that the ITLOS seems more desirous to play a progressive role in the development of the principles on the protection and preservation of the marine environment. It first declared, in the *Southern Bluefin Tuna* Order (1999) for provisional measures under article 290(5), that is pending the constitution of another arbitral tribunal, that the conservation of the living resources of the sea is an element in the protection and preservation of the marine environment; thus, it established a link between these two concepts[51]. Since the parties in the dispute, namely New Zealand, Australia and Japan, agreed that the stock of Southern Bluefin Tuna (SBT) is being severely depleted, the ITLOS prescribed provisional measures in that case consisting in the abstention from any action that

---

[49] The position of the ICJ has been relied upon by the Appellate Body of the World Trade Organization in the case of the *European Community Measures Concerning Meat and Meat Products*, the *Hormones* case, where this Body took note that "the Court did not identify the precautionary principle as one of those recently developed norms" and aligned itself with that position; Report of 16 January 1998, WTO documents WT/DS 26/AB/R, at 50, paragraph 123, n. 93, www.wto.org, as cited by Dupuy, *supra*, p. 807.

[50] R. Wolfrum, Provisional Measures of the International Tribunal of the Law of the Sea, *Indian Journal of International Law* 1997, pp. 420-434.

[51] Order of 27 October 1999, paragraph 70.

might prejudice the carrying out of any future decision that the arbitral tribunal (to be constituted) might render and limitation of the quantity of catch for all the three parties as well as the abstention from conducting experimental fishing programmes, except with the agreement of all parties to the dispute. Regrettably, the provisional measures prescribed by the ITLOS have been eventually revoked by the Arbitral Tribunal constituted under article 287 and Annex VII of the LOS Convention, which found that it did not have jurisdiction to adjudicate the case on the merits[52].

As already mentioned, the ICJ refrained from including the precautionary principle among the newly developed rules on protection of the environment. In the *Southern Bluefin Tuna* Order (1999), the ITLOS did not go as far as to prescribe as a provisional measure the duty for the parties to act in consistence with the precautionary principle in fishing for BFT pending a final settlement of the dispute, as requested by New Zealand and Australia. It nevertheless recognized that the parties "should in the circumstances act with prudence and caution to ensure that effective conservation measures are taken to prevent serious harm to the stock of Southern Bluefin Tuna"[53].

The *Mox Plant* case is about a dispute between Ireland and the UK concerning the authorization of a MOX (Mixed Oxide Fuel) Plant in the North-West of England on the coast of the Irish Sea, whose operation, including transportation of radioactive material to and from the plant, would, according to Ireland, pollute the Irish Sea. Pending the constitution of an arbitral tribunal under article 287 and Annex VII of the LOS Convention, Ireland asked the ITLOS to prescribe provisional measures under article 290 paragraph 5, consisting mainly in the suspension of the authorization of the plant and the cessation of marine transport of radioactive substances in connection with its operation.

In its *Mox Plant* Order on provisional measures (2001), the ITLOS declared that the duty to cooperate is a fundamental principle in the prevention of pollution of the marine environment under the LOS Convention and general international law[54]. On the other side, it also linked the requirement to cooperate for Ireland and the UK with the prudence and caution necessary for the prevention of serious harm to the marine environment. The ITLOS found that in this case there was no urgency requiring the measures re-

---

[52] ICSID, Award of the Arbitral Tribunal in the Case *Southern Bluefin Tuna*, of 4 August 2000, www.worldbank.org/icsid. For comments see B. Kwiatkowska, The Australia and New Zealand v. Japan Southern Bluefin Tuna (Jurisdiction and Admissibility) Award of the First LOSC Annex VII Arbitral Tribunal, 16 *TIJMCL* 2001, pp. 239-294.

[53] Order of 27 October 1999, paragraph 31(3).

[54] Order of 3 December 2001, paragraph 82.

quested by Ireland. It nevertheless prescribed a different provisional measure, consisting in improved cooperation and the provision of information[55].

Finally, the ITLOS unanimously prescribed a provisional measure under article 290 paragraph 5 of the LOS Convention in the case concerning *Land Reclamation by Singapore in and Around the Straits of Johor*, Malaysia v. Singapore (2003), consisting in the duty to cooperate and enter into consultations in order to establish a mechanism for exchanging information and on assessing the risks or effects of land reclamation on the marine environment[56]. Following the Order of the Tribunal, the two States established a Group of independent experts (GOE), which conducted a study on the reclamation activities and recommended, as required by the Order of the Tribunal, measures to deal with any adverse effects. Interestingly enough, this procedure enabled the two States to exchange views and information in such a way as to agree *ad referendum* on the text of a draft Settlement Agreement. Accordingly, in January 2005, the Arbitral Tribunal meanwhile established and for which the Permanent Court of Arbitration serves as registry, decided to abstain from further action on this case for the moment.

4. CONCLUDING REMARKS

In conclusion, one should emphasize the eminent role played by the ICJ (and other arbitral tribunals) to the progressive development of the international law of the sea. Especially in the area of maritime delimitation, the impact of the ICJ on the law making process, after an initial period of hesitation and staling, ended up in both clarification and unification of the law of the sea in that field.

As far as the ITLOS is concerned, its case law is mainly limited, for the moment, to prompt release judgments under article 292 of the LOS Convention and Orders on provisional measures under article 290 thereof. The Tribunal has nevertheless seized the opportunity to present interesting interpre-

---

[55] "The two States shall cooperate and enter into consultations in order to be informed of the possible consequences of the commissioning of the MOX plant and monitor risks of this operation for the marine environment as well as devise appropriate measures preventive from pollution that might result from the operation of the MOX plant"; *ibid.*, paragraph 89, a), b), c). It is to be noted that in June 2003 the Arbitral Tribunal constituted under article 287 and Annex VII of the LOS Convention, having recognized the existence of certain jurisdictional problems, suspended its proceedings but, acting under article 290 paragraph 5, affirmed the provisional measure prescribed in 2001 by the ITLOS; Order of the Arbitral Tribunal of 24 June 2003, Operative Part, paragraph 2, confirmed by the Order of 14 November 2003, www.pca-cpa.org.

[56] Order of 8 October 2003, paragraphs 96 and 99.

tations of relevant articles of the LOS Convention on the enforcement means in the EEZ and prescribe provisional measures, promoting the progressive development of the law of the protection and preservation of marine environment. Furthermore, the Tribunal serves also as a forum, which facilitates exchange of views and information between the parties and its provisional measures may act as a catalyst, through the creation of appropriate mechanisms, promoting the settlement of environmental disputes.

For the time being, the two courts, the ICJ and the ITLOS, coexist without major disturbances to their respective missions. Nevertheless, the increasing multiplication of judicial *fora*, through the 'forum shopping' organized by the LOS Convention settlement of disputes system, allows for the submission of the same dispute, or a part of it, to more than one judicial bodies. This is not an imaginary situation, the *MOX Plant* dispute, or parts of it, having been submitted before four different judicial bodies:

1. The ITLOS, under article 290 paragraph 5 of the LOS Convention, which prescribed provisional measures after having found that the arbitral tribunal which was to be constituted to adjudicate the dispute had *prima facie* jurisdiction to do so.

2. After having been constituted under Annex VII of the LOS Convention, the Arbitral Tribunal suspended its proceedings because of serious doubts concerning its jurisdiction, due to the fact that the dispute comprises also some aspects of European community law. It has been brought to the attention of the Arbitral Tribunal that the European Commission was studying the possibility to seize the Court of Justice of the European Communities under article 226 of the European Community Treaty. "Bearing in mind considerations of mutual respect and comity which would prevail between judicial institutions", in its Order of 24 June 2003, reiterated in November 2003, the Arbitral Tribunal suspended its own proceedings in order to have a clearer picture of the position regarding the European law and possible proceedings thereunder. As for the provisional measure prescribed by the ITLOS, the Arbitral Tribunal aligned itself to the ITLOS Order by affirming the measure[57].

3. Indeed, the European Commission decided to bring a case before the Court of Justice of the European Communities against Ireland, on the grounds of an alleged violation of Community Law, according to which the Member States of the European Union have the obligation to resolve their disputes in relation to community law through the means made available by the Community legal order, namely articles 292 of the EEC Treaty and article 193 of the EURATOM Treaty.

---

[57] *Supra* note 55.

4. Finally, a particular side of the dispute concerning the procedural aspects of the rights of the parties, and especially the right to information claimed by Ireland, was submitted by this State to another Arbitral Tribunal, in accordance with the dispute settlement provisions of the Convention on the Protection of the Marine Environment of the North East Atlantic (the OSPAR Convention). Although the Tribunal has declared that it had jurisdiction to adjudicate the case, it found that Ireland's claim for information did not fall within the relevant provisions of the OSPAR Convention and that, as a consequence, there was no violation of those provisions by the United Kingdom[58].

The LOS Convention offers to the States parties the possibility to choose, out of different existing judicial *fora*, the one to use for the settlement of their disputes. This "menu à la carte" offers certainly a flexibility that allows for and facilitates the settlement of disputes. For the time being, any discrepancy between the judgments of the ITLOS and the international arbitral tribunals is limited to matters of jurisdiction – as in the *MOX Plant* case and the *Southern Bluefin Tuna* cases. But in the future, the existence of multiple judiciary institutions that might be involved in a same case, or part of it, or even in a dispute arising from similar facts, may well lead to contradictory decisions as a result of different interpretations or application of the substantive law. In the international legal order, where, unlike the national legal orders, there are no courts of appeal and review, this might result in fragmentation and confusion of the law. Maybe the considerations of restraint and comity that have guided the Arbitral Tribunal in the *MOX Plant* case should be present in the minds of judges while performing their judicial duties. This attitude could help avoid in the future divergence in the case law of international courts and tribunals and maintain the necessary unity and the coherence of the international law of the sea.

---

[58] Final Award of the OSPAR Arbitral Tribunal of 2 July 2003, www.pca-cpa.org/ OSPAR Arbitration.

Chapter 10

STATE PRACTICE IN THE AFTERMATH OF THE UN CONVENTION ON THE LAW OF THE SEA: THE EXCLUSIVE ECONOMIC ZONE AND THE MEDITERRANEAN SEA

Budislav Vukas[*]

1. INTRODUCTION

The peoples that have lived on the coasts and islands of the Mediterranean Sea have valid reasons for being proud of their contribution to the developments of rules regulating the uses of the seas. In the distant past the *Lex Rhodia de jactu* must be mentioned and there are many initiatives coming from the Mediterranean that have contributed to the development of the Law of the Sea. For example, the Mediterranean Action Plan should always be remembered as the beginning of the whole system of protection of regional seas.

On the other hand, the attitude of the Mediterranean coastal States towards the regime of the exclusive economic zone (EEZ) proves that the behaviour of these States does not always contribute to a sound development and implementation of the legal order of the seas and oceans. Contrary to the States bordering all other seas, the Mediterranean States have had problems in accepting this regime although it has become part of general law of the sea a quarter of a century ago.

2. THE EXCLUSIVE ECONOMIC ZONE – A COMPROMISE REGIME

The regime of the EEZ has been established at the Third United Nations Conference on the Law of the Sea ("UNCLOS III") in the United Nations Convention on the Law of the Sea (hereafter cited as "LOS Convention") as the result of a compromise between the majority of the coastal States, mostly developing countries, and the main maritime powers. Developing coastal

[*] Former Judge and Vice-President of the International Tribunal for the Law of the Sea; Professor of International Law, University of Zagreb.

Anastasia Strati, Maria Gavouneli & Nikos Skourtos (eds.), *Unresolved Issues and New Challenges to the Law of the Sea*, Martinus Nijhoff Publishers 2006, 251-258.

States claimed an extensive territorial sea, in order to protect the living resources off their coasts from the fishing fleets of the most developed countries. On the other hand, the maritime powers wanted to preserve the freedom of the seas, and particularly the freedom of navigation.

The compromise arrived at UNCLOS III – the specific legal regime of the EEZ – has taken care of the main worries of both groups. This marine area, beyond the outer limits of the territorial sea – and therefore outside the State's territory – may be extended up to 200 nautical miles from the baselines from which the breadth of the territorial sea is measured. In the EEZ, the respective coastal State has "sovereign rights for the purpose of exploring and exploiting, conserving and managing the natural resources, whether living or non-living"[1]. On the other hand, freedom of navigation in the EEZ has been granted to ships flying the flags of all States[2].

In addition to those two basic provisions, Chapter V of the LOS Convention contains rules on other rights and duties of the coastal State and all other States in every EEZ. The coastal State has sovereign rights with regard to activities for the economic exploitation and exploration of the zone, such as the production of energy from the water, currents and winds. Moreover, the coastal State has jurisdiction with regard to the establishment and use of artificial islands, installations and structures, marine scientific research and the protection and preservation of the marine environment[3].

In addition to the freedom of navigation, all States, whether coastal or land-locked, enjoy the freedom of "overflight and of laying of submarine cables and pipelines, and other internationally lawful uses of the sea related to these freedoms, such as those associated with the operation of ships, aircraft and submarine cables and pipelines..."[4].

Be that as it may, the following opinion of the Chairman of the Italian Delegation at UNCLOS III, Ambassador Varvesi, expressed the view of the majority of the States participating at the Conference: "With regard to the rules governing the exclusive economic zone and the freedoms recognized for all States in it, we believe they constitute a well-balanced compromise solution between the aspirations of coastal States, and the requirements of maritime States"[5].

As already mentioned, the regime of the EEZ has become part of general customary international law. Such an opinion was expressed by the Interna-

---

[1] Article 56(1)(a) of the LOS Convention.
[2] Article 58(1) of the LOS Convention.
[3] Article 56 of the LOS Convention.
[4] Article 58(1) of the LOS Convention.
[5] UNCLOS III, *Official Records*, Vol. XVII, p. 121, paragraph 65.

tional Court of Justice (ICJ) already in 1985[6]. The reason for such a conclusion was the fact that, since the achievement of the said compromise at UNCLOS III, States bordering all the seas and oceans started proclaiming this regime beyond the limits of their territorial seas. According to the information provided by the United Nations in 2001, already 111 States had by that time proclaimed their EEZs[7].

3. THE MEDITERRANEAN STATES AND THE EEZ

The attitude of the Mediterranean States towards this new regime at sea has had a quite specific development. Egypt, one of the first States to ratify the LOS Convention, proclaimed its EEZ simultaneously with the ratification in 1983. It was natural to expect that other Mediterranean States would follow this example, particularly those which had unusually extended their territorial sea (Syria) or had already established fishery zones (Malta, Tunis, and later Algeria).

Even the States belonging to the European Community seemed to be open to the extension of the jurisdiction of coastal States. On 3 November 1977, the Council of the European Communities adopted a Resolution which required the extension of the limits of the fishery zone of the Member States to 200 nautical miles of their North Sea and North Atlantic coasts, "without prejudice to similar action being taken for the other fishing zones within their jurisdiction such as the Mediterranean"[8].

However, in the following years States belonging to the European Community as well as other coastal States have shown extreme restraint in proclaiming their EEZs in the Mediterranean. France and Spain proclaimed their EEZs off their coasts in other seas but not in the Mediterranean. Even Morocco, having established its EEZ off its Atlantic coast, has not clarified whether this regime is applicable beyond its territorial sea in the Mediterranean.

This hesitant attitude has not been shared by the States bordering the Black Sea, the easternmost part of the Mediterranean. Bulgaria, Romania, Russia, Turkey and Ukraine have established their EEZs[9].

Taking into account the establishment of the EEZs all over the world, it is important to find out the reasons for the different situation in the Mediterranean, which contradicts the statements of experts and representatives of the North African States, who confirm their right to proclaim their EEZs. The

---

[6] *Libya/Malta Continental Shelf* case, ICJ Reports 1985, p. 33.

[7] 45 *Law of the Sea Bulletin* 2001, pp. 115-129.

[8] OJ C 105 (181).

[9] See *supra* note 7.

rather small size of the Mediterranean and the fact that this sea can be qualified as an "enclosed or semi-enclosed sea" cannot be advanced as a reason
against the establishment of the EEZs in that sea. Namely, the existence of
EEZs has been included as an element of the definition of such seas, which
consist "entirely or primarily of the territorial seas and exclusive economic
zones of two or more coastal States"[10]. We, therefore, must share the opinion
of Professor Mirjam Škrk, who concludes that "the EEZ regime cannot be
'reserved' for the oceanic States but it represents a general rule of customary
law of the sea, embodied in the LOS Convention"[11].

The real reasons for the opposition of the developed Mediterranean coastal
States, members of the European Community, can be found in the writings
of the experts coming from these States.

The main argument, openly advanced by the Italian authors against the establishment of EEZs in the Mediterranean, was the supposed danger that
such a development could cause problems to the freedom of navigation in
the most important routes connecting Gibraltar, the Suez Canal and the
Straits of the Dardanelles, the Sea of Marmara and the Bosphorus[12].
Although all States enjoy the freedom of navigation in the EEZ[13], in exercising this right "States shall have due regard to the rights and duties of the
coastal State and shall comply with the laws and regulations adopted by the
coastal State in accordance with the provision of this Convention…"[14].

A special worry related to the freedom of navigation concerns the activity
of warships. Thus, in its Declarations made upon its signature (1984) and
ratification (1995) of the LOS Convention, Italy expressed its opinion that
the coastal State has not "the right to obtain notification of military exercises
or manoeuvres or to authorize them"[15].

---

[10] Article 122 of the LOS Convention.

[11] M. Škrk, Exclusive Economic Zone in Enclosed or Semi-Enclosed Seas, *The Legal Regime of Enclosed or Semi-Enclosed Seas: The Particular Case of the Mediterranean, Prinosi
za poredbeno proučavanje prava i međunarodno pravo*, Vol. XIX, No. 22, 1988, p. 168.

[12] U. Leanza, La délimitation des espaces maritimes dans la Méditerranée, *The Legal Regime of Enclosed or Semi-Enclosed Seas*, supra, pp. 84-85; Zona economica esclusiva e co-
operazione marittima nel Mediterraneo, *in* U. Leanza & U. Sico (eds.), *Zona economica esclusiva e mare Mediterraneo* (Editoriale Scientifica, Napoli 1989) p. 6; U. Lenza, *Il nuovo diritto
del mare e la sua applicazione nel Mediterraneo* (G. Giappichelli Editore, Torino 1993) p. 364;
T. Scovazzi, Les zones côtières en Méditerranée: évolution et confusion, 6 *Annuaire du Droit
de la Mer* 2001, p. 100; G. Andreone, The Legal Regime of Fishing in the Mediterranean: Some
Issues Concerning Italy, 11 *Italian YBIL* 2003, p. 232.

[13] Article 58(1) of the LOS Convention.

[14] Article 58(3) of the LOS Convention.

[15] 4 *Law of the Sea Bulletin* 1985, pp. 12-13; 25 *Law of the Sea Bulletin* 1994, p. 31; 27
Law of the Sea Bulletin 1995, p. 5.

The second reason advanced against the establishment of the EEZs in the Mediterranean was the necessity of delimiting these zones between States with opposite or adjacent coasts[16]. However, this is not a very convincing argument, because the delimitation of the EEZs should not cause more problems than the delimitation of the continental shelves of States bordering the Mediterranean. Although the delimitation of these two marine areas between the two neighbouring States should not necessarily follow the same line, the rules relative to the delimitation of the EEZs and the continental shelves are identical[17].

Finally, we come to the most important reason, at least for Italy. The distribution of the entire Mediterranean waters into the EEZs of the coastal States would reduce the freedom of fishing of the Italian fishermen only to the Italian EEZ (or fisheries zone). In the present situation, when the status of the high seas prevails in the waters of the Mediterranean, the Italian fishermen can still enjoy the freedom of fishing. And, as Professor Umberto Leanza wrote in 1993, Italy was harvesting 50% of all the living resources in the Mediterranean (the Black Sea excluded)[18].

Taking into account all the above mentioned facts, once again we have to agree with Professor Škrk, who concluded in 1988 that the reasons that the Mediterranean area, the whole Mediterranean – Adriatic – Aegean – Black Sea complex, was not divided into EEZs by its coastal States where "not legal, but political and economic"[19].

4. RECENT DEVELOPMENTS

Notwithstanding the initial interests of the developed Mediterranean coastal States to preserve the high seas in the Mediterranean, some of them have gradually changed their attitude towards the extension of the jurisdiction of the coastal States. This change has been based on individual, national interests but even more on the worries to preserve the marine environment of the Mediterranean and the living resource of its waters. Namely, the fishing fleets of Mediterranean and non-Mediterranean States have depleted the fish stocks of that sea and the navigation of ships carrying various dangerous cargos constantly endanger the marine environment of the Mediterranean.

---

[16] Andreone, *supra* note 12, p. 231 at note 3, pp. 232 and 260; Scovazzi, *ibid.*

[17] Articles 74 and 83 of the LOS Convention.

[18] Leanza, *Il nuovo diritto del mare e la sua applicazione nel Mediterraneo, supra* note 12, p. 335; see also Andreone, *ibid.*, p. 232; Scovazzi, *ibid.*

[19] Škrk, *supra* note 11, pp. 163 and 181.

Some States reacted to these threats individually and the European Community has also undertaken a collective action.

Already in 1994, in its Commentary of the Draft Act on the Ratification and Implementation of the LOS Convention, Italy stated that it should think about the "establishment of an exclusive economic zone or, perhaps, of a zone where it would exercise only some of the rights provided for such a zone (for example, in the field of the protection of the marine environment, as it has been done in the North Sea)"[20]. For the time being, Italy has not undertaken anything in applying the regime of the EEZ or some of its components. However, having in mind the quoted text from 1994, it is strange that Italy reacted unfavourably when in 2003 Croatia established its ecological and fisheries protection zone (EFPZ), based on the EEZ regime[21]. In a letter to the Secretariat of the United Nations, Italy reproached Croatia for having proclaimed such a zone before establishing cooperation with other Adriatic coastal States, as required by article 123 of the LOS Convention[22].

Such a reaction is a misinterpretation of article 123, which generally requires co-operation of States bordering an enclosed or semi-enclosed sea "in the performance of their rights and duties under this Convention". Those States should cooperate in respect of the exploitation of the living resources of the sea, the protection and preservation of the marine environment and the scientific research, whatever the extension of their national jurisdiction. Any State is free in establishing unilaterally its EEZ, or in using only some rights and jurisdictions contained in this regime. After having undertaken such a decision, it may be necessary to adjust the co-operation with neighbouring States to the new situation. Croatia has co-operated with the neighbouring States for a long time and the establishment of its EFPZ, and possible similar zones of some other Adriatic coastal States may require some adjustments in their co-operation.

As another Adriatic State, the Republic of Slovenia, also expressed some opposition to the establishment of the Croatian EFPZ[23], on 3 June 2004 the Croatian Government decided to apply its EFPZ regime in respect of the Members of the European Union only after the conclusion of a treaty on the

---

[20] For the text of the draft in Italian see in T. Treves, *Il diritto del mare e l'Italia* (Giuffrè Editore, Milano 1995) pp. 128-134.

[21] Decision on the Extension of the Jurisdiction of the Republic of Croatia in the Adriatic Sea, 53 *Law of the Sea Bulletin* pp. 68-69.

[22] Permanent Mission of Italy to the United Nations, Communication dated 16 April 2004 to the Secretariat of the United Nations, New York.

[23] Note verbale dated 7 November 2003 from the Permanent Mission of Slovenia to the United Nations addressed to the Secretary-General, 53 *Law of the Sea Bulletin* pp. 70-71.

partnership in fisheries between the European Union and the Republic of Croatia.

Croatia was not the first Mediterranean State to extend its jurisdiction beyond the outer limits of its territorial sea in the last years. In a way its EFPZ represents a synthesis of the contents of the two zones proclaimed by two Mediterranean States, members of the European Union, still within the limits of the EEZ regime. Spain in 1997 established its fisheries protection zone and France proclaimed its ecological zone in 2003, only some months before the Croatian Decision[24]. This new tendency has been resumed in a statement by Gemma Andreone:

> "... Mediterranean States prefer to extend national jurisdiction either through the actual proclamation of zones or by appealing to "potential exclusive rights" of exploitation or by claiming environmental protection. Recourse to unilateral proclamations or to bilateral agreements is legitimate under international law, and is also understandable in light of the need to avoid further delays in adopting strict measures for the protection of resources"[25].

The said unilateral acts of some Mediterranean States were adopted at the time when the European Community itself had already intensified its efforts to undertake new measures for the protection of the Mediterranean Sea and its living resources. Contrary to the earlier silent agreement of the coastal States members of the European Community to oppose to establishment of the EEZs in the Mediterranean, they now realized that the extension of the jurisdiction of the coastal States is the right way to protect the Mediterranean living resources. The establishment of fisheries protection zones would result in the application of the European Common Fisheries Policy to all fishing activities, and it would prevent fishing fleets belonging to non-Mediterranean States from enjoying the present freedom of fishing in the Mediterranean high seas[26].

A Communication from the Commission of the European Communities on the reform of the Common Fisheries Policy, called the "Road map" and adopted on 28 May 2002, stated the Commission's opinion that "consideration by the member States concerned of a co-ordinated initiative to establish

---

[24] Royal Decree No. 1395/1997, of 1 August 1997, establishing a fisheries protection zone in the Mediterranean Sea, 36 *Law of the Sea Bulletin* pp. 47-48; Département de la communication et d'information, Service de Presse, *La création d'une Zone de Protection Écologique en Méditerranée*, Dossier de Presse, 27 février 2002.

[25] Andreone, *supra* note 12, p. 235; see also Scovazzi, *ibid.*

[26] K. Turkalj, The extending of the jurisdiction on the Mediterranean Sea in the context of the reform of the EU Common Fisheries Policy, 9 *Croatian International Relations Review* 2003, *Dossier*, pp. 10-18.

wider fisheries protection zones" should be undertaken[27]. This Communication demonstrates the caution of the Commission concerning the variety of opinions of the Mediterranean member States. Although the Commission is aware of the fact that the establishment of fisheries protection zones is indispensable for the Mediterranean, the non-Mediterranean members of the European Union cannot impose such an opinion to the Mediterranean members. In this sense, even the Declaration of the Ministerial Conference for the Sustainable Development of Fisheries in the Mediterranean, adopted in Venice in November 2003, refers to the extension of national jurisdiction as to a rather complicated task for the Mediterranean States:

> "We consider that, without prejudice to the sovereign rights of States and in accordance with relevant national law, a more detailed examination should be made of the modalities for the creation of fisheries protection zones taking into account the precedents that exist, with a view to employing a concerted and regional approach suited to the needs of the fisheries concerned and based on dialogues and coordination"[28].

---

[27] European Commission, COM(2002)181 final, 28 May 2002, p. 8.
[28] Declaration adopted at the Conference, 25-26 November 2003, paragraph 10.

Comment

SOME THOUGHTS ON THE CONCEPT OF THE CONTIGUOUS ZONE AND ITS POTENTIAL APPLICATION TO THE GREEK SEAS

*Aristotelis B. Alexopoulos**

1. INTRODUCTION

By the time the 1982 United Nations Convention on the Law of the Sea (hereinafter cited as "LOS Convention") was adopted, the contiguous zone had no longer maintained its interest for most States, the reason being primarily the new concept of the exclusive economic zone (EEZ). A similar situation occurred but for different reasons, ever since the Geneva Convention on the Territorial Sea and the Contiguous Zone (hereinafter cited as "TSC")[1] had come into force. Article 24(2) of the latter states: "The contiguous zone may not extend beyond 12 miles from the baselines from which the breadth of the territorial sea is measured". Bearing in mind that State practice tended towards the adoption of a 12-mile limit for the territorial waters and knowing that the contiguous zone could not extend beyond 12 miles, it was apparent that the regime of the contiguous zone would lose its significance.

Although the LOS Convention followed in article 33(1) the same rule established by the TSC in article 24(1) with respect to the nature and scope of coastal rights within the contiguous zone (see *infra* section 3), the extension of its maximum breadth to 24 miles from the territorial sea baselines together with the insertion of a new provision on the protection of archaeological and historical objects under article 303(2) has brought new interest to the rights of coastal States in this area. This paper discusses the legal status of the contiguous zone in international law, including a brief account of its history, and its potential application to the seas surrounding Greece.

---

* Adjunct Assistant Professor, University of the Aegean.

[1] D.P. O'Connell, *International Law* (Volume II, Stevens Publishers, 1970) pp. 640-642.

Anastasia Strati, Maria Gavouneli & Nikos Skourtos (eds.), *Unresolved Issues and New Challenges to the Law of the Sea* Martinus Nijhoff Publishers 2006, pp. 259-270.

2. HISTORICAL PERSPECTIVE

State practice has shown in the past, even before the 1958 Geneva Convention, that raising a claim for a zone contiguous to the territorial sea was not unreasonable. It was based on the coastal State's need to exercise limited powers over the sea, mainly for the protection of its revenue and health interests[2]. It was felt that the narrow breadth of the territorial sea could not prevent activities such as smuggling and threats to public health. The first related regulations were the British Hovering Acts of 1718, which gave the authority to British warships to patrol the sea areas near the coastline in order to suppress unlawful acts such as the transport of slaves or prevent custom violations. This law was abolished when Britain claimed a 3-mile territorial sea. At a later stage, France and the United States followed with similar laws. The Greek corresponding law promulgating a customs zone can be traced back in 1918[3].

It seems that priority of control was given to the customs sector but those States in favour of establishing such zones expanded their jurisdiction in other sectors as well, notably for public health and security reasons. The tendency during that time was to treat these 'protection zones' as having a territorial-sea status[4]. A detailed discussion about the concept of the contiguous zone took place during the 1930 Hague Codification Conference; a compromise was reached at that time in a sense that the coastal State could not exercise sovereignty over this zone but rather limited powers of an administrative nature.

It took a lot of time until the international community accepted a right of exercising control outside the territorial sea, in the high seas; upon the initiative of G. Gidel, this new concept was named 'contiguous zone'. The US had already enacted related laws, the 1935 Anti-Smuggling Act, which dealt with the suppression of illegal acts, notably liquor activities, in a zone of 50

---

[2] E.D. Brown, *The International Law of the Sea* (Volume I: *Introductory Manual*, Dartmouth Publications, 1984) pp. 128-139.

[3] C. Economides, The Contiguous Zone Today and Tomorrow, *in* Christos Rozakis & C. Stephanou (eds.) *The New Law of the Sea* (Elsevier Science Publishers, 1983) pp. 69-81. As pointed out by Ioannou, "Law 1165/1918 did not use the term contiguous zone. It stipulated in its article 85(1) that within three kilometres from the coast the Customs Authorities have the right to visit navigating vessels for the purpose of examining their documents". K. Ioannou, The Greek territorial sea *in* T. Kariotis, *Greece and the Law of the Sea* (Martinus Nijhoff Publishers, 1977) pp. 115-152 at pp. 129 and 136.

[4] *Ibid.*, at 70-71.

miles measured from the coastline; at the time several individuals had already established 'floating cabarets' outside the territorial waters[5].

The main Geneva provisions with regard to the contiguous zone can be
found in Part II of the TSC: a sole article 24, which is regarded as the basis
for the concept of the contiguous zone. This article is complemented by article 23 of the Geneva Convention on the High Seas, which refers exclusively
to the right of hot pursuit. The LOS Convention does not grant a separate
part to the contiguous zone but rather refers to it in a final section, section 4
of Part II: *Territorial Sea and Contiguous Zone*, which consists of single article 33. Respectively, the hot pursuit provision is to be found in article 111
of Part VII: *High Seas*. However, the LOS Convention also includes a new
provision in article 303 of Part XVI: *General Provisions*, regarding archaeological and historical objects found on the bed of the contiguous zone.

Most importantly, articles 24 of the TSC and 33 of the LOS Convention
are regarded as rules of customary law binding upon all States. Until 15
March 2000, 69 States had adopted a contiguous zone, 63 of which have
claimed the 24-mile limit[6]. By 26 August 2005 the number of States claiming a contiguous zone had raised to 80[7], a fact which not only it cannot be
ignored but rather poses a challenge for further discussion on this subject.
Similarly to an EEZ and unlike the continental shelf where the rights of the
coastal State exist *ipso facto* and *ab initio,* a State must proclaim a contiguous zone, if it wishes to exercise the powers that are recognised by international law in this area. However, it is under no obligation to publicize its limits in official maps and navigational charts.

On 2 September 1999 President Clinton signed a proclamation, whereby
the outer edge of the US contiguous zone is formally extended from 12 to 24
nautical miles, except in areas in which such an extension would overlap the
territorial sea of another State. It is intended to advance law enforcement and
public health interests at sea and to protect submerged natural and cultural
resources. Within the 24-mile limit, the US Coast Guard may board and
search a foreign vessel suspected of violating domestic law, without first obtaining permission from the State in which the vessel is registered. The contiguous zone is a zone within the EEZ and adjacent to the territorial sea,

---

[5] E. Roucounas, *International Law* II (2nd. ed., Athens 2005) pp. 152-156 [in Greek].

[6] K. Ioannou & A. Strati, *The Law of the Sea* (2nd ed., Ant. N. Sakkoulas Publishers, Athens 2000) at p. 110 [in Greek]. However, these claims are not always compatible with the regime envisaged by the TSC and the LOS Convention; at least four States have extended their
legislative competence over the contiguous zone and/or include security among the protected
interests.

[7] See Table of claims to maritime jurisdiction, available at www.un.org.

within which the US may enforce customs, fiscal, immigration and sanitary laws and regulations. Such powers are exercised in conformity with the law of the sea and other rules of international law relating to innocent passage, transit passage, archipelagic sea lanes passage and protection of the marine environment[8].

3. THE RIGHTS OF THE COASTAL STATE

According to article 24 of the TSC , States are not permitted to extend their contiguous zone beyond 12 miles from the territorial sea baseline. In other words, the breadth of the contiguous zone depends entirely upon the breadth of the territorial sea[9], i.e. if a State claimed a 3-mile territorial limit then it could claim a 9-mile contiguous zone. It has been predicted during the First UN Conference on the Law of the Sea ("UNCLOS I") that the contiguous zone was nothing more than a temporary compromise for the extension of the territorial limits[10].

However, this approach has not been adopted during UNCLOS III. Article 3 of the LOS Convention allows States to establish a 12-mile territorial sea and article 33(2) gives them the right to extend the contiguous zone up to 24 miles from the territorial sea baselines. Under these circumstances, if Greece decided to claim a contiguous zone, the breadth of this zone would reach 18 miles beyond the outer limit of its 6-mile territorial sea..

3.1. Juridical nature of the contiguous zone

Article 33(1) of the LOS Convention refers to "...a zone contiguous to the territorial sea". There is no specification as to the legal status of the waters within the contiguous zone. To this effect, article 55 of the LOS Convention refers to the exclusive economic zone as being "...an area beyond and adjacent to the territorial sea". If a State claims an EEZ, the two zones will overlap and thus the significance of the contiguous zone is diminishing – it constitutes a part of the EEZ. As one author noted[11], the contiguous zone was extended under article 33 of the LOS Convention to 24 miles and, while its main features were retained, its 'residual status' is that of the EEZ.

---

[8] See www.csc.noaa.gov/opis/html/summary/cz.htm (26.02.2003)

[9] Brown, *supra* note 2, at p. 129.

[10] P. Reuter, *Droit international public* (Paris 1968) pp. 205-206.

[11] A.V. Lowe, The Development of the Concept of the Contiguous Zone, 52 *BYBIL* 1981, pp. 109-169.

In contrast, under article 24(1) of the TSC the contiguous zone is described as *a zone of the high seas* contiguous to the coastal State's territorial sea. Similarly, under the LOS Convention if a State has not claimed an EEZ, the contiguous zone is part of the high seas and remains governed by the principle of the freedom of the high seas. Under these circumstances, the rights of the coastal State in the contiguous zone constitute an exception to the overall applicable regime of the freedom of the high seas. In case of conflict, the latter would prevail[12]. However, according to another view[13], although the contiguous zone is a part of the high seas, it is still subject to that special regime which places specific restrictions on the freedom of the high seas (needless to say) to the advantage of the coastal State. On the other hand, once an EEZ is established, the situation is quite different. The EEZ is a *sui generis zone*, where the rights of both coastal and flag States may be balanced by reference to the LOS Convention.

Furthermore, article 33(1) of the LOS Convention states that "the coastal State may exercise the control necessary to: (a) prevent infringement of its customs, fiscal, immigration or sanitary laws and regulations *within its territory or territorial sea*; (b) punish the infringement of those laws committed *within its territory or territorial sea*". This provision is identical to that incorporated in article 24(1) of the TSC . The wording of these provisions leaves no room but to realize that the coastal State cannot exercise sovereignty or jurisdiction in the contiguous zone for violations committed in its territory or territorial sea. In addition, as Economides notes[14], a State may establish a contiguous zone to protect only one right, i.e. custom regulations, but it is not allowed to accord protection for a right that is not accepted by international law.

In this respect, special reference should be made to a draft article adopted by the First Committee of UNCLOS I in 1958: "In a zone of the high seas contiguous to its territorial sea, the coastal state may take measures necessary to prevent and punish infringements of its customs, fiscal, immigration or sanitary regulations, and *violations of its security*"[15]. If this formula were to be adopted by the Plenary,

---

[12] Brown, *supra* note 2, at p. 130.

[13] Economides, *supra* note 3, at p. 73.

[14] *Ibid.*, at p. 74.

[15] The International Law Commission had proposed that sanitary regulations should not be included in article 24 but the Geneva Conference, through a US initiative, decided to accept the protection of public health. Still, they have rejected a proposal to add in this article the right of security of the coastal State. At that time 14 States had expressed demands for the establishment of security zones but with the extension of the territorial sea limit, the subject was dropped. It is worth noting that in 1939 the US had established a security zone of 200 miles in the Atlantic, where they did not permit entrance of the warships of the belligerent states.

then the coastal State would have been entitled, as Oda put it, "to enact its own legislation relating to the subjects as enumerated within the contiguous zone, and to exercise its own police powers, including search and seizure"[16]. In other words, the aim was to deal with violations committed within the contiguous zone itself[17]. The result of the voting clearly showed that some States were not willing to attribute additional powers to the coastal State[18].

As a result, article 24 and more specifically the phrase "within its territory or territorial sea" limits coastal jurisdiction to the area landward of the outer limit of the territorial sea. Nevertheless, article 23 of the High Seas Convention recognizes a right of hot pursuit from the contiguous zone with respect to the four rights already specified.

3.2. Delimitation of the contiguous zone between opposite or adjacent States

Under article 24(3) of the TSC it is stated that: "Where the coasts of two States are opposite or adjacent to each other, neither of the two States is entitled, failing agreement between them to the contrary, to extend its contiguous zone beyond the median line, every point of which is equidistant from the nearest points on the baseline from which the breadth of the territorial seas of the two states is measured". Surprisingly, the LOS Convention has not followed the TSC on this matter and no provision concerning the delimitation of the contiguous zone between two States is to be found.

Many reasons could be brought up for this situation. A rather simplified approach was that the rights of the coastal State within the contiguous zone are not of an exclusive character and, even if the two zones overlap, there would be no conflict of interest. Another opinion expressed was that although no separate provision is made for the delimitation of the contiguous zone in the LOS Convention, it nevertheless forms part of the EEZ and even if an EEZ is not claimed, article 74 may still be expected to apply to the contiguous zone, if that is claimed[19]. In contrast, it is suggested[20] that the concept

---

[16] S. Oda, The concept of the continuous zone, 11 *ICLQ* 1962, pp. 131-151.

[17] As noted by Brown, *supra* note 2, this formula was rejected by a vote of 40 in favour to 27 against, with 9 abstentions; in other words, it failed to attract the 2/3 majority. In contrast, it was the US proposal that was adopted and became article 24 of the TSC..

[18] A similar view had been expressed in 1956 by François, the ILC Rapporteur, as an interpretation of article 24: "The coastal State enjoys certain specified rights over a 12-mile belt, even where that belt extends beyond its territorial sea into the high seas, and that it can exercise control over that zone, in custom and sanitary matters, in the same manner as in the territorial sea".

[19] P.B. Beazley (ed.), *Maritime Limits and Baselines: A Guide to their Delineation* (Hydrographic Society, Special Publication No. 2, 1987) pp. 44-51.

of the contiguous zone is not superseded by the concept of the EEZ and, that it is not reasonable two coastal States which exercise their rights according to international law within the contiguous zone to do so in the same sea area, particularly in the case where both States have adopted 24-mile archaeological zones under article 303(2) of the LOS Convention. Furthermore, the contiguous zone is connected with the territorial sea and so, *mutatis mutandis*, it is justified that the provisions relating to the delimitation of the territorial sea should be applied. To the same point, Brown suggests that, since the area is part of the contiguous zone of each of them, it could be assumed that each State is entitled to proceed to the removal of archaeological objects from the area of overlap and there is no apparent way of establishing an order of priority between them[21].

3.3. The Aegean Sea hypothesis

Although the origins of the contiguous zone are dating back in the early 18th century and have been discussed in detail during the period 1920-1930, the concept of the contiguous zone has never been a major issue in the Aegean or at least an issue of official debate between Greece and Turkey[22]. Nevertheless, Greece has always been in favour of establishing a contiguous zone and/or an archaeological zone. Article 303(2) of the LOS Convention, which establishes a *de facto* 24-mile archaeological zone, is based upon a Greek proposal submitted at the Geneva resumed ninth session (1980)[23]. Under its provisions, the coastal State in applying article 33 of the LOS Convention may presume that the removal of these objects could not take place without its approval; otherwise it would amount to an infringement of its laws and regulations[24].

In contrast, Turkey has not shown any interest in establishing a contiguous zone. This position has been justified on the basis that this zone has become obsolete due to the new institution of the EEZ; furthermore, the rights of the coastal State in the contiguous zone are limited and cannot affect the rights

---

[20] Ioannou & Strati, *supra* note 6, at pp. 335-336.

[21] Brown, *supra* note 2, at p. 138.

[22] A.M. Syrigos, *The Status of the Aegean Sea According to International Law* (Ant. N. Sakkoulas/Bruylant Publishers, Athens/Brussels 1998) pp. 25-27.

[23] C. Economides, *Issues of International Law and Greek Foreign Policy* (Ant. N. Sakkoulas Publications, Athens 1999) pp. 33-34 [in Greek and French].

[24] M. Michael, *Archaeological and Historical Objects of the Seabed. International Law and the Aegean Sea* (Ant. N. Sakkoulas Publishers, Athens 1983) pp. 89-97 [in Greek]. It is recalled that Greece claims a 10 nm territorial sea for aviation and policing matters (Decree of 1931) and a 6 nm territorial sea for general matters (Law of 1936).

of flag States on the high seas. Similarly, Turkey opposes the declaration of a contiguous zone for the purpose of controlling the traffic of archaeological objects, which in its opinion falls contrary to State practice and to customary rules of international law. As far as the delimitation of the contiguous zone is concerned, the two States follow a different approach. Turkey claims that the provisions applicable to the delimitation of an EEZ and the continental shelf should be enforced by analogy to the delimitation of the contiguous zone. Greece, on the other hand, strongly supports the view that the provisions to be applied in the delimitation of the contiguous zone should be the ones that are used for the delimitation of the territorial waters between opposite or adjacent States.

4. Preventive and Repressive Control

As already noted, article 33(1)(a) of the LOS Convention refers to certain administrative rights of the coastal State, which could be exercised only on foreign ships that are entering the territorial sea of a coastal State. If such a vessel remains in the contiguous zone and proceeds on her course or has no intention of entering the territorial sea of a State, she cannot have violated any of its laws or regulations. As G. Fitzmaurice put it, such administrative rights they could be qualified as 'exercising powers' rather than 'rights of the coastal State'[25]. It is control, not jurisdiction that is exercised. It seems reasonable to say that, if a foreign ship manages to avoid the coastal State's preventive control by heading for the high seas or an EEZ, the coastal State could not lawfully pursue it there. The right of hot pursuit is granted, when there has been an infringement of the laws of the coastal state committed within its territory or territorial sea. However, the coastal State may exercise whatever control is necessary to prevent violations of its laws and regulations, i.e. by inspecting a vessel, its cargo, crew or documents. It may even escort it to one of its ports, if weather conditions do not permit a thorough inspection. In case a vessel has proved guilty of a violation, the coastal State may exercise criminal jurisdiction.

Suffice to say that not all foreign ships crossing the contiguous zone of a coastal State will be inspected; only those that are approaching or leaving a port and those that are acting in a suspicious manner within this zone. The repressive control exercised by the coastal State under article 33(1)(b) of the LOS Convention refers to the foreign ships that have already left its territorial sea and are exposed to possible arrest since they have violated the laws and

---

[25] G. Fitzmaurice, Some Results of the Geneva Conference on the Law of the Sea, 8 *ICLQ* 1959, pp. 112-117.

regulations of the coastal State regarding customs, fiscal, immigration or sanitary matters in its territory or territorial sea[26]. In this case, hot pursuit from the contiguous zone would be permissible if the foreign ship has escaped[27].

5. FURTHER DEVELOPMENTS

The LOS Convention has undoubtedly introduced new elements into the concept of the contiguous zone: (a) the extension of its breadth to 24 miles; and (b) the protection of historical and archaeological objects found within this area. It has been suggested that, among the regulations that are enforced in the contiguous zone, the fiscal and custom ones are of primary importance from a practical point of view. In this study we intend to further examine the other two types of regulations, immigration and sanitary, with respect to the Greek interests.

a. With regard to *immigration regulations*, Greece faces serious problems almost on a daily basis. Despite the fact that a Protocol of Re-admittance and Cooperation has been signed between Greece and Turkey for the suppression of the transportation of illegal immigrants (for both mainland and sea borders),[28] the situation has not improved[29].

According to the Greek Ministry of Merchant Marine during the last two years over 10,000 illegal immigrants were interdicted. It seems that patrolling the Greek seas may prove more difficult than doing so in the mainland, the reasons being the long coastline of Greece (over 17,000 km), the congested sea lanes and the density of traffic, particularly during the summer periods as well as the right of innocent passage of foreign vessels through the territorial sea. The establishment of a contiguous zone will no doubt facilitate the prevention and the repression of illicit trafficking and make the exer-

---

[26] As pointed out by Economides, *supra* note 3 at p. 77, in this case the coastal State may exercise full jurisdiction.

[27] See the first judgment of the International Tribunal for the Law of the Sea in respect of the M/V *Saiga*, 37 *ILM* 1998, where the vessel was supplying gas oil to three fishing vessels "in all likelihood within the contiguous zone of Guinea".

[28] See Agreement between the Hellenic Republic and the Republic of Turkey on Co-operation of the Ministry of Public Order of the Hellenic Republic and the Ministry of Internal Affairs of the Republic of Turkey on Combating Crime, Illicit Drug Trafficking and Illegal Immigration, signed on 20 January 2002, approved in Greece by Law 2926/2001, *Official Gazette* A 139/2001.

[29] To set up an example, only for the year 2002, 837 inspections by air have been taken place, 362 of those for the protection of the marine environment and 128 for pinpointing vessels carrying illegal immigrants. At the same period, the Greek Coast Guard inspected 614 foreign vessels, 25 of those for pollution incidents and 64 for illegal immigrants found on board. See also the newspaper *Elefterotypia*, 21 January 2003 and 30 January 2003.

cise of jurisdiction within the territorial sea more effective. It is recalled that under article 19 paragraph (2)(g) of the LOS Convention:

> "Passage of a foreign ship shall be considered prejudicial......to the peace, good order or security of the coastal State, if in the territorial sea it engages in any of the following activities: the loading or unloading of any commodity, currency or person contrary to customs, fiscal, immigration or sanitary laws and regulations of the coastal State".

Furthermore, article 21(1)(h) enables the coastal State to adopt laws and regulations, in conformity with the provisions of the LOS Convention and other rules of international law, relating to innocent passage through the territorial sea in respect of "...the prevention of infringement of the customs, fiscal, immigration, sanitary regulations". Finally, article 25(2) states:

> "In the case of ships proceeding to internal waters or a call at a port facility outside internal waters, the coastal state has the right to take the necessary steps to prevent any breach of the conditions to which admission of those ships to internal waters or such a call is subject".

Although the jurisdiction of the coastal State is to be exercised on board a foreign ship for violations in the territorial sea, in practice it is not an easy task for the Coast Guard to identify which ship is acting in a suspicious manner or has committed a specific crime.

b. It has been suggested in the past that *sanitary control* may also encompass *pollution control*. To this effect Part XII of the LOS Convention "Protection and Preservation of the Marine Environment" should be considered. According to article 228(1) of the LOS Convention:

> "Proceedings to impose penalties in respect of any violation of applicable laws and regulations or international rules and standards relating to the prevention, reduction and control of pollution from vessels committed by a foreign vessel beyond the territorial sea of the State instituting proceedings shall be suspended upon the taking of proceedings to impose penalties in respect of corresponding charges by the flag State within six months of the date on which proceedings were first instituted...".

The phrase "beyond the territorial sea" may be interpreted to refer to either the EEZ or the contiguous zone, if the coastal State concerned has claimed such zones. One could, therefore, argue that in the event of major damage to the coastal State and if the flag State has failed to enforce the applicable international rules, the coastal State has the right to exercise criminal jurisdiction[30].

---

[30] In examining the historical scope of pollution incidents in the Greek seas, it is important to distinguish between accidental and intentional pollution. Accidents or near-miss situations that have occurred, mostly in port areas or close to the coastline, were mostly not of serious

On the other hand, however, it should be considered that article 228 of the LOS Convention presupposes the exercise of coastal jurisdiction over the protection of the marine environment within the EEZ. Even if we accept that the term "sanitary control" encompasses "pollution control", the coastal State cannot exercise such jurisdiction within the contiguous zone; it could only claim the control necessary to prevent or punish violations of its legislation within its territorial sea. Otherwise, the contiguous zone would be transformed into a full-jurisdictional zone. As a result, it is not possible to establish a contiguous zone for reasons relating directly to the protection of the marine environment. Only pollution regulations confined to the control and prevention of pollution that can cause the spread of diseases or other health problems could be covered under the term "sanitary regulations".

6. CONCLUDING REMARKS

It remains to be seen whether, in the context of the LOS Convention, the regime of the contiguous zone may affect future relations between opposite or adjacent States. As far as Greece is concerned, the establishment of a 24-mile contiguous zone will enable the exercise of more effective control over the seas surrounding its coasts, especially in matters of immigration and drug trafficking. The protection of archaeological and historical objects may provide another reason for such a proclamation. Finally, special attention should be paid to the possibility of exercising pollution control in the contiguous zone in conjunction with the prevention and punishment of sanitary regulations[31].

Quite recently, the problem of pollution has peaked again in the European context. Alarmed by a series of oil tanker disasters, France initially extended its competence to 80 nm from its coast to combat pollution from shipping. The French authorities intended to apply stricter controls over oil tankers in transit. This measure followed the decision by the European Union to ban

---

nature. In contrast, operational pollution cannot be easily discovered and controlled. See further A.B. Alexopoulos, G. Georgoulis & A. Drakopoulou, Combating Oil Spill Incidents in Greek Ports and Coastlines: A Holistic Approach, paper presented in the International Conference: *Mediterranean Ports*, 23-25 May, 2002, University of the Aegean, pp. 1-9.

[31] In examining the records of pollution incidents in the Greek seas, we come to the conclusion that accidents or near-miss situations that have occurred, mostly in port areas or close to the coastline, were mostly not of serious nature. In contrast, operational pollution cannot be easily discovered and controlled, in particularly the intentional discharge of dirty ballast or bilge water into the sea at night hours. A.B. Alexopoulos, G. Georgoulis & A. Drakopoulou, Combating Oil Spill Incidents in Greek Ports and Coastlines: A Holistic Approach, paper presented in the International Conference: *Mediterranean Ports*, 23-25 May, 2002, University of the Aegean, pp. 1-9.

large single-hull tankers carrying heavy grade oil to and from European ports. Subsequently, France adopted an ecological zone[32], whereby it applies the relevant provisions of the LOS Convention relating to the protection of the marine environment and marine scientific research within the EEZ. In addition, Croatia claimed a "fisheries protection and ecological zone" in the Adriatic.

---

[32] Loi no 2003-246 du 16 avril 2003 modifiant Loi 76-655 du 16 Julie 1976, relative à la création d'une zone de protection écologique au large des côtes du territoire de la République; Décret no 2004-33 du 8 janvier 2004, Décret portant création d'une zone de protection écologique au large des côtes du territoire de la République en Méditerranée, http://www.legi-france.com.

CONCLUDING REMARKS

Argyris A. Fatouros[*]

The organizers of this conference, the Aegean Institute for the Law of the Sea and Maritime Law and the Hellenic Branch of the International Law Association, deserve our thanks for a very interesting conference. Fascinating issues were raised and discussed and we learned a lot during this meeting. Several factors contributed to its success, over and above the good planning and the competent administration of the persons in charge.

An important factor was the presence of our foreign participants, all eminent people who have spent a lifetime of work on and with the law of the sea and the 1982 UN Convention on the Law of the Sea (hereinafter cited as "LOS Convention"). They brought with them a well-informed and perceptive point of view, reflecting their experience and their memories, their insights from the processes of preparation, negotiation, drafting and application of the LOS Convention, in which most of them had participated. They also brought with them a long-standing and, I would say, passionate commitment to the topic. The younger participants, my colleagues from Greece, were also remarkably knowledgeable and well-informed; yet, they came from a different context, they saw things from another angle. One significant feature of our meeting was that it ranged widely from technical issues to broad theoretical questions, from old much-discussed topics to new or future questions, never flinching from confronting the fundamental problems that arise in the international law of the sea.

It is hard to present conclusions about a meeting, which largely consisted of conclusions concerning particular facets of the Convention and of the law of the sea in general. And for good measure, the last panel essentially did my job for me by presenting a series of summaries and conclusions on the Convention and its operation. My task is therefore easier – or perhaps non-existent.

---

[*] Emeritus Professor of International Law, University of Athens.

Anastasia Strati, Maria Gavouneli & Nikos Skourtos (eds.), *Unresolved Issues and New Challenges to the Law of the Sea*, Martinus Nijhoff Publishers 2006, pp. 271-274.

I shall therefore restrict myself to offering some general comments on the Conference topic, on the basis of today's sessions, some impressions of the state of play – these are, moreover, the impressions of someone who does not pretend to be as knowledgeable and well-informed as most of the other participants. Like all international lawyers who lived through the heroic period of the negotiation and preparation of the Convention, from the nineteen sixties until the early eighties, I am not indifferent to the topic. Over the years, I have followed developments, even if from the margins, as it were, watching from the sidelines and not as a direct participant in the process of the creation of the LOS Convention. Nobody could stay indifferent to what was happening, I can assure you, we were all stirred by what was happening.

We deal today with the international law of the sea in a manner, which is quite different from the way we deal with most of international law certainly radically different from the way we approached the topic before the negotiation of the Convention. Today there is, to start with, a fundamental comprehensive legally binding text – a "Constitution", it was said in the discussions, a "legal monument," others called it – that covers one way or another the entire body of the international law of the sea. As a result, we address the law of the sea today as a coherent, albeit by no means perfect, body of law, where authoritatively formulated rules and principles are closely linked with functioning structures and procedures. This branch of international law is today in a different shape from most of the other branches or fields, its character and mode of functioning is perhaps closer to some parts of international economic law, even though radical differences persist.

Let us recall, moreover, that the LOS Convention was drafted and negotiated during a particularly creative period of international law. I am not being nostalgic of my younger years when I say that in the sixties and seventies there was in international law a special atmosphere of creativity, legal technique was informed by novel visions and significant objectives, whether we are thinking of the drive for economic development, the concern for the environment or the synthesis of the two that became known as "sustainable development". Something of the missionary zeal of those days was reflected in our discussions here today and marked indelibly this meeting.

The topics to which the papers and discussions in the meeting were devoted reflected the diversity of contents of the present-day law of the sea, reflected it indeed to the point of placing some papers to a place by themselves, with few direct links to the rest of the discussion. I am thinking, for example, of the interesting papers on the novel topic of the use of the sea for intelligence purposes. One could thus appreciate the variety of issues and problems covered, the differences in approach, the varying role of international rules, principles and institutions, as well as the multiplicity of meanings of established notions and terms, reflecting new uses and possibilities of uses – for example, that old term of the "high seas" that we thought we knew everything about. And of course, the classical issue of the constant interaction of national and international laws and policies came up again and again in our discussions.

The law and its application – its realization, I would say – moves at all levels at once in many forms: at the universal, regional and national level, in the form of hard law and soft law, through institutional and judicial channels. In the last panel, specific illustrations of the process and of its *problématique* were provided, dealing with the influence of courts on the law of the sea, the ways in which the LOS Convention provisions can accommodate new situations and new concerns as well as a case study of the evolution of the application of one innovation of the LOS Convention, the exclusive economic zone.

It is clear that what is changing is not only the policies of States or the positions of the courts. A host of other forces and factors are at work: New concerns, new technological possibilities, in particular, new contexts and functions of established rules. The problems of fisheries, for instance, are not new, God knows. Yet, the questions arising today often concern novel related issues. Freedom of navigation is not a novel notion, either; but the paper presented approached it in such broad terms that it acquired new meaning and importance.

Concern with the environment is one of the few relatively new questions the law of the sea deals with. In the past, references to the environment were few and indirect. Nowadays, national and international interests, partly as a result of the impact of technological developments, have brought environmental issues to the forefront of law of the sea concerns. Our meeting provided clear evidence of the high priority attributed to them today. Resulting complications are legion. The possibilities of establishing marine protected areas and other avenues for the protection of vulnerable marine ecosystems were well explored in our meeting and the debate on pertinent action in the high seas gave the opportunity for some very interesting exchanges.

International development, on the other hand, the other new topic of the sixties and seventies, appears to have lost some of its appeal. Concern with the developing countries was very much in evidence, in particular during the early years of the negotiation over the LOS Convention. Today, I regret to say – and I very much hope I am wrong – official statements and expressions of concern on this topic sound to me to be repeating older established approaches, if not *clichés*. It is true, however, that earlier concerns have found their way into the text of the Convention, so that they are still relevant and one can hope that they can be revived.

Other concerns are also present: to the saga of the – not too successful – efforts to protect and regulate underwater cultural heritage; the pertinent UNESCO Convention was recently added. Its success remains to be proven.

To sum up: Of the multitude of problems that the law of the sea addresses, many of which were discussed here, some are by no means new but may have acquired new forms or novel importance, others are the result of new conditions, new technological developments or even new needs. The UN Convention on the Law of the Sea seems capable of coping with most of them, although it remains useful to explore its possibilities and limits. At the same time, there are other legal contexts that are relevant – institutions, procedures, sets of rules. The proliferation of contexts for addressing the issues complicates things but, if wisely – and creatively – handled, may be most helpful.

Annexes

Annex I

UNESCO CONVENTION ON THE PROTECTION
OF THE UNDERWATER CULTURAL HERITAGE

The General Conference of the United Nations Educational, Scientific and Cultural Organization, meeting in Paris from 15 October to 3 November 2001, at its 31st session,

Acknowledging the importance of underwater cultural heritage as an integral part of the cultural heritage of humanity and a particularly important element in the history of peoples, nations, and their relations with each other concerning their common heritage,

Realizing the importance of protecting and preserving the underwater cultural heritage and that responsibility therefor rests with all States,

Noting growing public interest in and public appreciation of underwater cultural heritage,

Convinced of the importance of research, information and education to the protection and preservation of underwater cultural heritage,

Convinced of the public's right to enjoy the educational and recreational benefits of responsible non-intrusive access to *in situ* underwater cultural heritage, and of the value of public education to contribute to awareness, appreciation and protection of that heritage,

Aware of the fact that underwater cultural heritage is threatened by unauthorized activities directed at it, and of the need for stronger measures to prevent such activities,

Conscious of the need to respond appropriately to the possible negative impact on underwater cultural heritage of legitimate activities that may incidentally affect it,

Deeply concerned by the increasing commercial exploitation of underwater cultural heritage, and in particular by certain activities aimed at the sale, acquisition or barter of underwater cultural heritage,

Aware of the availability of advanced technology that enhances discovery of and access to underwater cultural heritage,

Believing that cooperation among States, international organizations, scientific institutions, professional organizations, archaeologists, divers, other interested parties and the public at large is essential for the protection of underwater cultural heritage,

Considering that survey, excavation and protection of underwater cultural heritage necessitate the availability and application of special scientific methods and the use of suitable techniques and equipment as well as a high degree of professional specialization, all of which indicate a need for uniform governing criteria,

Realizing the need to codify and progressively develop rules relating to the protection and preservation of underwater cultural heritage in conformity with international law and practice, including the UNESCO Convention on the Means of Prohibiting and Preventing the Illicit Import, Export and Transfer of Ownership of Cultural Property of 14 November 1970, the UNESCO Convention for the Protection of the World Cultural and Natural Heritage of 16 November 1972 and the United Nations Convention on the Law of the Sea of 10 December 1982,

Committed to improving the effectiveness of measures at international, regional and national levels for the preservation *in situ* or, if necessary for scientific or protective purposes, the careful recovery of underwater cultural heritage,

Having decided at its twenty-ninth session that this question should be made the subject of an international convention,

Adopts this second day of November 2001 this Convention.

Article 1
Definitions

For the purposes of this Convention:

1. (a) "Underwater cultural heritage" means all traces of human existence having a cultural, historical or archaeological character which have been partially or totally under water, periodically or continuously, for at least 100 years such as:

   (i) sites, structures, buildings, artefacts and human remains, together with their archaeological and natural context;

   (ii) vessels, aircraft, other vehicles or any part thereof, their cargo or other contents, together with their archaeological and natural context; and

   (iii) objects of prehistoric character.

(b) Pipelines and cables placed on the seabed shall not be considered as underwater cultural heritage.

(c) Installations other than pipelines and cables, placed on the seabed and still in use, shall not be considered as underwater cultural heritage.

2. (a) "States Parties" means States which have consented to be bound by this Convention and for which this Convention is in force.

(b) This Convention applies *mutatis mutandis* to those territories referred to in Article 26, paragraph 2(b), which become Parties to this Convention in accordance with the conditions set out in that paragraph, and to that extent "States Parties" refers to those territories.

3. "UNESCO" means the United Nations Educational, Scientific and Cultural Organization.

4. "Director-General" means the Director-General of UNESCO.

5. "Area" means the seabed and ocean floor and subsoil thereof, beyond the limits of national jurisdiction.

6. "Activities directed at underwater cultural heritage" means activities having underwater cultural heritage as their primary object and which may, directly or indirectly, physically disturb or otherwise damage underwater cultural heritage.

7. "Activities incidentally affecting underwater cultural heritage" means activities which, despite not having underwater cultural heritage as their primary object or one of their objects, may physically disturb or otherwise damage underwater cultural heritage.

8. "State vessels and aircraft" means warships, and other vessels or aircraft that were owned or operated by a State and used, at the time of sinking, only for government non-commercial purposes, that are identified as such and that meet the definition of underwater cultural heritage.

9. "Rules" means the Rules concerning activities directed at underwater cultural heritage, as referred to in Article 33 of this Convention.

Article 2

Objectives and general principles

1. This Convention aims to ensure and strengthen the protection of underwater cultural heritage.

2. States Parties shall cooperate in the protection of underwater cultural heritage.

3. States Parties shall preserve underwater cultural heritage for the benefit of humanity in conformity with the provisions of this Convention.

4. States Parties shall, individually or jointly as appropriate, take all appropriate measures in conformity with this Convention and with international law that are necessary to protect underwater cultural heritage, using for this

purpose the best practicable means at their disposal and in accordance with their capabilities.

5. The preservation *in situ* of underwater cultural heritage shall be considered as the first option before allowing or engaging in any activities directed at this heritage.

6. Recovered underwater cultural heritage shall be deposited, conserved and managed in a manner that ensures its long-term preservation.

7. Underwater cultural heritage shall not be commercially exploited.

8. Consistent with State practice and international law, including the United Nations Convention on the Law of the Sea, nothing in this Convention shall be interpreted as modifying the rules of international law and State practice pertaining to sovereign immunities, nor any State's rights with respect to its State vessels and aircraft.

9. States Parties shall ensure that proper respect is given to all human remains located in maritime waters.

10. Responsible non-intrusive access to observe or document *in situ* underwater cultural heritage shall be encouraged to create public awareness, appreciation, and protection of the heritage except where such access is incompatible with its protection and management.

11. No act or activity undertaken on the basis of this Convention shall constitute grounds for claiming, contending or disputing any claim to national sovereignty or jurisdiction.

Article 3

Relationship between this Convention and the United Nations Convention on the Law of the Sea

Nothing in this Convention shall prejudice the rights, jurisdiction and duties of States under international law, including the United Nations Convention on the Law of the Sea. This Convention shall be interpreted and applied in the context of and in a manner consistent with international law, including the United Nations Convention on the Law of the Sea.

Article 4

Relationship to law of salvage and law of finds

Any activity relating to underwater cultural heritage to which this Convention applies shall not be subject to the law of salvage or law of finds, unless it:

(a)   is authorized by the competent authorities, and

(b)   is in full conformity with this Convention, and

(c) ensures that any recovery of the underwater cultural heritage achieves its maximum protection.

Article 5
Activities incidentally affecting underwater cultural heritage

Each State Party shall use the best practicable means at its disposal to prevent or mitigate any adverse effects that might arise from activities under its jurisdiction incidentally affecting underwater cultural heritage.

Article 6
Bilateral, regional or other multilateral agreements

1. States Parties are encouraged to enter into bilateral, regional or other multilateral agreements or develop existing agreements, for the preservation of underwater cultural heritage. All such agreements shall be in full conformity with the provisions of this Convention and shall not dilute its universal character. States may, in such agreements, adopt rules and regulations which would ensure better protection of underwater cultural heritage than those adopted in this Convention.

2. The Parties to such bilateral, regional or other multilateral agreements may invite States with a verifiable link, especially a cultural, historical or archaeological link, to the underwater cultural heritage concerned to join such agreements.

3. This Convention shall not alter the rights and obligations of States Parties regarding the protection of sunken vessels, arising from other bilateral, regional or other multilateral agreements concluded before its adoption, and, in particular, those that are in conformity with the purposes of this Convention.

Article 7
Underwater cultural heritage
in internal waters, archipelagic waters and territorial sea

1. States Parties, in the exercise of their sovereignty, have the exclusive right to regulate and authorize activities directed at underwater cultural heritage in their internal waters, archipelagic waters and territorial sea.

2. Without prejudice to other international agreements and rules of international law regarding the protection of underwater cultural heritage, States Parties shall require that the Rules be applied to activities directed at underwater cultural heritage in their internal waters, archipelagic waters and territorial sea.

3. Within their archipelagic waters and territorial sea, in the exercise of their sovereignty and in recognition of general practice among States, States Parties, with a view to cooperating on the best methods of protecting State vessels and aircraft, should inform the flag State Party to this Convention and, if applicable, other States with a verifiable link, especially a cultural, historical or archaeological link, with respect to the discovery of such identifiable State vessels and aircraft.

Article 8
Underwater cultural heritage in the contiguous zone

Without prejudice to and in addition to Articles 9 and 10, and in accordance with Article 303, paragraph 2, of the United Nations Convention on the Law of the Sea, States Parties may regulate and authorize activities directed at underwater cultural heritage within their contiguous zone. In so doing, they shall require that the Rules be applied.

Article 9
Reporting and notification
in the exclusive economic zone and on the continental shelf

1. All States Parties have a responsibility to protect underwater cultural heritage in the exclusive economic zone and on the continental shelf in conformity with this Convention.

Accordingly:

(a) a State Party shall require that when its national, or a vessel flying its flag, discovers or intends to engage in activities directed at underwater cultural heritage located in its exclusive economic zone or on its continental shelf, the national or the master of the vessel shall report such discovery or activity to it;

(b) in the exclusive economic zone or on the continental shelf of another State Party:

(i) States Parties shall require the national or the master of the vessel to report such discovery or activity to them and to that other State Party;

(ii) alternatively, a State Party shall require the national or master of the vessel to report such discovery or activity to it and shall ensure the rapid and effective transmission of such reports to all other States Parties.

2. On depositing its instrument of ratification, acceptance, approval or accession, a State Party shall declare the manner in which reports will be transmitted under paragraph 1(b) of this Article.

3. A State Party shall notify the Director-General of discoveries or activities reported to it under paragraph 1 of this Article.

4. The Director-General shall promptly make available to all States Parties any information notified to him under paragraph 3 of this Article.

5. Any State Party may declare to the State Party in whose exclusive economic zone or on whose continental shelf the underwater cultural heritage is located its interest in being consulted on how to ensure the effective protection of that underwater cultural heritage. Such declaration shall be based on a verifiable link, especially a cultural, historical or archaeological link, to the underwater cultural heritage concerned.

Article 10
Protection of underwater cultural heritage
in the exclusive economic zone and on the continental shelf

1. No authorization shall be granted for an activity directed at underwater cultural heritage located in the exclusive economic zone or on the continental shelf except in conformity with the provisions of this Article.

2. A State Party in whose exclusive economic zone or on whose continental shelf underwater cultural heritage is located has the right to prohibit or authorize any activity directed at such heritage to prevent interference with its sovereign rights or jurisdiction as provided for by international law including the United Nations Convention on the Law of the Sea.

3. Where there is a discovery of underwater cultural heritage or it is intended that activity shall be directed at underwater cultural heritage in a State Party's exclusive economic zone or on its continental shelf, that State Party shall:

(a) consult all other States Parties which have declared an interest under Article 9, paragraph 5, on how best to protect the underwater cultural heritage;

(b) coordinate such consultations as "Coordinating State", unless it expressly declares that it does not wish to do so, in which case the States Parties which have declared an interest under Article 9, paragraph 5, shall appoint a Coordinating State.

4. Without prejudice to the duty of all States Parties to protect underwater cultural heritage by way of all practicable measures taken in accordance with international law to prevent immediate danger to the underwater cultural heritage, including looting, the Coordinating State may take all practicable measures, and/or issue any necessary authorizations in conformity with this Convention and, if necessary prior to consultations, to prevent any immedi-

ate danger to the underwater cultural heritage, whether arising from human activities or any other cause, including looting. In taking such measures assistance may be requested from other States Parties.

5. The Coordinating State:

(a) shall implement measures of protection which have been agreed by the consulting States, which include the Coordinating State, unless the consulting States, which include the Coordinating State, agree that another State Party shall implement those measures;

(b) shall issue all necessary authorizations for such agreed measures in conformity with the Rules, unless the consulting States, which include the Coordinating State, agree that another State Party shall issue those authorizations;

(c) may conduct any necessary preliminary research on the underwater cultural heritage and shall issue all necessary authorizations therefor, and shall promptly inform the Director-General of the results, who in turn will make such information promptly available to other States Parties.

6. In coordinating consultations, taking measures, conducting preliminary research and/or issuing authorizations pursuant to this Article, the Coordinating State shall act on behalf of the States Parties as a whole and not in its own interest. Any such action shall not in itself constitute a basis for the assertion of any preferential or jurisdictional rights not provided for in international law, including the United Nations Convention on the Law of the Sea.

7. Subject to the provisions of paragraphs 2 and 4 of this Article, no activity directed at State vessels and aircraft shall be conducted without the agreement of the flag State and the collaboration of the Coordinating State.

Article 11
Reporting and notification in the Area

1. States Parties have a responsibility to protect underwater cultural heritage in the Area in conformity with this Convention and Article 149 of the United Nations Convention on the Law of the Sea. Accordingly when a national, or a vessel flying the flag of a State Party, discovers or intends to engage in activities directed at underwater cultural heritage located in the Area, that State Party shall require its national, or the master of the vessel, to report such discovery or activity to it.

2. States Parties shall notify the Director-General and the Secretary-General of the International Seabed Authority of such discoveries or activities reported to them.

3. The Director-General shall promptly make available to all States Parties any such information supplied by States Parties.

4. Any State Party may declare to the Director-General its interest in being consulted on how to ensure the effective protection of that underwater cultural heritage. Such declaration shall be based on a verifiable link to the underwater cultural heritage concerned, particular regard being paid to the preferential rights of States of cultural, historical or archaeological origin.

Article 12
Protection of underwater cultural heritage in the Area

1. No authorization shall be granted for any activity directed at underwater cultural heritage located in the Area except in conformity with the provisions of this Article.

2. The Director-General shall invite all States Parties which have declared an interest under Article 11, paragraph 4, to consult on how best to protect the underwater cultural heritage, and to appoint a State Party to coordinate such consultations as the "Coordinating State". The Director-General shall also invite the International Seabed Authority to participate in such consultations.

3. All States Parties may take all practicable measures in conformity with this Convention, if necessary prior to consultations, to prevent any immediate danger to the underwater cultural heritage, whether arising from human activity or any other cause including looting.

4. The Coordinating State shall:

(a) implement measures of protection which have been agreed by the consulting States, which include the Coordinating State, unless the consulting States, which include the Coordinating State, agree that another State Party shall implement those measures; and

(b) issue all necessary authorizations for such agreed measures, in conformity with this Convention, unless the consulting States, which include the Coordinating State, agree that another State Party shall issue those authorizations.

5. The Coordinating State may conduct any necessary preliminary research on the underwater cultural heritage and shall issue all necessary authorizations therefor, and shall promptly inform the Director-General of the results, who in turn shall make such information available to other States Parties.

6. In coordinating consultations, taking measures, conducting preliminary research, and/or issuing authorizations pursuant to this Article, the Coordinating State shall act for the benefit of humanity as a whole, on behalf of all States Parties. Particular regard shall be paid to the preferential rights of

States of cultural, historical or archaeological origin in respect of the underwater cultural heritage concerned.

7. No State Party shall undertake or authorize activities directed at State vessels and aircraft in the Area without the consent of the flag State.

Article 13
Sovereign immunity

Warships and other government ships or military aircraft with sovereign immunity, operated for non-commercial purposes, undertaking their normal mode of operations, and not engaged in activities directed at underwater cultural heritage, shall not be obliged to report discoveries of underwater cultural heritage under Articles 9, 10, 11 and 12 of this Convention. However States Parties shall ensure, by the adoption of appropriate measures not impairing the operations or operational capabilities of their warships or other government ships or military aircraft with sovereign immunity operated for non-commercial purposes, that they comply, as far as is reasonable and practicable, with Articles 9, 10, 11 and 12 of this Convention.

Article 14
Control of entry into the territory, dealing and possession

States Parties shall take measures to prevent the entry into their territory, the dealing in, or the possession of, underwater cultural heritage illicitly exported and/or recovered, where recovery was contrary to this Convention.

Article 15
Non-use of areas under the jurisdiction of States Parties

States Parties shall take measures to prohibit the use of their territory, including their maritime ports, as well as artificial islands, installations and structures under their exclusive jurisdiction or control, in support of any activity directed at underwater cultural heritage which is not in conformity with this Convention.

Article 16
Measures relating to nationals and vessels

States Parties shall take all practicable measures to ensure that their nationals and vessels flying their flag do not engage in any activity directed at underwater cultural heritage in a manner not in conformity with this Convention.

Article 17
Sanctions

1. Each State Party shall impose sanctions for violations of measures it has taken to implement this Convention.

2. Sanctions applicable in respect of violations shall be adequate in severity to be effective in securing compliance with this Convention and to discourage violations wherever they occur and shall deprive offenders of the benefit deriving from their illegal activities.

3. States Parties shall cooperate to ensure enforcement of sanctions imposed under this Article.

Article 18
Seizure and disposition of underwater cultural heritage

1. Each State Party shall take measures providing for the seizure of underwater cultural heritage in its territory that has been recovered in a manner not in conformity with this Convention.

2. Each State Party shall record, protect and take all reasonable measures to stabilize underwater cultural heritage seized under this Convention.

3. Each State Party shall notify the Director-General and any other State with a verifiable link, especially a cultural, historical or archaeological link, to the underwater cultural heritage concerned of any seizure of underwater cultural heritage that it has made under this Convention.

4. A State Party which has seized underwater cultural heritage shall ensure that its disposition be for the public benefit, taking into account the need for conservation and research; the need for reassembly of a dispersed collection; the need for public access, exhibition and education; and the interests of any State with a verifiable link, especially a cultural, historical or archaeological link, in respect of the underwater cultural heritage concerned.

Article 19
Cooperation and information-sharing

1. States Parties shall cooperate and assist each other in the protection and management of underwater cultural heritage under this Convention, including, where practicable, collaborating in the investigation, excavation, documentation, conservation, study and presentation of such heritage.

2. To the extent compatible with the purposes of this Convention, each State Party undertakes to share information with other States Parties concerning underwater cultural heritage, including discovery of heritage, location of heritage, heritage excavated or recovered contrary to this Convention

or otherwise in violation of international law, pertinent scientific methodology and technology, and legal developments relating to such heritage.

3. Information shared between States Parties, or between UNESCO and States Parties, regarding the discovery or location of underwater cultural heritage shall, to the extent compatible with their national legislation, be kept confidential and reserved to competent authorities of States Parties as long as the disclosure of such information might endanger or otherwise put at risk the preservation of such underwater cultural heritage.

4. Each State Party shall take all practicable measures to disseminate information, including where feasible through appropriate international databases, about underwater cultural heritage excavated or recovered contrary to this Convention or otherwise in violation of international law.

Article 20
Public awareness

Each State Party shall take all practicable measures to raise public awareness regarding the value and significance of underwater cultural heritage and the importance of protecting it under this Convention.

Article 21
Training in underwater archaeology

States Parties shall cooperate in the provision of training in underwater archaeology, in techniques for the conservation of underwater cultural heritage and, on agreed terms, in the transfer of technology relating to underwater cultural heritage.

Article 22
Competent authorities

1. In order to ensure the proper implementation of this Convention, States Parties shall establish competent authorities or reinforce the existing ones where appropriate, with the aim of providing for the establishment, maintenance and updating of an inventory of underwater cultural heritage, the effective protection, conservation, presentation and management of underwater cultural heritage, as well as research and education.

2. States Parties shall communicate to the Director-General the names and addresses of their competent authorities relating to underwater cultural heritage.

Article 23

Meetings of States Parties

1. The Director-General shall convene a Meeting of States Parties within one year of the entry into force of this Convention and thereafter at least once every two years. At the request of a majority of States Parties, the Director-General shall convene an Extraordinary Meeting of States Parties.

2. The Meeting of States Parties shall decide on its functions and responsibilities.

3. The Meeting of States Parties shall adopt its own Rules of Procedure.

4. The Meeting of States Parties may establish a Scientific and Technical Advisory Body composed of experts nominated by the States Parties with due regard to the principle of equitable geographical distribution and the desirability of a gender balance.

5. The Scientific and Technical Advisory Body shall appropriately assist the Meeting of States Parties in questions of a scientific or technical nature regarding the implementation of the Rules.

Article 24

Secretariat for this Convention

1. The Director-General shall be responsible for the functions of the Secretariat for this Convention.

2. The duties of the Secretariat shall include:

(a) organizing Meetings of States Parties as provided for in Article 23, paragraph 1; and

(b) assisting States Parties in implementing the decisions of the Meetings of States Parties.

Article 25

Peaceful settlement of disputes

1. Any dispute between two or more States Parties concerning the interpretation or application of this Convention shall be subject to negotiations in good faith or other peaceful means of settlement of their own choice.

2. If those negotiations do not settle the dispute within a reasonable period of time, it may be submitted to UNESCO for mediation, by agreement between the States Parties concerned.

3. If mediation is not undertaken or if there is no settlement by mediation, the provisions relating to the settlement of disputes set out in Part XV of the United Nations Convention on the Law of the Sea apply *mutatis mutandis* to

any dispute between States Parties to this Convention concerning the interpretation or application of this Convention, whether or not they are also Parties to the United Nations Convention on the Law of the Sea.

4. Any procedure chosen by a State Party to this Convention and to the United Nations Convention on the Law of the Sea pursuant to Article 287 of the latter shall apply to the settlement of disputes under this Article, unless that State Party, when ratifying, accepting, approving or acceding to this Convention, or at any time thereafter, chooses another procedure pursuant to Article 287 for the purpose of the settlement of disputes arising out of this Convention.

5. A State Party to this Convention which is not a Party to the United Nations Convention on the Law of the Sea, when ratifying, accepting, approving or acceding to this Convention or at any time thereafter shall be free to choose, by means of a written declaration, one or more of the means set out in Article 287, paragraph 1, of the United Nations Convention on the Law of the Sea for the purpose of settlement of disputes under this Article. Article 287 shall apply to such a declaration, as well as to any dispute to which such State is party, which is not covered by a declaration in force. For the purpose of conciliation and arbitration, in accordance with Annexes V and VII of the United Nations Convention on the Law of the Sea, such State shall be entitled to nominate conciliators and arbitrators to be included in the lists referred to in Annex V, Article 2, and Annex VII, Article 2, for the settlement of disputes arising out of this Convention.

Article 26
Ratification, acceptance, approval or accession

1. This Convention shall be subject to ratification, acceptance or approval by Member States of UNESCO.

2. This Convention shall be subject to accession:

(a) by States that are not members of UNESCO but are members of the United Nations or of a specialized agency within the United Nations system or of the International Atomic Energy Agency, as well as by States Parties to the Statute of the International Court of Justice and any other State invited to accede to this Convention by the General Conference of UNESCO;

(b) by territories which enjoy full internal self-government, recognized as such by the United Nations, but have not attained full independence in accordance with General Assembly resolution 1514 (XV) and which have competence over the matters governed by this Convention, including the competence to enter into treaties in respect of those matters.

3. The instruments of ratification, acceptance, approval or accession shall be deposited with the Director-General.

Article 27
Entry into force

This Convention shall enter into force three months after the date of the deposit of the twentieth instrument referred to in Article 26, but solely with respect to the twenty States or territories that have so deposited their instruments. It shall enter into force for each other State or territory three months after the date on which that State or territory has deposited its instrument.

Article 28
Declaration as to inland waters

When ratifying, accepting, approving or acceding to this Convention or at any time thereafter, any State or territory may declare that the Rules shall apply to inland waters not of a maritime character.

Article 29
Limitations to geographical scope

At the time of ratifying, accepting, approving or acceding to this Convention, a State or territory may make a declaration to the depositary that this Convention shall not be applicable to specific parts of its territory, internal waters, archipelagic waters or territorial sea, and shall identify therein the reasons for such declaration. Such State shall, to the extent practicable and as quickly as possible, promote conditions under which this Convention will apply to the areas specified in its declaration, and to that end shall also withdraw its declaration in whole or in part as soon as that has been achieved.

Article 30
Reservations

With the exception of Article 29, no reservations may be made to this Convention.

Article 31
Amendments

1. A State Party may, by written communication addressed to the Director-General, propose amendments to this Convention. The Director-General

shall circulate such communication to all States Parties. If, within six months from the date of the circulation of the communication, not less than one half of the States Parties reply favourably to the request, the Director-General shall present such proposal to the next Meeting of States Parties for discussion and possible adoption.

2. Amendments shall be adopted by a two-thirds majority of States Parties present and voting.

3. Once adopted, amendments to this Convention shall be subject to ratification, acceptance, approval or accession by the States Parties.

4. Amendments shall enter into force, but solely with respect to the States Parties that have ratified, accepted, approved or acceded to them, three months after the deposit of the instruments referred to in paragraph 3 of this Article by two thirds of the States Parties. Thereafter, for each State or territory that ratifies, accepts, approves or accedes to it, the amendment shall enter into force three months after the date of deposit by that Party of its instrument of ratification, acceptance, approval or accession.

5. A State or territory which becomes a Party to this Convention after the entry into force of amendments in conformity with paragraph 4 of this Article shall, failing an expression of different intention by that State or territory, be considered:

(a) as a Party to this Convention as so amended; and

(b) as a Party to the unamended Convention in relation to any State Party not bound by the amendment.

Article 32
Denunciation

1. A State Party may, by written notification addressed to the Director-General, denounce this Convention.

2. The denunciation shall take effect twelve months after the date of receipt of the notification, unless the notification specifies a later date.

3. The denunciation shall not in any way affect the duty of any State Party to fulfil any obligation embodied in this Convention to which it would be subject under international law independently of this Convention.

Article 33
The Rules

The Rules annexed to this Convention form an integral part of it and, unless expressly provided otherwise, a reference to this Convention includes a reference to the Rules.

Article 34
Registration with the United Nations

In conformity with Article 102 of the Charter of the United Nations, this Convention shall be registered with the Secretariat of the United Nations at the request of the Director-General.

Article 35
Authoritative texts

This Convention has been drawn up in Arabic, Chinese, English, French, Russian and Spanish, the six texts being equally authoritative.

ANNEX
Rules concerning activities directed at underwater cultural heritage

I. *General principles*

Rule 1. The protection of underwater cultural heritage through *in situ* preservation shall be considered as the first option. Accordingly, activities directed at underwater cultural heritage shall be authorized in a manner consistent with the protection of that heritage, and subject to that requirement may be authorized for the purpose of making a significant contribution to protection or knowledge or enhancement of underwater cultural heritage.

Rule 2. The commercial exploitation of underwater cultural heritage for trade or speculation or its irretrievable dispersal is fundamentally incompatible with the protection and proper management of underwater cultural heritage. Underwater cultural heritage shall not be traded, sold, bought or bartered as commercial goods.

This Rule cannot be interpreted as preventing:

(a) the provision of professional archaeological services or necessary services incidental thereto whose nature and purpose are in full conformity with this Convention and are subject to the authorization of the competent authorities;

(b) the deposition of underwater cultural heritage, recovered in the course of a research project in conformity with this Convention, provided such deposition does not prejudice the scientific or cultural interest or integrity of the recovered material or result in its irretrievable dispersal; is in accordance with the provisions of Rules 33 and 34; and is subject to the authorization of the competent authorities.

Rule 3. Activities directed at underwater cultural heritage shall not adversely affect the underwater cultural heritage more than is necessary for the objectives of the project.

Rule 4. Activities directed at underwater cultural heritage must use non-destructive techniques and survey methods in preference to recovery of objects. If excavation or recovery is necessary for the purpose of scientific studies or for the ultimate protection of the underwater cultural heritage, the methods and techniques used must be as non-destructive as possible and contribute to the preservation of the remains.

Rule 5. Activities directed at underwater cultural heritage shall avoid the unnecessary disturbance of human remains or venerated sites.

Rule 6. Activities directed at underwater cultural heritage shall be strictly regulated to ensure proper recording of cultural, historical and archaeological information.

Rule 7. Public access to *in situ* underwater cultural heritage shall be promoted, except where such access is incompatible with protection and management.

Rule 8. International cooperation in the conduct of activities directed at underwater cultural heritage shall be encouraged in order to further the effective exchange or use of archaeologists and other relevant professionals.

II. *Project design*

Rule 9. Prior to any activity directed at underwater cultural heritage, a project design for the activity shall be developed and submitted to the competent authorities for authorization and appropriate peer review.

Rule 10. The project design shall include:

(a)   an evaluation of previous or preliminary studies;
(b)   the project statement and objectives;
(c)   the methodology to be used and the techniques to be employed;
(d)   the anticipated funding;
(e)   an expected timetable for completion of the project;
(f)   the composition of the team and the qualifications, responsibilities and experience of each team member;
(g)   plans for post-fieldwork analysis and other activities;
(h)   a conservation programme for artefacts and the site in close cooperation with the competent authorities;
(i)   a site management and maintenance policy for the whole duration of the project;
(j)   a documentation programme;

(k)   a safety policy;
(l)   an environmental policy;
(m)   arrangements for collaboration with museums and other institutions, in particular scientific institutions;
(n)   report preparation;
(o)   deposition of archives, including underwater cultural heritage removed; and
(p)   a programme for publication.

Rule 11. Activities directed at underwater cultural heritage shall be carried out in accordance with the project design approved by the competent authorities.

Rule 12. Where unexpected discoveries are made or circumstances change, the project design shall be reviewed and amended with the approval of the competent authorities.

Rule 13. In cases of urgency or chance discoveries, activities directed at the underwater cultural heritage, including conservation measures or activities for a period of short duration, in particular site stabilization, may be authorized in the absence of a project design in order to protect the underwater cultural heritage.

III. *Preliminary work*

Rule 14. The preliminary work referred to in Rule 10 (a) shall include an assessment that evaluates the significance and vulnerability of the underwater cultural heritage and the surrounding natural environment to damage by the proposed project, and the potential to obtain data that would meet the project objectives.

Rule 15. The assessment shall also include background studies of available historical and archaeological evidence, the archaeological and environmental characteristics of the site, and the consequences of any potential intrusion for the long-term stability of the underwater cultural heritage affected by the activities.

IV. *Project objective, methodology and techniques*

Rule 16. The methodology shall comply with the project objectives, and the techniques employed shall be as non-intrusive as possible.

V. *Funding*

Rule 17. Except in cases of emergency to protect underwater cultural heritage, an adequate funding base shall be assured in advance of any activity, sufficient to complete all stages of the project design, including conservation, documentation and curation of recovered artefacts, and report preparation and dissemination.

Rule 18. The project design shall demonstrate an ability, such as by securing a bond, to fund the project through to completion.

Rule 19. The project design shall include a contingency plan that will ensure conservation of underwater cultural heritage and supporting documentation in the event of any interruption of anticipated funding.

VI. *Project duration - timetable*

Rule 20. An adequate timetable shall be developed to assure in advance of any activity directed at underwater cultural heritage the completion of all stages of the project design, including conservation, documentation and curation of recovered underwater cultural heritage, as well as report preparation and dissemination.

Rule 21. The project design shall include a contingency plan that will ensure conservation of underwater cultural heritage and supporting documentation in the event of any interruption or termination of the project.

VII. *Competence and qualifications*

Rule 22. Activities directed at underwater cultural heritage shall only be undertaken under the direction and control of, and in the regular presence of, a qualified underwater archaeologist with scientific competence appropriate to the project.

Rule 23. All persons on the project team shall be qualified and have demonstrated competence appropriate to their roles in the project.

VIII. *Conservation and site management*

Rule 24. The conservation programme shall provide for the treatment of the archaeological remains during the activities directed at underwater cultural heritage, during transit and in the long term. Conservation shall be carried out in accordance with current professional standards.

Rule 25. The site management programme shall provide for the protection and management *in situ* of underwater cultural heritage, in the course of and upon termination of fieldwork. The programme shall include public information, reasonable provision for site stabilization, monitoring, and protection against interference.

IX. *Documentation*

Rule 26. The documentation programme shall set out thorough documentation including a progress report of activities directed at underwater cultural heritage, in accordance with current professional standards of archaeological documentation.

Rule 27. Documentation shall include, at a minimum, a comprehensive record of the site, including the provenance of underwater cultural heritage moved or removed in the course of the activities directed at underwater cultural heritage, field notes, plans, drawings, sections, and photographs or recording in other media.

X. *Safety*

Rule 28. A safety policy shall be prepared that is adequate to ensure the safety and health of the project team and third parties and that is in conformity with any applicable statutory and professional requirements.

XI. *Environment*

Rule 29. An environmental policy shall be prepared that is adequate to ensure that the seabed and marine life are not unduly disturbed.

XII. *Reporting*

Rule 30. Interim and final reports shall be made available according to the timetable set out in the project design, and deposited in relevant public records.

Rule 31. Reports shall include:

(a)   an account of the objectives;
(b)   an account of the methods and techniques employed;
(c)   an account of the results achieved;
(d)   basic graphic and photographic documentation on all phases of the activity;
(e)   recommendations concerning conservation and curation of the site and of any underwater cultural heritage removed; and
(f)   recommendations for future activities.

XIII. *Curation of project archives*

Rule 32. Arrangements for curation of the project archives shall be agreed to before any activity commences, and shall be set out in the project design.

Rule 33. The project archives, including any underwater cultural heritage removed and a copy of all supporting documentation shall, as far as possible, be kept together and intact as a collection in a manner that is available for professional and public access as well as for the curation of the archives. This should be done as rapidly as possible and in any case not later than ten years from the completion of the project, in so far as may be compatible with conservation of the underwater cultural heritage.

Rule 34. The project archives shall be managed according to international professional standards, and subject to the authorization of the competent authorities.

XIV. *Dissemination*

Rule 35. Projects shall provide for public education and popular presentation of the project results where appropriate.

Rule 36. A final synthesis of a project shall be:

(a)   made public as soon as possible, having regard to the complexity of the project and the confidential or sensitive nature of the information; and

(b)   deposited in relevant public records.

The White House, Office of the Press Secretary
Washington, DC
September 4, 2003

PROLIFERATION SECURITY INITIATIVE:
STATEMENT OF INTERDICTION PRINCIPLES

The Proliferation Security Initiative (PSI) is a response to the growing challenge posed by the proliferation of weapons of mass destruction (WMD), their delivery systems, and related materials worldwide. The PSI builds on efforts by the international community to prevent proliferation of such items, including existing treaties and regimes. It is consistent with and a step in the implementation of the UN Security Council Presidential Statement of January 1992, which states that the proliferation of all WMD constitutes a threat to international peace and security, and underlines the need for member states of the UN to prevent proliferation. The PSI is also consistent with recent statements of the G8 and the European Union, establishing that more coherent and concerted efforts are needed to prevent the proliferation of WMD, their delivery systems, and related materials. PSI participants are deeply concerned about this threat and of the danger that these items could fall into the hands of terrorists, and are committed to working together to stop the flow of these items to and from states and non-state actors of proliferation concern. The PSI seeks to involve in some capacity all states that have a stake in non-proliferation and the ability and willingness to take steps to stop the flow of such items at sea, in the air, or on land. The PSI also seeks cooperation from any state whose vessels, flags, ports, territorial waters, airspace, or land might be used for proliferation purposes by states and non-state actors of proliferation concern. The increasingly aggressive efforts by proliferators to stand outside or to circumvent existing non-proliferation norms, and to profit from such trade, require new and stronger actions by the international community. We look forward to working with all concerned states on measures they are able and willing to take in support of the PSI, as outlined in the following set of "Interdiction Principles".

INTERDICTION PRINCIPLES
FOR THE PROLIFERATION SECURITY INITIATIVE

PSI participants are committed to the following interdiction principles to establish a more coordinated and effective basis through which to impede and stop shipments of WMD, delivery systems, and related materials flowing to and from states and non-state actors of proliferation concern, consistent with national legal authorities and relevant international law and frameworks, including the UN Security Council. They call on all states concerned with this threat to international peace and security to join in similarly committing to:

1.   Undertake effective measures, either alone or in concert with other states, for interdicting the transfer or transport of WMD, their delivery systems, and related materials to and from states and non-state actors of proliferation concern. "States or non-state actors of proliferation concern" generally refers to those countries or entities that the PSI participants involved establish should be subject to interdiction activities because they are engaged in proliferation through: (1) efforts to develop or acquire chemical, biological, or nuclear weapons and associated delivery systems; or (2) transfers (either selling, receiving, or facilitating) of WMD, their delivery systems, or related materials.

2.   Adopt streamlined procedures for rapid exchange of relevant information concerning suspected proliferation activity, protecting the confidential character of classified information provided by other states as part of this initiative, dedicate appropriate resources and efforts to interdiction operations and capabilities, and maximize coordination among participants in interdiction efforts.

3.   Review and work to strengthen their relevant national legal authorities where necessary to accomplish these objectives, and work to strengthen when necessary relevant international law and frameworks in appropriate ways to support these commitments.

4.   Take specific actions in support of interdiction efforts regarding cargoes of WMD, their delivery systems, or related materials, to the extent their national legal authorities permit and consistent with their obligations under international law and frameworks, to include:

a.   Not to transport or assist in the transport of any such cargoes to or from states or non-state actors of proliferation concern, and not to allow any persons subject to their jurisdiction to do so.

b.   At their own initiative, or at the request and good cause shown by another state, to take action to board and search any vessel flying their flag in their internal waters or territorial seas, or areas beyond the territorial seas of any other state, that is reasonably suspected of transporting such cargoes to or from states or non-state actors of proliferation concern, and to seize such cargoes that are identified.

c.   To seriously consider providing consent under the appropriate circumstances to the boarding and searching of its own flag vessels by other states, and to the seizure of such WMD-related cargoes in such vessels that may be identified by such states.

d.   To take appropriate actions to (1) stop and/or search in their internal waters, territorial seas, or contiguous zones (when declared) vessels that are reasonably suspected of carrying such cargoes to or from states or non-state actors of proliferation concern and to seize such cargoes that are identified; and (2) to enforce conditions on vessels entering or leaving their ports, internal waters or territorial seas that are reasonably suspected of carrying such cargoes, such as requiring that such vessels be subject to boarding, search, and seizure of such cargoes prior to entry.

e.   At their own initiative or upon the request and good cause shown by another state, to (a) require aircraft that are reasonably suspected of carrying such cargoes to or from states or non-state actors of proliferation concern and that are transiting their airspace to land for inspection and seize any such cargoes that are identified; and/or (b) deny aircraft reasonably suspected of carrying such cargoes transit rights through their airspace in advance of such flights.

f.   If their ports, airfields, or other facilities are used as trans shipment points for shipment of such cargoes to or from states or non-state actors of proliferation concern, to inspect vessels, aircraft, or other modes of transport reasonably suspected of carrying such cargoes, and to seize such cargoes that are identified.

Annex II(b)

AGREEMENT BETWEEN THE GOVERNMENT OF THE UNITED
STATES OF AMERICA AND THE GOVERNMENT OF THE
REPUBLIC OF LIBERIA CONCERNING COOPERATION
TO SUPPRESS THE PROLIFERATION OF WEAPONS OF MASS
DESTRUCTION, THEIR DELIVERY SYSTEMS
AND RELATED MATERIALS BY SEA

Signed 11 February 2004;
Provisionally applied from 11 February 2004;
Entered into force 9 December 2004.

The Government of the United States of America and the Government of the Republic of Liberia (hereinafter, "the Parties");

Deeply concerned about the proliferation of weapons of mass destruction (WMD), their delivery systems, and related materials, particularly by sea, as well as the risk that these may fall into the hands of terrorists;

Recalling the 31 January 1992 United Nations Security Council Presidential statement that proliferation of all WMD constitutes a threat to international peace and security, and underlines the need for Member States of the UN to prevent proliferation;

Further recalling the International Ship and Port Facility Security Code, adopted by the International Maritime Organization on 12 December 2002;

Mindful of the Convention on the Prohibition of the Development, Production, Stockpiling and Use of Chemical Weapons and on their Destruction, done at Paris 13 January 1993; the Treaty on Non-proliferation of Nuclear Weapons, done at Washington, London and Moscow on 1 July 1968; and the Convention on the Prohibition of the Development, Production and Stockpiling of Bacteriological (Biological) and Toxin Weapons and on their Destruction, done at Washington, London and Moscow on 10 April 1972;

Acknowledging the widespread consensus that proliferation and terrorism seriously threaten international peace and security;

Convinced that trafficking in these items by States and non-state actors of proliferation concern must be stopped;

Inspired by the efforts of the International Maritime Organization to improve the effectiveness of the Convention for the Suppression of Unlawful Acts against the Safety of Maritime Navigation, done at Rome 10 March 1988;

Reaffirming the importance of customary international law of the sea, and mindful of the provisions in that respect of the 1982 United Nations Convention on the Law of the Sea;

Committed to cooperation to stop the flow by sea of WMD, their delivery systems, and related materials to or from States or non-state actors of proliferation concern;

Have agreed as follows:

Article 1
Definitions

In this Agreement, unless the context otherwise requires:

1. "Proliferation by sea" means the transportation by ship of weapons of mass destruction, their delivery systems, and related materials to or from States or non-state actors of proliferation concern.

2. "Weapons of mass destruction" (WMD) means nuclear, chemical, biological and radiological weapons.

3. "Related materials" means materials, equipment and technology, of whatever nature or type, that are related to and destined for use in the development, production, utilization or delivery of WMD.

4. "Items of proliferation concern" means WMD, their delivery systems, and related materials.

5. "States or non-state actors of proliferation concern" means those countries or entities that should be subject to interdiction activities because they are or are believed to be engaged in: (1) efforts to develop or acquire WMD or their delivery systems; or (2) trafficking (either selling, receiving or facilitating) of WMD, their delivery systems, or related materials.

6. "Security Force Officials" means:

a. for the United States, uniformed or otherwise clearly identifiable members of the United States Coast Guard and the United States Navy, who may be accompanied by clearly identifiable law enforcement officials of the Departments of Homeland Security and Justice, and other clearly identifiable officials duly authorized by the Government of the

United States of America and notified to the Competent Authority of the Republic of Liberia; and

b. for Liberia, uniformed or otherwise clearly identifiable members of the armed forces or law enforcement authorities of Liberia, duly authorized by the Government of the Republic of Liberia and notified to the Competent Authority of the United States.

7. "Security Force vessels" means warships and other vessels of the Parties, or of third States as may be agreed upon by the Parties, on which Security Force Officials of either or both Parties may be embarked, clearly marked and identifiable as being on government service and authorized to that effect, including any vessel and aircraft embarked on or supporting such vessels.

8. "Suspect vessel" means a vessel used for commercial or private purposes in respect of which there are reasonable grounds to suspect it is engaged in proliferation by sea.

9. "International waters" means all parts of the sea not included in the territorial sea, internal waters and archipelagic waters of a State, consistent with international law.

10. "Competent Authority" means for the United States, the Commandant of the United States Coast Guard (including any officer designated by the Commandant to perform such functions), and for Liberia, the Agent of the Commissioner of Maritime Affairs appointed under section 13 of Title 21 (the Maritime Law) of the Laws of the Republic of Liberia.

Article 2
Object and Purpose of Agreement

1. The object and purpose of this Agreement is to promote cooperation between the Parties to enable them to prevent the transportation by vessel of items of proliferation concern.

2. The Parties shall carry out their obligations and responsibilities under this Agreement in a manner consistent with the principles of international law pertaining to the sovereign equality and territorial integrity of States.

3. The Parties shall cooperate to the fullest extent possible, subject to the availability of resources and in compliance with their respective laws.

Article 3
Cases of Suspect Vessels

Operations to suppress proliferation by sea pursuant to this Agreement shall be carried out only against suspect vessels, including suspect vessels without nationality, suspect vessels assimilated to vessels without nationality, and suspect vessels registered under the law of one of the Parties under a bareboat charter notwithstanding an underlying registration in another State not party to this Agreement, but not against a vessel registered under the law of one of the Parties while bareboat chartered in another State not party to this Agreement.

Article 4
Operations in International Waters

1. *Authority to Board Suspect Vessels.* Whenever the Security Force Officials of one Party ("the requesting Party") encounter a suspect vessel claiming nationality in the other Party ("the requested Party") located seaward of any State's territorial sea, the requesting Party may request through the Competent Authority of the requested Party that it:

a. confirm the claim of nationality of the suspect vessel; and

b. if such claim is confirmed:

   i. authorize the boarding and search of the suspect vessel, cargo and the persons found on board by Security Force Officials of the requesting Party; and

   ii. if evidence of proliferation is found, authorize the Security Force Officials of the requesting Party to detain the vessel, as well as items and persons on board, pending instructions conveyed through the Competent Authority of the requested Party as to the actions the requesting Party is permitted to take concerning such items, persons and vessels.

2. *Contents of Requests.* Each request should contain the name of the suspect vessel, the basis for the suspicion, the geographic position of the vessel, the IMO number if available, the homeport, the port of origin and destination, and any other identifying information. If a request is conveyed orally, the requesting Party shall confirm the request in writing by facsimile or e-mail as soon as possible. The requested Party shall acknowledge to the Competent Authority of the requesting Party in writing by e-mail or facsimile its receipt of any written or oral request immediately upon receiving it.

3. *Responding to Requests.*

a. If the nationality is verified, the requested Party may:

   i. decide to conduct the boarding and search with its own Security Force Officials;

    ii. authorize the boarding and search by the Security Force Officials of the requesting Party;

    iii. decide to conduct the boarding and search together with the requesting Party; or

    iv. deny permission to board and search.

  b. The requested Party shall answer through its Competent Authority requests made for the verification of nationality within two hours of its acknowledgment of the receipt of such requests.

  c. If the nationality is not verified within the two hours, the requested Party may, through its Competent Authority:

    i. nevertheless authorize the boarding and search by the Security Force Officials of the requesting Party; or

    ii. refute the claim of the suspect vessel to its nationality.

  d. If there is no response from the Competent Authority of the requested Party within two hours of its acknowledgment of receipt of the request, the requesting Party will be deemed to have been authorized to board the suspect vessel for the purpose of inspecting the vessel's documents, questioning the persons on board, and searching the vessel to determine if it is engaged in proliferation by sea.

  4. *Right of Visit.* Notwithstanding the foregoing paragraphs of this Article, the Security Force Officials of one Party ("the first Party") are authorized to board suspect vessels claiming nationality in the other Party that are not flying the flag of the other Party, not displaying any marks of its registration or nationality, and claiming to have no documentation on board the vessel, for the purpose of locating and examining the vessel's documentation. If documentation or other physical evidence of nationality is located, the foregoing paragraphs of this Article apply. If no documentation or other physical evidence of nationality is available, the other Party will not object to the first Party assimilating the vessel to a ship without nationality consistent with international law.

  5. *Use of Force.* The authorization to board, search and detain includes the authority to use force in accordance with Article 9 of this Agreement.

  6. *Ship-boarding Otherwise in Accordance with International Law.* This Agreement does not limit the right of either Party to conduct boardings of vessels or other activities consistent with international law whether based, *inter alia*, on the right of visit, the rendering of assistance to persons, vessels, and property in distress or peril, or an authorization from the Flag or Coastal State, or other appropriate bases in international law.

Article 5

Exercise of Jurisdiction over Detained Vessels,
as well as Items and Persons on Board

1. *Jurisdiction of the Parties.* In all cases covered by Article 4 concerning the vessels of a Party located seaward of any State's territorial sea, that Party shall have the primary right to exercise jurisdiction over a detained vessel, cargo or other items and persons on board (including seizure, forfeiture, arrest, and prosecution), provided, however, that the Party with the right to exercise primary jurisdiction may, subject to its Constitution and laws, waive its primary right to exercise jurisdiction and authorize the enforcement of the other Party's law against the vessel, cargo or other items and persons on board.

2. *Jurisdiction in the contiguous zone of a Party.* In all cases not covered by Article 4 involving the vessel of a Party that arise in the contiguous zone of a Party and in which both Parties have authority to board and to exercise jurisdiction to prosecute--

a. except as provided in paragraph (b), the Party which conducts the boarding shall have the primary right to exercise jurisdiction;

b. in cases involving suspect vessels fleeing from the territorial sea of a Party in which that Party has the authority to board and to exercise jurisdiction, that Party shall have the primary right to exercise jurisdiction.

3. *Disposition Instructions.* Consultations as to the exercise of jurisdiction pursuant to paragraphs 1 and 2 of this Article shall be undertaken without delay between the Competent Authorities.

4. *Form of waiver.* Where permitted by its Constitution and laws, waiver of jurisdiction may be granted verbally, but as soon as possible it shall be recorded in a written note from the Competent Authority and be processed through the appropriate diplomatic channel, without prejudice to the immediate exercise of jurisdiction over the suspect vessel by the other Party.

Article 6

Exchange of Information and Notification of Results of Actions
of the Security Forces

1. *Exchange of Operational Information.* The Competent Authorities of both Parties shall endeavour to exchange operational information on the detection and location of suspect vessels and shall maintain communication with each other as necessary to carry out the purpose of this Agreement.

2. *Notification of Results*. A Party conducting a boarding and search pursuant to this Agreement shall promptly notify the other Party of the results thereof through their Competent Authorities.

3. *Status Reports*. The relevant Party, in compliance with its laws, shall timely report to the other Party, through their Competent Authorities, on the status of all investigations, prosecutions and judicial proceedings and other actions and processes, arising out of the application of this Agreement.

Article 7
Conduct of Security Force Officials

1. *Compliance with Law and Practices*. Each Party shall ensure that its Security Force Officials, when conducting boardings and searches pursuant to this Agreement, act in accordance with its applicable national laws and policies and consistent with international law and accepted international practices.

2. *Boarding and Search Teams*.

a. Boardings and searches pursuant to this Agreement shall be carried out by Security Force Officials from Security Force vessels and vessels and aircraft embarked on or otherwise supporting such Security Force vessels, as well as by vessels and aircraft of third States as agreed between the Parties.

b. The boarding and search teams may operate from Security Force vessels of the Parties and from such vessels of other States, according to arrangements between the Party conducting the operation and the State providing the vessel and notified to the other Party.

c. The boarding and search teams may carry arms.

Article 8
Safeguards

1. Where a Party takes measures against a vessel in accordance with this Agreement, it shall:

a. take due account of the need not to endanger the safety of life at sea;

b. take due account of the security of the vessel and its cargo;

c. not prejudice the commercial or legal interests of the Flag State;

d. ensure within available means, that any measure taken with regard to the vessel is environmentally sound under the circumstances;

e. ensure that persons on board are afforded the protections, rights and guarantees provided by international law and the boarding State's law and regulations;

f. ensure the master of the vessel is, or has been, afforded the opportunity to contact the vessels' owner, manager or Flag State at the earliest opportunity.

2. Reasonable efforts shall be taken to avoid a vessel being unduly detained or delayed.

Article 9
Use of Force

1. All uses of force pursuant to this Agreement shall be in strict accordance with the applicable laws and policies of the Party conducting the boarding and applicable international law.

2. Each Party shall avoid the use of force, except when and to the degree necessary to ensure the safety of Security Force Officials and vessels or where Security Force Officials are obstructed in the execution of their duties.

3. Only that force reasonably necessary under the circumstances may be used.

4. Boarding and search teams and Security Force vessels have the inherent right to use all available means to apply that force reasonably necessary to defend themselves or others from physical harm.

5. Whenever any vessel subject to boarding under this Agreement does not stop on being ordered to do so, the Security Force vessel should give an auditory or visual signal to the suspect vessel to stop, using internationally recognized signals. If the suspect vessel does not stop upon being signalled, Security Force vessels may take other appropriate actions to stop the suspect vessel.

Article 10
Exchange and Knowledge of Laws and Policies of Other Party

1. *Exchange of Information.* To facilitate implementation of this Agreement, each Party shall take steps necessary to ensure the other Party is appropriately informed of its respective applicable laws and policies, particularly those pertaining to the use of force.

2. *Knowledge.* Each Party shall take steps necessary to ensure that its Security Force Officials are knowledgeable concerning the applicable laws and policies in accordance with this Agreement.

Article 11
Points of Contact

1. *Information.* Each Party shall inform the other Party, and keep current, the points of contact for communication, decision and instructions under Articles 4 and 5, and notifications under Articles 6 and 10 of this Agreement. Such information shall be updated by and exchanged between the Competent Authorities.

2. *Availability.* The Parties shall ensure that the points of contact have the capability to receive, process and respond to requests and reports at any time.

Article 12
Disposition of Seized Property

1. Except as otherwise agreed by the Parties, cargo and other items seized in consequence of operations undertaken onboard vessels subject to the jurisdiction of a Party pursuant to this Agreement, shall be disposed of by that Party in accordance with its laws.

2. The Party exercising jurisdiction may, in any case, transfer forfeited cargo and other items or proceeds of their sale to the other Party. Each transfer generally will reflect the contribution of the other Party to facilitating or effecting the forfeiture of such assets or proceeds.

Article 13
Claims

1. *Injury or Loss of Life.* Any claim for injury to or loss of life of a Security Force Official of a Party while carrying out operations arising from this Agreement shall normally be resolved in accordance with the laws of that Party.

2. *Other Claims.* Any other claim submitted for damage, harm, injury, death or loss resulting from an operation carried out by a Party under this Agreement shall be resolved in accordance with the domestic law of that Party, and in a manner consistent with international law.

3. *Consultation.* If any loss, injury or death is suffered as a result of any action taken by the Security Force Officials of one Party in contravention of this Agreement, or any improper or unreasonable action is taken by a Party pursuant thereto, the Parties shall, without prejudice to any other legal rights which may be available, consult at the request of either Party to resolve the matter and decide any questions relating to compensation or payment.

Article 14
Disputes and Consultations

1. *Disputes.* Disputes arising from the interpretation or implementation of this Agreement shall be settled by mutual agreement of the Parties.

2. *Evaluation of Implementation.* The Parties agree to consult as necessary to evaluate the implementation of this Agreement and to consider enhancing its effectiveness. The evaluation shall be carried out at least once a year.

3. *Resolving Difficulties.* In case a difficulty arises concerning the operation of this Agreement, either Party may request, through the Competent Authorities, consultations with the other Party to resolve the matter.

Article 15
Effect on Rights, Privileges and Legal Positions

Nothing in this Agreement:

a. alters the rights and privileges due any person in any administrative or judicial proceeding conducted under the jurisdiction of either Party.

b. shall prejudice the position of either Party with regard to international law.

Article 16
Cooperation and Assistance

1. The Competent Authority of one Party may request, and the Competent Authority of the other Party may authorize, Security Force Officials to provide technical assistance, such as specialized assistance in the conduct of search of suspect vessels, for the boarding and search of suspect vessels located in the territory or waters of the requesting Party.

2. Nothing in this Agreement precludes a Party from authorizing the other Party to suppress proliferation in its territory, waters or airspace, or to take action involving suspect vessels or aircraft claiming its nationality, or from providing other forms of cooperation to suppress proliferation.

Article 17
Entry into Force and Duration

1. *Entry into Force.* This Agreement shall enter into force upon an exchange of notes indicating that the necessary internal procedures of each Party have been completed.

2. *Provisional Application.* Beginning on the date of signature of this Agreement, the Parties shall, to the extent permitted by their respective national laws and regulations, apply it provisionally. Either Party may discontinue provisional application at any time. Each Party shall notify the other Party immediately of any constraints or limitations on provisional application, of any changes to such constraints or limitations, and upon discontinuation of provisional application.

3. *Termination.* This Agreement may be terminated by either Party upon written notification of such termination to the other Party through the diplomatic channel, termination to be effective one year from the date of such notification.

4. *Continuation of Actions Taken.* This Agreement shall continue to apply after termination with respect to any administrative or judicial proceedings regarding actions that occurred during the time the Agreement was in force.

Article 18
Rights for Third States

1. The Parties agree that the Government of the Republic of Liberia may extend, *mutatis mutandis*, all rights concerning suspect vessels claiming its nationality under the present Agreement to such third States as it may deem appropriate, on the understanding that such third States shall likewise comply with all conditions set forth in the present Agreement for the exercise of such rights, and subject to agreement by that Party and such third States on the designation of points of contact in accordance with Article 11.

2. Such third States shall enjoy rights and be subject to all conditions governing their exercise as set forth in paragraph 1 of this Article effective on the date of a notification by the third State to that Party that it will comply with the conditions for the exercise of those rights.

3. Such rights shall be revocable by that Party or the third State in writing. Such rights shall be revoked, and the conditions governing their exercise shall cease to apply, effective on the date of notification.

4. Such rights shall be subject to modification by mutual concurrence in writing of that Party and the third State. Upon establishment of such mutual written concurrence by that Party and the third State in question, such rights shall be modified effective on the date agreed between that Party and the third State.

IN WITNESS WHEREOF, the undersigned, being duly authorized by their respective Governments, have signed this Agreement.

DONE AT Washington, this eleventh day of February 2004, in duplicate, both texts being equally authentic.

Annex II(c)

AGREEMENT BETWEEN THE GOVERNMENT OF THE UNITED
STATES OF AMERICA AND THE GOVERNMENT OF THE REPUBLIC
OF THE MARSHALL ISLANDS CONCERNING COOPERATION
TO SUPPRESS THE PROLIFERATION OF WEAPONS
OF MASS DESTRUCTION, THEIR DELIVERY SYSTEMS AND
RELATED MATERIALS BY SEA

Signed 13 August 2004;
Provisionally applied from 13 August 2004;
Entered into force 24 November 2004.

The Government of the United States of America and the Government of the Republic of the Marshall Islands, (hereinafter, "the Parties");

Deeply concerned about the proliferation of weapons of mass destruction (WMD), their delivery systems and related materials, particularly by sea, as well as the risk that these may fall into the hands of terrorists;

Recalling the 31 January 1992 United Nations Security Council Presidential statement that proliferation of all WMD constitutes a threat to international peace and security, and underlines the need for Member States of the UN to prevent proliferation;

Also recalling United Nations Security Council Resolution 1540 (2004), which calls on all States, in accordance with their national legal authorities and legislation and consistent with international law, to take cooperative action to prevent illicit trafficking in nuclear, chemical or biological weapons, their means of delivery, and related materials;

Recalling further the Convention on the Prohibition of the Development, Production, Stockpiling and Use of Chemical Weapons and on their Destruction, done at Paris on 13 January 1993; the Treaty on Non-Proliferation of Nuclear Weapons, done at Washington, London and Moscow on 1 July 1968; and the Convention on the Prohibition of the Development, Production and Stockpiling of Bacteriological (Biological) and Toxin Weapons and on their Destruction, done at Washington, London and Moscow on 10 April 1972;

Further recalling the International Ship and Port Facility Security Code, adopted by the International Maritime Organization on 12 December 2002;

Acknowledging the widespread consensus that proliferation and terrorism seriously threaten international peace and security;

Convinced that trafficking in these items by States and non-state actors of proliferation concern must be stopped;

Guided by the Statement of Interdiction Principles for the Proliferation Security Initiative;

Inspired by the efforts of the International Maritime Organization to improve the effectiveness of the Convention for the Suppression of Unlawful Acts against the Safety of Maritime Navigation, done at Rome 10 March 1988;

Reaffirming the importance of customary international law of the sea as reflected in the 1982 United Nations Convention on the Law of the Sea, done at Montego Bay on 10 December 1982;

Committed to cooperation to stop the flow by sea of WMD, their delivery systems, and related materials to or from States or non-state actors of proliferation concern;

Have agreed as follows:

Article 1
Definitions

In this Agreement, unless the context otherwise requires:

1. "United States" means the Government of the United States of America.

2. "Marshall Islands" means the Government of the Republic of the Marshall Islands.

3. "Proliferation by sea" means the transportation by ship of weapons of mass destruction, their delivery systems, and related materials to or from States or non-state actors of proliferation concern.

4. "Weapons of mass destruction" (WMD) means nuclear, chemical, biological and radiological weapons.

5. "Related materials" means materials, equipment and technology, of whatever nature or type, that are related to and destined for use in the development, production, utilization or delivery of WMD.

6. "Items of proliferation concern" means WMD, their delivery systems, and related materials.

7. "States or non-state actors of proliferation concern" means those countries or entities that should be subject to interdiction activities because they are or are believed to be engaged in: (1) efforts to develop or acquire WMD

or their delivery systems; or (2) trafficking (either selling, receiving, or facilitating) of WMD, their delivery systems, or related materials.

8. "Security Force" means:

a. for the United States, the United States Coast Guard and the United States Navy; and

b. for the Marshall Islands, the National Police Force of the Marshall Islands.

9. "Security Force Officials" means:

a. for the United States, uniformed or otherwise clearly identifiable members of the US Security Force, who may be accompanied by uniformed or otherwise clearly identifiable members of the Departments of Homeland Security and Justice, and others duly authorized by the United States and notified to the Competent Authority of the Marshall Islands; and

b. for the Marshall Islands, uniformed or otherwise clearly identifiable members of the law enforcement authorities of the Marshall Islands Security Force.

10. "Security Force vessels" means warships and other vessels of the Parties, or of third States as may be agreed upon by the Parties, on which Security Force Officials of either or both Parties may be embarked, clearly marked and identifiable as being on government service and authorized to that effect, including any vessel and aircraft embarked on or supporting such vessels.

11. "Warship" means ships belonging to the armed forces of a State bearing the external marks distinguishing such ships of its nationality, under the command of an officer duly commissioned by the government of the State and whose name appears in the appropriate service list or its equivalent, and manned by a crew that is under regular armed forces discipline.

12. "Suspect vessel" means a vessel used for commercial or private purposes in respect of which there are reasonable grounds to suspect it is engaged in proliferation by sea.

13. "International waters" means all parts of the sea not included in the territorial sea, internal waters and archipelagic waters of a State, consistent with international law.

14. "Competent Authority" means for the United States, the Commandant of the United States Coast Guard (including any officer designated by the Commandant to perform such functions), and for the Marshall Islands, the Commissioner of Maritime Affairs of the Office of the Maritime Administrator (including any officer designated under Marshall Islands law to perform such functions) appointed under Sections 103, 104 and 105 of Title 47 (The Maritime Act 1990, as amended) of the Laws of the Marshall Islands.

Article 2
Object and Purpose of Agreement

1. The object and purpose of this Agreement is to promote cooperation between the Parties to enable them to prevent the transportation by sea of items of proliferation concern.

2. The Parties shall carry out their obligations and responsibilities under this Agreement in a manner consistent with the principles of international law pertaining to the sovereign equality and territorial integrity of States.

3. The Parties shall cooperate to the fullest extent possible, subject to the availability of resources and in compliance with their respective laws.

Article 3
Cases of Suspect Vessels

Operations to suppress proliferation by sea pursuant to this Agreement shall be carried out only against suspect vessels, including suspect vessels without nationality, and suspect vessels assimilated to vessels without nationality, but not against a vessel registered under the law of one of the Parties while bareboat charter registered in another State not party to this Agreement.

Article 4
Operations in International Waters

1. *Authority to Board Suspect Vessels.* Whenever the Security Force Officials of one Party ("the requesting Party") encounter a suspect vessel claiming nationality in the other Party ("the requested Party") located seaward of any State's territorial sea, the requesting Party may request through the Competent Authority of the requested Party that it:

a. confirm the claim of nationality of the suspect vessel; and

b. if such claim is confirmed:

    i. authorize the boarding and search of the suspect vessel, cargo and the persons found on board by Security Force Officials of the requesting Party; and

    ii. if evidence of proliferation is found, authorize the Security Force Officials of the requesting Party to detain the vessel, as well as items and persons on board, pending instructions conveyed through the Competent Authority of the requested Party as to the actions the requesting Party is permitted to take concerning such items, persons and vessels.

2. *Contents of Requests.* Each request should contain the name of the suspect vessel, the basis for the suspicion, the geographic position of the vessel, the IMO number if available, the homeport, the port of origin and destination, and any other identifying information. If a request is conveyed orally, the requesting Party shall confirm the request in writing by facsimile or e-mail as soon as possible. The requested Party shall acknowledge to the Competent Authority of the requesting Party in writing by e-mail or facsimile its receipt of any written or oral request immediately upon receiving it.

3. *Responding to Requests.*

a. If the nationality is verified, the requested Party may:

    i. decide to conduct the boarding and search with its own Security Force Officials;

    ii. authorize the boarding and search by the Security Force Officials of the requesting Party;

    iii. decide to conduct the boarding and search together with the requesting Party; or

    iv. deny permission to board and search.

b. The requested Party shall answer through its Competent Authority requests made for the verification of nationality within four hours of its acknowledgment of the receipt of such requests. The requesting Party shall acknowledge to the Competent Authority of the requested Party in writing by e-mail or facsimile its receipt of any written or oral response from the Requesting Party immediately upon receiving it.

c. If the nationality is not verified within the four hours, the requested Party may, through its Competent Authority:

    i. nevertheless authorize the boarding and search by the Security Force Officials of the requesting Party; or

    ii. refute the claim of the suspect vessel to its nationality.

d. If there is no response from the Competent Authority of the requested Party within four hours of its acknowledgment of receipt of the request, the requesting Party will be deemed to have been authorized to board the suspect vessel for the purpose of inspecting the vessel's documents, questioning the persons on board, and searching the vessel to determine if it is engaged in proliferation by sea.

4. *Right of Visit.* Notwithstanding the foregoing paragraphs of this Article, the Security Force Officials of one Party ("the first Party") are authorized to board suspect vessels claiming nationality in the other Party that are not flying the flag of the other Party, not displaying any marks of its registration or nationality, and claiming to have no documentation on board the vessel, for the purpose of locating and examining the vessel's documentation. If docu-

mentation or other physical evidence of nationality is located, the foregoing paragraphs of this Article apply. If no documentation or other physical evidence of nationality is available, the other Party will not object to the first Party assimilating the vessel to a ship without nationality consistent with international law.

5. *Use of Force.* The authorization to board, search and detain includes the authority to use force in accordance with Article 9 of this Agreement.

6. *Ship-boarding Otherwise in Accordance with International Law.* This Agreement does not limit the right of either Party to conduct boardings of vessels or other activities consistent with international law whether based, *inter alia*, on the right of visit, the rendering of assistance to persons, vessels, and property in distress or peril, or an authorization from the Flag or Coastal State, of any other party, or other appropriate bases in international law.

Article 5
Exercise of Jurisdiction over Detained Vessels,
as well as Items and Persons on Board

1. *Jurisdiction of the Parties.* In all cases covered by Article 4 concerning the vessels of a Party located seaward of any State's territorial sea, that Party shall have the primary right to exercise jurisdiction over a detained vessel, cargo or other items and persons on board (including seizure, forfeiture, arrest, and prosecution), provided, however, that the Party with the right to exercise primary jurisdiction may, subject to its Constitution and laws, waive its primary right to exercise jurisdiction and authorize the enforcement of the other Party's law against the vessel, cargo or other items and persons on board.

2. *Jurisdiction in the Contiguous Zone of a Party.* In all cases not covered by Article 4 involving the vessel of a Party that arise in the contiguous zone of a Party and in which both parties have authority to board and to exercise jurisdiction to prosecute-

a. except as provided in paragraph (b), the Party which conducts the boarding shall have the primary right to exercise jurisdiction.

b. in cases involving suspect vessels fleeing from the territorial sea of a Party in which that Party has the authority to board and to exercise jurisdiction, that Party shall have the primary right to exercise jurisdiction.

3. *Disposition Instructions.* Consultations as to the exercise of jurisdiction pursuant to paragraphs 1 and 2 of this Article shall be undertaken without delay between the Competent Authorities.

4. *Form of waiver*. Where permitted by the Constitution and laws of a Party, waiver of jurisdiction may be granted verbally, but as soon as possible it shall be recorded in a written note from the Competent Authority and be processed through the appropriate diplomatic channel, without prejudice to the immediate exercise of jurisdiction over the suspect vessel by the other Party.

Article 6
Exchange of Information and Notification of Results of Actions of the Security Forces

1. *Exchange of Operational Information*. The Security Forces of both Parties shall endeavour to exchange operational information on the detection and location of suspect vessels and shall maintain communication with each other as necessary to carry out the purpose of this Agreement.

2. *Notification of Results*. A Party conducting a boarding and search pursuant to this Agreement shall promptly notify the other Party of the results thereof through their Competent Authorities.

3. *Status Reports*. The relevant Party, in compliance with its laws, shall timely report to the other Party, through their Competent Authorities, on the status of all investigations, prosecutions and judicial proceedings and other actions and processes, arising out of the application of this Agreement.

Article 7
Conduct of Security Force Officials

1. *Compliance with Law and Practices*. Each Party shall ensure that its Security Force Officials, when conducting boardings and searches pursuant to this Agreement, act in accordance with its applicable national laws and policies and consistent with international law and accepted international practices.

2. *Boarding and Search Teams*.

a. Boardings and searches pursuant to this Agreement shall be carried out by Security Force Officials from Security Force vessels and vessels and aircraft embarked on or otherwise supporting such Security Force vessels, as well as by vessels and aircraft of third States as agreed between the Parties.

b. The boarding and search teams may operate from Security Force vessels of the Parties and from such vessels of other States, according to arrangements between the Party conducting the operation and the State providing the vessel and notified to the other Party.

c. The boarding and search teams may carry arms.

Article 8
Safeguards

1. Where a Party takes measures against a vessel in accordance with this Agreement, it shall:

a. take due account of the need not to endanger the safety of life at sea, including, but not limited to:

   i. taking precautions not to hazard unduly the vessel or the vessel's crew while boarding; and

   ii. taking account of vessel location, *e.g.,* in a traffic separation scheme, to avoid inadvertently endangering other vessels in the vicinity in the course of boarding;

b. take due account of the security of the vessel and its cargo;

c. not prejudice the commercial or legal interests of the Flag State;

d. ensure within available means, that any measure taken with regard to the vessel is environmentally sound under the circumstances;

e. ensure that persons on board are afforded the protections, rights and guarantees provided by international law and the boarding State's law and regulations;

f. ensure that the master of the vessel is, or has been, afforded the opportunity to contact the vessels' owner, manager or Flag State at the earliest opportunity and provided the necessary information to file a claim pursuant to Article 13, paragraph 2.

2. Reasonable efforts shall be taken to avoid a vessel being unduly detained or delayed.

Article 9
Use of Force

1. All uses of force pursuant to this Agreement shall be in strict accordance with the applicable laws and policies of the Party conducting the boarding and applicable international law.

2. Each Party shall avoid the use of force except when and to the degree necessary to ensure the safety of Security Force vessels and officials and where Security Force Officials are obstructed in the execution of their duties.

3. Only that force reasonably necessary under the circumstances may be used.

4. Boarding and search teams and Security Force vessels have the inherent right to use all available means to apply that force reasonably necessary to defend themselves or others from physical harm.

Article 10
Exchange and Knowledge of Laws and Policies of Other Party

1. *Exchange of Information*. To facilitate implementation of this Agreement, each Party shall endeavour to ensure the other Party is appropriately informed of its respective applicable laws and policies, particularly those pertaining to the use of force.

2. *Knowledge*. Each Party shall endeavour to ensure that its Security Force Officials are knowledgeable concerning the applicable laws and policies in accordance with this Agreement.

Article 11
Points of Contact

1. *Information*. Each Party shall inform the other Party, and keep current, the points of contact for communication, decision and instructions under Articles 4 and 5, and notifications under Articles 6 and 10 of this Agreement. Such information shall be updated by and exchanged between the Competent Authorities.

2. *Availability*. The Parties shall ensure that the points of contact have the capability to receive, process and respond to requests and reports at any time.

Article 12
Disposition of Seized Property

1. Except as otherwise agreed by the Parties, cargo and other items seized in consequence of operations undertaken onboard vessels subject to the jurisdiction of a Party pursuant to this Agreement, shall be disposed of by that Party in accordance with its laws.

2. The Party exercising jurisdiction may, in any case, transfer forfeited cargo and other items or proceeds of their sale to the other Party. Each transfer generally will reflect the contribution of the other Party to facilitating or effecting the forfeiture of such assets or proceeds.

Article 13
Claims

1. *Injury or Loss of Life*. Any claim for injury to or loss of life of a Security Force Official of a Party while carrying out operations arising from this Agreement shall normally be resolved in accordance with the laws of that Party.

2. *Other Claims.* Any other claim submitted for damage, harm, injury, death or loss, including for loss or damage suffered as a result of a vessel being unduly detained or delayed as provided in Regulation XI-2/9.3.5.1 annexed to the International Convention for the Safety of Life at Sea, 1974 as amended, resulting from an operation carried out by a Party under this Agreement shall be resolved in accordance with the domestic law of that Party, and in a manner consistent with international law, provided the vessel has not committed any act justifying the measures taken. All such claims shall be forwarded to the relevant addressees included in the information provided pursuant to Article 8, paragraph 1(f).

3. *Consultation.* If any damage, harm, injury, death or loss is suffered as a result of any action taken by the Security Force Officials of one Party in contravention of this Agreement, or any improper or unreasonable action is taken by a Party pursuant thereto, the Parties shall, without prejudice to any other legal rights which may be available, consult at the request of either Party to resolve the matter and decide any questions relating to compensation or payment.

Article 14
Disputes and Consultations

1. *Disputes.* Disputes arising from the interpretation or implementation of this Agreement shall be settled by mutual agreement of the Parties.

2. *Evaluation of Implementation.* The Parties agree to consult as necessary to evaluate the implementation of this Agreement and to consider enhancing its effectiveness. The evaluation shall be carried out at least once a year.

3. *Resolving Difficulties.* In case a difficulty arises concerning the operation of this Agreement, either Party may request consultations with the other Party to resolve the matter.

Article 15
Effect on Rights, Privileges and Legal Positions

Nothing in this Agreement:

a. shall alter the rights and privileges due any person in any administrative or judicial proceeding conducted under the jurisdiction of either Party.

b. shall prejudice the position of either Party with regard to international law.

Article 16
Cooperation and Assistance

1. The Competent Authority of one Party may request and the Competent Authority of the other Party may authorize Security Force Officials to provide technical assistance, such as specialized assistance in the conduct of search of suspect vessels, for the boarding and search of suspect vessels located in the territory or waters of the requesting Party.

2. Nothing in this Agreement precludes a Party from authorizing the other Party to suppress proliferation in its territory, waters or airspace, or to take action involving suspect vessels or aircraft claiming its nationality or from providing other forms of cooperation to suppress proliferation.

Article 17
Entry into Force and Duration

1. *Entry into Force.* This Agreement shall enter into force upon an exchange of notes indicating that the necessary internal procedures of each Party have been completed.

2. *Provisional Application.* Beginning on the date of signature of this Agreement, the Parties shall apply it provisionally. Either Party may discontinue provisional application at any time. Each Party shall notify the other Party immediately of any constraints or limitations on provisional application, of any changes to such constraints or limitations, and upon discontinuation of provisional application.

3. *Termination.* This Agreement may be terminated by either Party upon written notification of such termination to the other Party through the diplomatic channel, termination to be effective one year from the date of such notification.

4. *Continuation of Actions Taken.* This Agreement shall continue to apply after termination with respect to any administrative or judicial proceedings regarding actions that occurred during the time the Agreement was in force.

Article 18
Rights for Third States

1. The Parties agree that the Government of the Republic of the Marshall Islands may extend, *mutatis mutandis*, all rights concerning suspect vessels claiming its nationality under the present Agreement to such third States as it may deem appropriate, on the understanding that such third States shall likewise comply with all conditions set forth in the present Agreement for the exercise of such rights, and on the understanding that the Government of

the Republic of the Marshall Islands and such third States agree on the designation of points of contact in accordance with Article 11.

2. Such third States shall enjoy rights and be subject to all conditions governing their exercise as set forth in paragraph 1 of this Article, effective on the date of notification by the third State to the Government of the Republic of the Marshall Islands that it will comply with the conditions for the exercise of those rights.

3. Such rights shall be revocable by the Government of the Republic of the Marshall Islands or renounceable by the third State in writing. Such rights shall be revoked, and the conditions governing their exercise shall cease to apply, effective on the date of notification.

4. Such rights shall be subject to modification by mutual concurrence in writing of the Government of the Republic of the Marshall Islands and the third State. Upon establishment of such mutual written concurrence, such rights shall be modified on a mutually agreed date, which shall be specified in the written concurrence.

IN WITNESS WHEREOF, the undersigned, being duly authorized by their respective Governments, have signed this Agreement.

DONE at Honolulu, this thirteenth day of August 2004, in duplicate, both texts being equally authentic.

Annex II(d)

AGREEMENT BETWEEN THE GOVERNMENT OF THE UNITED
STATES OF AMERICA AND THE GOVERNMENT OF THE REPUBLIC
OF CROATIA CONCERNING COOPERATION TO SUPPRESS THE
PROLIFERATION OF WEAPONS OF MASS DESTRUCTION, THEIR
DELIVERY SYSTEMS AND RELATED MATERIALS BY SEA

Signed 1 June 2005; will enter into force on the date of receipt of the last written notification through diplomatic channels by which the Parties inform each other that the necessary internal procedures of each Party for its entry into force have been completed.

The Government of the United States of America and the Government of the Republic of Croatia (hereinafter, "the Parties");

Deeply concerned about the proliferation of weapons of mass destruction (WMD), their delivery systems, and related materials, particularly by sea, as well as the risk that these may fall into the hands of terrorists;

Recalling the 31 January 1992 United Nations Security Council Presidential statement that proliferation of all WMD constitutes a threat to international peace and security, and underlines the need for Member States of the UN to prevent proliferation;

Also recalling United Nations Security Council Resolution 1540 (2004), which calls on all States, in accordance with their national legal authorities and legislation and consistent with international law, to take cooperative action to prevent illicit trafficking in nuclear, chemical or biological weapons, their means of delivery, and related materials;

Mindful of the Convention on the Prohibition of the Development, Production, Stockpiling and Use of Chemical Weapons and on their Destruction, done at Paris 13 January 1993; the Treaty on Nonproliferation of Nuclear Weapons, done at Washington, London and Moscow 1 July 1968; and the Convention on the Prohibition of the Development, Production and Stockpiling of Bacteriological (Biological) and Toxin Weapons and on their Destruction, done at Washington, London and Moscow 10 April 1972;

Further recalling the International Ship and Port Facility Security Code, adopted by the International Maritime Organization on 12 December 2002;

Acknowledging the widespread consensus that proliferation and terrorism seriously threaten international peace and security;

Convinced that trafficking in these items by States and non-state actors of proliferation concern must be stopped;

Guided by the Statement of Interdiction Principles for the Proliferation Security Initiative;

Inspired by the efforts of the International Maritime Organization to improve the effectiveness of the Convention for the Suppression of Unlawful Acts against the Safety of Maritime Navigation, done at Rome 10 March 1988;

Reaffirming the importance of customary international law of the sea as reflected in the 1982 United Nations Convention on the Law of the Sea;

Aware of the Ecological and Fisheries Protection Zone established by the Republic of Croatia in the waters of the Adriatic Sea beyond its territorial sea;

Committed to cooperation to stop the flow by sea of WMD, their delivery systems, and related materials to or from States or non-state actors of proliferation concern;

Have agreed as follows:

Article 1
Definitions

In this Agreement, unless the context otherwise requires:

1. "Proliferation by sea" means the transportation by ship of WMD, their delivery systems, and related materials to or from States or non-state actors of proliferation concern.

2. "Weapons of mass destruction" (WMD) means nuclear, chemical, biological and radiological weapons.

3. "Related materials" means materials, equipment and technology, of whatever nature or type, that are related to and destined for use in the development, production, utilization or delivery of WMD.

4. "States or non-state actors of proliferation concern" means those States or entities that should be subject to interdiction activities because they are or are believed to be engaged in: (1) efforts to develop or acquire WMD or their delivery systems; or (2) trafficking (either selling, receiving, or facilitating) of WMD, their delivery systems, or related materials.

5. "Security Force Officials" means:

a. for the Republic of Croatia, uniformed or otherwise clearly identifiable members of the Croatian Navy, duly authorized by the Government of the

Republic of Croatia and notified to the Competent Authority of the United States of America; and

b. for the United States of America, uniformed or otherwise clearly identifiable members of the United States Coast Guard and the United States Navy, who may be accompanied by clearly identifiable law enforcement officials of the Department of Homeland Security and/or the Department of Justice, and/or other clearly identifiable officials duly authorized by the Government of the United States of America and notified to the Competent Authority of Republic of Croatia.

6. "Security Force vessels" means warships and other vessels of the Parties, or of third States as may be agreed upon by the Parties, on which Security Force Officials of either or both Parties may be embarked, clearly marked and identifiable as being on government service and authorized to that effect, including any vessel and aircraft embarked on or supporting such vessels.

7. "Suspect vessel" means a vessel used for commercial or private purposes in respect of which there are reasonable grounds to suspect it is engaged in proliferation by sea.

8. "Competent Authority" means for the United States of America, the Commandant of the United States Coast Guard (including any official designated by the Commandant to perform such functions), and for the Republic of Croatia, the Commandant of the Croatian Navy (including any official designated by the Commandant to perform such functions).

Article 2
Object and Purpose of Agreement

1. The object of this Agreement is to promote cooperation between the Parties to enable them to prevent the transportation by ship of WMD, their delivery systems, and related materials.

2. The Parties shall carry out their obligations and responsibilities under this Agreement in a manner consistent with the principles of freedom of navigation and of international law pertaining to sovereign equality and territorial integrity of States, and non-intervention in the domestic affairs of other States.

3. The Parties shall cooperate to the fullest extent possible, subject to the availability of resources and in compliance with their respective laws.

Article 3
Scope of Agreement

1. Except as otherwise provided in this Agreement, operations to suppress proliferation by sea pursuant to this Agreement shall be carried out beyond any State's territorial sea only against suspect vessels claiming nationality in one of the Parties, suspect vessels without nationality, and suspect vessels assimilated to vessels without nationality.

2. Except as otherwise agreed between the Competent Authorities on a case-by-case basis, this Agreement does not apply to passenger vessels, including roll-on/roll-off (ro-ro) passenger vessels, of a Party engaged in international voyages between ports in the Adriatic Sea, and other Croatian flag vessels navigating in the Ecological and Fisheries Protection Zone in the Adriatic Sea.

Article 4
Operations Beyond the Territorial Sea

1. A Party that has reasonable grounds to suspect that a vessel claiming its nationality, located beyond any State's territorial sea, is engaged in proliferation by sea may request assistance of the other Party in suppressing the vessel's use for that purpose. The Party so requested shall render such assistance within the means available to it.

2. Whenever the Security Force Officials of one Party ("the requesting Party") encounter a suspect vessel claiming nationality in the other Party ("the requested Party") located beyond any State's territorial sea, the requesting Party may request through the Competent Authority of the requested Party that it:

a. confirm the claim of nationality of the requested Party; and

b. if such claim is confirmed:

    i. authorize the boarding and search of the suspect vessel, cargo and the persons found on board by Security Force Officials of the requesting Party; and

    ii. if evidence of proliferation is found, authorize the Security Force Officials of the requesting Party to detain the vessel, cargo and persons on board, pending instructions conveyed through the Competent Authority of the requested Party as to the exercise of jurisdiction in accordance with Article 5 of this Agreement.

3. *Contents of Requests.* Each request should be in writing and contain sufficiently reliable information forming the basis for the suspicion, the geographic position of the vessel, the name and physical description of the suspect vessel, and, if available, the registration number/call sign, the IMO

number, home port, the port of origin and destination, and any other identifying information. Nevertheless, in urgent circumstances, a request may be made orally, but shall be confirmed in writing forthwith. The time limits established in paragraph 4 of this Article shall commence on receipt of a written request by the Competent Authority of the requested Party. The requested Party shall immediately acknowledge in writing to the Competent Authority of the requesting Party its receipt of all written requests.

4. *Responding to Requests.*

a. If the nationality is verified and the requested Party is satisfied with the basis for suspicion that the vessel is a suspect vessel, and that the information provided by the requesting Party is sufficiently reliable, the requested Party may:

  i. decide to conduct the boarding and search with its own Security Force Officials;

  ii. authorize the boarding and search by the Security Force Officials of the requesting Party;

  iii. decide to conduct the boarding and search together with the requesting Party; or

  iv. deny permission to board and search.

b. The requested Party shall answer through its Competent Authority requests made for the verification of nationality and authorization to board and search within four (4) hours of the receipt of such written requests.

c. Either Party, consistent with the other provisions of this Agreement, may subject its authorization under this paragraph to conditions, including obtaining additional information from the requesting Party, and conditions relating to responsibility for and the extent of measures to be taken. Information to be provided in response to such a request shall be exchanged in a timely manner between the Competent Authorities.

d. Except as otherwise permitted by international law, the requesting Party shall not board the vessel without the express written authorization of the Competent Authority of the requested Party.

e. Written communications between the Competent Authorities may be made by facsimile or e-mail.

5. In deciding where to conduct the boarding, the Parties shall take into account the dangers and difficulties in boarding the ship and searching its cargo at sea and the safeguards set out in Article 8 of this Agreement, and give consideration to whether the boarding should more appropriately be undertaken in the next port of call or elsewhere.

6. *Right of Visit.* Notwithstanding the foregoing paragraphs of this Article, the Security Force Officials of one Party ("the first Party") are authorized to

board suspect vessels claiming nationality in the other Party that are not flying the flag of the other Party, not displaying any marks of its registration or
nationality, and claiming to have no documentation on board the vessel, for
the purpose of locating and examining the vessel's documentation. If documentation or other physical evidence of nationality is located, the foregoing
paragraphs of this Article apply. If no documentation or other physical evidence of nationality is located, the other Party will not object to the first
Party assimilating the vessel to a ship without nationality in accordance with
international law.

7. *Use of Force.* The authorization to board, search and detain includes the
authority to use force in accordance with Article 9 of this Agreement.

8. *Indicia of Authority.* Security Force vessels of a Party operating with the
authorization of the other Party pursuant to this Article shall, during such
operations, also fly, in the case of the United States of America, the flag of
the Republic of Croatia, and in the case of the Republic of Croatia, the
United States Coast Guard ensign.

9. *Authority to Detain Suspect Vessels.* If evidence of proliferation by sea
is found, the Security Force Officials of the first Party may detain the vessel,
cargo, and persons on board pending expeditious disposition instructions
from the other Party.

10. *Ship-boarding Otherwise in Accordance with International Law.* This
Agreement does not limit the right of either Party to conduct boardings of
vessels or other activities consistent with international law whether based,
inter alia, on the right of visit, the rendering of assistance to persons, vessels,
and property in distress or peril, the consent of the vessel master, or an authorization from the coastal State.

11. *Notification to the Master.* Prior to the boarding being conducted, the
requested Party may, in coordination with the requesting Party, transmit to
the Master of the suspect vessel notice that it has authorized the requesting
Party to board the vessel.

Article 5
Jurisdiction over Detained Vessels

1. *Jurisdiction of the Parties.* In all cases covered by Article 4 concerning
the vessels of a Party located beyond any State's territorial sea, that Party
shall have the right to exercise jurisdiction over a detained vessel, cargo
and/or persons on board (including seizure, forfeiture, arrest, and prosecution). The Party with the right to exercise jurisdiction may, subject to its
Constitution and laws, waive its right to exercise jurisdiction and authorize

the enforcement of the other Party's law against the vessel, cargo and/or persons on board.

2. *Jurisdiction in the contiguous zone of a Party*. In cases arising in the contiguous zone claimed by a Party, not involving suspect vessels fleeing from the waters of that Party or suspect vessels claiming the nationality of that Party, in which both Parties have the authority to exercise jurisdiction to prosecute, the Party which conducts the boarding and search shall have the right to exercise jurisdiction.

3. *Disposition Instructions*. Instructions as to the exercise of jurisdiction pursuant to paragraphs 1 and 2 of this Article shall be given without delay through the Competent Authorities.

Article 6
Exchange of Information and Notification of Results of Actions of the Security Forces

1. *Exchange of Operational Information*. The Competent Authorities of both Parties shall endeavour to exchange operational information on the detection and location of suspect vessels and shall maintain communication with each other as necessary to carry out the purpose of this Agreement.

2. *Notification of Results*. A Party conducting a boarding and search pursuant to this Agreement shall promptly notify the other Party of the results thereof through their Competent Authorities.

3. *Status Reports*. Each Party, in compliance with its laws, shall timely report to the other Party, through their Competent Authorities, on the status of all investigations, prosecutions and judicial proceedings and other actions and processes, arising out of the application of this Agreement.

Article 7
Conduct of Security Force Officials

1. *Compliance with Law and Practices*. Each Party shall ensure that its Security Force Officials, when conducting boardings and searches pursuant to this Agreement, act in accordance with its applicable national laws and policies and with international law and accepted international practices.

2. *Boarding and Search Teams*.

a. Security Force Officials from Security Force vessels shall carry out boardings and searches pursuant to this Agreement, and may be assisted by crew members from such vessels, including the vessels of third States as arranged between the Parties.

b. The boarding and search teams may operate from Security Force vessels of the Parties and from such vessels of other States, according to arrangements between the Party conducting the operation and the State providing the vessel and notified to the other Party.

c. The boarding and search teams may carry arms.

Article 8
Safeguards

1. Where a Party takes measures against a vessel in accordance with this Agreement, it shall:

a. take due account of the need not to endanger the safety of life at sea;

b. take due account of the security of the vessel and its cargo;

c. not prejudice the commercial or legal interests of the Flag State;

d. ensure within available means, that any measure taken with regard to the vessel is environmentally sound under the circumstances;

e. ensure that persons on board are afforded the protections, rights and guarantees provided by international law and the boarding State's law and regulations;

f. ensure that the master of the vessel is, or has been, afforded at any time the opportunity to contact the vessel's Flag State, and, subject to preserving the safety and security of operations, is, or has been, afforded the opportunity to contact the vessel's owner or manager.

2. Reasonable efforts shall be taken to avoid a vessel being unduly detained or delayed.

Article 9
Use of Force

1. *Rules*. When carrying out the authorized actions under this Agreement, the use of force shall be avoided except when necessary to ensure the safety of its officials and persons on board, or where the officials are obstructed in the execution of the authorized actions. Any use of force pursuant to this Agreement shall not exceed the minimum degree of force which is necessary and reasonable in the circumstances.

2. *Self-defence*. Nothing in this Agreement shall impair the exercise of the inherent right of self-defence by Security Force or other officials of either Party.

Article 10
Exchange and Knowledge of Laws and Policies of Other Party

1. *Exchange of Information*. To facilitate implementation of this Agreement, each Party shall ensure that the other Party is fully informed of its re-

spective applicable laws and policies, particularly those pertaining to the use of force.

2. *Knowledge*. Each Party shall ensure that its Security Force Officials are knowledgeable concerning laws and policies applicable to implementation of this Agreement.

Article 11
Points of Contact

1. *Identification*. Each Party shall inform the other Party, and keep current, the points of contact for communication, decision and instructions under Articles 4 and 5, and notifications under Articles 6 and 16 of this Agreement. Such information shall be updated by and exchanged between the Competent Authorities.

2. *Availability*. The Parties shall ensure that the points of contact have the capability to receive process and respond to requests and reports at any time.

Article 12
Disposition of Seized Property

1. Assets seized in consequence of operations undertaken on board vessels subject to the jurisdiction of Republic of Croatia pursuant to this Agreement, shall be disposed of in accordance with the laws of Republic of Croatia.

2. Assets seized in consequence of operations undertaken on board vessels subject to the jurisdiction of the United States of America pursuant to this Agreement shall be disposed of in accordance with the laws of the United States of America.

3. To the extent permitted by its laws and upon such terms as it deems appropriate, the seizing Party may, in any case, transfer forfeited assets or proceeds of their sale to the other Party. Each transfer generally will reflect the contribution of the other Party to facilitating or effecting the forfeiture of such assets or proceeds.

Article 13
Claims

1. *Injury or Loss of Life*. Any claim for injury to or loss of life of a Security Force Official of a Party while carrying out operations arising from this Agreement shall normally be resolved in accordance with the laws of that Party.

2. *Other Claims*. Any other claim submitted for damage, harm, injury, death or loss, asserted to have resulted from an operation carried out by a Party under this Agreement may be submitted to the boarding Party or the

flag State Party, and the claim shall be processed in accordance with the domestic law of the Party in which the claim is submitted and in a manner consistent with international law.

3. *Consultation*. If any damage, harm, injury, death or loss is suffered as a result of any action asserted to have been taken by the Security Force Officials of one Party in contravention of this Agreement, including action taken on unfounded suspicions, or if any improper, disproportionate or unreasonable action is asserted to have been taken by a Party, the Parties shall, without prejudice to any other legal recourse which may be available, consult at the request of either Party with a view to resolving the matter and deciding any questions relating to compensation or payment.

Article 14
Disputes and Consultations

1. *Disputes*. Disputes arising from the interpretation or implementation of this Agreement shall be settled by mutual agreement of the Parties.

2. *Evaluation of Implementation*. The Parties agree to consult as necessary to evaluate the implementation of this Agreement and to consider enhancing its effectiveness. The evaluation shall be carried out at least once a year.

3. *Resolving Difficulties*. In case a difficulty arises concerning the operation of this Agreement, either Party may request, through the Competent Authorities, consultations with the other Party to resolve the matter.

Article 15
Effect on Rights, Privileges and Legal Positions

Nothing in this Agreement:

a. is intended to alter the rights and privileges due any individual in any administrative or judicial proceeding;

b. shall prejudice the position of either Party with regard to international law of the sea, or affect the territorial or maritime boundaries or claims of either Party, as between them or with third States;

c. shall prejudice the position of either Party with regard to the Ecological and Fisheries Protection Zone of the Republic of Croatia in the Adriatic Sea.

Article 16
Cooperation and Assistance

The Competent Authority of one Party may request, and the Competent Authority of the other Party may authorize, Security Force Officials to provide technical assistance, such as specialized assistance in the conduct of search of suspect vessels, for the boarding and search of suspect vessels located in the territory or waters of the requesting Party.

Article 17
Entry into Force and Duration

1. *Entry into Force.* This Agreement shall enter into force on the date of receipt of the last written notification through diplomatic channels by which the Parties inform each other that the necessary internal procedures of each Party for its entry into force have been completed.

2. *Termination.* This Agreement may be terminated by either Party by written notification of such termination to the other Party through diplomatic channels. Such termination shall take effect six months from the date of receipt of such notification.

3. *Continuation of Actions Taken.* This Agreement shall continue to apply after termination with respect to any administrative or judicial proceedings regarding actions that occurred while it was in force.

IN WITNESS WHEREOF, the undersigned, being duly authorized by their respective Governments, have signed this Agreement.

DONE at Washington, this first day of June 2005, in duplicate in the English and Croatian languages, both texts being equally authentic.

INDEX

Publications on Ocean Development

1. R.P. Anand: *Legal Regime of the Sea-Bed and the Developing Countries*. 1976
    ISBN 90-286-0616-5

2. N. Papadakis: *The International Legal Regime of Artificial Islands*. 1977
    ISBN 90-286-0127-9

3. S. Oda: *The Law of the Sea in Our Time*. Volume I: *New Developments, 1966-1975*.
    1977   ISBN 90-286-0277-1

4. S. Oda: *The Law of the Sea in Our Time*. Volume II: *The UN Seabed Committee, 1968-
    1973*. 1977   ISBN 90-286-0287-9

5. C.O. Okidi: *Regional Control of Ocean Pollution*. Legal and Institutional Problems and
    Prospects. 1978   ISBN 90-286-0367-0

6. N.S. Rembe: *Africa and the International Law of the Sea*. A Study of the Contribution
    of the African States to the 3rd UN Conference on the Law of the Sea. 1980
    ISBN 90-286-0639-4

7. R.P. Anand: *Origin and Development of the Law of the Sea.* History of International
    Law Revisited. 1983   ISBN 90-247-2617-4

8. A.M. Post: *Deepsea Mining and the Law of the Sea*. 1983   ISBN 90-247-3049-X

9. S.P. Jagota: *Maritime Boundary*. 1985   ISBN 90-247-3133-X

10. A.O. Adede: *The System for Settlement of Disputes under the UN Convention on the
    Law of the Sea*. A Drafting History and a Commentary. 1987   ISBN 90-247-3324-3

11. M. Dahmani: *The Fisheries Regime of the Exclusive Economic Zone*. 1987
    ISBN 90-247-3374-X

12. S. Oda: *International Control of Sea Resources*. Reprint with a New Introduction.
    1989   ISBN 90-247-3800-8

13. D.G. Dallmeyer and L. DeVorsey, Jr. (eds.): *Rights to Oceanic Resources*. Deciding
    and Drawing Maritime Boundaries. 1989   ISBN 0-7923-0019-X

14. B. Kwiatkowska: *The 200 Mile Exclusive Economic Zone in the New Law of the Sea*.
    1989   ISBN 0-7923-0074-2

15. H.W. Jayewardene: *The Regime of Islands in International Law*. 1990
    ISBN 0-7923-0130-7

16. D.M. Johnston and M.J. Valencia: *Pacific Ocean Boundary Problems*. Status and Solu-
    tions. 1990   ISBN 0-7923-0862-X

17. J.A. de Yturriaga: *Straits Used for International Navigation*. A Spanish Perspective.
    1991   ISBN 0-7923-1141-8

18. C.C. Joyner: *Antarctica and the Law of the Sea*. 1992   ISBN 0-7923-1823-4

Publications on Ocean Development

19. D. Pharand and U. Leanza (eds.): *The Continental Shelf and the Exclusive Economic Zone:* Delimitation and Legal Regime/*Le Plateau continental et la Zone économique exclusive:* Délimitation et régime juridique. 1993   ISBN 0-7923-2056-5

20. F. Laursen: *Small Powers at Sea*. Scandinavia and the New International Marine Order. 1993   ISBN 0-7923-2341-6

21. J. Crawford and D.R. Rothwell (eds.): *The Law of the Sea in the Asian Pacific Region.* 1995   ISBN 0-7923-2742-X

22. M. Munavvar: *Ocean States*. Archipelagic Regimes in the Law of the Sea. 1995
        ISBN 0-7923-2882-5

23. A. Strati: *The Protection of the Underwater Cultural Heritage:* An Emerging Objective of the Contemporary Law of the Sea. 1995   ISBN 0-7923-3052-8

24. A.G. Oude Elferink: *The Law of Maritime Boundary Delimitation*. A Case Study of the Russian Federation. 1994   ISBN 0-7923-3082-X

25. Y. Li: *Transfer of Technology for Deep Sea-Bed Mining*. The 1982 Law of the Sea Convention and Beyond. 1994   ISBN 0-7923-3212-1

26. T.O. Akintoba: *African States and Contemporary International Law*. A Case Study of the 1982 Law of the Sea Convention and the Exclusive Economic Zone. 1996.
        ISBN 90-411-0144-6

27. J.A. Roach and R.W. Smith: *United States Responses to Excessive Maritime Claims.* Second Edition. 1996   ISBN 90-411-0225-6

28. T. Treves (ed.): *The Law of the Sea*. The European Union and its Member States. 1997
        ISBN 90-411-0326-0

29. A. Razavi: *Continental Shelf Delimitation and Related Maritime Issues in the Persian Gulf.* 1997   ISBN 90-411-0333-3

30. J.A. de Yturriaga: *The International Regime of Fisheries*. From UNCLOS 1982 to the Presential Sea. 1997   ISBN 90-411-0365-1

31. M.J. Valencia, J.M. Van Dyke and N.A. Ludwig: *Sharing the Resources of the South China Sea*. 1997   ISBN 90-411-0411-9

32. E.C. Farrell: *The Socialist Republic of Vietnam and the Law of the Sea*. An Analysis of Vietnamese Behavior within the Emerging International Oceans Regime. 1997
        ISBN 90-411-0473-9

33. P.B. Payoyo: *Cries of the Sea*. World Inequality, Sustainable Development and the Common Heritage of Humanity. 1997   ISBN 90-411-0504-2

34. H.N. Scheiber (ed.): *Law of the Sea*. The Common Heritage and Emerging Challenges. 2000   ISBN 90-411-1401-7

35. D.R. Rothwell and S. Bateman (eds.): *Navigational Rights and Freedoms and the New Law of the Sea*. 2000   ISBN 90-411-1499-8

Publications on Ocean Development

36. M.J. Valencia (ed.): *Maritime Regime Building*. Lessons Learned and their Relevance for Northeast Asia. 2001   ISBN 90-411-1580-3

37. A.G. Oude Elferink and D.R. Rothwell (eds.): *The Law of the Sea and Polar Maritime Delimitation and Jurisdiction*. 2001   ISBN 90-411-1648-6

38. Robert Kolb, *Case Law on Equitable Maritime Delimitation/Jurisprudence sur les délimitations maritimes selon l'équité*: Digest and Commentaries/Répertoire et commentaires. 2002   ISBN 90-411-1976-0

39. Simon Marr, *The Precautionary Principle in the Law of the Sea*: Modern Decision Making in International Law. 2002   ISBN 90-411-2015-7

40. Sun Pyo Kim: *Maritime Delimitation and Interim Arrangements in North East Asia*. 2003   ISBN 90-04-13669-X

41. Roberta Garabello and Tullio Scovazzi (eds.): *The Protection of the Underwater Cultural Heritage*. Before and After the 2001 UNESCO Convention. 2003
ISBN 90-411-2203-6

42. Nuno Marques Antunes: *Towards the Conceptualisation of Maritime Delimitation*. Legal and Technical Aspects of a Political Process. 2003   ISBN 90-04-13617-7

43. Geir Hønneland: *Russian Fisheries Management*. The Precautionary Approach in Theory and Practice. 2004   ISBN 90-04-13618-5

44. Alex G. Oude Elferink and Donald R. Rothwell (eds.): *Oceans Management in the 21st Century*. 2004   ISBN 90-04-13852-8

45. Budislav Vukas: *The Law of the Sea*. 2004   ISBN 90-04-13863-3

46. Rosemary G. Rayfuse: *Non-Flag State Enforcement in High Seas Fisheries*. 2004
ISBN 90-04-13889-7

47. David. D. Caron and Harry N. Scheiber (eds.): *Bringing New Law to Ocean Waters*. 2004   ISBN 90-04-14088-3

48. Zou Keyuan: *China's Marine Legal System and the Law of the Sea*. 2005
ISBN 90-04-14423-4

49. Florian H.Th. Wegelein: *Marine Scientific Research*. The Operation and Status of Research Vessels an Other Platforms in International Law. 2005
ISBN 90-04-14521-4

50. Guifang Xue: *China and International Fisheries Law and Policy*. 2005
ISBN 90-04-14814-0

51. Aldo Chircop and Olof Linden (eds.): *Places of Refuge for Ships*. Emerging Environmental Concerns of a Maritime Custom. 2006   ISBN 90-04-14952-X

52. Tore Henriksen, Geir Hønneland and Are Sydnes: *Law and Politics in Ocean Governance*. The UN Fish Stocks Agreement and Regional Fisheries Management Regimes. 2006   ISBN 90-04-14968-6

Publications on Ocean Development

53. Rainer Lagoni and Daniel Vignes (eds.): *Maritime Delimitation*. 2006
ISBN 90-04-15033-1

54. Anastasia Strati, Maria Gavouneli and Nikolaos Skourtos (eds.): *Unresolved Issues and New Challenges to the Law of the Sea*. Time Before and Time After. 2006
ISBN 90-04-15191-5